Financial Markets Operations Management

The Wiley Finance series contains books written specifically for finance and investment professionals as well as sophisticated individual investors and their financial advisors. Book topics range from portfolio management to e-commerce, risk management, financial engineering, valuation and financial instrument analysis, as well as much more. For a list of available titles, visit our Web site at www.WileyFinance.com.

Founded in 1807, John Wiley & Sons is the oldest independent publishing company in the United States. With offices in North America, Europe, Australia and Asia, Wiley is globally committed to developing and marketing print and electronic products and services for our customers' professional and personal knowledge and understanding.

Financial Markets Operations Management

KEITH DICKINSON

WILEY

Library of Congress Cataloging-in-Publication Data

Dickinson, Keith.
    Financial markets operations management / Keith Dickinson.
      pages cm
    Includes index.
    ISBN 978-1-118-84391-8 (cloth)
  1. Investment advisors.   2. Financial services industry–Management.   3. Finance.   I. Title.
    HG4621.D53 2015
    332.64068–dc23   2014039881

A catalogue record for this book is available from the British Library.

ISBN 978-1-118-84391-8 (hbk) ISBN 978-1-118-84390-1 (ebk)
ISBN 978-1-118-84389-5 (ebk)

Cover Design: Wiley
Cover Image Top: © iStock.com/Mani_CS2
       Bottom: © agsandrew/Shutterstock

Set in 10/12pt, Times by Aptara Inc., New Delhi, India
Printed in Great Britain by TJ International Ltd, Padstow, Cornwall, UK

To Nicole

Contents

CHAPTER 8
Settlement and Fails Management

Preface

I have been involved in Operations for over forty years as a practitioner, an executive education trainer and university lecturer. In my practitioner days, there was very little by way of reference books that addressed Operations; in addition, the Internet had yet to enter our collective consciousness. As a consequence, it was difficult for those working in Operations to find any literature that dealt with their topic.

Today, we can research any topic we choose, including Operations, by accessing the Internet, clicking through websites managed by exchanges, depositories, custodians, regulators and various trade associations. In spite of this, and with one or two notable exceptions, there is a dearth of books that enable Operations professionals to navigate the settlement and post-settlement environment for securities and derivatives.

This book, *Financial Markets Operations Management*, fills that information gap.

The intended audience is fourfold. Firstly, the text may be used in a teaching context as a course reader for staff already working in an operational environment. Secondly, as a reference guide for students taking a financially focused first degree or Masters course. Thirdly, for staff working in non-operational areas that are interested in what happens "after the trade has been executed". Finally, for those who are about to enter the financial world or who simply have a passing interest in the subject, this book is for those readers.

The text covers the trade lifecycle for securities and derivatives products from trade capture, pre-settlement and settlement through to the custody of assets and asset servicing. It is divided into four parts, as follows:

- Part One: An understanding of operations in the context of financial instruments, data management and the different types of organisation.
- Part Two: The post-trade processing of financial instruments; trade capture, clearing and settlement.
- Part Three: The post-settlement environment of safekeeping, asset servicing and asset optimisation.
- Part Four: A consideration of two key controls – accounting for securities and asset reconciliation.

Chapters are broken down as follows:

- Chapter 1 looks at the organisational structure of a typical investment company and at the Operations Department in particular. We consider the internal and external relationships that Operations manage.

- Chapter 2 defines the main financial instruments, explains the operational features and shows the transaction calculations including accrued interest for bonds.

- Chapter 3 considers the importance of data and its management.

- Chapter 4 explains how the various intermediaries and market infrastructures enable lenders and borrowers to operate.

- Chapter 5 starts the post-trade processing phase by looking at the clearing systems and distinguishing between clearing houses and central counterparties.

- Chapter 6 continues looking at the infrastructure and in particular the securities depositories.

- Chapter 7 follows the initial post-trade processes of clearing and the pre-settlement forecasting of cash and securities.

- Chapter 8 describes the different types of settlement including "delivery versus payment", the reasons why trades fail to settle and what actions can be taken to manage the fails.

- Chapter 9 changes focus from securities to derivatives with a look at how exchange-traded and over-the-counter derivative products are cleared.

- Chapter 10 looks at the safekeeping of securities including the use of nominee names and the relationships between the beneficial owner and the securities issuer, together with the intermediaries such as custodians and securities depositories.

- Chapter 11 introduces the reader to what is considered to be the most risky area within Operations – corporate actions. This chapter looks at the complexities, processing requirements and information flows of this topic.

- Chapter 12 describes the different forms of securities financing and includes user motivations and the lifecycle. Securities financing is not risk-free; this chapter addresses the risks and the ways in which these risks are mitigated.

- Chapter 13 looks at the impact of securities transactions on the Profit & Loss Statement and Balance Sheet together with the transaction lifecycle from an accounting perspective.

- Chapter 14 explains the importance of efficient and timely asset reconciliation and how it might be used as a predictive tool to prevent problems from occurring.

To cover the entire operational spectrum would require a text containing many hundreds, if not thousands, of pages. In order to overcome this problem I have concentrated on what I consider to be the main operational processes for securities and derivatives. Whilst I do not cover every type of equity, bond and derivative, there is sufficient detail to enable the reader to understand what happens in the engine room of the financial markets, i.e. after the trade is executed.

Therefore, I have not included regulation other than by occasional reference. We are subjected to regulation for a variety of reasons – for example, to maintain confidence in the financial system – and it is both complex and technical. Furthermore, in a global context, there are different and sometimes conflicting regulations from country to country.

I have also excluded commodities for two reasons. Firstly because in the physical world, types of commodities behave in different ways – think of the processes that enable you to pump petrol/gas into your car or electricity to light up your home. By contrast, commodities derivatives are cleared in similar ways to financial derivatives. Secondly, there is already an excellent book written by a friend and colleague, Neil Schofield.[1]

Finally, this book does not cover funds administration. This relates to activities that support the running of a collective investment scheme (for example, a traditional mutual fund, hedge fund, pension fund, unit trust or similar variation).

In any event, there is more than enough material within the regulatory, commodities and funds administration world for an additional three books.

Students and instructors can find additional resources at www.wiley.com.

---

[1] Schofield, N. C. (2007) *Commodity Derivatives: Markets and Applications*. Published by Wiley Finance (ISBN 978-0-470-01910-8).

Acknowledgements

Thanks to John Evans, FMT, who suggested the idea of writing the book, and to Colin Hill, Shelby Limited, who reviewed the first draft of the manuscript. At Wiley, I'd like to acknowledge the work of Development Editor Meg Freeborn, Acquisitions Editor Thomas Hyrkiel, Assistant Editor Jennie Kitchin, Senior Production Editor Tessa Allen and Copy-Editor Helen Heyes.

Introduction to Operations

1.1 INTRODUCTION

For every action there is a reaction. For every transaction, there has to be an appropriate sequence of processes such as a payment, a delivery of an asset, an exchange of information or a combination of these. We refer to this as an *operational process*. In this introductory chapter, we will see how an investment company's Operations Department relates to other departments within the company and other external organisations.

Firstly, we need to distinguish the operations of an organisational entity and the entity's post-transactional operations.

What do the following types of business actually do?

- Vineyard?
- Publisher?
- Hotel?
- Insurance company?

In simple terms, these businesses produce something (often referred to as *outputs*):

- Vineyards produce wine;
- Publishers produce books, newspapers and computer software;
- Hotels produce satisfied customers;
- Insurance companies help customers reduce their financial risks.

These outputs are the results of the transformation of a variety of *inputs*, including some of the following (the list is not exhaustive):

- Vineyard – grapes, yeast, water, sugar, etc.
- Publisher – authors, ideas, paper, digital resources, etc.
- Hotel – premises (rooms, dining areas), food, staff (front of house, catering, cleaning), ambiance, etc.
- Insurance company – products, sales staff, research & development staff, distribution channels, etc.

This is what businesses "do"; we know this as the business operations and the transformation of inputs into outputs are how each business operates.

Q&A

Question

An investment company is also a business operation. What do you think are the inputs and outputs? How might an investment company be profitable?

Answers

Table 1.1 gives the answers.

TABLE 1.1 Inputs and outputs of an investment company

Inputs	▪ Managing portfolios for clients (asset management) ▪ Trading for the company's own account (proprietary trading in securities, cash, foreign exchange, derivatives) ▪ Advising issuer clients re capital raising (equity or debt) ▪ Advising corporate clients re mergers and acquisitions either as target or bidder (takeovers) ▪ Designing new products (innovation) ▪ Employing strategies to protect assets (hedging)
Outputs	▪ Increased profitability ▪ Increased wealth for clients ▪ Portfolios protected from market risk ▪ Successful new issuance of securities on behalf of issuer clients ▪ Innovative solutions to investment challenges and changes in regulation
Sources of Revenue	▪ Interest from loans to counterparties and clients ▪ Trading profits (bid/offer spread) ▪ Charging fees to clients ▪ Income from deposits, dividends (equities) and coupons (bonds) ▪ Commissions levied on new issues, etc.

What is missing here is the processing that occurs after the inputs have taken place. A trader executes a transaction; the decision-making that led to the requirement to transact, the negotiation with a counterparty and the final execution of the transaction are all part of the business operation. What happens next is the completion of that deal. By completion, we mean the settlement, the exchange of the financial instrument for cash. This processing, this completion, is what financial market operations is all about. It is what we in the Operations Department do.

There is, therefore, a distinction between the operations of a business and Operations in the sense of processing most of the inputs. In this opening chapter you will learn:

- How an investment company is typically structured;
- What the departments' roles are;
- What relationships Operations have with internal departments and external entities;
- Other service functions within the business.

1.2 ORGANISATIONAL STRUCTURE OF AN INVESTMENT COMPANY

There is no right or wrong way to organise the structure of an investment company. It depends on the size of the company, the products in which it deals and the locations of its offices.

The biggest companies, for example the investment banks, will have several thousand staff located in offices based around the world. By contrast, the smallest, such as a hedge fund, might have less than 100 staff working from one office.

What is usually certain is that there will be one department that generates business for the company and one that ensures that the business is administered in an efficient, controlled, timely and risk-free manner. In many companies there will be a third department that supports these two.

We refer to these three departments or offices as follows:

- Front Office – the business generator;
- Middle Office – the administrator;
- Back Office[1] – the supporter.

1.2.1 Front Office

The Front Office generates revenue and is responsible for the buying and selling of financial products.

Within the Front Office (see Figure 1.1) there are generally five areas:

1. **Corporate Finance** – This area helps clients to raise funds in the capital markets and advises clients on mergers and acquisitions. Corporate finance can be divided into industry coverage (e.g. financial institutions, industrials, healthcare, etc.) and product coverage (e.g. leveraged finance, equity, public finance, etc.).
2. **Sales** – The sales desk will suggest trading ideas to clients (institutional and high-net-worth individuals) and take orders. Orders must be executed at the best possible price and this can mean placing an order internally or with an external trading desk.
3. **Trading** – The trading desk (aka the dealing desk) executes trades on behalf of the investment organisation (known as principal, proprietary or own-account trading). The traders can take both long and short positions in financial instruments that they have been

---

[1] Although there is a logical progression from Front to Middle to Back, the term Back Office has been effectively replaced by the term *Operations* in today's lexicon.

authorised to trade in. This desk also executes trades on behalf of the sales desk, as noted above.

4. **Repo Desk** – The repo desk supports the traders by helping to finance their positions. When the traders go long, they need to borrow cash. The repo traders borrow cash through repo. Conversely, when the traders go short, they need to borrow securities. The repo traders borrow securities through reverse repo.

5. **Research** – Research is undertaken for a variety of reasons. For example, equity research review companies write reports about their prospects and make "buy", "sell" or "hold" recommendations. Predominantly, research is a key service in terms of advice and strategy; it covers credit research and fixed-income research amongst others.

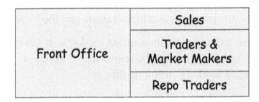

FIGURE 1.1   Investment organisation – structure

There are other, similar types of Front Office used by organisations, such as:

- **Stockbrokers** – These act in an agency capacity on behalf of clients. They can offer "execution only" (without any advice) brokerage, non-discretionary services (provide advice but can only trade subject to a client's instructions) and fully discretionary services (the broker decides what to do based on the client's overall investment objectives without seeking case-by-case instructions).
- **Market makers** – These make their money by using their company's capital to quote bid and offer (buy and sell) prices in pre-specified securities. Market makers are obliged to make a two-way price in any and all market conditions.
- **Investment managers** – These use their clients' cash to make investment decisions in accordance with the clients' investment objectives. Having made the investment decisions, orders are placed with their brokers for execution in the market.
- **Broker/Dealers** – These can act as both a dealer (trading for the organisation's own account) and as a broker (on behalf of clients).
- **Inter-dealer brokers** – These are specialised intermediaries that execute transactions on behalf of sell-side institutions such as broker/dealers and market makers. The IDBs provide anonymity so that the market is not aware of the sell-side institution's positions.

In whatever capacity it is acting, the Front Office executes transactions either on a stock exchange or in the over-the-counter (OTC) markets.

1.2.2   Middle Office

Not every investment company is obliged to have a Middle Office, but the larger the company, the more likely it is to have one. The Middle Office is the link between the Front Office and the various operational departments (see Figure 1.2).

Front Office	Sales
	Traders & Market Makers
	Repo Traders
Middle Office	Trade Confirmation & Risk Information

FIGURE 1.2   Investment organisation – structure

It both supports and controls output from the Front Office; it ensures that any trade is correctly booked and the economic consequences of the trade comply with various pre-agreed limits, for example:

- The value of the trade must be within counterparty limits;
- The value of the trade must be within the trader's limits;
- The trader must be authorised to trade that asset.

The Middle Office monitors existing trades and identifies any that do not meet these limits. Assets held in the dealers' blotters should be checked and revalued daily. The Middle Office needs to ensure that pricing data are correct and investigate prices that do not look right.

The Middle Office will exchange confirmations of executed trades with the counterparties and, where necessary, identify discrepancies, obtain the dealer's confirmation of the change and update the trading systems accordingly. Changes cannot be made without reference back to the trading floor, as it could appear that the Middle Office is actually trading rather than simply making a correction to a trade.

As part of the monitoring process, the Middle Office ensures that all the trades executed during one particular day are fully booked in the system, that valuations have been made and that reports have been produced.

Q&A

You work in the Middle Office of Masham Dealers (account number 859327) and the following transaction appears on your system:

Purchase: USD 1 million ABC 5% bonds due 15 September 2021

Price: 99.1250 plus 72 days of accrued interest (Annual, 30/360)

Trade date: 30 June 2015

Settlement date: 03 July 2015

Counterparty: Skipton Bank Limited (account number 132546)

Total cost: USD 1,031,125.00)

A few moments later, the confirmation arrives from your counterparty:

> Confirmation from: Skipton Bank International (account number 132654)
>
> Sale: USD 1 million ABC 5% bonds due 15 September 2021
>
> Price: 99.0625 plus 72 days of accrued interest (Annual, 30/360)
>
> Trade date: 30 June 2015
>
> Settlement date: 03 July 2015
>
> Counterparty: Masham Dealers (account number: 859327)
>
> Total cost: USD 1,030,625.00

Question

What, if anything, is wrong with the confirmation, who is correct and what action would you take?

Answer

There are two discrepancies:

1. Counterparty – you have Skipton Bank Limited and the incoming confirmation has come from Skipton Bank International. Although both counterparties are from the same banking group, they are different counterparties.
2. Price – You have 99.1250 and they have 99.0625.

There is no sure way of knowing what the correct situation should be:

- Counterparty – You may have traded with both entities in the recent past, so either might be right.
- Price – If the market was showing 99.140625 (bid) and 99.203125 (offer) at the time the trade was executed, whose trade is more likely to be correct? If we are the sell-side (and therefore Skipton the buy-side), our price looks more likely to be correct. As the sell-side dealer, we would purchase at close to the bid (i.e. lower) price.

Our only course of action is to talk to the trader concerned and get him or her to check the details by contacting, if necessary, the counterparty dealer. Our dealer will have to authorise any alteration to the contract. Then, and only then, can you make the corrections in the system.

In most cases where there are discrepancies in transaction details, the Middle Office would have to investigate with the Front Office. In Table 1.2 there is a list of typical types of query together with the department that is responsible for making any changes.

TABLE 1.2 Primary responsibilities for resolving trade discrepancies

Settlement Instruction Component	Trade Detail from which Settlement Instruction Component is Derived	Primary Responsibility
Depot account no.	Trading company	Front Office and/or Operations
Nostro account no.	Trading company	Front Office and/or Operations
Trade reference	N/A	N/A
Deliver/Receive	Purchase or Sale	Front Office
Settlement basis	DVP or RVP or FoP	Front Office
Settlement date	Settlement date	Front Office
Quantity	Quantity	Front Office
Security reference	Security	Front Office
Settlement currency	Settlement currency	Front Office
Total net amount (Principal)	Price	Front Office
Total net amount (accrued interest)	Accrued interest	Operations
Counterparty's depot account	Counterparty (Cpty)	Cpty = Front Office Cpty account = Operations
Counterparty's nostro account	Counterparty (Cpty)	Cpty = Front Office Cpty account = Operations

1.2.3 Back Office/Operations

For those organisations that do not have a Middle Office, the initial trade capture from the dealing systems would start here in the Operations area (see Figure 1.3). It is here that all the post-trade processing takes place, and this includes activities such as settlement of all transactions. Settlement requires the receipt and delivery of securities together with the payment and receipt of cash; as we will see later, we expect the movements of securities to occur at the same time as the corresponding movements of cash. We refer to this as *delivery versus payment* or *receipt versus payment* (DVP and RVP, respectively).

More often than not, securities held centrally in a type of organisation known as a central securities depository (CSD) are recorded as electronic records by the CSD. For this reason,

Front Office	Sales
	Traders & Market Makers
	Repo Traders
Middle Office	Trade Confirmation & Risk Information
Back Office (Operations)	Settlement, Custody & Administration

FIGURE 1.3 Investment organisation – structure

Operations will also have responsibility for ensuring that when transactions settle, the correct amount of securities is either credited (for purchase) or debited (for a sale) at the relevant CSD.

Operations may or may not be a direct participant within a CSD; if not, Operations will make use of an organisation such as a custodian bank that does have direct participation with the CSD. So we now have a custody or safekeeping responsibility in addition to settlements.

As we will see throughout this book, many of the operational responsibilities refer to the processing and final completion of transactions that have come out of the Front Office. There are other aspects to consider as well:

- Monitoring and control – Operations must make sure that any payments and deliveries are made with the appropriate level of authorisation. Authorisation can include a tested telex, an authenticated email, an authenticated fax, a signed (and possibly countersigned) hardcopy instruction or a message delivered through a secure and automated electronic messaging system such as SWIFT.
- Reconciliation – This is a key control designed to ensure that the organisation can verify that assets recorded in the books and records of the organisation agree with external statements received from counterparties, banks, custodians, etc.
- Protection of revenues – Revenues are generated in the Front Office and there will be certain, known costs that each transaction will be subject to. Examples of these costs can include brokerage fees, transaction fees, custody charges, clearing fees and stamp duty.

These represent the cost of doing business; however, if there are processing errors, there is every likelihood that there will be penalty costs associated with this. In a perfectly efficient environment where no mistakes are made, there should be no need for any penalty costs to be incurred. If, for example, a payment is made late, then it is quite possible for the interest charge to be greater than the profit made on the underlying transaction. Operations staff members have to pay great attention to detail in their attempts to avoid problems such as these.

1.3   OPERATIONS' RELATIONSHIPS

The Operations Department does not and cannot operate in isolation. It has to maintain relationships with many different types of organisation including:

- Clients – external;
- Clients – internal;
- Counterparties;
- Suppliers;
- The authorities.

1.3.1   Clients – External

These are your fee-paying clients; you provide a service for which you are compensated. Table 1.3 lists some examples.

You could be in contact with your clients on a regular basis for a variety of reasons, such as responding to their queries, taking instructions for an optional corporate action events and sending them securities and/or cash statements including evaluations and performance-related information.

TABLE 1.3 Examples of external clients

Your Organisation	Your Client (example)	Revenue
Investment manager	Pension fund	■ Management fee ■ Administration fees
Dealer/Sales	Corporate	■ Commission or loading the bid/offer spread
Broker	High-net-worth individual	■ Commission on value of transactions
Custodian bank	Insurance company	■ Transaction charges ■ Custody fees

1.3.2   Clients – Internal

Internal clients would include your colleagues in other departments such as the Front Office. The Front Office looks to you for reports and you look to it for decisions on certain types of transaction query or voluntary corporate action event. Therefore, this relationship is based on information swapping rather than fee generation. Other business functions (see below) would also be regarded as internal clients.

1.3.3   Counterparties

The term "counterparty" can have two meanings. On the one hand, a counterparty is one party to any transaction and your organisation is the second party. The term can also refer to any legal entity to which you could be exposed financially (this is known as counterparty or credit risk).

Please refer back to the transaction that Masham Dealers entered into with Skipton Bank Limited. In this case you would regard Skipton Bank as your counterparty with whom you had exchanged confirmations of the trade in ABC bonds and whom you would have contacted as a result of the discrepancies in the contract terms.

Regardless of how competitive the business is, it is always a good idea to maintain good working relationships with your counterparties.

In our example we would have a financial exposure to Skipton Bank.

Q&A

Question

What exposure(s) might you be exposed to?

Answer

If we pay Skipton Bank on the settlement date and the bank fails to deliver the bonds to us, we run the risk that the bank might decide not to deliver the bonds to us or that it has gone into default and is not able to. We call this *counterparty risk*, and it is a variation on the term *credit risk*.

If, however, we agree to receive the bonds "against payment" and the bank is unable or unwilling to deliver, then we retain the cash. This is a lower type of risk, *settlement risk*, which might expose us to *market risk* if we subsequently have to go back into the market and purchase the bonds at a higher price.

For this reason, our organisation would analyse any counterparty from a credit perspective and establish some trading limits with the counterparty. So long as the value of all our transactions with the same counterparty is within the limit, the organisation will be comfortable with this. These limits should be under constant review and if the creditworthiness of a counterparty deteriorates, the trading limits should be reduced accordingly.

1.3.4 Suppliers

The financial markets depend on a wide range of intermediaries (suppliers) to enable investment organisations to do their jobs. Table 1.4 shows a small selection of typical suppliers.

TABLE 1.4   Typical suppliers

Supplier	Description
Custodians	Typically commercial banks, custodians hold assets on behalf of their clients.
Central Securities Depository (CSD)	Securities issued in any one particular market are typically held centrally by a locally based CSD. It is here that settlement occurs having been cleared by the appropriate clearing system.
Registrar	Equities are issued by corporate entities as one way of raising capital. The issuer must know who its shareholders are. To achieve this, a register of shareholders is maintained by a registrar on behalf of the issuer.
Paying Agent	An issuer of bonds is obliged to pay interest periodically to its bondholders. The issuer pays the total amount of interest to its paying agent, who, in turn, pays the bondholders (or their custodians).
Legal profession	A vast number of legal documents are required in the financial markets for many activities such as new issues of securities. Whilst there are standard (or master) agreements available, it is still necessary for solicitors to prepare/review documentation.
Clearing systems	As part of the settlement process, clearing systems will match both sides to any transaction and check that there is sufficient asset availability before advising a CSD that the transaction can settle. Some clearing systems assume the counterparty risk from both the original counterparties – we know these clearers as *central counterparties* (CCPs).

1.3.5 The Authorities

The final relationship is that with the various governmental and market organisations that have the power to regulate, supervise and censure organisations which come under their authority.

The majority of markets require organisations to be authorised in order to participate in certain regulated activities and to be subjected to regular inspections. Failure to meet requirements and breaches of the rules can expose organisations to financial penalties, public censure and even a restriction in their business activities.

Organisations must submit reports to their regulators and comply with their rule books.

Financial organisations are businesses that are liable to pay corporation tax on profits made. There therefore needs to be a good working relationship with the tax authorities in the organisation's country of incorporation.

Corporation tax is not the only tax to deal with; other taxes include:

- Stamp duty, which might be payable in certain circumstances (typically on purchases of securities based on a pre-specified percentage of the market value of the transaction).
- Withholding tax (WHT) is often deducted from dividends paid to shareholders. Depending on the shareholder's tax status, it might be possible to reclaim some or all of this tax. In which case, the Operations Department will have to submit reclaim documentation to the appropriate tax authorities.
- Financial transaction tax (FTT), which is levied on certain types of transaction (stamp duty is one such example). The European Commission has proposed the introduction of an EU FTT that would impact transactions between financial institutions. The charge for equities and bond transactions would be 0.1% and derivatives contracts 0.01%. In 2011, it was expected that this FTT would raise EUR 57 billion annually.[2] The proposal, supported by eleven EU Member States, has been approved by both the European Parliament and the Council of the European Union. Details, however, have yet to be decided.

1.4 OTHER BUSINESS FUNCTIONS

There are other business functions that work outside of the direct Front Office/Middle Office/Back Office triangle but are nevertheless important elements in a well-run investment organisation. Again, the exact management of these functions depends on the size of the organisation and how it chooses to run its own business.

These functions include:

- Accounting
- Compliance
- Human Resources
- Information Technology/Systems
- Internal Audit
- Risk Management
- Treasury.

See Table 1.5 for details.

---

[2]Source: EU Inside (online). "The EU Expects 57 Billion Euros a Year from a New Financial Tax." Available from www.euinside.eu/en/news/the-eu-expects-57-billion-euros-a-year-by-a-new-bank-tax. [Accessed Thursday, 10 April 2014]

TABLE 1.5 Other business functions

Business Function	Overview
Accounting	Financial Accounting: Recording business transactions in the general ledger and preparing financial accounts (Profit & Loss, Balance Sheet, etc.). Reporting tends to be backward-looking (e.g. information for a previous period).
	Management Accounting: Measures, analyses and reports information to enable managers to make decisions on future business objectives. Reporting tends to be forward-looking (e.g. budget for the next 12 months).
Compliance	This function ensures that the organisation complies with appropriate regulations, laws, internal policies and contracts, identifies non-compliance and initiates corrective action.
Human Resources	A key resource in any organisation, it is the management of staff recruitment, learning and development, assessment and compensation.
Information Technology/Systems	The financial industry is concerned with the storage, retrieval, transmission, interpretation and security of information. Computers with databases, spreadsheets, telecommunications, etc. enable this to happen and have replaced paper-based storage (ledgers) and manual processes.
	High-speed networks have led to electronic and algorithmic trading that can execute thousands of transactions in milliseconds.
	The Internet has enabled instructions and information to be sent quickly and securely, making many proprietary transmission systems redundant.
Internal Audit	Provides independent assurance that an organisation's risk management, governance and internal control processes are operating effectively. Internal audit is independent from the business operations and reports to the organisation's board and senior management.
Risk Management	Financial institutions are exposed to a number of risks, including:
	▪ Credit risk,
	▪ Market risk,
	▪ Liquidity risk,
	▪ Business environment risk, and
	▪ Operational risk.
	The primary objective of the operational risk management function is to minimise the occurrence and impact of operational risk events, in particular avoiding extreme or catastrophic events, in order to support the organisation in achieving its strategic objectives.
Treasury	A Treasury Department focuses on customer dealing business, servicing the organisation's banking book, supporting credit business by offering treasury products, managing liquidity (daily cash flow) and conducting limited trading activities.

1.5 SUMMARY

An Operations Department is the "engine room" of an investment organisation and the conduit along which transactions that have been executed in the Front Office flow.

Operations have a processing role – ensuring that these transactions are completed (settled) in an accurate and timely manner.

Operations also have a supporting role – they help the Front Office by reducing costs and making sure that any profits are not reduced through late interest claims.

Operations have a safekeeping role – ensuring that assets are held in custody and are only released on properly authorised instructions.

Operations do not work alone – they provide information to other functions and require resources such as staff (Human Resources) and cash (e.g. Treasury). To do this effectively, Operations maintain many different types of relationship, both internally (e.g. with the Front Office) and externally (e.g. with counterparties, clients, custodians, etc.).

CHAPTER 2

Financial Instruments

2.1 INTRODUCTION

Financial instruments are negotiable (i.e. they can be traded) assets that can be divided into cash instruments and derivative instruments. Cash instruments are issued in response to a legal entity, a corporate or a government raising capital and are either securities or loans. We will concentrate on securities.

Derivative instruments derive their value from the value and characteristics of one or more underlying entities, for example, a security, an interest rate or a market index. Derivatives are not created by the issuers of the underlying entity; rather they are created either by a derivatives exchange (known as exchange-traded derivatives – ETDs) or by participants in the market (OTC derivatives – OTCDs).

Another way to look at these examples is to consider the differences between the money markets and the debt and equity markets (both collectively known as the capital markets). We can differentiate the money markets from the capital markets on the basis of maturity, the credit instruments and the purpose of the financing (see Table 2.1).

TABLE 2.1   Money market and capital market differentiators

Differentiator	Market	Description
Maturity	Money	Deals in the lending and borrowing of short-term finance for up to 12 months.
	Capital	Deals in the lending and borrowing of long-term finance for more than one year.
Credit instruments	Money	Collateralised cash loans, bankers' acceptances, certificates of deposit, commercial paper and bills of exchange.
	Capital	Equity, corporate bonds and government securities.
Purpose	Money	Short-term credit needs of business; it provides working capital to the industrialists.
	Capital	Long-term credit needs of business; it provides capital to buy fixed assets such as land, machinery, etc. Helps provide adequate capital to meet statutory minimum capital standards.

(continued)

TABLE 2.1   *(Continued)*

Differentiator	Market	Description
In addition, there are differences in emphasis regarding:		
Risk	Money	These are short-term instruments. Credit risk is lower than in the capital markets, as there is less time for the credit to default.
	Capital	Long-term instruments. Credit risk is greater than in the money markets, as there is more time for the credit to default.
Basic role of the market	Money	Adjustment of liquidity.
	Capital	Putting capital to work.

2.2   WHY DO WE ISSUE FINANCIAL INSTRUMENTS?

As we are going to see in this chapter, there is a great variety of financial instruments, each with a varying degree of complexity from an operational point of view. For what purpose, though, are these instruments issued?

Entities that issue financial instruments do so for one fundamental reason and that is to raise capital. If you take a look at a company's annual report and accounts, you will notice on the Balance Sheet that the company has assets that are matched by liabilities. Assets are what the company owns and liabilities reflect the ways that the assets have been financed. Depending on the individual circumstances, a company can finance its assets by issuing securities (equity, bonds, etc.), borrowing cash or a combination of both.

The type of securities issued depends on the purpose for which the cash is being raised and the time horizon for which the cash is needed. Table 2.2 shows some examples.

TABLE 2.2   Purposes and time horizons of securities

Purpose of Cash	Time Horizon	Type of Security
Working capital	Short term, less than 12 months	Money market instrument such as a certificate of deposit
Finance an infrastructure project	Long term, say 10 years	Debt instrument such as a bond issue with a term of 10 years
Business expansion	No definitive time horizon, but certainly long term	Equity instrument such as ordinary shares

A "soft" benefit of issuing securities is that the issuer gains a presence in a particular market; there is a certain cachet for a company that has its shares listed on a major stock market, such as Tokyo, New York or London.

One of the features of equity and bonds is that these are negotiable and the investor community is free to buy and sell these instruments under rules and regulations laid down in the markets where the instruments are issued. We refer to this as a *secondary market*.

Investing is an inherently risky business. The market price might move away from the investor, resulting in a loss if the investor decides to sell the asset. It is also risky in the sense that the issuer might default, leaving the investor with a worthless asset, and risky in the sense that the benefits of ownership may either not be received or not be as high as expected.

By contrast, derivative financial instruments are issued by the market rather than the issuer of the underlying asset from which the derivative derives its value. The market issues and uses derivatives for a number of purposes, including:

- To hedge an existing position in a related underlying asset;
- To obtain exposure to an underlying asset;
- To create an option of doing something;
- To speculate and make a profit.

It is not the purpose of this book to teach you about the reasons why entities issue debt and equity securities; there are excellent books that fulfil this purpose. Rather, it is to illustrate that the ways in which we administer financial instruments are determined by some of the features of these instruments. The main learning objective is to know enough about any particular instrument to enable you to understand the main processes within a settlements or custody or asset servicing context.

By the end of this chapter you should be able to:

- Define the different types of financial instrument;
- Describe the operational features of these instruments;
- Calculate accrued interest on debt securities using the correct day-count conventions;
- Calculate the transaction amounts of a selection of financial instruments.

2.3 MONEY MARKET INSTRUMENTS

Together with the capital markets, the money markets form the financial markets. The main distinction between the two is that the money markets focus on short-term debt financing, whereas the capital markets focus on the longer term through the issuance and subsequent trading of equity, bonds and all the other types of securities.

In this section, we will look at the main money-market instruments including deposits, coupon securities (such as certificates of deposit) and discount securities (such as treasury bills and commercial paper). Due to the short-term nature of these instruments, interest can be paid to the lender in one of two ways:

- Instruments are issued at a discount to their face value and, on maturity, the repayment will be at par (i.e. the face value). We refer to these as *discount instruments*.
- Instruments are issued at their face value and mature at par together with interest. We refer to these as *accrual instruments*.

2.3.1 Euro-Currency Deposits

Any currency that is traded outside the country of the currency is referred to as a *Euro-currency* trade. For example, if you are a dealer based in Tokyo wishing to borrow US dollars, you would be borrowing Euro-dollars.

Euro-currency deposits are non-negotiable and there is no secondary market as such. Title to a deposit cannot be assigned or transferred without the approval of the lender and borrower. This makes it a rather complex situation if either party wishes to liquidate the deposit; the normal practice if one party wishes to "cancel" the deposit is to enter into an equal-and-opposite transaction for the same maturity.

Euro-currency rates are quoted on a percentage per annum basis based on inter-bank offered rates and bid rates. Traditionally, the key benchmark rate has been the London Interbank Offered Rate (LIBOR – the rate which the market charges to lend money) and the London Interbank Bid Rate (LIBID – the rate which the market pays for taking money).

LIBOR and LIBID rates for the major currencies (see Table 2.3) are fixed every day in London by groups of banks known as *panel banks* (see Table 2.4) across a range of maturities (see Table 2.5).

TABLE 2.3   British Bankers' Association – LIBOR currencies

AUD	Australian Dollar	GBP	Sterling
CAD	Canadian Dollar	JPY	Japanese Yen
EUR	Euro	NZD	New Zealand Dollar
CHF	Swiss Franc	SEK	Swedish Krona
DKK	Danish Krone	USD	US Dollar

Source: www.bbalibor.com.

TABLE 2.4   Panel banks for EUR LIBOR

Euro Panel Banks		**Last Reviewed May 2012**
Abbey National plc	Deutsche Bank AG	Rabobank
Bank of Tokyo-Mitsubishi UFJ Ltd	HSBC	Royal Bank of Canada
Barclays Bank plc	JP Morgan Chase	Société Générale
Citibank NA	Lloyds Banking Group	The Royal Bank of Scotland Group
Credit Suisse	Mizuho Corporate Bank	UBS AG

Source: www.bbalibor.com.

TABLE 2.5   Range of maturities

Overnight (O/N)	Starting today and maturing tomorrow
Tom–Next (T/N)	Starting tomorrow and maturing the next day
Spot–Next (S/N)	Starting on the spot date
1 w	Starting on the value date, maturing 1 week later
1 m	Starting on the value date, maturing 1 month later
2 m	Starting on the value date, maturing 2 months later
3 m	Starting on the value date, maturing 3 months later
6 m	Starting on the value date, maturing 6 months later
12 m	Starting on the value date, maturing 12 months later

Fixing, Value and Maturity Dates   When a deposit is transacted, there will be a difference between the dates on which the transaction is executed (the fixing date), the start date of the deposit (the value date) and the finish date of the deposit (the maturity date).

In general, there are two business days between the fixing date and the value date. The maturity date will be the number of days/months after the value date, as noted in the transaction (e.g. three months). In the BBA's LIBOR guidance notes, the period between the fixing and the value date for the ten currencies is as noted in Table 2.6.

TABLE 2.6   Period between fixing and value dates

Currency	Period between Fixing and Value Dates
All currencies except EUR and GBP	Two London business days after fixing
EUR	Two TARGET2 business* days after fixing
GBP	The fixing date and value date are the same

Source: bbalibor (online). Available from www.bbalibor.com/technical-aspects/fixing-value-and-maturity. [Accessed Monday, 2 December 2013]
* A TARGET2 business day is when the Eurozone payment system is open in all participating countries. It is closed on 1 January, Good Friday, Easter Monday, 1 May and Christmas (25 and 26 December).

Calculations   There are two calculations to be aware of:

- Simple interest (Equation (2.1))
- Repayment (Equation (2.2)).

Simple Interest Calculation   Interest is calculated on a simple interest basis based on the actual number of days in the deposit period divided by 360 days (365 days for GBP):

$$\text{Interest} = \text{Face Amount of Deposit} \times \left(\frac{\text{Interest Rate}}{100} \right) \times \left(\frac{\text{Actual Days in Period}}{360} \right) \quad (2.1)$$

Repayment Calculation

$$\text{Repayment Amount} = \text{Face Value} + \text{Interest}$$
$$\text{Repayment Amount} = FV + \left(FV \times r \times \frac{d}{360} \right)$$
$$\text{restated as :} \quad (2.2)$$
$$\text{Repayment Amount} = FV \times \left[1 + \left(r \times \frac{d}{360} \right) \right]$$

Where:

FV = Face value of deposit
d = number of days from value date to maturity date
r = interest rate per annum ÷ 100 (i.e. 5.00% is stated as 0.05).

The following two exercises will check your understanding of:

- Fixing dates, value dates and maturities;
- Interest and repayment calculations.

Q&A

Question

Please complete Table 2.7 with the appropriate dates.

TABLE 2.7   Fixing, value and maturity dates

CCY	Term	Fixing Date	Value Date	Maturity
GBP	3 m	18 June 2014		
EUR	1 m		30 May 2014	
USD	6 m			30 October 2014

Answers

Table 2.8 gives the answers.

TABLE 2.8   Fixing, value and maturity dates – answers

CCY	Term	Fixing Date	Value Date	Maturity
GBP	3 m	18 June 2014	18 June 2014	18 September 2014
EUR	1 m	28 May 2014	30 May 2014	30 June 2014
USD	6 m	28 April 2014	30 April 2014	30 October 2014

Q&A

Exercise

Please calculate the interest and repayment amount for deposits made on the above fixing dates (rounded to two decimal places) and complete Table 2.9.

TABLE 2.9   Interest and repayment amounts

CCY	FV	r	d	Interest	Repayment
GBP	1,000,000	0.05150			
EUR	2,500,000	0.08357			
USD	5,000,000	0.03930			

Answers

Table 2.10 gives the answers.

TABLE 2.10   Interest and repayment amounts – answers

CCY	FV	r	d	Interest	Repayment
GBP	1,000,000	0.05150	92	GBP 12,980.82	GBP 1,012,980.82
EUR	2,500,000	0.08357	31	EUR 17,990.76	EUR 2,517,990.76
USD	5,000,000	0.39300	183	USD 99,887.50	USD 5,099,887.50

2.3.2 Certificates of Deposit

A *certificate of deposit* (CD) is a type of time deposit where a bank issues a receipt certifying that a deposit has been made. Unlike the time deposit that we saw previously with a Euro-currency deposit, a CD can be sold prior to the final maturity. Therefore, instead of waiting until maturity, depositors may sell them in the market for cash. The holder of a CD receives interest at a fixed or floating rate.

CDs are quoted on a discount-to-yield basis and, on maturity, the holder receives the face value plus interest (either at a fixed rate or a floating rate). Interest on a CD is calculated in the same way as for a Euro-currency deposit, as the example in Table 2.11 illustrates.

TABLE 2.11 Example of a certificate of deposit

Issuer	Nycredit Bank
Face value	EUR 1,000,000
Interest rate	0.16%
Tenor	180 days

On maturity, the holder will receive EUR 1,000,800.00 (i.e. the face value EUR 1,000,000.00 plus interest of EUR 800.00):

$$\text{Maturity} = \text{Face Value} \times \left[1 + \left(\text{Coupon} \times \frac{\text{Tenor Days}}{\text{Days in Year}}\right)\right]$$

$$\text{Maturity} = 1,000,000 \times \left[1 + \left(0.0016 \times \frac{180}{360}\right)\right] \qquad (2.3)$$
$$\text{Maturity} = 1,000,800.00$$

Let us assume that the holder sells the CD at a yield of 0.15% with 90 days remaining until maturity. The maturity amount is discounted by the yield for the remaining period:

$$\text{Proceeds} = \text{Face Value} \times \left[\frac{1 + \left(\text{Coupon} \times \frac{\text{Tenor Days}}{\text{Days in Year}}\right)}{1 + \left(\text{Yield} \times \frac{\text{Days Remaining}}{\text{Days in Year}}\right)}\right]$$

$$\text{Proceeds} = \text{EUR } 1,000,000 \times \left[\frac{1 + \left(0.0016 \times \left(\frac{180}{360}\right)\right)}{1 + \left(0.0015 \times \left(\frac{90}{360}\right)\right)}\right] \qquad (2.4)$$

$$\text{Proceeds} = \text{EUR } 1,000,000 \times \frac{1.000800}{1.000375}$$
$$\underline{\underline{\text{Proceeds} = \text{EUR } 1,000,424.84}}$$

2.3.3 Commercial Paper

Commercial paper (CP) is a short-term unsecured instrument issued by corporate entities. As CP does not normally pay interest, it is issued at a discount to its face value and on maturity the holder receives the full face value. The discount represents the investor's interest.

Although CP is negotiable and can be sold in the secondary market, most CP is held to maturity.

There are two major markets for CP:

1. The US dollar domestic market (US-CP), and
2. The Euro commercial paper market (ECP).

US Dollar Commercial Paper   The market price of US-CP is quoted as a discount rate. This is the rate of discount to face value at which the CP is being issued or sold. At a 7% per annum discount rate, US-CP with a one-year tenor would be issued at 93.00 (100% less 7%). At a discount rate of 7% per annum, US-CP with a 180-day tenor would be issued at 96.50 (100 minus 7.00 x 180/360).

Euro Commercial Paper   Most ECP issues are denominated in US dollars and range in maturities from 7 days to 12 months, with 90 days being typical. ECP is priced on a discount-to-yield basis (like CDs) and not on a discount to par, as with US-CP. The day-count convention for non-GBP ECP is actual/360; it is actual/365 for sterling.

The cost of ECP will be the face value discounted by the yield and the tenor of the CP.

Example

The cost of an investor purchasing a GBP 500,000 ECP with a 90-day tenor and yielding 0.65% would be:

$$\text{Cost} = \frac{\text{Face Value}}{\left[1 + \left(\dfrac{\text{Yield} \times \text{Tenor}}{100 \times 365}\right)\right]}$$

$$\text{Cost} = \frac{500,000}{\left[1 + \left(\dfrac{0.65 \times 90}{100 \times 365}\right)\right]}$$

$$\text{Cost} = \frac{500,000}{\left[1 + \left(\dfrac{58.50}{36,500}\right)\right]}$$

$$\text{Cost} = \frac{500,000}{1 + 0.001603}$$

$$\text{Cost} = \text{GBP } 499,199.91 \text{ (a discount of GBP 800.09)} \qquad (2.5)$$

2.3.4   Treasury Bills

Treasury bills (T-bills) are issued and guaranteed by governments as part of their debt-financing activities. T-bills are issued on a regular basis by auction with maturities out to 52 weeks and priced at a discount from the face value.

T-bills are not interest-bearing, and the difference between the face value and the purchase cost represents the interest earned on the bill.

USA   There are four terms of T-bill that investors can bid for.[1] These are shown in Table 2.12 together with cash management bills.

TABLE 2.12   US Treasury bills auction frequency

Term	Auction Frequency	
4-week	Every week	Competitive bid (investor specifies the discount rate) or non-competitive (investor accepts the discount rate determined at the auction).
13-week	Every week	
26-week	Every week	
52-week	Every four weeks	
Cash management bills	No regular schedule; CMBs are auctioned as required.	

For example, if a USD 1,000 26-week bill were to sell at auction for a 0.145% discount rate, the purchase price would be USD 999.27, a discount of USD 0.73. The purchase price can be determined from the following formula:

$$P = F[1 - (dxt/360)] \tag{2.6}$$

$$P = \text{USD } 1,000^*[1 - (0.00145 \times 182/360)], \text{ solving}$$
$$P = \text{USD } 999.27$$

Where:

P = Price

F = Face value

d = Rate of discount

t = Days to maturity

During periods when Treasury cash balances are particularly low, the Treasury may sell *cash management bills* (or CMBs). These are sold at a discount and by auction just like weekly Treasury bills. They differ in that they are irregular in amount, term (often less than 21 days) and day of the week for auction, issuance and maturity.

UK   Treasury bills are zero-coupon bearer government securities issued in minimum denominations of GBP 5,000 at a discount to their face value for any period up to one year. Prices

---

[1] See www.treasurydirect.gov/instit/marketables/tbills/tbills.htm.

are based on a money market yield to maturity calculation priced around prevailing General Collateral (GC) repo rates, adjusted by a spread reflecting recent Treasury bill tender results and, if applicable, any specific supply and demand factors.

Although they are usually issued for 3 months (91 days), they have occasionally been issued for 28 days, 63 days and 182 days.

They are issued:

- By allotment to the highest bidder at a weekly (Friday) tender to a range of counterparties;
- In response to an invitation from the Debt Management Office[2] to a range of counterparties;
- At any time to government departments (non-marketable bills only).

The secondary market in Treasury bills has, in recent years, become illiquid and representative rates are no longer obtainable other than those for the most recently issued 91-day bills.

2.4 DEBT INSTRUMENTS

Now that we have seen the money market instruments and noted that the tenor of these instruments tends to be at the short end with a maximum tenor of typically 12 months, we will turn our attention to the capital markets by looking at the various debt instruments. The word "debt" simply means "loan" and loans can be subdivided into three types:

1. A bilateral loan is where, for example, a customer borrows cash from its bank.
2. A syndicated loan is where a corporate customer borrows not from one bank but from a group of banks.
3. A securitised loan is represented by the issuance of a bond. This bond is divisible into smaller portions of the total loan and can be bought and sold by other investors.

It is the third type of loan that we are interested in; we will not be covering bilateral or syndicated loans in this book.

2.4.1 A Bond Defined

A bond is a security that represents the indebtedness of the issuer of the bond (i.e. the borrower) to the holder of the bond (i.e. the investor). The issuer has an obligation to service its indebtedness by paying interest on a regular basis and repaying the debt when it falls due.

It should be noted that the holders of bonds do not have any voting interest in the issue unless the situation arises where the issuer is in a distress situation and is unable to service the debt. Bondholders are creditors to the issuer and rank senior to investors who own shares in the issuer.

---

[2]The UK Debt Management Office (DMO) is responsible for government wholesale sterling debt issuance.

2.4.2 Bond Issuance

Bonds can be issued by a variety of entities including:

- Governments and government agencies;
- Sovereign states;
- Corporations;
- Supranational institutions;
- Public authorities.

Government bonds tend to be issued through an auction process. Depending on the market, either market makers only can bid for these bonds through a competitive process or market makers can bid competitively along with other investors who can bid non-competitively.

By contrast, other types of bonds can be issued through an underwriting process where a syndicate of banks and securities houses buys the issue of bonds and sells them to other investors. A smaller group within the syndicate, known as book runners, will act as adviser to the issuer and arranger of the bond with direct links to the syndicate and other investors.

With government bond issuance, under the auction process, potential investors will bid for the bonds and will either be successful or not. The difference from the other types of bonds, which are syndicated, is that the book runners take the risk of the whole issue onto their books until such time as they can sell the bonds to other investors.

We refer to this activity as bond issuance in the primary markets; once the bond has been issued (and the issuer has received the cash) it automatically goes into the secondary markets until such time as the bond is repaid. So the primary markets are for the new issuance of bonds and the secondary markets for the subsequent trading and investment activities.

2.4.3 Types and Features of Bonds

There are various ways to categorise bonds, including:

- Domicile
- Interest rate
- Maturity.

Domicile   From the point of view of the issuer, bonds can be issued either in their domestic currency or in a foreign currency. We can classify these bonds into one of three types:

- **Domestic bonds:** These are bonds issued in the country of the issuer, the currency of the issuer and using a syndicate of domestic banks and investors.
- **Foreign bonds:** These are international bond issues underwritten by a syndicate of banks primarily from one country, denominated in that country's currency and sold principally in that country. The issue, however, is domiciled outside of that country. For example, if the European Investment Bank wishes to raise US dollars in New York, the issue will be called a foreign dollar bond. Foreign bonds are usually referred to in terms of some local characteristic, for example, a US-dollar-denominated bond issued by a non-US entity in

the US market is referred to as a Yankee bond. Other foreign bonds include Samurai (Japan), Bulldog (UK) and Matrioshka (Russia) to name but a few.

- **Eurobonds:** Like foreign bonds, Eurobonds are international bond issues, but they differ from other types of international bonds, in that they are underwritten by an international syndicate of commercial and investment banks and they are sold principally in countries other than the country of the currency in which they are denominated. For example, if the European Investment Bank wishes to raise dollars outside of the USA, the issue will be underwritten by the international syndicate of banks and will be sold on initial distribution in countries outside of the USA. From an investor's point of view, the differences between Eurobonds and foreign bonds are largely technical. The main differences relate to the composition of the underwriting syndicates and the selling features.

Interest Rate   Also known as a *coupon*, this is the rate of interest that the issuer pays to the bondholder. The term "coupon" refers to the fact that when bonds are in paper form (certificated), the bondholder has to remove (or "clip") a coupon from the bond certificate and present it to the appropriate paying agent in order to receive the interest. Depending on the type of bond, coupons are usually paid on a semi-annual or annual basis.

When the bond is issued, the coupon rate can be set at a rate that will not change during the life of the bond. This is a *fixed-interest bond*. Conversely, there are bonds where the coupon rate changes periodically. These are *floating-rate bonds*. The most common type is a *floating-rate note* (FRN), which usually pays coupons on a semi-annual basis but can also pay quarterly.

Maturity   This refers to the date on which the issuer is obliged to repay the principal amount. Bonds, which are long-term securities, typically have maturities greater than seven years. Traditionally, most bonds have a term in the 25- to 30-year period, but there are bonds which have been issued with 50 years' maturity and there are even some bonds issued with no maturity at all. These are known as *undated*, *perpetual* or *irredeemable bonds*.

2.4.4 Other Key Characteristics of Bonds

- **Principal:** This is the amount on which the issuer pays interest and repays the loan at the end of the term. Repayment is usually the principal amount (at par). The term "principal" is synonymous with the terms nominal, par value and face amount; please note that the principal amount is not the same as the market value; we will look at this in more detail later on.
- **Yield:** The yield is the rate of return received from investing in a bond. There are two types of yield:
  - current yield (running yield) – this is the annual interest payment divided by the current market price of the bond;
  - yield to maturity (redemption yield) – in addition to the current market price, this yield also takes into account the amount and timing of all remaining coupon payments and the length of time to maturity.
- **Market price:** The market price of a bond is quoted in percentage terms and is calculated by considering all future cash flows (i.e. coupon payments and maturity payment) and

converting them into a net present value (NPV). This NPV is the market price of the bond. Whilst the market price is, in fact, a percentage, it is quoted as a number to four decimal places.

For example, the UK Treasury 4.5% 2042 bond has a price of 115.4500 and a yield to redemption of 3.64%. You will notice that whilst this bond pays a coupon of 4.5% per annum, the yield is only 3.64%. This is because the price is above par (i.e. 115.4500) and has the effect of reducing the impact of the interest rate. We will look at this relationship between yield and price in more detail in Section 2.4.8.

2.4.5 Types of Bond

There are many types of bond, but we will concentrate on some of the major types. The descriptions that you will see below are not mutually exclusive and any particular bond might have more than one type associated with it.

- **Fixed-rate bonds:** The interest rate is set when the bonds are first issued and stays the same throughout the life of the bond. (Please note that the term "coupon" is synonymous with the term "interest".)

Example

GE Capital 5.00% USD bond due January 2016. This bond will pay a coupon of 5% per annum from the time it was issued up until January 2016, when the bond will be repaid.

- **Floating-rate notes (FRNs):** The interest rate varies periodically and is linked to a reference rate of interest such as LIBOR or EURIBOR. Depending on the creditworthiness of the issuer, the bond might also have an additional margin, for example the coupon rate might be fixed linked to six-month LIBOR plus 0.15%. In this particular case, the interest rate would be recalculated (re-fixed) every six months.

Example

ENEL USD FRN (6L+15) due 15 May 2024. With this FRN, on 15 May and 15 November (and every year until May 2024), the previous coupon is paid and the next coupon is fixed. If, for example, in May the six-month USD LIBOR rate is 0.3734%, then the coupon will be 0.5234% per annum for the next six months (i.e. 0.3734% + 0.15%). In the November, the coupon of 0.5234% p.a. will be paid, covering the six-month period, and the next coupon from November to May will be fixed.

- **Zero-coupon bonds:** These bonds do not carry any coupon and are issued at a substantial discount to par value. For example, if a zero-coupon bond is issued at a price of 80%, it will be repaid at par (i.e. 100%). The gain of 20% is treated as interest rather than capital for tax purposes.
- **High-yield bonds:** So-called because these bonds earn a higher yield due to the fact that they are rated below investment grade by the credit-rating agencies.

Example

A company known as Kazkommerts International issued a Euro-denominated bond with a B+ credit rating (Standard & Poor's), a coupon rate of 6.88% and a repayment due in February 2017. With a price of 96.65% it is yielding 8.02%. If you compare this yield with that of an investment-grade issuer with a similar maturity date, you will see that the yield is in the region of 2.5% – a significant difference.

- ▪ **Convertible bonds:** These bonds have a fixed coupon rate, maturities usually between 10 and 15 years and are structured so that there is the right to convert the bonds into ordinary shares of a company. Typically, it is the bondholder that has this right and the ordinary shares are those issued by the issuer of the bond. There are convertible bonds, however, that give the bond issuer the right to convert and it is possible to convert the bond into shares of another company other than the issuer. The conversion price and the conversion period are fixed at the time of issue.

2.4.6   Form of Bonds and Interest Payment

Traditionally, bonds would be issued in the form of certificates. It is more usual today for bonds to be issued with a single global certificate with deliveries and receipts reflected in a book entry format.

Domestic and foreign bonds together with government bonds tend to be in registered form, where the bond issuer (through a third-party organisation known as a *registrar* or *transfer agent*) keeps a record of the investors and all movements on to and away from the register. Interest on these bonds is usually payable half-yearly, but note that with some FRNs, interest is paid quarterly depending on the terms of the issue.

Eurobonds are always issued in bearer form with no corresponding bond register and the bondholder is presumed to be the owner of the bond. Interest on Eurobonds is usually paid annually and is paid gross without deduction of withholding tax or any other taxes.

Bond prices are quoted as a percentage of par, to which must be added accrued interest where appropriate.

Bonds are usually issued in multiples (denominations) of 1,000 units of currency; however, depending on the terms of issue, the denominations could be smaller (e.g. UK gilts are transferable in denominations of GBP 0.01) or larger (e.g. in denominations of USD 10,000 or more). A small denomination can be helpful to an investor who wishes to invest a set amount of cash rather than purchase a set denomination of the bond, as the following examples illustrate for an investor who has USD 10,000.00 in cash to invest (see Tables 2.13 and 2.14).

TABLE 2.13   Example 1: Bond denomination is USD 0.01

Cash Available	Bond Price	Principal Amount of Bond Purchased
USD 10,000.00	97.1250	USD 10,296.01

In Example 1 (Table 2.13), the investor is able to spend USD 10,000 and the amount of bonds purchased reflects the price of the bond to the nearest cent.

TABLE 2.14 Example 2: Bond denomination is USD 1,000

Principal Amount of Bond Purchased	Bond Price	Cash Paid
USD 10,000	97.1250	USD 9,712.50
Cash available to invest:		USD 10,000.00
Uninvested cash:		USD 287.50

In Example 2 (Table 2.14), the investor could only buy the bond in multiples of 10,000, which would have left the investor with USD 287.50 uninvested.

2.4.7 Maturity and Redemption Provisions

The bond issuer repays the bond in accordance with the terms of issue. These can be either repayable in one amount at maturity (a bullet maturity) or in stages during the life of the bond. In the latter case, redemptions may be mandatory as in the case of a sinking fund, or conditional as in the case of a purchase fund.

   Sinking fund: The issuer is obliged to redeem a specified amount of the bond within pre-set time limits, for example, it may have to purchase 10% of the issue in each of years three and four, 20% in each of years five and six and the balance at maturity (see Table 2.15).

TABLE 2.15 Example of a sinking fund repayment schedule

ABC Bonds due 2020			Issue Size	USD 1,000,000,000
2016	**2017**	**2018**	**2019**	**2020**
10%	10%	20%	20%	40%
USD 100,000,000	USD 100,000,000	USD 200,000,000	USD 200,000,000	USD 400,000,000
			Total:	USD 1,000,000,000

   If the bonds are trading below par, the borrower will usually buy the required number of bonds in the market. Alternatively, the bonds can be drawn by lot and repaid at par with the relevant central securities depository advising those investors whose bonds have been drawn.

   Purchase fund: The issuer is only required to buy up to a specified amount of bonds if the bonds are trading in the market at a price below par during any particular year.

   There is an optional element where the bond issuer sometimes has the right to accelerate repayment of the bonds in part or in whole, in which case they usually pay a premium varying with the length of time by which repayment is accelerated. The conditions under which a bond repayment might be accelerated will be specified in the terms of the bond. The term we use to describe this right is a *call option*. There is a second optional element that gives the bondholder the right to surrender the bond back to the issuer at a price less than par. We refer to this as a *put option*. (More details can be found in Chapter 11: Corporate Actions.)

2.4.8 Calculations

The settlement amount for purchases and sales comprises two elements:

1. The market value (consideration) of the transaction. This is the face amount of the bond multiplied by the price (quoted as a percentage to par). We refer to this price as the *clean price*.
2. The amount of interest that has accrued and is due to the seller.

Before we explore the topic of accrued interest in more detail, the following example illustrates the calculation of the amount payable by the buyer to the seller.

Example

Transaction details

Dealer A sells USD 5,000,000 EDF 4.60% bonds due 27 January 2020 to Client B at a price of 112.1560 on trade date 09 September 2014. The accrued interest amount is shown in Table 2.16.

TABLE 2.16   Accrued interest

Transaction Details		Comments
Settlement date	12 September 2014	The asset is a Eurobond and the settlement convention is T+3
Face value	USD 5,000,000	
Price	112.1560	Strictly speaking, the correct quotation style should be 112.1560%. This is the "clean price".
Consideration	USD 5,607,800.00	This is the market value of the bond – the "clean value".
Number of days' accrued interest	225	Using the 30E/360 convention
Accrued interest	USD 143,750.00	
Total net amount (TNA)	USD 5,751,550.00	Total cash amount payable by Client B to Dealer A on 12 September 2014

In the above example we use the terms *clean price* and *clean value* and note that this represents the market value of the bond. The accrued interest has nothing to do with a market value of the bond; it is the means by which the seller is compensated for holding the bond for a particular number of days. However, the TNA does disguise the market value of the bond, and so we refer to this as the *dirty value*.

Q&A

Question

What do you think the dirty price of this bond is?

Answer

The dirty price is 115.0310 (divide the TNA USD 5,751,550.00 by the face value USD 5,000,000 as a percentage).

Market convention is that bonds are traded using the clean price. It is the Settlements Department's job to calculate the correct amount of accrued interest and to apply it to the transaction.

2.4.9 Accrued Interest

Issuers pay interest on their bonds in accordance with the terms of the issue and this can be annually (e.g. Eurobonds), semi-annually (e.g. government bonds) or, more rarely, quarterly (e.g. FRNs).

Take the example of the EDF bond traded above. Recall that we were talking about a Eurobond, which pays interest annually. We can tell on which date the interest is paid because it will coincide with the day and month shown in the maturity date (i.e. annually every 27 January). Although we do not know when Dealer A originally purchased the bond, we make the assumption that Dealer A has held the bond since the last coupon was paid. For this particular transaction, we can say that the last coupon payment date was 27 January 2014 (and the next coupon payment date will be 27 January 2015).

During the period from 27 January 2014 update until the above transaction was due to settle, Dealer A was entitled to benefit from the interest that was accruing on the bond. In the example above, this amounted to 225 days.

Q&A

Question

Do you agree with this figure? Please attempt the calculation making a note of how you arrived at your figure.

Answer

The correct answer for this particular type of bond is 225 days. This might appear counter-intuitive if you are new to the concept of accrued interest. The difficulty is that there are two methods of calculating the number of days between the last coupon payment date and the settlement date. The choice is either to calculate the actual, calendar days (i.e. 228 days in the example) or to assume every month consists of 30 days regardless of the actual days in any particular month (i.e. 225 days). In Table 2.17, we can compare both conventions on a month-by-month basis.

TABLE 2.17　Accrued interest day count

Last Coupon Date	Settlement Date	Number of Days (30 days/month)	Number of Days (Actual)
27 January 2014	12 September 2014	225	228
Analysis of calculation:			
Days accrued in:	January	4	5
	February	30	28
	March	30	31
	April	30	30
	May	30	31
	June	30	30
	July	30	31
	August	30	31
	September	11	11
	Totals:	**225**	**228**

Our EDF transaction therefore accrued 225 days' interest. How, then, did we arrive at the figure of USD 143,750.00?

1. The accrued interest is calculated on the face value of the bond and not on the market value of the bond.
2. Interest accrues on a daily basis up until the next coupon is paid. We therefore need to know how many days there are in that coupon period. With a Eurobond, there are 30 days in a month and therefore 360 days in a year and the calculation would be:

$$\text{Accrued Interest} = \text{Face Value} \times \frac{\text{Coupon Rate}}{100} \times \frac{\text{Number of Days Accrued}}{\text{Number of Days in Year}}$$

$$\text{Accrued Interest} = \text{USD } 5,000,000 \times \frac{4.60}{100} \times \frac{225}{360}$$

$$\text{Accrued Interest} = \text{USD } 143,750.00$$

We can therefore summarise that a US-dollar-denominated, fixed-interest Eurobond accrues interest on a 30E/360 basis. As US-dollar-denominated, fixed-interest bonds are not the only type, we need a set of rules that apply to all types.

The International Capital Market Association (ICMA), which represents members who are active in the international capital market, deals with the calculation of accrued interest in Section 250: Calculation of Accrued Interest Rules and Recommendations.

When interest starts to accrue and when it ends is covered in Rule 251.1. This states that: "The number of days accrued shall be calculated from and including the date of the last paid interest coupon or the day from which interest is to accrue for a new issue, up to but excluding the value date of the transaction".[3]

Let us apply this rule to the example of the EDF transaction above. The last coupon payment date was 27 January 2014 and therefore the 27th represented one day of accrued interest, with a total of four days for that month. The settlement date was 12 September 2014 and therefore there were 11 days of accrued interest (as we exclude the 12th). For the months of February through to August there were seven months, each of 30 days.

Rule 251 makes the distinction between different types of bond and bonds that were issued before and after the introduction of the single European currency in January 1999. The "number of days accrued" and the "number of days in the year" conventions described in Rule 251 can be found in Table 2.18 and are summarised in Figure 2.1.

TABLE 2.18 ICMA rule on accrued interest conventions

Bond Type	When Issued	Number of Days Accrued	Number of Days in a Year
All convertible bonds	Before 01 Jan 1999	360-days-per-year basis (a month is 30 days)	360 days
All straight bonds	Before 01 Jan 1999	360-days-per-year basis (a month is 30 days)	360 days
Euro sterling FRNs	Any time	Calendar days (incl. leap year)	Actual number of days in the calendar year
All FRNs (except Euro sterling FRNs)	Any time	Calendar days (incl. leap year)	360 days
Non-USD-denominated convertible bonds	After 31 Dec 1998	Calendar days (incl. leap year)	Actual calendar days in coupon period multiplied by number of coupon periods in the year
Non-USD-denominated straight bonds	After 31 Dec 1998	Calendar days (incl. leap year)	Actual calendar days in coupon period multiplied by number of coupon periods in the year
USD-denominated convertible bonds	After 31 Dec 1998	360-days-per-year basis (a month is 30 days)	360 days
USD-denominated straight bonds	After 31 Dec 1998	360-days-per-year basis (a month is 30 days)	360 days

---

[3]*Source:* ICMA Group (online). "ICMA Rule Book" available to members and subscribers only. Available from www.icmagroup.org/Regulatory-Policy-and-Market-Practice/Secondary-Markets/ICMA-Rule-Book.

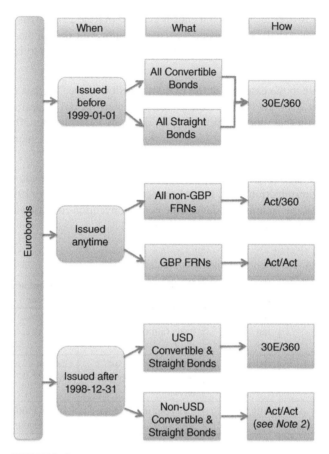

FIGURE 2.1   Summary of ICMA accrued interest rules

Note 1: Day basis (the "How" in Figure 2.1) is explained in Table 2.19.

TABLE 2.19   Day basis

Convention	Explanation
30E/360	30 days in a month, 360 days in a year, using the European method for dates falling on the 31st of a month (European 30/360).
Actual/360	Actual calendar days in each month, 360 days in a year.
Actual/Actual	Actual calendar days in each month, actual days in each year (both including the extra day in leap years).
Other variations include:	
Actual/365	Actual calendar days in each month, 365 days in a year.
30/360	30 days in a month, 360 days in a year, using the NASD method for dates falling on the 31st of a month.

Note 2: The full text of "/Actual" is: "… actual calendar days in the coupon period multiplied by the number of coupon periods in the year". So, for example, if the coupon period contains 181 days and the bond is a semi-annual coupon payer, then the divisor is 362 days.

Note 3: "Actual" includes the extra day in a leap year.

Day/year conventions also differ when we consider government bonds and domestic corporate bonds.

- **Actual/Actual:** Applicable to most government bonds and many corporate bonds.
- **30/360:** Used by many corporate bonds. Assumes 30 days for each month, even for those months that have 28, 29 or 31 days.
- **30E/360:** A slight modification of the 30/360 convention common in the Eurobond market. If either the previous coupon date or the settlement date falls on the 31st of any month, it is assumed to be the 30th.
- **Actual/360:** Used by some supranational and corporate bonds.
- **Actual/365:** Used by some supranational and corporate bonds.

2.4.10 First Short Coupon

Depending on the payment frequency, the first coupon is paid either six or twelve months after the bond was issued. For example, if a semi-annual bond was issued on 15 January 2014, the first coupon payment would fall due six months later on 15 July 2014 (thereafter on 15 January 2015, 15 July 2015, etc.).

The situation can be complicated when an issuer, typically a government, authorises a bond but only makes part of it (the first tranche) immediately available to investors. The balance of the issue (second tranche) can be made available at some future time. This type of bond is referred to as a *tap bond* or *tap issue*.

In Table 2.20 we show the details of a fictitious bond issued in two tranches.

TABLE 2.20 Details of ABC 5.00% bonds due 2024

	1st Tranche	2nd Tranche
Issuer:	ABC	
Issue date:	15 January 2014	15 October 2014
Maturity date:	15 January 2024	
Coupon rate:	5.00%	
First coupon date:	15 July 2014	15 January 2015
Day count convention:	Actual/Actual	
Days in coupon period:	181 days	92 days

We can see here that whilst the first tranche has the full semi-annual number of days (i.e. 181 days from 15 January 2014 to 15 July 2014), the second tranche only has 92 days. With effect from 15 January 2015, both tranches will be consolidated into the single bond and the coupon payments will be made on the normal six-monthly cycle.

2.4.11 First Long Coupon

Taking the ABC example again (see Table 2.21), if the second tranche had been issued on 15 December 2014, the issuer might not wish to go to the trouble and expense of paying a first short coupon only one month later (on 15 January 2015). Instead, the issuer might delay the first coupon payment until 15 July 2015. This would result in the first coupon being paid more than six months after issue and we refer to this as a *first long coupon*.

TABLE 2.21 Details of ABC 5.00% bonds due 2024

	1st Tranche	2nd Tranche
Issuer:	ABC	
Issue date:	15 January 2014	15 December 2014
Maturity date:	15 January 2024	
Coupon rate:	5.00%	
First coupon date:	15 July 2014	15 July 2015
Day count convention:	Actual/Actual	
Days in coupon period:	181 days	212 days

Q&A

Question

On what date would both tranches be consolidated?

Answer

15 July 2015 (and not 15 January 2015 as in the first short coupon scenario).

2.5 EQUITY INSTRUMENTS

2.5.1 Equity Defined

Equity, also known as shares, is the third asset class that stands alongside cash (plus near-cash instruments) and debt instruments. Debt, as you will recall, represents the borrowing of cash; by contrast, corporate entities that issue equity are, in fact, selling a stake in the entity to investors in exchange for cash.

When a company is first established, it can raise finance by selling shares to external investors. There will be a limit to the total share capital that the company is authorised to issue, and therefore the number of shares that it can sell. The amount of share capital will be published in the company's Memorandum and Articles of Association, as the example below illustrates.

ABC LIMITED SHARE CAPITAL

ABC Ltd has an authorised share capital of GBP 10 million.

The authorised share capital is subdivided into shares, each with a par value of 25p (i.e. 40 million ordinary shares).

ABC Ltd is not obliged to issue all of the authorised share capital at once. It will issue sufficient shares to raise the expected amount of cash.

Q&A

Question

Let us assume that the company's advisers estimate that the company is worth GBP 20 million. On that basis, how much would each of the 40 million shares be worth?

Answer

Each share would be worth 50p (GBP 20,000,000 ÷ 40,000,000 shares).

Q&A

Question

If the company wishes to raise GBP 10 million in cash, it would not have to issue all the shares. How many shares would the company need to issue?

Answer

If each share is estimated to be worth 50p, then only 20 million shares need to be issued (20 million shares multiplied by 50p).

At the end of this share-issuing exercise, ABC Ltd would show the following position in its financial reporting:

- Authorised share capital GBP 10 million (40 million shares);
- Issued share capital GBP 5 million (20 million shares);
- Unissued share capital GBP 5 million (20 million shares).

We have used the term *par value* in this example. Par value represents the capital value of each share (as opposed to the market value). In the example above, ABC Ltd had decided that each pound sterling of share capital would be represented by four shares, each with a par value of 25p. At some later stage, ABC could decide to make the shares more liquid by subdividing the shares into a lower par value, for example, 10p. Each one pound would be represented by 10 shares and the total number of shares authorised would be 100 million shares (GBP 10 million multiplied by 10 shares).

Whereas bond issuers have an obligation to pay interest and the principal amount of the loan as and when due, equity issuers have no such obligation. Bondholders know how much cash they will receive and when they will receive it. Shareholders, on the other hand, can only expect to benefit if the company distributes profits by way of a cash dividend. Shares do not have a maturity date, so, apart from the expectation of cash dividends, the only other predictable benefit is that shareholders have the right to vote at Annual General Meetings (AGMs) and Extraordinary General Meetings (EGMs).

Share prices do fluctuate for a variety of reasons and can be highly volatile at times. Shareholders can benefit, as the value of the shares they hold will increase if the market price is above the original purchase price. The shareholder could then sell the shares and make a profit. However, if the share price is below the original price and the shareholder decides to sell, then there will be a loss.

What is the maximum loss that a shareholder can suffer? As the share price cannot go below zero, the maximum loss will be the total investment that the shareholder made. What about the maximum profit? Depending on the individual circumstances for the company, the share price can increase without any upper limit.

Q&A

Question

As a potential investor, which asset class is generally the riskier – debt or equity?

Answer

In general terms, as an asset class, equity is more risky than debt.

See Table 2.22 for a comparison of equity with debt from an investor's point of view.

TABLE 2.22   Debt vs. equity characteristics

Equity	Characteristic	Debt
Dividends Voting rights	Benefits	Coupon receipts.
Dividends – uncertain Voting rights – certain	Certainty of benefit	Certain, assuming issuer is able to pay.

TABLE 2.22 *(Continued)*

Equity	Characteristic	Debt
Dividends – annual/semi-annual/ quarterly depending on market convention and/or issuer preference Voting rights – AGM/EGM	Timing of benefit	Predictable, as noted in issuing prospectus. FRN coupons are fixed periodically against a known benchmark interest rate.
No maturity – shares can be bought out by issuer, surrendered in a takeover or deleted through liquidation	Maturity/ Redemption	Except for perpetual bonds, maturity proceeds are predictable and certain with the caveat noted above.
Ranks junior to all other asset classes	Seniority re liquidation	Ranks more senior to equity, with secured debt ranking above unsecured debt.

You might wonder why any investor would wish to risk his money buying shares. A cursory glance at a typical institutional investor's portfolio could very well show that over 60% of the portfolio is invested in shares, with 30% in bonds and the remaining 10% in cash/near-cash instruments/alternative investments and, perhaps, derivative instruments.

From an operational point of view, we do not need to be concerned about why investments are made, only that they have been made and need to be processed. As a matter of interest, investors will invest in equities in the hope (but without any certainty) that the market value of their holdings increases and that companies pay cash dividends on a regular basis. We saw that there is no theoretical limit to how high the share price can go over time, and it is the anticipation of such a price increase over time that can motivate an investor.

As a comparison, investors in bonds are looking for a degree of certainty: certainty of income (coupon payments), certainty of timing and certainty of repayment. You could argue that the "cost" of this certainty is a relatively stable bond price and a known coupon rate. Remember that the price of a bond is linked primarily to the yields in the market. As yields go up, the price of the bond goes down and as yields go down, then the price of the bond will go up. You can appreciate that there are limits to how high or low yields can go.

2.5.2 Classes of Equity

There are two main classes of equity:

- Ordinary shares
- Preference shares.

Ordinary Shares　　Ordinary shares (also known as common stock in the USA or just simply shares) are the basic class of share. An example of this class of equity:

Lloyds Banking Group plc, ordinary shares of 10p each

Total number of voting shares: 71,367,953,697 (as at 30 April 2014)

ISIN: GB0008706128

SEDOL: 0870612

London Stock Exchange ticker code: LLOY:LSE

Registrar: Equiniti

Preference Shares   Preference shares (aka preferred stock) can be regarded as a hybrid security, in that they contain some features of ordinary shares and some features of bonds. Not every company will issue preference shares, and those that do will issue more ordinary shares than preference shares.

The main features of preference shares are listed in Table 2.23 together with the asset type of which they are a hybrid.

TABLE 2.23   Main features of preference shares

Feature	Description	Hybrid of:
Dividends	Preference shares can be either a fixed amount or a floating amount.	Debt
	Dividends are paid on preference shares before ordinary shares are paid.	–
Cumulative dividends	If the issuer does not pay a cumulative preference share, it must pay it at a later time before paying any other dividends.	–
Non-cumulative dividends	This does not happen with non-cumulative preference shares; the dividend is lost (this is similar to the situation with ordinary shares).	Equity
Voting rights	Most preference shares are non-voting. However, some do gain the right to vote under certain circumstances, e.g. when the dividends are in arrears.	Equity
Convertibility	Some preference shares are convertible into ordinary shares.	Debt
Seniority	Preference shares are senior to ordinary shares but junior to debt instruments.	–
Maturity	Preference shares can be either redeemable or irredeemable (perpetual).	Debt/Equity
Credit rating	Preference shares are rated by the various credit-rating agencies, but are rated lower than bonds.	Debt

An example of a company that has issued both ordinary and preference shares is the Chilean-based copper-mining company, Antofagasta plc. The company is listed on the London Stock

Exchange (ANTO:LSE) and is a constituent of the FTSE 100 index. As at 31 December 2013,[4] the company had the following share capital issued and fully paid:

Ordinary shares: 985,856,695 ordinary shares of 5p each;

Preference shares: 2,000,000 5% cumulative preference shares of GBP 1 each. These preference shares are non-redeemable and pay an annual dividend of GBP 100,000.

2.5.3 Equity Issuance

When a company issues shares for the first time, we refer to this as an *Initial Public Offering* (IPO). The same company can subsequently issue more shares and we would refer to this as a secondary issue of shares (e.g. a *rights issue*). We will cover rights issues in Chapter 11: Corporate Actions.

A company becomes a public company through an IPO and shares are sold to investors in exchange for cash. Details of any proposed IPO must be disclosed in a prospectus document. The prospectus explains the company's performance to potential buyers, including an overview of its financial history and is generally approved by the local regulatory authority. The prospectus provides sufficient information to enable a prospective investor to make a judgement as to whether an investment should be made.

The company will not arrange an IPO on its own. It will employ the services of an investment bank, which will act as an underwriter and provide advice on the best method of issuing the IPO, assess the share price at which the shares will be offered and arrange for the shares to be sold. The company will also employ a law firm to obtain securities-related legal advice.

One method of issuing shares is through an *open offer* whereby, after a period of advertising the issue through the media and by meetings with potential institutional investors, investors are invited to apply for shares at a price that is not advertised until a few days before the issue is due to close. An interested investor will then apply for a quantity of shares and arrange for the appropriate amount of cash to be paid to the issuer's agent. If the preliminary public relations exercise has gone well and there is a high level of investor interest, then the price might be set at the higher end of the anticipated price range. Even so, the number of shares applied for might very well exceed the number of shares being offered, in which case the company needs to decide how it is going to allocate the shares.

On the other hand, if the market conditions are not right and/or there is little investor appetite to buy the shares, then fewer shares will be sold and the underwriters will be expected to buy the unallocated shares. This way, the issuing company is able to issue sufficient shares to get the amount of cash it was hoping for.

A recent example of an IPO was the British Government's GBP 1.7bn privatisation of the Royal Mail Group in October 2013. There was a great deal of interest in the issue and the shares were priced at 330p per share (at the higher end of expectations). The institutional tranche was twenty times over-subscribed, with allocations scaled back or no allocation made at all. The retail offer was seven times over-subscribed, with only those who had applied for

---

[4]*Source:* Company's annual report (online). Available from www.antofagasta.co.uk/~/media/Files/A/ Antofagasta/pdf/annual-reports/ar-2013.pdf. [Accessed Tuesday, 29 April 2014]

less than GBP 10,000 worth of shares being successful. On the first day of trading, the share price rose to 459p before closing at 431p per share.

The largest IPOs have occurred in China and the USA, with the largest half dozen shown in Table 2.24.

TABLE 2.24   Largest IPOs

Company	Year	Amount (USD billions)
Agricultural Bank of China	2010	22.1
Industrial and Commercial Bank of China	2006	21.9
American International Assurance	2010	20.5
Visa	2008	19.7
General Motors	2010	18.1
Facebook	2012	16.0

2.5.4   Pricing and Calculations

Equity trades are priced in units of currency per share. For example, the price of ABC Corporation shares might be EUR 5.50 per share. The one exception to this rule occurs in the UK where shares are priced in pence per share (not pounds sterling per share), so shares in Barclays Bank might be priced at 250p per share.

In order to make the correct calculation, we need to know the local market convention regarding brokerage fees and any local stock exchange/tax charges. Let us pretend that a trade has been executed in an imaginary market where the brokerage fee is charged at 25 basis points on the market value and that a local tax of 50 basis points is also charged on the market value of any purchase.

How much, then, would we have to pay if we were to buy 10,000 XYZ Corporation shares at 3.25 per share? To calculate the market value of this transaction, we multiply the number of shares traded by the price per share. In addition, we need to calculate the brokerage fees and, separately, any local taxes. The results are shown in Table 2.25.

TABLE 2.25   Total cost of purchasing 10,000 XYZ Corporation shares

Description	Quantity	Price/Fee/Tax Rate	Amount
Purchase: XYZ Corporation shares	10,000	3.25	32,500.00
Brokerage (bp)		25	81.25
Local tax (bp)		50	162.50
Total cost			32,743.75

Q&A

Question

How much cash would you receive if you sold 50,000 Barclays Bank shares at a price of 266p per share and you were charged a brokerage fee of 15 basis points? (Please note that in the UK, no local tax is charged for a sale.)

Answer

The answer is GBP 132,800.50 (see Table 2.26). Remember that these are UK shares and are (a) priced in pence per share and (b) there is no local tax on sales of shares. Note also that brokerage is deducted (not added) from the market value.

TABLE 2.26   Total proceeds calculation

Description	Quantity	Price/Fee/Tax Rate	Amount
Sale: Barclays Bank shares	50,000	266	GBP 133,000.00
Brokerage (bp)		15	GBP (199.50)
Local tax (bp)		0	GBP 0.00
Total proceeds:			GBP 132,800.50

2.5.5 Examples of Local Taxes

There are different tax regimes in each country, as the examples show. It is usual that the local clearing house collects the tax and periodically remits it to the appropriate government agency. Table 2.27 shows some examples of these taxes.

TABLE 2.27   Examples of local taxes

Country	Stamp Duty (on consideration)	Payable by
USA	N/A	N/A
UK	0.5% (stamp duty reserve tax – SDRT) (See note below)	Purchaser
China	A shares 0.1% B shares 0.1%	Seller Seller
Germany	N/A	N/A
Japan	N/A	N/A
Singapore	Transfer stamp duty: 0.2% on contract value is payable for share certificates sent for registration.	This is not applicable to securities settled on a book-entry basis.

Note: The London Stock Exchange abolished stamp duty on shares admitted to the AIM and the High Growth with effect from 28 April 2014.

2.5.6 Disclosure

As ownership of shares with voting rights represents an actual interest in the issuing company, it is important for the company to know which investors have substantial shareholdings. An investor with an interest of over 50% of the voting rights has control of the issuing company; a situation that the issuing company may not be comfortable with. There are, therefore, disclosure rules that oblige any shareholder with more than a predefined percentage interest to disclose that fact to the issuing company and possibly the local stock exchange and regulator. The requirements do vary from market to market, but typically shareholdings below a 3% threshold are not required to be disclosed (see Table 2.28).

TABLE 2.28 Disclosure limits

Country	Disclosure Threshold Levels	Deadline after Transaction Date
USA	$\geq 5\%$ per class	To SEC within ten days
UK	(a) $\geq 3\%$ plus each 1% movement (b) $\geq 15\%$	(a) LSE and issuer company within two business days (b) By 12:00 one business day later
China	Three levels: 1. 5% 2. $> 5\% < 20\%$ 3. $> 20\% < 30\%$	To relevant stock exchange, CSRC, issuer and media within three business days Subsequent increase or decrease by 5% requires the same response
Germany	Exceeds or falls below the 3%, 5%, 10%, 15%, 20%, 25%, 30%, 50% or 75% thresholds of the voting rights	BaFin and issuer within four business days of having reached, exceeded or fallen below any of the thresholds
Japan	(a) FX and Foreign Trade Act Article 55-5 – Non-residents: $> 10\%$ (b) Financial Instruments and Exchange Law Article 27-23 (1) – Residents and non-residents: $> 5\%$	(a) Bank of Japan within 15 business days (b) Local finance bureau within five business days Additionally, any increase or decrease of 1%, as above
Singapore	$> 5\%$	To stock exchange and issuer within two business days

Not only is disclosure required when investors acquire shares that cross the specified thresholds, but also when investors dispose of shares that likewise cross the threshold.

In Chapter 3: Data Management, you will notice that one of the data fields contains information on the total number of shares in issue. It is this figure against which the investor's holding is compared in order to calculate the percentage interest. Failure to disclose as and when required can lead to fines and holdings being frozen in terms of deliveries and benefits.

2.5.7 Summary of Cash Market Instruments

So far in Chapter 2 we have seen the three main types of cash market instruments, including both the money markets and the capital markets. These financial instruments cover a time horizon from short term to long term; from certificates of deposit to long-term debt and equities.

The issuers of these financial instruments range from corporate issuers to government treasuries.

Q&A

Question

Which instrument is never issued by a government or its agencies?

> **Answer**
>
> Equities. Governments can borrow money but cannot issue share capital.

One further common factor is that these instruments are issued because the issuer requires cash/capital for whatever purpose. Investors can purchase these instruments and become either a holder of an issuer's debt and/or a stakeholder in the issuer company.

We will now continue our look at financial instruments by turning our attention to the derivatives market.

2.6 DERIVATIVE INSTRUMENTS

2.6.1 Introduction

Whilst issuers are directly involved in the issuance of cash market instruments, they have no such role with derivatives. So what, you might ask, are derivatives? There are many different types of derivatives and we can define the whole class as follows:

> A derivative is a financial contract that derives its value from the performance of another entity, called the "underlying".

If you are comfortable with this definition, here is another from the Office of the Comptroller of the Currency (a department of the US Treasury):

> A derivative is a financial contract whose value is derived from the performance of underlying market factors, such as interest rates, currency exchange rates, and commodity, credit, and equity prices. Derivative transactions include an assortment of financial contracts, including structured debt obligations and deposits, swaps, futures, options, caps, floors, collars, forwards, and various combinations thereof.[5]

What can we learn from the OCC's definition? There are two learning outcomes:

1. The underlying covers a very broad range of asset types, e.g. interest rates, stock market indices, commodities, share prices, etc.

---

[5]*Source:* The Office of the Comptroller of the Currency (online). Derivatives definition. Available from www.occ.gov/topics/capital-markets/financial-markets/trading/derivatives/index-derivatives.html. [Accessed Thursday, 12 December 2013]

2. Derivative transactions fall into four types:
   - Forwards
   - Futures
   - Options
   - Swaps.

We can also differentiate derivatives in further ways. Firstly, there are types of derivative product that are constructed by an exchange, traded on the exchange and cleared by a central clearing system. We refer to these as *exchange-traded derivatives*.

Secondly, there are other types of derivative product that are constructed by financial entities such as banks and traded away from an exchange between the buyer and the seller. We refer to these as *Over-The-Counter (OTC) derivatives*.

Not only are OTC derivatives traded between buyer and seller, but all the post-trade activities also take place between the buyer and the seller, i.e. no central clearing system is involved. This situation is changing, with many of the more straightforward OTC contracts being cleared centrally and the more exotic OTC contracts yet to be decided.

It is not possible in this book to look at every single derivative product; we will, however, look at one or two examples of ETDs and OTCs. It is sufficient for you to be able to define the four main types of derivatives and understand the prime reasons for using them.

2.6.2 Definitions

We saw that there are four headline types of derivative product and each one can be defined as follows:

> 1. **Forwards:** A forward contract is a legally binding obligation to buy or sell an agreed amount of an agreed asset at a certain future time for a certain price agreed today.

This derivative type is OTC.

> 2. **Futures:** A futures contract is a legally binding obligation to buy or sell a standard amount of a standard asset at a specific time in the future for a certain price that is agreed today.

This derivative type is ETD.

Notice how the definition of a future is similar to that of a forward. The key difference is that the terms of a futures contract are much more standardised with regards to the:

- Standard quantity/amount;
- Standard (underlying) asset/commodity;
- Specific delivery date.

3. Options: A call option gives the buyer (the *holder*) the right to purchase an asset for a specified price on or before a specified expiration date.

A put option gives the holder the right to sell an asset for a specified price on or before a specified expiration date.

This derivative type can be either ETD or OTC.

Call options and put options can also be sold; the seller is known as the *writer* of the contract.

4. Swaps: This is a derivative product in which two counterparties exchange certain benefits of one party's financial assets for those of the counterparty's assets.

The cash flows are calculated on a notional principal amount and these cash flows are known as the *legs* of a swap.

This derivative type is OTC.

2.6.3 Derivative Usage

Hedging: A broad range of market participants use derivatives to hedge or reduce their exposure to future market conditions, for example, an airline will ask its bank to design a combination of option contracts against rising jet fuel prices. If the fuel price increases to a predetermined amount, then the bank, in effect, refunds the difference between the cash price of the fuel and the strike price of the option contract. We will look at an example later in this chapter. As a further example, a fund manager can hedge a portfolio of bonds against a decrease in value by selling an appropriate number of futures contracts. If the portfolio does, in fact, decrease in value, then the fund manager will receive benefit from an increase in the value of the futures contract. A perfect hedge would therefore be a decrease in the portfolio value of X, mirrored by an increase in the value of the futures contracts also of X.

Dealing: Both ETD and OTC contracts are traded by dealers who work for banks and securities houses. Their role is to trade on behalf of their employer companies and to advise and trade on behalf of their clients. They will have expertise in a wide variety of derivative products ranging from standard ETDs to complex combinations of OTC contracts.

Speculation: It can be time-consuming and expensive to buy or sell the underlying assets such as equities and bonds. For a speculator it can be a lot more straightforward to purchase a derivative contract and benefit by selling it when the price increases. It may not be possible to sell the underlying asset "short"; by contrast, it is just as easy to sell the derivative short as it is to buy long. Furthermore, these transactions can be executed much more quickly and more cheaply.

A common variant of speculative trading is *spread trading,* whereby there is a combination of buys and sells in the same product but with two different aspects, for example:

Two different delivery months (e.g. March and June);

Two different stock market indices (e.g. DAX and CAC);

Two different commodities (e.g. West Texas Intermediate and Brent crude).

Arbitrage: Arbitrageurs attempt to exploit the price differences between two similar products traded in two different markets. By way of comparison, in Table 2.29 we can see how an arbitrageur might benefit from the price differences on an interest-rate future and an underlying government bond.

TABLE 2.29   Arbitrage government bond and futures contract

Government Bond	Bond Price	Long-Dated Bond Future	Futures Price
Japan 10-year	99.44	Japan 10yr contract	114.14
If the prices change as follows…			
Price decreases to:	99.40	Price increases to:	114.20
The arbitrageur would buy the bonds believing the price will rise…		The arbitrageur would short the futures believing the price will fall…	
Buy bonds @	99.40	Sell futures @	114.20
If prices then settle back to approximately where they were, the arbitrageur will sell the bond position and close-out the futures position.			
Sell bonds @	99.43	Buy futures @	114.15
The sale of the bond has made a profit…		The close-out of the futures has made a profit…	
Profit:	0.03	Profit:	0.05

The arbitrageur has made a profit by benefiting from price differences that might only remain for a short period of time. Note that the arbitrageur has closed out both positions at the conclusion of this transaction.

Asset allocation: An institutional client such as an insurance company might be holding a portfolio of securities in one particular market. It might wish to reduce its exposure to that market and increase exposure in another market. There are two ways that the insurance company can achieve this:

1. The insurance company can sell securities in the first market and with the cash buy securities in the second. This can be expensive in terms of transaction costs, time-consuming in selecting appropriate securities and uncertain in terms of pricing. Furthermore, it may not be part of the insurance company's investment strategy to reallocate funds for a long-term time horizon. In other words, this might be a short-term strategy.
2. The insurance company can reduce exposure in the first market by selling an appropriate number of futures contracts and can increase exposure in the second by buying an appropriate number of futures contracts. This can be achieved by two transactions and can be quick to execute with low transaction charges. If the insurance company wishes to revert to the original allocation, then it simply needs to close out the two futures contracts.

Changing risk: A corporation might be borrowing money at a variable rate of interest and may be concerned that interest rates will increase. It could enter into an interest rate swap, in which it would swap its variable interest payments with, for example, a fixed rate of interest. In this way, if interest rates do increase as feared, the corporation is protected by paying interest at a fixed rate.

In April 2009, the International Swaps and Derivatives Association (ISDA) announced the results of its Derivatives Usage Survey of the world's biggest 500 companies. It found that 94% of these companies were users of derivative products. Table 2.30 shows the usage by industry sector and the type of derivative used and Table 2.31 shows the usage by country.

TABLE 2.30   Usage by industry sector and type of derivative

Sector Name	Total Companies	Derivatives Overall	Interest Rate	Forex	Commodity	Credit	Equity
Basic materials	86	97%	70%	85%	79%	0%	6%
Consumer goods	88	91%	81%	84%	39%	1%	9%
Financial	123	98%	94%	96%	63%	76%	80%
Healthcare	25	92%	80%	72%	8%	4%	20%
Industrial goods	49	92%	86%	86%	37%	2%	20%
Services	40	88%	75%	85%	35%	3%	13%
Technology	65	95%	86%	92%	15%	6%	15%
Utilities	24	92%	92%	88%	83%	0%	8%
Total	**500**	**94%**	**83%**	**88%**	**49%**	**20%**	**29%**

Source: ISDA (online). News release, 23 April 2009 re derivatives usage by the world's top 500 companies. Available from www2.isda.org/functional-areas/research/surveys/end-user-surveys. [Accessed Thursday, 12 December 2013]

TABLE 2.31   Numbers and percentage of users per country

Country	Users	Usage
Canada	14	100.0%
France	39	100.0%
Japan	64	100.0%
Netherlands	13	100.0%
Switzerland	14	100.0%
UK	34	100.0%
Germany	36	97.3%
USA	140	91.5%
South Korea	13	86.7%
China	18	62.1%

Source: ISDA (online). News release, 23 April 2009 re derivatives usage by the world's top 500 companies. Available from www2.isda.org/functional-areas/research/surveys/end-user-surveys. [Accessed Thursday, 12 December 2013]

These are the main uses and users of derivative products. From an operational point of view, the reasons for using derivatives tend to be of secondary importance, however interesting these reasons might be. We are more concerned by what needs to happen once a derivatives transaction has taken place. The best way to approach this is to consider exchange-traded derivative transactions separately from OTC transactions, remembering that more and more of the latter are being cleared centrally rather than bilaterally between the buyer and seller.

2.7 EXCHANGE-TRADED DERIVATIVES

2.7.1 Introduction

Before we look at exchange-traded derivatives (ETDs) in more detail, please refresh your memories regarding the definitions of two types of ETD, i.e. futures and options.

Q&A

Question

What words or phrases in the definitions re-occur?

Answer

Here are the definitions that you saw above, with the key words or phrases highlighted in *italic*:

- A futures contract is a legally binding *obligation* to buy or sell a *standard amount of a standard asset* at a *specific time in the future* for a certain *price that is agreed today.*
- A call option gives the buyer (the "holder") *the right* to purchase an asset for a *specified price* on or before a *specified expiration date.*
- A put option gives the holder *the right* to sell an asset for a *specified price* on or before a *specified expiration date.*

Let us examine the similarities and differences between futures and options.

1. A futures contract is an obligation to do something; an option is a right or choice to do something. We will see that, in many cases, the buyers and sellers of futures contracts do not wish to make or take delivery of the underlying asset. To remove their obligation, the buyers and sellers must "close out" their obligations by selling (by the original buyer) and buying (by the original seller) the same quantity of contracts and, most importantly, informing the counterparty that these are closing transactions.

2. Both types refer to "standard amounts" and "specified prices and dates". This would suggest that an entity other than the buyers and sellers has previously specified what these amounts, prices and dates should be. In other words, these derivative contracts have been designed and specified by a third party. This third party is a derivatives exchange.

2.7.2 The Role of the Derivatives Exchanges

ETD contracts are designed by the exchange on which they are traded. The standard nature of each contract refers to the contract specifications set out in Table 2.32.

TABLE 2.32 Contract specifications

Contract Specification	Description
Underlying asset:	The name of the asset that would be delivered/received
Contract size:	The quantity of the asset represented in one contract
Delivery details:	(Also known as Expiry) The process for delivering the underlying asset, e.g. the date(s) when delivery can be made, the price at which deliveries will be made and who initiates delivery (the buyer or the seller)
Trading details:	Details such as the first and the last trading dates, exchange trading hours and the ways in which trading takes place (i.e. open outcry or electronic or a combination of both)
Pricing details:	The currency in which the contract will be traded, pricing style and the minimum price movement (known as the minimum tick value)

2.7.3 Major Derivatives Exchanges

It is usual for there to be a derivatives exchange in a market that has a stock exchange either as two separate entities or one combined entity (see Table 2.33).

In November 2013, the Intercontinental Exchange Group (ICE) announced the successful completion of its acquisition of NYSE Euronext.[6] The stock-and-cash transaction had a total value of approximately USD 11 billion.

The combined company operates 16 global exchanges and five central clearing houses. ICE and NYSE Euronext businesses will continue to operate under their respective brand names. As previously announced, the company expected to conduct an IPO for the Euronext group of Continental European exchanges as a standalone entity (in 2014), subject to market conditions and regulatory approval.

---

[6]*Source:* Intercontinental Exchange Group (online press release, 13 November 2013). "Intercontinental Exchange Completes Acquisition of NYSE Euronext." Available from http://ir.theice.com/investors-and-media/press/press-releases/press-release-details/2013/IntercontinentalExchange-Completes-Acquisition-of-NYSE-Euronext/default.aspx. [Accessed Friday, 15 November 2013]

TABLE 2.33 Examples of derivatives exchanges

Country	Exchange Name
Australia	ASX and ASX24
Belgium	Euronext Brussels (ex BXS)
Brazil	BmfBovespa-Derivatives
Canada	ICE Canada, Montreal Exchange (MX)
China	Shanghai Stock Exchange and Shenzhen Stock Exchange
China	China Financial Futures Exchange
France	Euronext Paris (ex MATIF MONEP)
Germany	Eurex
Hong Kong	Hong Kong Futures Exchange (HKEx Group)
India	National Stock Exchange and Bombay Stock Exchange
Italy	Italian Derivatives Market (IDEM)
Japan	Japan Exchange Group (Tokyo Stock Exchange, Osaka Securities Exchange) and Tokyo Financial Exchange
Korea	Korea Exchange
Malaysia	Bursa Malaysia
Mexico	Mexican Derivatives (MexDer)
Netherlands	Euronext Amsterdam (ex AEX)
Russia	Moscow Exchange MICEX-RTS
Singapore	Singapore Exchange Derivatives Trading (SGX-DT)
South Africa	Johannesburg Stock Exchange
Spain	Mercado Español de Futuros Financieros (MEFF)
Sweden	NASDAQ OMX Stockholm
Switzerland	N/A (Stake in Eurex sold to Deutsche Börse in 2011)
Turkey	Turkish Derivatives Exchange (TurkDex)
UK	NYSE LIFFE UK
UK	ICE Europe
USA	CME Group
USA	NYSE LIFFE US
USA	NYSE ARCA Options
USA	International Securities Exchange
USA	Chicago Board Options Exchange
USA	OneChicago

CME Group – Taking a Closer Look Although it is not the intention to examine each and every derivatives exchange in any detail, it is nevertheless a good idea to look at perhaps the largest exchange, CME Group (www.cmegroup.com). The Group was formed from the merger of two Chicago-based exchanges in 2007: the Chicago Mercantile Exchange and the Chicago Board of Trade.

In terms of products listed on the exchange, there are in excess of 1,800 contracts, divided into ten categories. These categories, together with some examples, are shown in Table 2.34.

TABLE 2.34   Products listed on CME

	Sub-Categories	Examples
Agriculture	▪ Cereals ▪ Livestock ▪ Dairy ▪ Forest ▪ Commodity indices ▪ Softs	▪ Corn ▪ Live cattle ▪ Cash-settled cheese ▪ Random length lumbar ▪ DJ-UBS Commodity Index ▪ Coffee
Energy	▪ Crude oil ▪ Natural gas ▪ Refined products ▪ Biofuels ▪ Coal ▪ Electricity ▪ Emissions ▪ Freight ▪ Petrochemicals	▪ WTI financial futures ▪ Natural gas options ▪ NY Harbor ULSD futures ▪ Ethanol futures ▪ Coal futures ▪ PJM 50 MW Calendar-Month LMP option ▪ European Union aviation allowance futures ▪ Freight Route TC2 (Baltic) futures ▪ Mont Belvieu natural gasoline futures
Equity index	▪ US indices ▪ International indices ▪ Sectors	▪ S&P 500 ▪ Nikkei 225 (Dollar) ▪ E-mini industrial select sector
Foreign exchange	▪ Majors ▪ Emerging markets ▪ Cross rates ▪ E-micros	▪ EUR/USD ▪ USD/RMB ▪ EUR/GBP ▪ E-micro EUR/USD
Interest rates	▪ STIR ▪ US Treasuries ▪ Swap futures	▪ Eurodollar Mar 2014 ▪ US Treasury bond ▪ 10-year deliverable interest rate swap
Metals	▪ Precious ▪ Base ▪ Ferrous ▪ Coking coal ▪ Other	▪ Gold futures ▪ Copper options ▪ Iron ore 62% Fe, CFR China futures ▪ Australian coking coal (Platts) futures ▪ UxC Uranium U308 futures
Options	▪ Agriculture ▪ Energy ▪ Equity index ▪ FX ▪ Interest rates ▪ Metals	▪ Soybean options ▪ WTI average price options ▪ S&P 500 options ▪ Euro FX option (American) ▪ Eurodollar options ▪ Gold options
OTC	▪ Interest rate swaps ▪ Credit default swaps ▪ FX NDFs and CSFs ▪ Energy ▪ Agricultural swaps ▪ Metals ▪ Commodity index swaps	▪ USD, EUR, GBP fixed/float out to 51 years ▪ CDX IG Series 8: 7 and 10 years ▪ USD NDF including CNY, TWD, RUB, etc. ▪ See Energy above ▪ Corn cleared OTC calendar swaps (Asian style) ▪ See Metals above ▪ Cleared OTC commodity index swaps

(continued)

TABLE 2.34 *(Continued)*

	Sub-Categories	**Examples**
Weather	▪ Temperature ▪ Hurricanes ▪ Frost ▪ Snowfall ▪ Rainfall	▪ US cooling/heating monthly/seasonal ▪ Hurricane monthly/seasonal ▪ Frost monthly/seasonal ▪ Snowfall monthly/seasonal ▪ Rainfall monthly/seasonal

As you can appreciate, the CME Group covers a wide variety of products and sub-categories. You may also have noticed that some of these are based on commodities, a topic that is not covered in this book.[7]

In addition to providing products, derivatives exchanges provide the facilities for trading (mostly electronic trading platforms with some exchanges providing physical trading by open outcry). The exchanges will provide pricing data that are either real time or delayed, together with volume and open interest information.

We will cover the clearing and settlement in Chapter 9, but derivatives exchanges either maintain their own clearing services or have links to third-party clearing systems. In the case of CME, clearing is handled by CME Clearing.

2.7.4 Open Interest and Trading Volumes

Unlike the cash markets where there are finite amounts of shares and bonds in issue and available for trading and other purposes, ETD contracts are not issued. They are created as they are needed and destroyed when open interest decreases.

Every day, contracts are bought and sold. These trades either create an exposure (an open interest) or cancel an exposure (close) and in total represent volume in the contract being traded. *Open interest* is therefore the total quantity of contracts that have been traded but not closed or delivered on any particular day.

Open interest is not the same as volume, as illustrated in Tables 2.35a and 2.35b.

TABLE 2.35a Open interest and volume

Day	Trading Activity	Open Interest	Volume
1	**A** buys one contract from B and **B** sells one contract to A	1	1
2	**C** buys five contracts from D and **D** sells five contracts to C	5	5
3	**A** sells one option to D (to close) and **D** buys one option from A	−1	1
4	**E** buys five contracts from C and **C** sells five contracts to E (to close)	0	5
	Totals:	5	12

[7]For an excellent book on this topic, I can recommend Schofield, N. (2007) *Commodity Derivatives: Markets and Applications*. Published by John Wiley & Sons (ISBN 978-0470019108).

TABLE 2.35b   From the individual traders' perspective

Trader	Contracts Purchased	Contracts Sold	Open Long Interest	Open Short Interest
A	1	1	0	0
B	0	1	0	−1
C	5	5	0	0
D	1	5	0	−4
E	5	0	5	0
Totals:	12	12	5	−5

There are two points to note here:

1. The volume is calculated so that one purchase plus one sale equals one quantity of volume.
2. Notice that the sum of the total open long interest and total open short interest is zero. This is a meaningless figure and so we only consider the open long interest figure, i.e. five in the example above.

Q&A

Question

What are the volume and open interest figures for the trades shown in Table 2.36?

TABLE 2.36   Five days' trading activity

Day	Trading Activity	Open Interest	Volume
1	A buys 50 contracts and B sells 50 contracts		
2	C buys 30 contracts and D sells 30 contracts		
3	A sells 20 contracts and E buys 20 contracts		
4	A sells 20 contracts and D buys 20 contracts		
5	D buys 10 contracts and F sells 10 contracts		
	Totals:		

Answers

Total volume – 130 contracts

Open interest – 60 contracts

See Table 2.37 for the calculations.

TABLE 2.37 Calculation of total volume and open interest

Trader	Contracts Purchased	Contracts Sold	Open Long Interest	Open Short Interest
A	50	40	10	0
B	0	50	0	−50
C	30	0	30	0
D	30	30	0	0
E	20	0	20	0
F	0	10	0	−10
Totals:	130	130	60	−60

We saw that exchanges such as CME Group handle a wide range of product types, most of which fall into two types of derivative: futures and options. We will look at these in turn, concentrating on a typical set of contract specifications and looking at an example or two of each type.

2.7.5 Futures

Q&A

Question

Can you recall the definition of a future?

Answer

A futures contract is a legally binding obligation to buy or sell a standard amount of a standard asset at a specific time in the future for a certain price that is agreed today.

When a derivatives exchange develops a new product, the contract specifications have to have sufficient information for a user to understand the contract. A good example to look at would be an interest rate derivative for which the underlying asset is a government security. In Table 2.38, you will see headline contract specifications for three long-dated government securities as issued by three separate derivatives exchanges.

TABLE 2.38 Comparison of USD, GBP and EUR bond futures contracts

	US Treasury Bond Futures	Long Gilt Futures	Eurobond Futures
Exchange	CME Group	NYSE LIFFE	EUREX
Underlying unit (face value)	USD 100,000	GBP 100,000	EUR 100,000

TABLE 2.38 *(Continued)*

	US Treasury Bond Futures	Long Gilt Futures	Eurobond Futures
Deliverable grade (See Note)	US T-bond with a notional 6% coupon with a maturity from 15 to 25 years	UK gilt with a notional 4% coupon with a maturity from 8.75 to 13 years	German bund with a notional 6% coupon with a maturity from 8.5 to 10.5 years
Price quote	Points and 1/32nd of a point (e.g. 120−16 is 120 16/32)	As a percentage of the par value	As a percentage of the par value
Tick size	1/32 of one point (USD 31.25)	0.01 (GBP 10.00)	0.01 (EUR 10.00)
Contract months	First three consecutive contracts (i.e. up to nine months) in the March, June, September and December cycle		
Last trading day	Closes at 12:01, seventh business day preceding the last business day in the delivery month	Closes at 11:00, two business days prior to the last business day in the delivery month	Closes at 12:30 CET, two exchange days prior to the last business day in the delivery month
Last delivery day	Last day in the delivery month	Any business day in the delivery month (at seller's choice)	Tenth calendar day in the delivery month

Note: A delivery obligation arising out of a short position may only be fulfilled by the delivery of certain debt securities issued by Germany, Italy, France or Switzerland. Each country's bonds have slightly different maturities.

By making a comparison of these three futures contracts you can see that there are both similarities and differences between them. First of all, these are the similarities:

1. The deliverables are all long-dated government bonds.
2. The face value of each underlying unit (contract) is 100,000.
3. The price quote convention mirrors that of the underlying bond.
4. The contract months follow the same March quarterly cycle.
5. The tick size follows a similar pattern, although the USA convention is to quote in 1/32nd whilst the other two countries quote in decimals.

Secondly, here are the differences:

1. The notional coupon rate is different for the long gilt future at 4%.
2. In the delivery month, the CME and EUREX contracts are deliverable on one particular day whereas the NYSE LIFFE contract is deliverable on any business day in the delivery month. There are also differences in terms of which day is the last day for the CME and EUREX contracts.

Deliverable Bonds Closer examination of the contract specifications will show that there is no one particular bond designated as being the deliverable bond. The implication is that there is a choice of one or more bonds which meet the criteria to a certain extent.

In all probability there is no such bond that has a coupon rate as stated and with a maturity that fits within the timeline. The exchange overcomes this problem by publishing a list of bonds that would be suitable for any particular delivery month.

Take, for example, the June 2014 long gilt futures contract, remembering that the contract specifies a 4% coupon with a maturity from 8 years and 9 months out to 13 years. Therefore, for this particular contract, we are looking at an underlying security maturing from March 2023 to June 2027. NYSE LIFFE published its initial list of two deliverable gilts in September 2013,[8] with an update in March 2014.[9] The list now contains three securities:

- 2.25% Treasury bond due 7 September 2023;
- 2.75% Treasury bond due 7 September 2024; and
- 5.00% Treasury bond due 7 March 2025.

On occasion, there can be up to four or five different deliverable securities.

Questions now arise as to which of these three bonds would be delivered and at what price.

We saw from the contract specification that it is the seller who chooses when to deliver. In the case of the June 2014 contract, the seller can choose one of these three bonds. However, the delivered bond tends to be the one that has been calculated as the cheapest to deliver (CTD). We will look at CTD in the next section on futures pricing. From an Operations point of view, this is an example of a transformation from a derivative product into a cash market product. Normally, users tend to close out their long and short positions before the last date for trading, removing the need to deliver/receive against the contract.

The price at which the delivered bond is traded is dictated by the exchange and this price is known as the *exchange delivery settlement price* (EDSP). We will describe how the EDSP works in practice in Chapter 9: Derivatives Clearing and Settlement.

Futures Pricing   Futures contracts are priced using the same pricing convention as the underlying bond. At the same time, the underlying deliverable gilts are also similarly priced.

Listed in Table 2.39 are the closing prices for the June 2014 contract together with the three underlying deliverable gilts.

TABLE 2.39   NYSE LIFFE June 2014 long gilt futures contract

Product	Price	Source	Date
Long gilt future June 2014	110.66	NYSE LIFFE	2014-04-25
2.25% Treasury bond 7 Sep 2023	96.84	DMO reference prices	2014-04-25
2.75% Treasury bond 7 Sep 2024	99.88	DMO reference prices	2014-04-25
5.00% Treasury bond 7 Mar 2025	121.05	DMO reference prices	2014-04-25

Sources: NYSE LIFFE (online) Settlement prices. Available from https://globalderivatives.nyx.com/en/products/bond-futures/R-DLON/settlement-prices. [Accessed Tuesday, 29 April 2014]
DMO (online) Reference prices. Available from DMO (online) Reference prices. Available from www.dmo.gov.uk/rpt_parameters.aspx?rptCode=D3B&page=Gilts%2fDaily_Prices. [Accessed Tuesday, 29 April 2014]

---

[8]Available from NYSE LIFFE (online). LON3742 Initial List of Deliverable Gilts. Available from https://globalderivatives.nyx.com/en/bond-derivatives/nyse-liffe/deliverable-bonds. [Accessed Saturday, 14 December 2013]
[9]Available from NYSE LIFFE (online). LON3806 Update to Initial List of Deliverable Gilts. Available from https://globalderivatives.nyx.com/sites/globalderivatives.nyx.com/files/lon3806.pdf. [Accessed Tuesday, 29 April 2014]

Prices on futures contracts are regarded as being linear, meaning that if you buy a futures contract and the price goes up, you have an unrealised profit; if the price goes down, you have an unrealised loss (see Figure 2.2).

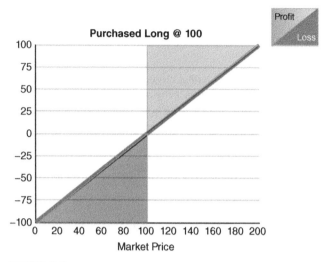

FIGURE 2.2   Long futures contract purchased at a price of 100

The reverse is true if you have a short futures position. If the price goes up, you lose and if the price goes down, you gain. This is approximately the same economic position as if you had purchased or sold the underlying asset (see Figure 2.3).

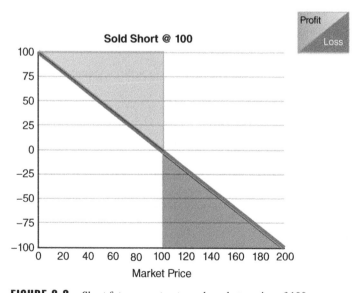

FIGURE 2.3   Short futures contract purchased at a price of 100

When you trade in the underlying asset, you are expected to settle the full economic value of the transaction almost straight away (e.g. T+3). Once settled, the legal contract is finalised and the original counterparty risk exposure removed. With derivatives such as a futures contract, the full economic value is not settled straight away. It will only be settled if and when the contract goes to delivery and if that happens, it will be several months away. This creates a counterparty risk exposure that would be unacceptable if it were not for the fact that a clearing house assumes the counterparty risk for the purchaser and for the seller (we refer to this as *novation*).

Until such time as the futures contract is either closed or delivered, both the buyer and the seller will reflect changes in the value of the contracts by a system known as *margin*. If a contract has gone up in value for a counterparty, the clearing house will credit that counterparty's account with the difference. Conversely, if a contract has gone down in value for a counterparty, the clearing house will debit that counterparty's account with the difference.

In effect, a counterparty is taking its profits and paying its losses on a day-by-day basis. This is in contrast with the underlying asset, where the profits or losses are not taken until the asset is either sold (from a long position) or purchased (for a short position).

Price (or Conversion) Factors   For the June 2014 contract,[10] we have seen that there are three bonds that have been selected as deliverable. In order to make these bonds "look like" the 4% gilt, each gilt is given a price factor (PF). These PFs are fixed from the outset and do not change throughout the life of the contract. The PF for a gilt with a coupon less than 4% will be less than 1 and for a gilt with a coupon greater than 4%, the PF will be greater than 1. In the case of the three deliverable gilts, the PFs were stated as:

2.25% gilt due 7 September 2023	PF is 0.8655782
2.75% gilt due 7 September 2014	PF is 0.8955672
5.00% gilt due 7 March 2025	PF is 1.0867250

On exercise, the exchange will announce the exchange delivery settlement price (EDSP) and this is multiplied by the price factor. Accrued interest is then factored into the calculation:

$$\text{Invoicing amount} = (\text{face value} \times \frac{\text{EDSP}}{100} \times \text{PF}) + \text{Accrued interest}$$

$$= (100,000 \times \frac{\text{EDSP}}{100} \times \text{PF}) + \text{Accrued interest}$$

This formula is valid for futures contracts that have one delivery date only; in the case of the long gilt future, the contract is deliverable on any business day in the delivery month. The formula must be adjusted to reflect interest that accrues to the delivery date chosen:

$$\text{IA} = (100,000 \times \frac{\text{EDSP}}{100} \times \text{PF}) + \text{Acc'd int (Daily accrued} \times \text{Delivery day in month)}$$

This can be restated as:

$$\text{IA} = (1,000 \times \text{EDSP} \times \text{PF}) \times \text{Acc'd int (Daily accrued} \times \text{Delivery day in month)}$$

---

[10]For sources, see Table 2.29 above.

If we take the first of the three gilts and the EDSP is 110.66, then the invoicing amount on ten contracts will be GBP 963,901.83 for delivery 14 June 2014 (see Table 2.40).

TABLE 2.40 Invoicing amount for the first of the three gilts

Parameters	EDSP	Price Factor	Initial Interest	Daily Interest	No. Contracts	Delivery Day
2.25% due 7 Sep 2023	110.66	0.8655782	519.701087	6.114130	10	14
Invoicing amount:	GBP 963,901.83					
Formula per GBP 100,000:	(1,000 × EDSP × PF) + Initial accrued interest + (days × daily interest)					

Q&A

Question

What will the invoicing amounts be for the remaining two deliverable gilts if the EDSP is also 110.66? You will require the (amended) list of deliverable gilts – see footnote 8.

Answers

The invoicing amounts are GBP 998,059.12 (2.75% 2024; see Table 2.41) and GBP 1,216,020.97 (5.00% 2025; see Table 2.42).

TABLE 2.41 Invoicing amount for the second of the three gilts

Parameters	EDSP	Price Factor	Initial Interest	Daily Interest	No. Contracts	Delivery Days
2.75% due 07 Sep 2024	110.66	0.8955672	597.826087	7.472826	10	14
Invoicing amount:	GBP 998,059.12					

TABLE 2.42 Invoicing amount for the third of the three gilts

Parameters	EDSP	Price Factor	Initial Interest	Daily Interest	No. Contracts	Delivery Days
5.00% due 07 Mar 2025	110.66	1.0867250	1154.891304	13.586957	10	14
Invoicing amount:	GBP 1,216,020.97					

Cheapest to Deliver (CTD) Whilst bonds with different maturities tend to have different yields, the conversion factors are based on pricing all the deliverable bonds at the same yield. The result of this is that one of the bonds tends to be the "cheapest to deliver" bond and this CTD bond is what tends to be delivered against a short futures position. At its simplest, a CTD bond is one that would make the most amount of money if it were purchased on credit and delivered against a short futures position.

Operationally, we do not need to know how the CTD bonds are identified. If a delivery were to take place, we would be told the EDSP and from that we could calculate the total invoicing amount. In reality, the majority of open contracts are closed before expiry and only comparatively few contracts are actually delivered.

2.7.6 Options

Q&A

Question

Can you recall the definition of an option?

Answer

A call option gives the buyer (the "holder") the right to purchase an asset for a specified price on or before a specified expiration date.

A put option gives the holder the right to sell an asset for a specified price on or before a specified expiration date.

Options have a language of their own; for example, we refer to a buyer and a seller as being a *holder* and a *writer* of an options contract respectively. We will come across other terminology as we go through the section. In the above definition we are referring to an option from the holder's point of view, i.e. the holder has the right to purchase an asset (call option) or the right to sell an asset (put option). But for every purchaser there must be a writer (seller).

It is normal practice for the holder to decide whether to exercise or not. If the holder wishes to exercise, then the writer is obliged to deliver.

Q&A

Question

In theory, who has the more attractive proposition – the holder or the writer?

Answer

As it is the holder who makes the choice, then it is the holder who has the more attractive proposition. For this reason, the holder is expected to partially compensate the writer by paying a premium to the writer when the trade is made.

For the holder, the premium is the price paid to take a view on whether it would be advantageous to exercise the contract at the appropriate time. For the writer, the premium is the price received as partial compensation if they are obliged to exercise the contract. We refer to options as *premium settled*.

More terminology: the price of an options contract is known as the *premium*.

Example

An investor holds a call option giving him the right (but not the obligation) to buy an asset in June 2014 at a strike price of 100. The spot price of the asset is 115. The investor pays a premium of 10 to the writer. This payment is made on the day after the contract is made (T+1).

We can fast forward to June 2014 and examine two scenarios:

1. If the spot price of the asset has dropped to 95, the holder is unlikely to exercise the contract and the option will lapse. For the holder, the total loss is the premium originally paid, i.e. 10. For the writer, no delivery is required and the premium is retained.
2. If the spot price of the asset has risen to 130, the holder is very likely to exercise. He gains an asset worth 130 in the market by exercising the option at 100. The total gain is 20 (130 spot price − 100 exercise price − 10 premium paid). The writer is obliged to sell an asset worth 130 in the market at 100. His loss is 20 (100 exercise price − 130 spot price + 10 premium earned at the start).

Q&A

Question

What can you conclude about the profit or loss possibilities for the holder and writer in the above example?

Answer

Table 2.43 outlines the answers.

TABLE 2.43   Profit and loss possibilities for the holder and the writer

Position	Maximum Profit	Maximum Loss
Holder	In theory, this is unlimited; the higher the spot price, the greater the profit.	The maximum loss amounts to the premium paid, as the holder is not obliged to exercise at a lower price.
Writer	The maximum profit is the premium received.	The lower the spot price, the greater the loss. The maximum loss would occur as the spot price approached zero.

Here we have an example of a nonlinear price relationship. If we look at a break-even chart, we will observe that the profit or loss line is broken at the point denoted by the premium amount.

The following four figures illustrate the pay-offs for the call and put options (all with a strike price of 100 and a premium of 10):

- Long call option (see Figure 2.4);
- Short call option (see Figure 2.5);
- Long put option (see Figure 2.6);
- Short put option (see Figure 2.7).

The value of a call option rises as the underlying market price rises. If you buy a call option, you make money as the underlying market price rises. If the market price falls, your loss is limited to the premium you paid.

If you sell a call option, you lose money as the underlying market price rises. If the market price falls, your profit is limited to the premium you received. Not a particularly attractive

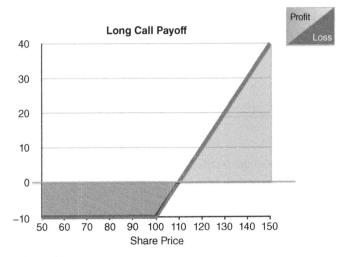

FIGURE 2.4   Long call option

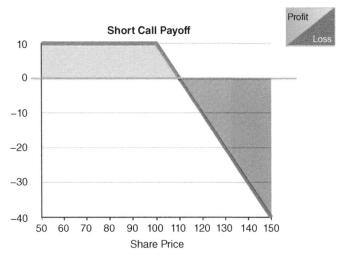

FIGURE 2.5 Short call option

risk/reward profile – but not dissimilar to the insurance business. The level of premium/price received is key.

The value of a put option rises as the underlying market price falls. If you buy a put option, you make money as the underlying market price falls. If the market price rises, your loss is limited to the premium you paid.

The value of a put option rises as the underlying market price falls. If the market price rises, your profit is limited to the premium you received.

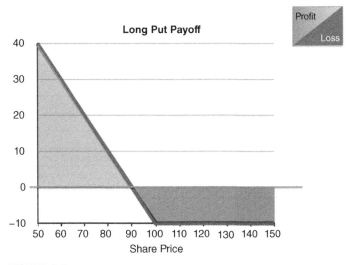

FIGURE 2.6 Long put option

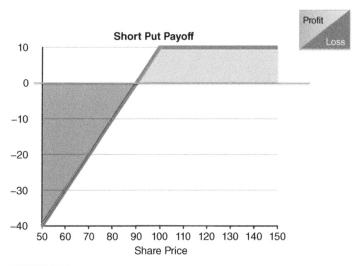

FIGURE 2.7   Short put option

Options Specifications   In the same way that futures contracts are specified by a derivatives exchange, so, too, are options contracts. Options contracts will usually contain the specifications outlined in Table 2.44.

TABLE 2.44   Options contract specifications

Contract Specification	Description
Option type	Call option (holder has the right to buy) Put option (holder has the right to sell)
Option style	American style – the option can be exercised at any time up to expiry of the option European style – the option can only be exercised on one date in the exercise month
Quantity and class of the underlying asset	For example, one contract relates to 1,000 ABC ordinary shares
Strike price (or exercise price)	The price at which the underlying transaction will be exercised
Minimum tick size	The minimum price movement
Contract month	Usually based on a quarterly cycle
Expiry date	This is the last date on which the contract can be exercised
Settlement terms	Whether settlement is by the actual delivery of the underlying asset (against cash) or by an equivalent amount of cash only

For an example of the underlying shares for an options contract including Canon Inc., see Table 2.45.

TABLE 2.45   Canon Inc. option contract specifications

Contract Specification	Description
Option type	Call and put options based on listed securities selected by the Tokyo Stock Exchange
Option style	European style
Quantity and class of the underlying asset	100 Canon Inc. shares Local code: 7751 ISIN code: JP3242800005
Strike price (or exercise price)	Exercise prices with the intervals based on the last execution price of the underlying security set on the first trading day
Minimum tick size	Depends on the size of the option premium, e.g. if the premium is between JPY 1,000 and JPY 3,000 per share, then the tick size is JPY 1
Contract month	Two closest serial months plus two closest quarterly months (March, June, September, December)
Expiry date	The last trading day (i.e. European-style option)
Last trading date	The business day prior to the second Friday of the respective contract month
Settlement terms	Cash settlement and physical delivery of the underlying on the fifth day counting from the day of exercise

Source: Tokyo Stock Exchange (online). Available from www.tse.or.jp/english/rules/derivatives/eqoptions/index.html. [Accessed Sunday, 15 December 2013]

Options Pricing   Before we look at the pricing of options, we need to introduce some further terminology.

There is a relationship between the price of an underlying asset and the strike price of an option. The ITM and OTM positions in Table 2.46 refer to the holder of the option. It will be the opposite for writers.

TABLE 2.46   ITM/OTM/ATM for option holders

In-the-money	ITM	▪ For a call option: when the strike price is below the spot price. ▪ For a put option: when the strike price is above the spot price.
At-the-money	ATM	▪ When the strike price is the same as the current spot price of the underlying security. (As this rarely happens in reality, we actually mean "near-the-money".)
Out-of-the-money	OTM	▪ For a call option: when the strike price is above the spot price of the underlying security. ▪ For a put option: when the strike price is below the spot price.

Q&A

Question

In the situations shown in Table 2.47, are your options ITM, ATM or OTM?

TABLE 2.47   Six situations

Situation	Strike Price	Spot Price
You hold call options	340	350
You write call options	235	260
You hold put options	75	100
You write put options	225	245
You hold call options	78	77
You write put options	1350	1351

Answers

Table 2.48 gives the answers.

TABLE 2.48   ITM, ATM and OTM decisions for the six situations in Table 2.47

Situation	Strike Price	Spot Price	Answer
You hold call options	340	350	ITM
You write call options	235	260	OTM
You hold put options	75	100	OTM
You write put options	225	245	ITM
You hold call options	78	77	ATM
You write put options	1350	1351	ATM

We can now summarise the risks associated with futures and options contracts (see Figure 2.8).

Q&A

Question

In Figure 2.8, why are some of the risks and rewards "almost" unlimited?

Answer

Because the underlying market price cannot go below zero (shares, bonds, commodities, interest rates, etc.) or above infinity.

Summary of Risk

Position	Risk	Reward
Long Call	Limited to premium	Unlimited
Long Put	Limited to premium	Almost unlimited
Short Call	Unlimited*	Limited to premium
Short Put	Almost unlimited	Limited to premium
Long Future	Almost unlimited	Unlimited
Short Future	Unlimited	Almost unlimited

*Unless covered.

FIGURE 2.8 Comparison of the risks of futures and options

2.7.7 Summary of Exchange-Traded Derivatives

ETD products are predominantly futures and options contracts that have been created by derivatives exchanges and centrally cleared through a clearing house. These products are standardised in terms of underlying assets, exercise dates and trading – all elements of the product's contract specification.

These contracts are created as required by the users; there are no limits regarding total contracts. However, to gain an idea of the depth of the market, users need to know trading volumes and open interest. This information, together with opening, closing, highest and lowest prices, is published by the derivatives exchange that created the product.

For the final part of this chapter, we turn our attention to the second type of derivative – over-the-counter, or OTC, derivatives.

2.8 OTC DERIVATIVES

2.8.1 Introduction

Unlike exchange-traded derivatives, OTC derivatives are not created by an exchange with standardised contract specifications, trading rules, etc. Instead, OTC derivatives are privately negotiated between buyer and seller away from any exchange. This results in issues that have concerned the industry's regulators:

- As the contracts are not cleared centrally, there is no central counterparty.
- Each counterparty to a trade relies on the other party to perform, and as some OTC contracts can last for many years before termination, there is a high degree of counterparty risk involved.
- As the contracts are not traded on an exchange, there has been no requirement to report trades.

- OTC derivatives can be relatively straightforward in design and content; however, many are highly complex in structure with risks that are correspondingly complex.
- The specification of OTC derivatives is established at the time of the trade. Nevertheless, the more "vanilla" contracts do follow basic templates.

This situation is changing. Due to pressure from the regulators, OTC contracts are migrating to central clearing systems, trades are expected to be reported (whether centrally cleared or not) and there is the possibility that trading itself might migrate to exchanges.

The big question concerns the more complex derivative structures (the exotic derivatives). As there is no central, exchange-published pricing, OTC derivatives can be very difficult to value. If the clearing houses do not understand the risks of the products and find it difficult to value them, they might decide not to clear them. Consequently, the usage of exotic derivatives could decrease or disappear altogether.

When we trade forward and swap products, we talk about a *notional amount*. With the exception of currency swaps, the notional amount is never exchanged – only the payments generated by the notional amount are exchanged.

A good source of information regarding notional amounts outstanding and gross market values of OTC derivatives can be found in the statistical annex of the Bank for International Settlements' "Quarterly Review".[11] In the BIS Quarterly Review for December 2013, Table 19, "Amounts outstanding of over-the-counter (OTC) derivatives", showed the amounts and values for the main risk categories given in Table 2.49.

Interest rate contracts have by far the greatest number of notional amounts outstanding and gross market values, at USD 561,299 billion and USD 15,155 billion respectively.

2.8.2 Forwards

Q&A

Question

Can you recall the definition of a forward?

Answer

A forward contract is a legally binding obligation to buy or sell an agreed amount of an agreed asset at a certain future time for a certain price agreed today.

We will look at two examples of a forward contract:

1. A forward rate agreement (FRA);
2. A currency forward.

---

[11] The BIS Quarterly Review is available at the Publications & Research area of the www.bis.org website.

TABLE 2.49 BIS – Amounts outstanding of OTC derivatives

Risk Category / Instrument	Notional amounts outstanding					Gross market values				
	Jun 2011	Dec 2011	Jun 2012	Dec 2012	Jun 2013	Jun 2011	Dec 2011	Jun 2012	Dec 2012	Jun 2013
Total contracts	**706,884**	**647,811**	**639,396**	**632,579**	**692,908**	**19,518**	**27,307**	**25,417**	**24,740**	**20,158**
Foreign exchange contracts	**64,698**	**63,381**	**66,672**	**67,358**	**73,121**	**2,336**	**2,582**	**2,240**	**2,304**	**2,424**
Forwards and forex swaps	31,113	30,526	31,395	31,718	34,421	777	919	771	803	953
Currency swaps	22,228	22,791	24,156	25,420	24,654	1,227	1,318	1,184	1,247	1,131
Options	11,358	10,065	11,122	10,220	14,046	332	345	285	254	339
Interest rate contracts	**553,240**	**504,117**	**494,427**	**489,703**	**561,299**	**13,244**	**20,001**	**19,113**	**18,833**	**15,155**
Forward rate agreements	55,747	50,596	64,711	71,353	86,334	59	67	51	47	168
Interest rate swaps	441,201	402,611	379,401	369,999	425,569	11,861	18,046	17,214	17,080	13,663
Options	56,291	50,911	50,314	48,351	49,396	1,324	1,888	1,848	1,706	1,325
Equity-linked contracts	**6,841**	**5,982**	**6,313**	**6,251**	**6,821**	**708**	**679**	**645**	**605**	**693**
Forwards and swaps	2,029	1,738	1,880	2,045	2,321	176	156	147	157	206
Options	4,813	4,244	4,434	4,207	4,501	532	523	497	448	487
Commodity contracts	**3,197**	**3,091**	**2,994**	**2,587**	**2,458**	**471**	**481**	**390**	**358**	**386**
Gold	468	521	523	486	461	50	75	61	53	30
Other commodities	2,729	2,570	2,471	2,101	1,997	421	405	328	306	306
Forwards and swaps	1,846	1,745	1,659	1,363	1,327					
Options	883	824	812	739	670					
Credit default swaps	**32,409**	**28,626**	**26,931**	**25,069**	**24,349**	**1,345**	**1,586**	**1,187**	**848**	**725**
Single-name instruments	18,105	16,865	15,566	14,309	13,135	854	958	715	527	430
Multi-name instruments	14,305	11,761	11,364	10,760	11,214	490	628	472	321	295
of which index products	12,473	10,514	9,731	9,663	10,170					
Unallocated	**46,498**	**42,613**	**42,059**	**41,611**	**24,860**	**1,414**	**1,978**	**1,842**	**1,792**	**775**
Memorandum Item:										
Gross Credit Exposure						2,971	3,939	3,691	3,609	3,900

Source: BIS Quarterly Review March 2014 (online). Available from www.bis.org/publ/qtrpdf/r_qt1403.htm. [Accessed Monday, 5 May 2014]

An FRA is an obligation to settle the difference between two interest rates calculated on a notional amount. FRAs are used by banks and corporates to hedge interest rate exposures. For example, you are the Treasurer of a corporate that wishes to borrow USD 10,000,000 for six months. If you wanted to borrow today, you would expect to pay the six-month spot rate. Suppose, though, you needed to borrow in three months' time (and not today); what is your risk? Answer: interest rates might rise over the next three months, making the cost of borrowing more expensive.

In order to buy protection against a rate rise, you buy an FRA at a price of 2.00% p.a. (the *fixed rate*) on the notional amount of USD 10,000,000. The price reflects the interest rate on a loan that starts in three months' time and has a term of six months – a 3x9 FRA (nine months less three months = six months).

In three months' time, you observe the spot six-month interest rate to be 2.50% p.a. (the *reference rate*). The rate has increased, as you had previously feared.

The difference in price is 0.50% p.a. (2.50% – 2.00%) and therefore, under the terms of the FRA, the seller pays this difference on the notional amount to the buyer. Once this amount has been paid, the FRA is finished with no further payments to make.

Intuitively, the seller would pay:

$$\text{Notional amount} \times \text{interest rate difference for six months}$$

However, the amount payable is paid at the *start* of the six-month loan period and not at the *end* as would normally be the case in lending. In order to make an adjustment to correct this anomaly, the amount payable is discounted by the reference rate. In our example, the amount payable by the seller to you would therefore be USD 24,962.28:

$$\text{Payment} = \text{Notional Amount} \times \left(\frac{(\text{Ref} - \text{Fixed}) \times \text{Day Count}}{1 + (\text{Ref} \times \text{Day Count})} \right)$$

$$\text{Payment} = \text{USD } 10,000,000 \times \left(\frac{(2.5\% - 2.0\%) \times \dfrac{182}{360}}{1 + \left(2.5\% \times \dfrac{182}{360} \right)} \right)$$

$$\text{Payment} = \text{USD } 10,000,000 \times \left(\frac{0.0025}{1.0126} \right)$$

$$\text{Payment} = \text{USD } 24,962.28$$

This is assuming 182 actual days in the six-month period.

There are two observations to make:

1. If you had wanted to borrow USD 10 million, you would borrow at the spot rate of 2.50% and receive the FRA difference. This would bring your cost down to almost 2.00%, i.e. the original fixed rate.
2. If you simply wanted to speculate on the direction interest rates would go, you would receive the USD 24,962.28 as your winnings on the bet.

Q&A

Question

What would the situation have been if the reference rate was 1.50%?

Answer

The buyer would pay the seller USD 25,087.53

$$\text{Payment} = \text{USD } 10,000,000 \times \left(\frac{(1.5\% - 2.0\%) \times \frac{182}{360}}{1 + \left(1.5\% \times \frac{182}{360}\right)} \right)$$

$$\text{Payment} = -\text{USD } 10,000,000 \times \left(\frac{0.0025}{1.0076} \right)$$

$$\text{Payment} = -\text{USD } 25,087.53$$

Although the payment is not settled until the start of the loan period (the *effective date*), both parties have an interest risk from the moment they enter into the transaction up to the effective date. To cover this risk, the FRA is revalued daily and the party at risk receives collateral. We will cover the topic of collateral later in the book.

In the above example, we used the notation 3×9 to denote the effective date and the termination date. See Table 2.50 for further examples of this notation using LIBOR as the benchmark rate (we could equally have used another interbank rate depending on the circumstances).

TABLE 2.50   FRA notation using LIBOR

Effective Date	Termination Date	Interest Rate	Notation
1 month	4 months	3-LIBOR	1 × 4
1 month	7 months	6-LIBOR	1 × 7
3 months	6 months	3-LIBOR	3 × 6
3 months	9 months	6-LIBOR	3 × 9
6 months	12 months	6-LIBOR	6 × 12
12 months	18 months	6-LIBOR	12 × 18

In summary, by entering into an FRA, you can lock in an interest rate to protect against an interest rate increase (as in our example). To do this, you would buy an FRA. Conversely, you can lock in an interest rate to protect against an interest rate decrease by selling an FRA.

2.8.3 Swaps

Q&A

Question

Can you recall the definition of a swap?

Answer

A swap is a derivative product in which two counterparties exchange certain benefits of one party's financial assets for those of the counterparty's assets.

The cash flows are calculated on a notional principal amount and these cash flows are known as the *legs* of a swap.

There are several types of swap depending on the underlying asset type. Each one of these swap types complies with our above definition; see Table 2.51 for some examples.

TABLE 2.51 Types of swap

Underlying Asset	OTC Swap	Definition
Equity	Equity swap	The performance of shares or a stock market index swapped with financing (e.g. LIBOR)
Interest rate	Interest rate swap	A fixed IRS swapped with a floating interest rate (e.g. 3m Euribor) or floating vs. floating (e.g. 1m LIBOR vs 6m LIBOR)
Credit	Credit default swap	CDS: the CDS buyer makes a series of payments ("fee") to the CDS seller who will compensate the buyer only in the event of a loan default or other credit event
Foreign exchange	Currency swap	Swap the principal amount plus interest in one currency with that of another. There are variations as to the structures used.
Commodity	Commodity swap	Similar in concept to a fixed/floating IRS. A floating (spot) price for a commodity (e.g. crude oil) is swapped for a fixed price in the same commodity.

We have seen that of all the OTC derivative types, interest rate swaps are by far the greatest component. Used for both hedging and speculating purposes, there are several types of interest rate swap (IRS) (see Table 2.52).

TABLE 2.52 Types of interest rate swap

Leg 1		Leg 2	Currency
Fixed	for	Floating	Same currency
Fixed	for	Floating	Different currencies
Floating	for	Floating	Same currency
Floating	for	Floating	Different currencies
Fixed	for	Fixed	Different currencies

We will examine the first of these, fixed for floating in the same currency, in more detail.

Q&A

Question

What is the risk for ABC Corporation, which has borrowed USD 10 million on a floating-rate basis at 6-LIBOR plus 200 basis points? The corporation is concerned that interest rates will steadily increase over the next five years.

Answer

If interest rates do increase, the interest costs for the corporate will also increase, as the interest rate is floating. It is possible that the corporate could close the floating loan and borrow at a fixed rate of interest. This may not be practical as it might breach the terms and conditions of the floating loan and/or the cost of taking out a fixed-rate loan might result in a high fixed-interest rate.

An alternative solution to ABC's funding problem would be to retain the floating-rate loan and enter into a fixed/floating interest rate swap in US dollars.

Here, ABC Corporation is using an IRS to hedge an existing position. The notional amount of the IRS will be USD 10 million, the term of the contract will be five years and ABC will want to end up in a situation where it pays a fixed rate of interest overall. In theory, ABC Corporation would need to find a counterparty with the opposite requirement, i.e. the counterparty has a fixed interest liability, believing that interest rates will go down. In practice, however, ABC Corporation would approach a swap dealer, who would act either as a principal or as a broker.

ABC will receive a floating rate of interest to partially or fully offset the existing floating rate loan and pay a fixed rate of interest. ABC is referred to as the *receiver*. The swap bank will therefore be the *payer* of fixed-rate interest.

The contract terms of the IRS might look something like those in Table 2.53.

TABLE 2.53   Contract terms of ABC's interest rate swap

Receiver	ABC Corporation	Receives "fixed"
Payer	Swap Bank	Pays "fixed"
Fixed rate	1.60% p.a.	30/360. Payable semi-annually on <DATE1> and <DATE2>, both netted against the fixed.
Floating rate	6-month LIBOR plus 50 bp	30/360. Payable semi-annually on <DATE1> and <DATE2>, both netted against the floating.
Notional	USD 10,000,000	
Term	5 years	

(Please note that the rates quoted above are illustrative only. When the swap transaction is executed, the swap will be priced in such a way that the net present value of the transaction is zero.)

Through this IRS transaction, ABC Corporation has effectively changed from a floating interest rate situation into a fixed rate one. We know that ABC is currently paying 6L+200 and we can use a "plumbing diagram" (see Figure 2.9) to track the interest flows and calculate the new interest rate for ABC.

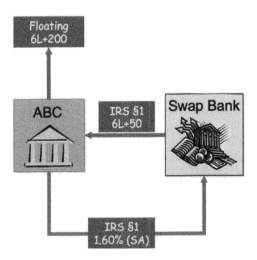

FIGURE 2.9   IRS plumbing diagram

We can see that paying the current rate and receiving the floating leg eliminates the six-month LIBOR rate, leaving a net 150 bp as a cost. Add that to the fixed leg of 1.60% and we arrive at a total fixed interest rate of 3.10% p.a. for ABC (as shown in Table 2.54).

TABLE 2.54   Total fixed interest rate for ABC

Details	Pay/Receive	Interest	±	Basis Points	Balance
Current rate	Paying	6L	+	200	−(6L+200)
Floating leg	Receiving	6L	+	50	−150
Fixed leg	Paying	1.60%	−		−3.10%

Let us assume that Swap Bank has a second counterparty/client, XYZ Inc., which has a loan and is paying 1.80% fixed. XYZ enters into an IRS transaction with Swap Bank on the terms shown in Table 2.55.

TABLE 2.55   Terms of XYZ's interest rate swap

Receiver	Swap Bank	Receives "fixed"
Payer	XYZ Inc	Pays "fixed"
Fixed rate	1.58% p.a.	30/360. Payable semi-annually on \<DATE1\> and \<DATE2\>, both netted against the fixed.
Floating rate	6-month LIBOR plus 50 bp	30/360. Payable semi-annually on \<DATE1\> and \<DATE2\>, both netted against the floating.
Notional	USD 10,000,000	
Term	5 years	

Q&A

Exercise

Please calculate the following:

- The total cost for XYZ Inc.
- The profit/loss for Swap Bank.

Answers

The cost to XYZ Inc will be 6L+72 (paying 1.80% and receiving 1.58% leaves a cost of 22 basis points to which is added the floating rate of 6L plus 50 basis points) – see Table 2.56.

TABLE 2.56   Cost to XYZ Inc

Details	Pay/Receive	Interest	±	Basis Points	Balance
Current rate	Paying	1.80%			−1.80%
Floating leg	Receiving	1.58%			1.58%
Fixed leg	Paying	6L	+	50	6L+72

If we now combine both IRS transactions (see Figure 2.10), we can see how much Swap Bank, in the role of agent, will make or lose.

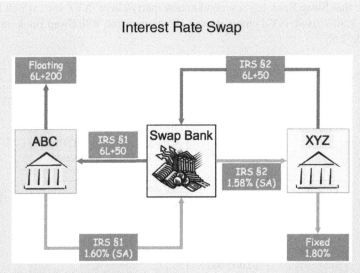

FIGURE 2.10   Swap Bank as agent

Swap Bank, in executing two swap transactions, will earn USD 10,000.00 for the five-year period, as shown in Table 2.57.

TABLE 2.57   Swap Bank's profit for the five years

Legs	Transaction §1	Transaction §2	Net
Floating	Pays 6L+50	Receives 6L+50	Flat
Fixed	Receives 1.60%	Pays 1.58%	+ 0.02%
	Total profit:	0.02% p.a. for five years	
	USD	10,000.00	
	i.e. USD	2,000.00 p.a.	

No matter whether interest rates increase or decrease during the term of the transactions, Swap Bank will make this profit. What can go wrong? The bank is exposed to both counterparties for the term, and if one or other (or both) were to default, then the bank would be put at risk. This situation would not arise if the swap transactions were centrally cleared, as we will cover later in the book.

The other types of swap follow the same general principles as the fixed/floating IRS but with characteristics unique to the swap type.

2.8.4   Summary of OTC Derivatives

OTC derivatives are privately negotiated contracts transacted away from an exchange. This has the advantage of enabling users to tailor their transactions to suit their situation. Unlike the transparency of exchange-traded derivatives, OTC derivatives are opaque to the market and the regulators. This situation is changing with the move to centrally clear the more straightforward, vanilla-type contracts. Whether this will lead to the contracts being traded on an exchange remains to be seen.

One disadvantage of OTC is that the terms and conditions of every transaction must be clearly stated in the transaction confirmation; even down to the granular level of specifying day-count conventions.

The ISDA Bookstore (www.isda.org/publications/pubguide.aspx) contains a wide range of publications that cover the ISDA Master Agreement, definitional booklets and confirmations and regulatory documentation.

2.9 SUMMARY

2.9.1 Financial Products in General

Financial products can be issued for a particular purpose and subsequently traded.

2.9.2 Cash Markets

The cash markets are divided into short-term and long-term products and these are issued by governments (and their various agencies), supranational organisations and corporations to enable them to satisfy their particular financial requirements.

We tend to refer to the issuance and trading of short-term products as the money markets and these include:

- Cash loans/deposits;
- Commercial paper;
- Certificates of deposit;
- Bankers' acceptances;
- Treasury bills;
- Bills of exchange.

By contrast, we refer to the longer-term products as the securities markets and these include:

- Equities (ordinary shares/common stock);
- Debt (corporate bonds, treasury bonds, supranational bonds);
- Hybrids (preference shares, convertible bonds, equity warrants).

Securities are traded for cash settlement, as payment is expected in full and within a few days following the trade date.

2.9.3 Derivatives Markets

Derivatives are financial contracts that derive their value from underlying assets such as equities, bonds, interest rates, stock market indices, etc. Derivative contracts are not issued by the issuers of the underlying assets; rather, they are issued either by an exchange (exchange-traded derivatives – ETDs) or privately between two counterparties (OTC derivatives).

There are four types of derivative contract:

1. Forwards (OTC);
2. Futures (ETD);
3. Options (ETD and OTC);
4. Swaps (OTC).

This market is changing; OTC derivative contracts are becoming more transparent as they are increasingly being reported to a trade repository and cleared through a central clearing house system. ETDs have always been traded on an exchange and cleared centrally.

Derivative contracts are either exercised (into the underlying assets or cash) or closed out prior to the last trading day. In the meantime, the financial risks associated with these products are covered, depending on the product type, by a system of margin calls, premium payments and collateral exchanges. The full economic value of the contract is not settled on the trade date.

CHAPTER 3

Data Management

3.1 INTRODUCTION

In today's financial world, the typical Operations Department has to capture and process vast amounts of data and information. In our personal lives we have to remember a multitude of login IDs, passwords, PIN numbers, telephone numbers, addresses of family, friends, customers, etc. How do we remember any or all of these different types of information? We can either memorise them (open to forgetfulness) or write them down (open to losing the paperwork). Either way, we run the risk of not having the correct information at the moment when we actually require it.

We are probably able to correctly identify our personal telephone numbers, home address and our most frequently used PIN numbers; we might possibly think we can remember some of our less frequently used information but have little chance of remembering occasionally used information. What, then, can we do? The obvious solution would be to develop a database into which we can enter a variety of different types of information that can be accessed easily when needed. Straight away you might be able to identify a problem with this approach – your database might be appropriate for your needs but inappropriate for everybody else's! In one sense, this is what has happened in the industry: banks, securities houses, fund management companies and all the other types of participant have developed their own databases focusing on their own requirements. What is needed, however, is a high degree of standardisation, where information can be generated from one source and be understood by all those individuals and institutions that require it.

By the end of this chapter, you will:

- Appreciate the importance of data and the information that comes from them;
- Know the different types of data and how they impact on the Operations Department;
- Understand how data are managed;
- Have learnt about the new global standard for legal entity identification.

3.2 IMPORTANCE OF REFERENCE DATA AND STANDARDISATION

3.2.1 Introduction

In the early 1980s, the author was working in a Eurobond Settlements Department where manual ledgers were still being used to record Eurobond purchases and sales. He remembers that:

> *"Euroclear, who held our Eurobonds, would publish a thick, hard-copy directory every six months containing basic details of every security that they were prepared to hold.*
>
> *Every time a transaction ticket came down from the trading floor, the first thing we had to do was to find the particular bond in the Euroclear directory. From this, we could find the following information:*
>
> ▪ *The correct name of the bond, including the coupon rate and full maturity date);*
> ▪ *The securities identification number (unique to Euroclear);*
> ▪ *The last coupon payment date.*
>
> *This would enable us to calculate the accrued interest, arrange for a confirmation note to be typed up and prepare the appropriate delivery/receipt instructions. These would be transmitted to Euroclear's proprietary system (known as Euclid) via an acoustic coupler (an interface device for coupling electrical signals by acoustical means) that was hooked up to a telephone handset.*
>
> *In effect, we were using the directory as a manual version of a securities database. The main drawback was that this process took quite some time, especially as there was only one directory book for the whole department! The situation improved when the department was computerised; however, the system that we purchased used the Euroclear securities identification system (as we had done previously in the manual environment). This gave us problems when we were communicating with Cedel (now known as Clearstream Banking Luxembourg). Cedel had its own directory and unique numbering system ..."*

3.2.2 Basic Securities Transactions

Let us consider a basic securities transaction, thinking about the information that is provided by the Front Office and comparing that with the information we need to be able to settle the transaction effectively. In today's environment, the majority of transaction information will arrive in the Operations area in an automated and electronic fashion. To help with the visualisation of the information, it is worth considering a transaction example using a hard copy dealing ticket.

Q&A

Question

What information would a dealer provide for a transaction of your choice? You should only include information that the dealer might provide.

Answer

There are some suggestions noted in Table 3.1, together with some additional information that we will need.

TABLE 3.1   Contents of a dealing ticket

Dealing Ticket		Comments
Trader:	AKD	Is this trader authorised and has he exceeded his trading limits?
Trade date:	10 March 2014	There are various formats for quoting dates including: 2014-03-10 (SWIFT) 10-03-2014 (Europe, etc.) 03-10-2014 (USA)
Trade time:	09:16	Is this EST, GMT or CET or some other time zone?
Trade venue:	ICMA/OTC	Important if there are multiple trading venues
Direction:	Sale	An incorrect direction impacts the financial economics of the transaction
Security:	EDF 4.60% bonds 2020	There might be more than one EDF 4.60% bond due for redemption in 2020. It is better to quote the full date (27 January 2020 in this case) plus a unique identification number
Quantity (USD):	5,000,000	What is the board lot size for this security and therefore deliverable as a multiple of this size?
Yield to maturity:	2.3663%	Most bonds are traded as a percentage to par basis. We would need to restate the YTM as a price if our system required it (112.1070 for this trade)
Counterparty:	ABC Trading Company	Is this trade within limits for this counterparty? What account number do we need to use?
Proprietary book/client:	Trading book	Is this the appropriate book? It would be a different situation if we were to sell from a held-to-maturity book
Some extra thoughts…		
Accrued interest:	USD 29,388.89	This is calculated using the appropriate convention (for a USD-denominated Eurobond under ICMA Rule 251, this would be on a 30E/360 day basis)

(continued)

TABLE 3.1   (*Continued*)

Dealing Ticket		Comments
Settlement date:	13 March 2014	This is the convention for a Eurobond (i.e. T+3)

Settlement method:	Delivery vs. payment	Using one or both ICSDs:
		■ Internal delivery
		  - (E/E or CBL/CBL)
		■ Bridge delivery
		  - (E/CBL or CBL/E)

Then ask yourself whether there are sufficient details on the dealing ticket to enable you to settle the transaction. The answer should be "No"; it will, therefore, be our responsibility to add the appropriate elements of information so that we can prepare, for example, confirmation notes and settlement instructions, update our books and records and all the other various processes.

3.3   TYPES OF REFERENCE DATA

3.3.1   Required Reference Data

From the transaction in the previous section, we can create a list of examples of the required reference data (see Table 3.2).

TABLE 3.2   Required reference data

Data Type	Data Elements
Transaction data	■ Price ■ Quantity ■ Counterparty ■ Customer (if appropriate) ■ Exchange/trading venue ■ Settlement instructions
Security identification	■ Local market identifier ■ International identifier ■ Security class ■ Maturity
Counterparty information	■ Credit ratings (internal and external) ■ Account details ■ Transaction history
Customer information	■ Credit ratings (internal) ■ Account details ■ Demographic information ■ Transaction history
Settlement information	■ Clearing house(s) ■ Clearing model (BIS) ■ Timing (trade date plus n days) ■ Calculation conventions

We will now consider what data we require for three of these data types:

- Securities;
- Counterparties and customers;
- Settlement information.

The challenge for the industry is to enable information to be classified and standardised in such a way that the users of information can access it and interpret it no matter what type of industry participant they are or in which market they are located.

3.3.2 Data Requirements – Securities

We will look at two issues regarding securities: the identification of securities and the classification of securities. Traditionally, securities issued in one particular market would be identified by a national numbering system unique to that market. Table 3.3 shows some examples of local numbering systems.

TABLE 3.3   Examples of local numbering systems

Country	Numbering System	Description
USA	CUSIP (Committee on Uniform Security Identification Procedures)	9-character alphanumeric code
UK	SEDOL (Stock Exchange Daily Official List)	7-character alphanumeric code
Germany	WKN (Wertpapierkennnummer)	6-character alphanumeric code

Whilst national numbering systems work well in a local context, a unique identifier is required in an international context. The internationally recognised standard for securities is the International Securities Identification Numbering system (ISIN). ISINs are issued by national numbering agencies (NNAs) using guidelines published by the Association of National Numbering Agencies (www.anna-web.org). An ISIN consists of 12 characters: a country code (two letters), nine characters taken up by the local number of the security and a final character acting as a check digit.

The NNA will typically be located in the country where the securities issuer is legally registered or, for debt securities, the NNA might be one of the international securities clearing organisations.

The international standard appropriate to ISINs is the International Organization for Standardization (ISO) 6166.

ANNA also acts as the registration authority for ISO 10962 – the Classification of Financial Instruments (CFI) Codes. CFI codes are allocated by the agency that allocates the ISIN and consist of six alphabetical characters that enable users to identify the type of financial instrument, its characteristics and attributes (see Table 3.4).

TABLE 3.4   CFI codes

Character Number	Classification Level	
First character	Category of instrument	Equities (E) Debt (D) Rights (R) Options (O) Futures (F) Structured products (S) Referential instruments (R) Miscellaneous (M)
Second character	Instrument group	Example – Equities: ■ Shares (S) ■ Preferred shares (P) ■ Preference shares (R) ■ Convertible shares (C) ■ Preferred convertible shares (F) ■ Preference convertible shares (V) ■ Units, e.g. mutual funds (U) ■ Others (miscellaneous) (M) Example – Debt: ■ Bonds (B) ■ Convertible bonds (C) ■ Bonds with warrants (W) ■ Medium-term notes (T) ■ Money market instruments (Y) ■ Asset-backed securities (A) ■ Mortgage-backed securities (G) ■ Others (miscellaneous) (M)
Third to sixth characters	Attributes	Up to four attributes applicable to the financial instrument

Source: ISO 2006. "Securities and related financial instruments – Classification of Financial Instruments (CFI code) – [Revision of ISO 10962:2001]." Available from www.fixtradingcommunity.org/mod/file/view.php?file_guid=43074. [Accessed Monday, 25 November 2013]

Tables 3.5a and 3.5b give some CFI classification examples.

TABLE 3.5a   Equities

ISIN	US4592001014	IBM International
CFI	ESVUFR	E = Equities S = Shares, i.e. common/ordinary V = Voting U = Unrestricted (no ownership/transfer restrictions) F = Fully paid R = Registered

TABLE 3.5b Debt

ISIN	GB0002146073	Commonwealth Bank of Australia, exchangeable floating-rate notes 1988-perpetual
CFI	DCVTQB	D = Debt C = Convertible/exchangeable bonds V = Variable interest rate T = Government/Treasury guaranteed Q = Perpetual with call feature B = Bearer form

In summary, for every type of financial instrument there will be a unique identifier and classification that enables users to standardise the information. However, there is yet more information that we need to know about the securities we are processing. We will look at this for examples involving a debt security (see Figure 3.1) and an equity security (see Figure 3.2).

Static Data Item	Example of a Bond	Typical Use of Data
Full Name of Security	British Land Company Co Ltd., 8.875% Bonds 2023	The formal description of the issue, used on trade confirmations & other correspondence with clients
ISIN	XS0047184964	The commonly known security identification number used for external communication, such as trade confirmations & trade instructions
CFI Code	DBFUGB	D = Debt, B = Bond, F = Type of Interest (Fixed), U = Guarantee (Unsecured), G = Redemption (Fixed maturity with call feature) & B = Bearer
Issued Currency	GBP	Quoted on trade confirmations & settlement instructions. Internally, represents the currency of the trading position & the cash owed by/to counterparties
Issued Quantity	150,000,000	Provides a measure of the position held in the issue as a percentage of the total issued amount
Security Type	Bond	Provides internal statistics & reporting by type of security
Security Group	Eurobond (GBP)	Enables distinguishing of security for static data defaulting
Coupon Rate Type	30E/360	Enables attachment of attributes such as accrued interest calculations
Coupon Rate	8.8750%	Enables calculation of cash value of accrued interest on trades & coupon payments
Coupon Frequency	Semi-Annual	Enables calculation of accrued interest on trades & coupon payments
Cpn Payment Date(s)	25 March & 25 September	Enables calculation of accrued interest on trades & coupon payments
Primary Value Date	15-Nov-93	Earliest value date of a new issue & the point from which accrued interest (on bonds) starts to accrue

FIGURE 3.1 Reference data – bonds

Static Data Item	Example of a Bond	Typical Use of Data
First Coupon Date	25-Mar-94	Enables determination of (first) long, (first) short or regular coupon periods
Maturity Date	25-Sep-23	Identifies date of final capital repayment
Early Redemption	Yes	Call feature at any time, subject to notice, at the higher of either par or a GRY equal to that of a specified Reference Bond
Maturity Price	100%	Identifies the price of the bond payable by the issuer at maturity
Board Lot Size(s)	100,000 10,000	Ensures trades are executed in acceptable denominations
Default Book	Trading Book	Enables defaulting of the internal book that typically trades this security
Credit Rating	A+	Enables calculation of collateral values of this security. Ensures security is valid from a risk management perspective

FIGURE 3.1 (*Continued*)

Static Data Item	Example of an Equity	Typical Use of Data
Full Name of Security	Barclays plc, ordinary shares 25p fully paid	The formal description of the issue, used on trade confirmations & other correspondence with clients
Ticker	BARC:LSE	
NSIN	3134865	The local/national identifier of the individual security (UK = SEDOL)
ISIN	GB0031348658	The commonly known security identification number used for external communication, such as trade confirmations & trade instructions
CFI Code	ESVUFR	E = Equity, S = Ordinary Shares, V = Voting (one share: one vote), U = Free (unrestricted ownership of transfer), F = Fully paid, R = Registered.
Settlement Currency	GBP	Quoted on trade confirmations & settlement instructions. Internally, represents the currency of the trading position & the cash owed by/to counterparties. (NB – shares priced in GBX in the UK)
Shares Outstanding	16.10 bn	Provides a measure of the position held in the issue as a percentage of the total issued amount. Can have regulatory implications (disclosure requirements)
Security Type	Equity	Provides internal statistics & reporting by type of security
Div Payment Date(s)	Interims: Jun, Sep & Dec Final: Mar	Identifies date(s) of dividend payment (subject to announcement)
Listing Date	31-Dec-53	Listing/admission to trading
Board Lot Size(s)	1	Minimum transferable number of shares
Exchange Market Size	10,000	Normal market size – ensures trades are executed in acceptable denominations
Default Book	Trading Book	Enables defaulting of the internal book that typically trades this security

FIGURE 3.2 Reference data – equities

3.3.3   Data Requirements – Counterparties and Customers

There is a requirement that information on counterparties and customers should be sufficient to enable:

1. Financial institutions to effectively communicate with their counterparties and customers.
2. Financial institutions to verify counterparty/customer identification information.
3. Counterparties/customers to operate within anti-money-laundering regulations.
4. Customer due diligence to be undertaken.
5. The identification of politically exposed persons (PEPs).
6. The submission of suspicious activity reports (SARs) to the appropriate authority.

Q&A

Question

Think about yourself. What personal attributes will never change throughout your life?

Answer

Table 3.6 gives some suggestions.

TABLE 3.6   Personal attributes

Attribute	Comments
Family name	Recorded on your birth certificate. Can be changed through marriage or deed poll.
Given name(s)	As above.
Date of birth	Determines certain rights and responsibilities, e.g. to vote, obtain a driving licence, attain the age of majority, etc.
Social security number	A unique personal number issued to residents of a country. May be used for identification purposes and/or as a tax reference number.
Nationality	Usually denotes the country of birth but can change through later residency in another country.

Of course there are other attributes, including addresses, telephone numbers, passport details, driving licence details, bank account details and occupation. These can and do change throughout the lifetime of an individual.

For businesses, we need to keep identification information such as:

- Full name of the business entity;
- The entity's designation (e.g. Limited, plc, SA, Inc. etc.);

- Trading name;
- Registered number;
- VAT and/or tax reference number;
- Country of incorporation;
- Business/trading address;
- Registered office address;
- Names of directors;
- Details of any individuals who own/control/exercise control over the management of the entity.

This information enables us to identify individuals, counterparties, customers and, not least of all, the companies for whom we are working. There is still information that we need to know, and this can include the following:

- Short name and reference number for counterparties and customers (used for internal reporting purposes);
- The type of counterparty (e.g. institutional client, broker, trading organisation, etc.);
- Any companies associated with a counterparty (plus the relationship);
- Names and locations of custodians together with account numbers for both securities and cash;
- Standing settlement instructions (the media through which instructions are sent to custodians and clearing houses);
- Membership of exchanges (for reporting purposes).

3.3.4 Data Requirements – Settlement Information

We saw earlier that we can codify financial instruments through the use of CFIs. This tells us nothing, however, about how financial instruments are typically cleared and settled. Table 3.7 shows a template for a country's central counterparty(ies) and central securities depository(ies).

TABLE 3.7 CCP and CSD template

	CCP	**CSD**
Country	Country name	Country name
System name	CCP name	CSD name
Product(s) cleared	Securities Derivatives Repo	
Securities held (domestic/international)		Bonds Government securities Money market instruments Equities Others

TABLE 3.7   *(Continued)*

	CCP	CSD
Currency(ies)	Domestic/International	Domestic/International
DVP model(s)		DVP1 DVP2 DVP3
Settlement lag		T+0 T+1 T+2 T+3, etc.
Cash settlement agent		Central bank Bank or Other agency

Source: Committee on Payment and Settlement Systems (September 2013 (online). "Statistics on payment, clearing & settlement systems in the CPSS countries." Available from http://www.bis.org/publ/cpss112.htm.

3.3.5   Sources of Reference Data

Reference data can be captured from a variety of different sources that range from the counterparties themselves to specialist information vendors which provide market data and securities reference data.

Information on counterparties and customers can be obtained by approaching the entities directly. Some information will be in the public domain (e.g. annual report and accounts) whilst other information will be confidential (e.g. custodian/bank account details for securities and cash). Where possible, information verification is desirable as part of the due diligence process, especially with regards to know your customer (KYC) and anti-money-laundering (AML) regulations and requirements.

Investment managers, brokers/dealers and custodian banks can automatically share accurate account and standing settlement instructions (SSI) information worldwide by interfacing with the Omgeo ALERT system. The interface is either web-based or direct using Java API. Omgeo is a wholly owned subsidiary of the Depository Trust & Clearing Corporation.

Information on securities can be obtained from a variety of sources, including the issuer (either direct or through its prospectus/offering circular), the appropriate central securities depository, custodians and market participants such as market makers and brokers. This is a rather laborious and time-consuming task. A more efficient alternative is to download the information from one or more information vendors, and some examples are noted below.

You will see a list of information vendors, together with their URLs and a selection of their services, in Table 3.8.

TABLE 3.8 Information vendors

Company	URL	Information Service(s)
Bloomberg	www.bloomberg.com	■ Market data ■ Reference data ■ Security master data ■ Pricing and valuation

Interactive Data	www.interactivedata.com	■ Reference data
		  ■ Terms and conditions
		    ■ Corporate actions
		    ■ Business entity
		■ Pricing services
		■ Fair value information
		■ Derivatives valuation

Six Financial Information	www.six-financial-information.com	■ Reference data ■ Corporate actions ■ Pricing and real-time valuations ■ Market data ■ News service
Standard & Poor's	www.standardandpoors.com	■ Security reference data ■ Entity reference data ■ Valuations and pricing ■ Credit ratings and research
Thomson Reuters	www.thomsonreuters.com	■ Company data ■ Financial analytics ■ Financial news ■ Market data ■ Pricing and valuation data ■ Market indices

3.4   DATA MANAGEMENT

3.4.1   What is Data Management?

Data management refers to the governance, oversight and monitoring of data to ensure accuracy and consistency. Information can become redundant and therefore a high degree of manual maintenance is called for. There is a risk that different departments within an organisation might very well be acquiring, maintaining and using the same information. This can lead to information redundancy. Information coming into the organisation needs to be verified for accuracy, which, again, calls for a high degree of manual maintenance.

3.4.2   Approaches to Data Management

There are three traditional approaches to data management:

■ **Transactional:** Process-based, known as *extract, transform and load* (ETL). ETL systems obtain data from multiple sources using different data structures across multiple financial instruments.

- **Analytical:** Storage-based, known as *warehouse*. In a warehouse-based system, all incoming information is held within a common data structure. This requires the information to be processed in order to fit this structure; in addition, it might be difficult to include complex financial instruments that may not fit within the structure.
- **Hybrid:** A combination of ETL and warehouse designed with the best features of both approaches. The disadvantages might include the pre-processing of data before they enter the warehouse and/or the re-structuring of the data as they leave the warehouse.

3.4.3   Data Processing

The logical process from data acquisition to data delivery must include appropriate levels of maintenance and support within the following stages:

1. Data acquisition from multiple sources including information vendors and counterparty/ customer data systems.
2. Matching to ensure a consistent view of security, issue, counterparty or customer.
3. Validation of incoming data to ensure accuracy, completeness and quality.
4. Composition, where the data are made to fit within the users' data structures.
5. Data made available to those authorised to use them, for example, the trading desks, the operational departments and data management maintenance teams.

3.5   LEGAL ENTITY IDENTIFICATION

3.5.1   Background to Legal Entity Identification

Before we turn to the final section in this chapter, recall that we recognise certain "entities" using a unique identification number. For example, there are several types of entity listed in Table 3.9.

TABLE 3.9   Types of entity

Entity Type	Identification Method
1. Securities	International securities identification number (ISIN) and local/national numbering systems
2. Book (hardback or paperback)	International standard book number (ISBN)
3. Patient in a hospital	Linear bar code on an identification wristband
4. Goods in a shop	Linear bar code on the product
5. Smartphone scanner	2D matrix bar code (e.g. QR code)
6. You or your employer	Your name or your employer's company name

With the exception of number six, all the above entity types have a unique identification system. This might suggest that we do not need a unique identification system, as we could record individuals, counterparties and customers by their name plus our own version of a short name and account number.

However, this would give us some potential problems, as the following examples will illustrate:

- There is no standardisation as to the number of letters contained in a name.
- The order in which names are quoted can vary, e.g. given name(s) followed by family name or family name followed by given name(s).
- An organisation such as the World Bank can also be recognised by the acronyms IBRD and BIRD. Furthermore, does it make a difference if it is IBRD or I.B.R.D?
- Many companies maintain a complex organisational structure, each unit of which has different business objectives. Banks, for example, can be structured as commercial banks, investment banks, insurance companies, asset managers, credit card companies, customers of other banks, etc.
- All these entities can be customers of more than one supplier, and each supplier will know its customer using an internal identification system.

With this "ad hoc" way of identifying these entities, there is every chance that entity details may be duplicated or mis-categorised, or that the entity's risk profile may be understated from a country or global perspective. What is required, therefore, is a unique identification system that allocates one ID to an entity no matter where the entity is domiciled or where in the world it undertakes business. The entity's risk exposures should be collated from all its global exposures.

3.5.2 The "Legal Entity"

The International Standards Organization's ISO 17442 refers to Entity §6 (in Table 3.9 above) as a *legal entity*. Legal entities are defined as those entities that are legally or financially responsible for the performance of financial transactions or have the legal right in their jurisdiction to enter independently into legal contracts.

These entities therefore include:

- Financial intermediaries;
- Banks;
- Finance companies;
- Issuers and guarantors of all asset classes;
- Entities listed on exchanges or trading venues;
- Counterparties;
- Investment vehicles (including umbrella structures);
- All entities under the supervision of a financial regulator and their affiliates, subsidiaries and holding companies.

3.5.3 The Global Legal Entity Identifier System (GLEIS)

In 2012, the G20 group of leading nations mandated the Financial Stability Board to co-ordinate the establishment of a global LEI system. The FSB published a number of principles together with 35 recommendations for the development of the GLEIS.

The GLEIS is structured in three operational levels (see Figure 3.3).

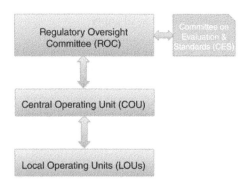

FIGURE 3.3   The global LEI system structure

- **Regulatory Oversight Committee:** Financial regulators from jurisdictions across the globe.
- **Central Operating Unit:** Co-ordinates and oversees the actions of local operating units.
- **Local Operating Units:** Responsible for assigning and maintaining LEIs. They are based in their national jurisdictions and sponsored by their local regulators.

Until the GLEIS becomes operational, an interim stage has been agreed whereby local regulators will authorise a "Pre-LOU" to issue "Pre-LEIs". In due course, the pre-LEIs will be converted into official LEIs.

3.5.4   LEI Structure

ISO 17442 has specified that each LEI must be a 20-digit, alphanumeric code, guaranteed to be unique, which provides access to key reference information and enables clear identification of the company concerned.

These 20 digits are made up as follows:

- 01 to 04: A prefix assigned to each LOU;
- 05 to 06: Two reserved characters set to zero/zero;
- 07 to 18: A randomly generated alphanumeric code;
- 19 to 20: Two check digits (as described in the ISO 17442 standard).

Table 3.10 shows the structure of an LEI and Table 3.11 an example of an LEI.

TABLE 3.10   LEI structure

Prefix	Reserved Digits	Alphanumeric Code	Check Digits
1234	00	A1B2C3D4E5F6	78

The LEI contains the following reference data:

- The official name of the legal entity;
- The address of the headquarters of the legal entity;
- The address of legal formation;
- The official business registry where the foundation of the legal entity is mandated to be recorded on formation of the entity, where applicable;
- The reference in the official business registry to the registered entity, where applicable, e.g. company registration number;
- Last updated date;
- Previous legal name (if applicable);
- Date and reason for expiry.

TABLE 3.11   An example of an LEI issued for ING Bank Anonim şirketi based in Istanbul, Turkey

Pre-LEI	7890001L64KNSIBT1H47
Official legal name	ING Bank Anonim Şirketi
Anglicised legal name	ING BANK Anonim Sirketi
Business register address	Reşitpaşa Mahallesi Eski Büyükdere Caddesi No: 8/Sarıyer
Post code	34467
City	İstanbul
Country	Türkiye
Official business address	Reşitpaşa Mahallesi Eski Büyükdere Caddesi No: 8/Sarıyer
Post code	34467
City	İstanbul
Country	Türkiye
Entity status	Active
Company legal form/fund type	Anonim Şirketi
Record status (validated/not validated)	LEITR_validated
First code assigned date	25 October 2013
Last code update date	25 October 2013
Next code certification date	7 January 2014
LEI code expiration date	7 January 2014
Reason for LEI expiry	–
Legal entity date of expiry, if applicable	–
LEI assigned by another pre-LOU/LOU	–
Place of trade registry	İstanbul
Other identifier-business register ID	269682
Other identifier-MERSIS ID	2332-9421-6542-8742
Other identifier-MKK ID	12658493
Other identifier-Takasbank Fund ID	–

TABLE 3.11 *(Continued)*

NACE sector code	64.19.01
Parent company	ING Bank NV/Amsterdam
LEI of the parent company	3TK20IVIUJ8J3ZU0QE75
Legal entity website	www.ingbank.com.tr

Source: Takasbank (online) "Turkey Legal Entity LEI List EN". Available from www.takasbank.com .tr/en/Pages/Numaralandirma.aspx. [Accessed Friday, 29 November 2013]

3.6 SUMMARY

We have seen that any financial transaction involves the collection and distribution of information which encompasses financial instruments and counterparties/customers. Today, the financial industry is truly global, and it is important that any information is in a standardised format so that it can be readily recognisable by our processing systems in a straight-through processing environment.

Information on financial instruments, counterparties and customers can be obtained from a variety of sources, ranging from direct access or indirect access to one of the information vendor companies.

We have also seen that financial instruments have, by and large, been standardised using the ISIN and local numbering systems together with the classification codes (CFI codes). However, the standardisation of counterparties and customers (the so-called legal entities) has only been addressed in recent years. The LEI initiative set up by the G20 countries and the FSB is now in progress, with the allocation of pre-LEIs by some LOUs (e.g. the UK and Turkey).

CHAPTER 4

Market Participation

4.1 INTRODUCTION

In the financial world, there is a relationship between those entities that require funds and those that have funds. We can refer to these entities as *borrowers* and *lenders* respectively.

Q&A

Question

Why might borrowers and lenders find it difficult to deal directly with each other?

Answer

There are three main reasons for this:

1. Size: Lenders tend to have smaller amounts of funds available to lend whereas borrowers require much larger amounts of funds.
2. Maturity: Lenders tend to have deposit or savings accounts on a "demand" basis (i.e. at call) whereas borrowers require funds across a maturity range that starts at call and ends at long term (e.g. for 25 years or more).
3. Risk: Lenders are exposed to the risk that borrowers may not be willing or able to repay amounts of borrowed funds. This is known as *credit risk* and can result in lenders losing all of their funds. Furthermore, lenders may not be able to assess the credit risk of existing and potential borrowers.

For these reasons, there will be a number of intermediaries that stand between the lenders and borrowers and help to transform the size of loans from small to large, transform the short-term wishes of the lenders into the longer-term needs of the borrowers and, finally, provide the ability to diversify the credit risk of the borrowers.

These relationships are shown in Figure 4.1 and we will discuss these in subsequent sections of this chapter.

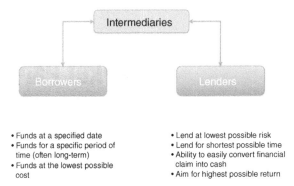

• Funds at a specified date
• Funds for a specific period of time (often long-term)
• Funds at the lowest possible cost

• Lend at lowest possible risk
• Lend for shortest possible time
• Ability to easily convert financial claim into cash
• Aim for highest possible return

FIGURE 4.1   Borrowers, lenders and intermediaries

By the end of this chapter, you will:

■ Understand the different types of lender and borrower and what motivates them;
■ Know why intermediaries are necessary, who they are and what functions they perform;
■ Understand the market infrastructures and the roles they perform.

4.2 MARKET PLAYERS

4.2.1 Retail Clients

Bank Accounts   Most of us have bank accounts into which our salaries, wages and other income is paid and out of which our day-to-day expenses such as rent, mortgage repayments, food, mobile telephone bills, etc. are deducted. These accounts are often referred to as *current accounts* or (in the USA) as *checking accounts*. The balances on these accounts might be rather small; however, we can transfer cash into and out of these current accounts very easily as we do not have to give our bank any forewarning (known as *notice*) of these activities. The banks for their part will use the credit balances on their clients' current accounts as part of their funding activities, i.e. lending the cash to those who need to borrow. For example, a client needs to borrow EUR 10,000 and requests the bank to lend this amount. The bank does not debit the current accounts directly; instead, the clients' cash balances are held collectively in a nostro account and it is from this account that the borrower is credited with the loan. Please note that the current account holders are not directly lending funds; however, many banks will credit these accounts with interest. These rates will be less than the interest the bank will charge the borrower. The difference (or spread) in these rates represents the net interest income on the bank's Profit & Loss account.

In addition to our current accounts, we might have a deposit or savings account. We would use this to hold cash that we may not require straight away; indeed, it could be used to build up a considerable balance in order to pay for a deposit on a property, or other significant purpose. Not only will there be higher balances compared with the current account balances, but the balances will tend to remain in the account for longer periods. The bank will utilise these balances as well in the knowledge that the deposit account holder will not require the cash straight away (unlike the current account holder).

Direct Investment   How else might a retail client use his funds? If, for example, the client has more cash than he needs for his day-to-day expenses, he might decide to purchase some investments. He might do this using a broker, either directly or online. The client now becomes an investor. His motivation might include benefiting from:

- Income from the investment (dividends or interest);
- Capital growth (the price of the investment increasing).

It is arguable that the direct investor requires access to a comparatively large amount of cash in order to diversify his investments; perhaps in the order of many tens of thousands of units of cash. Potential investors are often advised never to invest any cash that (a) is required for other, more immediate purposes and (b) that the investor cannot afford to lose. What can an investor do if he does not have sufficient cash to invest directly in shares and bonds, etc.? There is an alternative – indirect investment.

Indirect Investment   There is a wide range of investment products that are known as collective investments. Examples include mutual funds, unit trusts, investment trusts, exchange trade funds, open-ended funds, etc.

What these collective investments all have in common is that financial entities (e.g. investment managers) invest their clients' cash in one or more collective investment funds. The cash is used to buy appropriate securities that are held within the fund and, in exchange, the fund manager gives shares/units in the fund to the clients. In this way, one particular client with a small amount of cash can benefit from the investment expertise of the fund manager and hold shares within a fund that is diversified in terms of underlying products and markets.

As we will see later, the risks associated with these three fundamental types of cash usage differ from a comparatively low level of risk (bank accounts) to a comparatively high level of risk (e.g. equities/shares).

4.2.2   Institutional Clients

Collectively, institutional investors are organisations that invest large pools of money on behalf of their clients into various classes of investment such as securities, property, commodities and so-called "alternative investments". The institutional investors invest the money into "funds" that contain a broad, diverse range of assets tailored to meet predefined investment objectives. The idea behind asset diversification is that it helps to reduce the risk that the fund will suffer if a constituent investment defaults; the more diversified the fund, the lower the risk.

An example of an undiversified fund would be a fund that contains only one asset. If that asset lost, say, 50% of its value, then the fund would also lose 50% of its value. However, a diversified fund of, say, 25 assets including the one that loses 50% of its value, would only lose a fraction of its value. (Investment risk is an interesting topic and includes "hedging" as well as "fund diversification".)

Investment Managers   Investment management companies employ investment managers who invest and divest their clients' assets. This can be discretionary (where the manager decides what action to take without reference to the client) or non-discretionary (where the manager suggests a course of action for approval by the client prior to taking action). In either situation, the investment manager will have assessed each client's individual investment needs and risk profile.

It is the investment manager's role to manage clients' assets in such a way that the clients' investment objectives are met. To do this, the manager will allocate assets across a range of asset classes, commonly divided into:

- Cash/money market instruments
- Equities
- Bonds
- Property
- Commodities.

In addition, there are two broad investment management styles:

Active management: Active management (also called active investing) refers to a portfolio management strategy where the manager makes specific investments with the goal of outperforming an investment benchmark index. There are various strategies that the active manager can use; however, the essential idea is to exploit market inefficiencies (purchase *undervalued* assets and/or sell *overvalued* assets).

Passive management: By contrast, the passive manager creates a fund which only invests in the assets that constitute a particular stock market index. This way, the passive manager mimics the performance of the chosen index.

Whilst passive managers have traditionally used equity indices (of which there are many to choose from), there are indices that cover bonds, commodities and hedge funds.

Hedge Funds   Hedge fund managers employ an alternative investment style to the more traditional investment managers that we discussed above. The first hedge fund was established in 1949 by a Mr Alfred W. Jones, who designed the classic "long–short" strategy. Jones would take a long position in an asset and hedge the risk of the long position by taking a short position in another asset. For example, you could buy shares long in Company "A" (running the risk that the share price goes down) and sell shares short in Company "B" (running the risk that the share price goes up).

Example

In terms of price movements, there will be a "best outcome" and a "worst outcome", as follows:

Best outcome (Variation 1): Company "A" price goes up (making a profit) and Company "B" price goes down (making a profit).

Worst outcome (Variation 2): Company "A" price goes down (making a loss) and Company "B" price goes up (making a loss).

Q&A

Question

The variations noted above are two of nine possible variations of profit and loss outcomes. What might the remaining seven variations be?

Answer

Table 4.1 gives the answers.

TABLE 4.1   The seven remaining variations of profit and loss outcomes

Variation 3	Share Price	Profit or Loss	Outcome
Company "A"	flat	none	Neither a profit nor a loss
Company "B"	flat	none	

Variation 4	Share Price	Profit or Loss	Outcome
Company "A"	flat	none	You make a loss
Company "B"	goes up	loss	

Variation 5	Share Price	Profit or Loss	Outcome
Company "A"	flat	none	You make a profit
Company "B"	down	profit	

Variation 6	Share Price	Profit or Loss	Outcome
Company "A"	up	profit	You make a profit
Company "B"	flat	none	

Variation 7	Share Price	Profit or Loss	Outcome
Company "A"	down	loss	You make a loss
Company "B"	flat	none	

Variation 8	Share Price	Profit or Loss	Outcome
Company "A"	up	profit	You make a profit only if "A" goes up more than "B"
Company "B"	up	loss	

Variation 9	Share Price	Profit or Loss	Outcome
Company "A"	down	loss	You make a profit only if "B" falls more than "A"
Company "B"	down	profit	

Hedge fund managers can either adopt a single investment strategy approach (such as the long–short described above) or a multi-strategy approach. Whilst there are many variations, the main strategies are:

Global macro: Managers take large positions in securities in anticipation of global macroeconomic events. To do this, managers might have to borrow sizeable amounts of cash (leverage).

Directional: Managers select investments based on market movements, trends or inconsistencies across markets.

Event-driven: Managers aim to take advantage of pricing inconsistencies due to corporate action events such as distressed securities, mergers, acquisitions, etc.

Relative value: Managers aim to take advantage of the discrepancies between related securities.

Hedge fund managers can make substantial profits through using these investment styles; however, the reverse is also true – they can make substantial losses. The risk is that if the losses are too great, the fund might fail. For this reason, hedge funds are not generally available to retail investors.

The hedge fund industry manages over USD 2.9 trillion of assets (AUM) as at the 1Q 2014;[1] the ten largest hedge fund managers are shown in Table 4.2.

TABLE 4.2   Ten largest hedge fund managers by AUM

Rank	Hedge Fund	AUM USD bns
1	Bridgewater Associates (Westport, Connecticut)	77.6
2	Man Group (London)	64.5
3	JP Morgan Asset Management (New York)	46.6
4	Brevan Howard Asset Management (London)	32.6
5	Och-Ziff Capital Management Group (New York)	28.5
6	Paulson & Co. (New York)	28.0
7	BlackRock Advisors (New York)	27.7
8	Winton Capital Management (London)	27.0
9	Highbridge Capital Management (New York)	26.1
10	BlueCrest Capital Management (London)	25.0

Pension Funds   A pension fund is designed to provide retirement income to individuals who have reached retirement age. There are different classifications including open, closed, public and private pension funds. You do not need to understand these classifications for this module, but you should be aware of some of the investment challenges experienced by the funds themselves.

---

[1]*Source:* eVestment (online). "Hedge Fund Asset Flows" dated 17 April 2014. Available from www.evestment.com/docs/default-source/resources/monthly-hedge-fund-research/evestment-global-hedge-fund-asset-flows-report---march-2014.pdf?sfvrsn=2. [Accessed Wednesday, 30 April 2014]

In basic terms, an employer contributes cash into a pension fund on a regular basis (e.g. monthly) and a fund manager invests that cash in the markets. In addition, individuals can contribute either as employees into their employer's fund or into a personal pension fund. The objective is to provide the individual with an income at some specified time in the future, typically once the individual reaches retirement age.

The challenge for the employer is to decide how much cash to contribute now in order for the retiree to draw a pension in the future. In a *defined benefits* scheme, the retiree will receive a specified monthly benefit that is predetermined by a formula based on three factors: the employee's earnings history, tenure of service and age. The employer cannot know these factors in advance; to cover the cost of a defined benefits scheme, it has to make investment decisions based on advice given by actuarial professionals.

By contrast, in a *defined contribution* scheme, the employer contributes a specified amount of cash and relies on investment returns to provide a pension for the employee. The cost for the employer is therefore known; however, the benefit for the employee is unknown until retirement occurs and the calculations made.

Whichever scheme is adopted, the contributions are invested in order to provide a sufficient amount of cash with which an annuity is purchased. It is the annuity that provides the income during retirement. In the meantime, the fund managers will invest the contributions in a range of investment products including short-term instruments (money markets), long-term instruments and equities (cash markets), derivative products and alternative investments. There are rules as to which investment products can be invested in and limits as to how much can be invested in the product (see Table 4.3).

TABLE 4.3   Example of investment allocation for a pension fund

Investment Product	% per Investment Product	Fund % Holding
Equities		60%
... of which	Domestic – 70% International – 30% Sub-total – 100%	
Bonds		30%
... of which	Domestic government – 30% Domestic corporate – 25% International government – 25% International corporate – 15% Eurobonds – 5% Sub-total – 100%	
Cash and money markets		5%
... of which	Cash – 50% Certificates of deposit – 50% Sub-total – 100%	
Derivatives and alternatives		5%
... of which	Financial futures – 40% Commodities – 40% Forestry – 20% Sub-total – 100%	
Total:		100%

Based on OECD data and TheCityUK's estimates,[2] global pension assets totalled USD 31.5 trillion at the end of 2011. This compares with global conventional assets under management of the global fund management industry of USD 79.8 trillion (with a forecast of USD 85.2 trillion for 2012). This illustrates the importance of the pension fund industry to the financial markets.

The largest pension fund in the world is the Japanese Government Pension Investment Fund with total assets of JPY 123,922.8 billion (USD 1,188.4 billion).[3]

Insurance Companies   "Insurance" can be defined as the equitable transfer of the risk of a contingent, uncertain loss from one entity (the insured entity) to another (the insurer entity) in exchange for payment (the premium). The premia are invested in order to settle any future insurance claims.

There are many different types of insurance, but they can be divided into two principal categories, as the following examples illustrate:

Life

Life insurance: A lump sum is paid to a decedent's designated beneficiary (e.g. a family member).

Annuity: Regular payments are made to a beneficiary (e.g. retirement pension income).

Non-Life

Property insurance: Home, aviation, flood, earthquake, marine, etc.

Vehicle insurance: Third party, fire and theft, comprehensive.

Liability insurance: Public liability, professional liability, etc.

Credit insurance: Mortgage, credit card, trade credit, etc.

Other types of insurance include travel, legal expenses, divorce, etc.

Insurance companies make their money through underwriting and investing, with their profits being earned by deducting incurred losses and underwriting expenses from the premia and investment income.

Based on OECD data and TheCityUK's estimates,[4] global insurance fund assets totalled USD 24.4 trillion at the end of 2011. This compares with global conventional assets under management of the global fund management industry of USD 79.8 trillion. This illustrates the importance of the insurance fund industry to the financial markets. The ten largest insurers by assets are listed in Table 4.4.[5]

---

[2]*Source:* TheCityUK (November 2012), "Fund Management 2013". Available from www.thecityuk.com. [Accessed Tuesday, 06 August 2013]
[3]*Source:* GPIF (online), Investment Results for 2Q 2013, dated 29 November 2013. Available from www.gpif.go.jp/en. [Accessed Thursday, 16 January 2014]
[4]*Source:* TheCityUK (November 2012), "Fund Management 2013". Available from www.thecityuk.com. [Accessed Tuesday, 06 August 2013]
[5]*Source:* Forbes (online) "The World's Biggest Public Companies". Available from www.forbes.com/global2000. [Accessed Tuesday, 06 August 2013]

TABLE 4.4   Top ten insurers by assets

Company	Country	Assets (USD bns)	Sector
ING Group	Netherlands	1,533.7	Life and Health
AXA Group	France	1,005.4	Diversified
Allianz	Germany	915.8	Diversified
MetLife	United States	836.8	Diversified
Prudential Financial	United States	709.3	Life and Health
Generali Group	Italy	582.4	Diversified
Legal & General Group	United Kingdom	562.9	Life and Health
American International Group	United States	548.6	Diversified
Aviva	United Kingdom	512.7	Life and Health
Prudential	United Kingdom	489.4	Life and Health

Sovereign Wealth Funds   According to the Sovereign Wealth Fund Institute,[6] a sovereign wealth fund (SWF) is a state-owned investment fund or entity that is commonly established from balance of payments surpluses, official foreign currency operations, the proceeds of privatisations, governmental transfer payments, fiscal surpluses and/or receipts resulting from resource exports. The definition of a sovereign wealth fund excludes, among other things, foreign currency reserve assets held by monetary authorities for the traditional balance of payments or monetary policy purposes, state-owned enterprises in the traditional sense, government employee pension funds and assets managed for the benefit of individuals.

One example of an SWF is the Kuwait Investment Authority, established in 1953 from its oil revenues. In fact, the sources of SWF funds are either oil/gas-related or non-oil/gas-related, as the list of the ten largest SWFs by assets under management[7] in Table 4.5 demonstrates.

TABLE 4.5   Largest SWFs by AUM

Country	Name	Assets (USD bns)	Origin
Norway	Government Pension Fund	737.2	Oil
Saudi Arabia	SAMA Foreign Holdings	675.9	Oil
Abu Dhabi	Abu Dhabi Investment Authority	627.0	Oil
China	China Investment Corporation	575.2	Non-commodity
China	SAFE Investment Company	567.9	Non-commodity
Kuwait	Kuwait Investment Authority	386.0	Oil
China/Hong Kong	HK Monetary Authority Investment Portfolio	326.7	Non-commodity
Singapore	Government of Singapore Investment Corporation	247.5	Non-commodity
Russia	National Welfare Fund	175.5	Oil
Singapore	Temasek Holdings	173.3	Non-commodity

---

[6]For more information, click through to www.swfinstitute.org.
[7]*Source:* SWF Institute (online). Largest SWFs. Available from www.swfinstitute.org/fund-rankings. [Accessed Tuesday, 06 August 2013]

Based on OECD data and TheCityUK's estimates,[8] global SWFs totalled USD 4.8 trillion at the end of 2011. This compares with global conventional assets under management of the global fund management industry of USD 79.8 trillion. This illustrates the importance of the SWF fund industry to the financial markets.

Private Wealth Management   A group of economists at the United Nations' International Labour Organization[9] has calculated that the world's average salary is just under purchasing power parity USD 18,000 per annum.[10] Allowing for various data limitations and missing data from some countries, the report shows that the average salary is low. By the time the salary earner has paid the usual monthly bills, there is not much cash left in the household budget to save or invest. Therefore, the main investment vehicle available to most people is the collective investment route of mutual funds.

There are, however, a substantial number of wealthy individuals who own large amounts of assets of one form or another. Based on the annual CapGemini/RBC Wealth Management Report for 2013,[11] there were some 12.0 million people described as "high-net-worth individuals" (HNWIs) with a total investable wealth of USD 46.2 trillion. OECD data and TheCityUK estimate[12] that global conventional assets and alternative assets under management of the global fund management industry were USD 120.0 trillion. This illustrates the importance of the private wealth industry to the financial markets.

An HNWI is someone defined as having investable assets[13] worth USD 1 million or more, and "Ultra-HNWIs" are people with investable assets in excess of USD 30 million.

The Wealth Management Report authors surveyed some 4,400 individuals across 21 major wealth markets and found that the source of their respondents' wealth included:

- Salary and bonuses;
- Investments;
- Real estate (excluding primary residence);
- Business ownership;
- Stock options;
- Inheritance;
- Proceeds from selling off a business.

Salary, bonuses, business ownership and investments made up more than two-thirds of the source of wealth for respondents.

---

[8]*Source:* TheCityUK (November 2012), "Fund Management 2013". Available from www.thecityuk.com. [Accessed Tuesday, 06 August 2013]

[9]*Source:* BBC News (online). "Where are you on the global pay scale?" dated 29 March 2012. Available from www.bbc.co.uk/news/magazine-17512040?oo=0. [Accessed Wednesday, 14 August 2013]

[10]The purchasing power parity (PPP) dollars concept is explained in the BBC's report. One PPP dollar is equal to USD 1 spent in the USA.

[11]*Source:* CapGemini/RBC Wealth Management (online) "World's Wealth Report 2013". Available from www.capgemini.com/sites/default/files/resource/pdf/wwr_2013_0.pdf. [Accessed Tuesday, 13 August 2013]

[12]*Source:* TheCityUK (November 2012), "Fund Management 2013", Available from www.thecityuk .com. [Accessed Tuesday, 06 August 2013]

[13]Investable wealth does not include the value of personal assets and property such as primary residences, collectables, consumables and consumer durables.

Who are the managers and what do HNWIs expect from their wealth managers? Wealth management is provided by financial institutions such as banks, professional trust companies and brokerage companies. The largest managers by assets under management are shown in Table 4.6.

TABLE 4.6 Largest managers by AUM

Rank	Firm	AUM (USD billion)
1	UBS AG	1,705.0
2	Bank of America Corp.	1,673.5
3	Wells Fargo & Co.	1,400.0
4	Morgan Stanley	1,308.0
5	Credit Suisse Group AG	854.6
6	Royal Bank of Canada	628.5
7	HSBC Holdings plc.	398.0
8	Deutsche Bank AG	387.3
9	BNP Paribas SA	346.9
10	Pictet & Cie.	322.2
11	JP Morgan Chase & Co.	318.0
12	Citigroup Inc.	250.0
13	Goldman Sachs Group Inc.	240.0
14	ABN AMRO Bank NV	212.7
15	Barclays plc	201.4
16	Julius Baer Group Ltd	200.8
17	Northern Trust Corp.	197.7
18	Bank of NY Mellon Corp.	179.0
19	Lombard Odier & Cie.	175.5
20	Banco Santander SA	172.7

Source: Bloomberg (online). "UBS Leapfrogs Bank of America to Top Wealth Manager Ranks" dated 10 July 2013. Available from www.bloomberg.com/news/2013-07-09/ubs-leapfrogs-bank-of-america-to-top-global-wealth-manager-ranks.html. [Accessed Wednesday, 14 August 2013]

Financial assets of HNWIs for 1Q 2014 globally can be broken down into the classes of asset shown in Table 4.7.

TABLE 4.7 Financial assets of HNWIs

Asset Class	%	Notes
Cash/deposits	26.6	
Equities	24.8	
Real estate	18.7	Excluding primary residence
Fixed income	16.4	
Alternative investments	13.5	Includes structured products, hedge funds, derivatives, foreign currency, commodities, private equity

Source: World Wealth Report 2014, Capgemini and RBC Wealth Management.

The breakdown of HNWI alternative investments is shown in Table 4.8.

TABLE 4.8 Alternative investments – breakdown

Investment Class	%
Structured products	19.3
Private equity	18.6
Foreign exchange	18.4
Commodities	16.2
Hedge funds	13.4
Other alternative investments	14.1

Source: World Wealth Report 2014, Capgemini and RBC Wealth Management.

HNWIs' attitudes towards their relationships with their wealth managers and the services they use are summarised in Table 4.9.

TABLE 4.9 HNWI attitudes

Attitude	%	As opposed to	%
Prefer customised services	29.2	Standardised services	24.1
Work with a single firm	41.3	Work with multiple firms	12.3
Prefer direct contact	29.9	Digital contact	26.4
Wealth preservation focus	28.6	Wealth growth focus	27.6

Source: World Wealth Report 2014, Capgemini and RBC Wealth Management.

The main investment objectives tend to focus on asset safety and wealth preservation/growth. In addition, HNWIs look for highly personalised everyday banking services, loans, wealth planning and specialist advice on sectors, such as:

- Trust and fiduciary services.
- Charities and foundations.
- Media and entertainment.
- Diamonds and jewellery.

The largest private foundation in the world is the Bill & Melinda Gates Foundation (see www.gatesfoundation.org) founded by the Gateses in 1994 with the primary aims, globally, to enhance healthcare and reduce extreme poverty, and in America, to expand educational opportunities and access to information technology. The Foundation had an endowment of USD 36.4 billion as at 31 December 2012, with Bill Gates's donation amounting to USD 28 billion.

Mutual Funds For those of us who are not regarded as high-net-worth individuals, our access to the investment world might be regarded as being rather limited. With a few hundred dollars, it is certainly possible to purchase some shares in a company.

Q&A

Question

To what risks might you be exposed if you purchased, say, 500 shares in Company "X" at USD 1.00 per share?

Answer

There are several risks associated with a purchase of a single security, including:

- If the share price drops below USD 1.00 per share, you will see your capital shrink and you will be losing value.
- If the share price drops to zero, you will lose 100% of your investment.
- If Company "X" does not or cannot pay a dividend, you will not earn any income.
- You are 100% concentrated, i.e. all of your funds are invested in one investment.
- There is no diversification in your securities portfolio as there is only one holding.

So that you can overcome these problems, you should create a portfolio of a diverse number of securities that will spread the risk associated with holding a small number of investments. Ideally, the investments should be spread across types of securities (equities, bonds, etc.), markets (your domestic market and foreign markets) and industries (banking, manufacturing, telecommunications, etc.). Perhaps you can appreciate that you might need more cash than you can afford to invest in order to create the ideal portfolio of investments!

There is an alternative approach that you can take; together with other investors, you can pool your collective amounts of cash and use that larger amount of cash to purchase a more diverse portfolio of suitable securities. For example, instead of buying 500 Company "X" shares at a cost of USD 500 (as above), you pay the USD 500 into a pool of, say, USD 5,000,000. This five million dollars is invested in a selection of securities that are focused on earning dividends in the USA. Let's call this collection of securities a *fund*, to be known as the North American Equity Fund. Your investment is no longer in Company "X"; rather, it is in the fund and your holding will be shares in the fund. How many shares will you own? That depends on the value of the fund (USD 5 million) and the value of each share. If you and the other investors decide to issue shares at a price of USD 1.00 per share, then there are 5 million shares in total, with you having a holding of 500 shares. As the constituent companies held by the fund increase or decrease in value and/or pay dividends from time to time, then you will benefit from this in proportion to your holding of the fund's shares.

You can summarise this by saying that if you diversify your capital, you lower your capital risk. This diversification is one of the main advantages of a collective investment. An investment in a single asset (your Company "X") may do well, but it may collapse for any number of reasons. By investing in a range of securities you reduce your capital risk.

Depending on the country in which you have invested your cash, the fund might be known as a mutual fund, investment fund or managed fund; however, all of these variations are known generically as *collective investment schemes*.

Collective investment schemes may be formed under company law, by legal trust or by statute. Typically, the structure of a scheme contains the following:

- A fund manager (investment manager) who manages the investment decisions;
- A fund administrator who manages the trading, reconciliations, valuation and unit pricing;
- A board of directors or trustees who safeguard the assets and ensure compliance with laws, regulations and rules;
- The shareholders (or unit-holders) who own (or have rights to) the assets and associated income;
- A "marketing" or "distribution" company to promote and sell shares/units of the fund.

The largest global investment managers, as at the end of 2010, are shown in Table 4.10.

TABLE 4.10   The largest global investment managers

Rank	Company	Market	Assets (USD bns)
1	BlackRock	US	3,561
2	State Street Global	US	2,010
3	Allianz Group	Germany	2,010
4	Fidelity Investments	US	1,812
5	Vanguard Group	US	1,765
6	Deutsche Bank	Germany	1,562
7	AXA Group	France	1,463
8	BNP Paribas	France	1,314
9	JP Morgan Chase	US	1,303
10	Capital Group	US	1,223
11	Bank of New York Mellon	US	1,172
12	UBS	Switzerland	933
13	HSBC Holdings	UK	925
14	Amundi Asset Mgmt	France	915
15	Goldman Sachs Group	US	840

Source: TheCityUK (online) "Fund Management – 2012". Available from www.thecityuk.com/research/our-work/reports-list. Secondary sources: Pension & Investments and Towers Watson.

Based on OECD data and TheCityUK's estimates,[14] mutual fund assets totalled USD 23.8 trillion at the end of 2011. This compares with global conventional assets under management

---

[14]*Source:* TheCityUK (November 2012), "Fund Management 2013". Available from www.thecityuk.com. [Accessed Tuesday, 06 August 2013]

of the global fund management industry of USD 79.8 trillion and illustrates the importance of the mutual fund industry to the financial markets.

4.2.3　Banks

At the start of this chapter, we discussed the relationship between the lender and borrower. In addition to this, we added the term *intermediary* – see Figure 4.1. The question then is: "Who is the intermediary?"

The purpose of this section is to define what a bank is and to describe some of the main services offered by the banking industry.

Banks　　The simple answer to the question raised above is that it is a bank which acts as the intermediary. Banks do this by accepting deposits and using them for lending activities, either directly by lending to borrowers or indirectly through the capital markets. A bank, therefore, connects clients with excess capital with clients with a capital deficit.

From a borrower's perspective, there is a barrier to "direct financing", mainly through (a) the difficulty and expense of matching the complex needs of individual borrowers and lenders and (b) the incompatibility of the financial needs of lenders and borrowers. Without exploring the details, we can summarise the needs of lenders and borrowers as follows.

Lenders　　Lenders want to lend their assets for short periods of time and for the highest possible return. They wish to:

- Minimise credit risk (e.g. borrower default) and market risk (e.g. assets dropping in value);
- Minimise the cost of lending and maximise the returns on lending;
- Hold assets that are more easily converted into cash (liquid).

Borrowers　　In contrast, borrowers demand liabilities that are cheap and for longer periods. They wish to:

- Obtain funds at a particular, specified time in order to meet their borrowing requirements;
- Obtain funds for a specific period of time (either short term for working capital requirements or long term for capital equipment, etc.);
- Obtain funds at the lowest possible cost.

You can appreciate that there are conflicting points of view between lenders and borrowers; hence the need for an intermediary (i.e. the banks) that can transform small-scale, low-risk and liquid deposits into large-scale, riskier and more illiquid loans.

What do the banks offer the clients by way of products and services? As we will see later, the banks tend to classify their clients in terms of size, as shown in Table 4.11.

TABLE 4.11   Client classification

Banking Focus	Product/Service	Examples
Personal banking	Everyday banking	Current accounts Savings accounts Credit/debit cards International currency Payment services
	Borrowing	Overdrafts Personal loans Student loans Mortgages
	Investing	Investment funds Online trading Investment advice
	Insurance	Property Family Car Travel
	Planning	Retirement Marriage Growing wealth
Business banking	Starting a business	Some or all of these: Bank/deposit accounts Finance and borrowing Debit/credit cards Payment services Business insurance International business Company pensions Cash-flow management Leveraged finance Trade finance Equity and debt issuance, etc.
	Business banking for clients with up to GBP 2 m turnover	
	Commercial banking (turnover from GBP 2 m to GBP 30 m)	
	Corporate banking (turnover over GBP 30 m)	

There are several ways that the banks are able to deliver their services through so-called *delivery channels*. These include one or more of the following:

- In-branch, face-to-face contact;
- Postal banking;
- Telephone banking;
- Internet banking;
- Mobile telephone banking.

The world's 14 largest banks by market capitalisation are listed in Table 4.12.

TABLE 4.12   World's largest banks as at 31 March 2014

Rank	Bank	Country	Market Cap (USD bn)
1	Wells Fargo & Co	USA	261.72
2	JP Morgan Chase & Co	USA	229.90
3	ICBC	China	196.21
4	HSBC	UK	191.43
5	Bank of America	USA	181.77
6	China Construction Bank	China	160.83
7	Citigroup	USA	144.63
8	Agricultural Bank of China	China	126.41
9	Bank of China	China	115.92
10	Commonwealth Bank of Australia	Australia	115.35
11	Banco Santander	Spain	110.57
12	Westpac Banking Corporation	Australia	99.22
13	BNP Paribas	France	96.03
14	Royal Bank of Canada	Canada	95.18

Source: Relbanks (online). Available from www.relbanks.com/worlds-top-banks/
market-cap. [Accessed Wednesday, 30 April 2014]

Following the banking crisis of the mid-2000s, organisations such as the Financial Stability Board (FSB) have been asked by the leaders of the G20 countries to: "… develop a policy framework to address the systemic and moral hazard risks associated with systemically important financial institutions (SIFIs)".

In November 2011, the FSB published a document entitled *Policy Measures to Address Systemically Important Financial Institutions*[15] in which SIFIs were defined as: "… financial institutions whose distress or disorderly failure, because of their size, complexity and systemic interconnectedness, would cause significant disruption to the wider financial system and economic activity. To avoid this outcome, authorities have all too frequently had no choice but to forestall the failure of such institutions through public solvency support. As underscored by this crisis, this has deleterious consequences for private incentives and for public finances." The initial list of G-SIFIs contains nothing but banks.

We will examine the different types of bank; please be aware that whilst there are banks that operate in perhaps only one of these capacities, many banks operate in most, if not all, of them. Experience has shown that combining investment banking with retail, commercial and corporate banking can cause problems, hence the introduction in the USA of the 1933 Banking Act (known as the Glass–Steagall Act, after the Act's two legislative sponsors). Most elements of this Act were later repealed by US President Bill Clinton in 1999, and it has been argued that allowing banks to re-combine banking-, insurance- and securities-related businesses led

---

[15]*Source:* FSB (online) Available from www.financialstabilityboard.org/publications/r_111104bb.pdf.
[Accessed Thursday, 29 August 2013]

to the banking crisis mentioned earlier. The arguments "for" and "against" the repeal are topics for another time and place.

Retail Banking   In today's world, you and I have a relationship with a bank. You might take some or all of the services shown in Table 4.13.

TABLE 4.13   Typical retail banking services

Your Banking Needs	Bank's Service	
Monthly salary	Current account	Employer instructs its bank to pay your salary into your current account maintained by your bank.
Excess cash/cash to be saved	Deposit/savings account	You request your bank to transfer funds from your current account to your deposit account.
Earn interest on your cash	Interest	Bank pays interest into your account(s) on a periodic basis (monthly, annually, etc.).
Need to borrow cash	Credit cards, overdrafts and short-term loans	These can be secured or unsecured but are readily available and repayable.
Need to buy a property	Mortgages	Bank will lend you part of the market value of your property for a long period of time using the property as collateral.
Legal tax-avoidance schemes	Funds designed to meet Inland Revenue schemes that permit cash and certain non-cash products to attract gross (tax-free) benefits	Cash and cash invested in certain investments are "wrapped" in a tax-free package. Interest and dividends are paid gross.

Whether you take one or more of these services and products, the key point is that the bank is dealing with you as an individual and not as a company. The downside, however, is that the products and services are not tailored to suit particular client needs; they are designed to be mass produced and mass purchased.

Private Banking   We discussed high-net-worth individuals earlier, in the section on Private Wealth Management. Private banking is an extension of personal banking; there are certain similarities (e.g. bank accounts) but differences too. Whilst most personal bank accounts can be opened with as little cash as GBP 1.00, the minimum amount of assets required for an HNWI to benefit from the services of a private bank can be measured in millions of US dollars or equivalent. Even here, the clientele will be sub-divided into "mass affluent" at the lower end and "ultra affluent" at the top end. The key features of private banking can be summarised as follows:

- Services are tailored to meet the clients' individual needs; these might be transactional (see Retail Banking above) and/or advisory;

- Clients have a named private banker allocated to their account (i.e. personal contact);
- The private banker is often expected to anticipate the client's requirements;
- The client and private banker might expect to have a long-term relationship.

Corporate Banking By contrast to retail and private banking, corporate banking focuses on companies, be they regarded as small, medium or large firms. In addition, for the larger firms, the banks will offer services specific to the type of industry the firm is involved in.

Q&A

Question

In what way(s) might the banking services offered to the following types of firm differ from one another?

- Airline
- Import/export company
- Pharmaceutical company
- Energy company.

Answer

Table 4.14 gives some answers.

TABLE 4.14 Banking services offered to different types of firm

Type of Company	Service/Product
Airline	Aircraft leasing Jet fuel cost hedging Foreign exchange management Equity finance Debt finance
Import/export company	Trade finance Foreign exchange management
Pharmaceutical company	Foreign exchange management Equity finance Debt finance Trade finance
Energy company	Upstream business – finance for energy exploration, drilling, infrastructure, transport, etc. Downstream business – finance for refining, distribution and marketing activities.

The larger the client firm, the more specialised the services required. We will refer to some of these needs later when we cover products.

Products and services for the smaller firm include:

- **Payment services:** Similar to personal banking but additionally give access to payment systems (high-value, same-day value, bulk payments, etc.).
- **Debt finance:** Hire purchase, leasing, invoice discounting and factoring.
- **Equity finance:** Private equity and venture capital.
- **Specialist finance:** Financing where there might be government initiatives involved, such as financing for technology-based or bio-chemical-based start-up firms.

Products and services for the medium-sized and larger firms include:

- Most of those offered to the smaller firms;
- Cash management services;
- Loans (bilateral and syndicated), short-term financing (overdrafts, commercial paper issuance) and bonds;
- Bank commitments and guarantees;
- Foreign exchange and interest rate transactions;
- Securities issuance and underwriting;
- Fund management services.

Investment Banking   We have seen that the types of services and products offered by the banks to their commercial and retail banking clients are similar, i.e. deposit taking and lending, but differ in variety, complexity and scale. Investment banks, by contrast, are in the business of:

- **Proprietary trading:** Investing the bank's own money (in asset classes such as equities, bonds, derivatives, commodities) and taking long and short positions.
- **Asset management:** Managing wholesale investments (e.g. a pension on behalf of a corporate client).
- **Securities financing:** Securities lending and borrowing, repurchase ("repo")/reverse repo and sell/buy-backs.
- **Issuing securities for clients:** Assisting clients to raise capital through the issuance of share capital and/or debt capital.
- **Underwriting new issues of securities:** Partially or fully guaranteeing that a new issue of securities will take place.
- **Advising clients on mergers and acquisitions (M&As).**

Unlike the commercial/retail banks, investment banks do not hold retail deposits. The various business lines, noted above, are associated with higher levels of risk when compared with the commercial/retail banking business.

Q&A

Question

What risks might be associated with the above six business lines?

Answer

Table 4.15 shows a selection of risks; this list is by no means exhaustive.

TABLE 4.15 A selection of risks

Business Activity	Risks (Examples)
Proprietary trading	The value of long positions can fall (and rise for short positions), resulting in losses.
Asset management	Poor performance can result in the client moving to another bank or, at worst, being taken to court.
Securities financing	Securities lent may not be returned. If loaned securities were under-collateralised and the borrower defaulted, the lender could be exposed to loss.
Issuing securities	The fees from issuing securities may not fully compensate the bank for its time and effort.
Underwriting new issues	The bank, as an underwriter, will be obliged to take up securities that are not otherwise sold to investors. The fees earned may be outweighed by the losses on the underwritten securities.
Advising clients on M&As	The bank might suffer financial losses if the project it is advising on fails to be completed satisfactorily.

In the USA, specialist investment banks dominated this business, as commercial banks were not permitted to provide investment banking (refer to the Glass–Steagall Act, 1933). Since the Act was repealed in 1999, commercial banks have taken over investment banks; for example, Citigroup includes Citibank (commercial), Salomon Brothers (investment bank) and Smith Barney (brokerage firm).

According to the *Financial Times*,[16] five of the top ten investment banks (by fees earned) are from the USA, with two Swiss banks, one German, one Canadian and one British, as shown in Table 4.16.

---

[16]*Source:* FT.com (online). League Tables, Top 10 Banks – 1H 2014 Fees for M&A, Equity, Bonds and Loans Products. Available from http://markets.ft.com/investmentBanking/tablesAndTrends. asp?ftauth=1398866069529. [Accessed Wednesday, 30 April 2014]

TABLE 4.16   Top ten investment banks

Bank	Fees (USDm)	\% of Fees Earned by Product in 1Q 2014			
		M&A	Equity	Bonds	Loans
JP Morgan	1,369.47	25	22	30	22
Goldman Sachs	1,319.09	40	25	23	12
Bank of America Merrill Lynch	1,159.28	22	19	31	28
Morgan Stanley	1,058.50	28	33	28	11
Deutsche Bank	904.00	18	23	33	25
Citi	873.24	18	25	37	19
Credit Suisse	862.55	26	24	29	20
Barclays	817.76	28	19	33	20
UBS	488.96	24	28	29	19
RBC Capital Markets	449.26	27	24	27	22
Total:	9,302.11				

Source: FT.com (online). League Tables, Top 10 Banks – 1H 2014 Fees for M&A, Equity, Bonds and Loans Products. Available from http://markets.ft.com/investmentBanking/tablesAndTrends.asp?ftauth=1398866069529. [Accessed Wednesday, 30 April 2014]

These ten banks can be regarded as "full-service" investment banks; in addition there are financial service conglomerates that combine commercial banking, investment banking and, sometimes, insurance (e.g. Daiwa Securities, Crédit Agricole, Rabobank and Standard Chartered Bank), and independent investment banks (e.g. Cantor Fitzgerald, Cowen Group, Investec and Piper Jaffray).

Notable casualties from the 2008 banking crisis were investment banks such as:

- Bear Stearns – collapsed in 2008, assets acquired by JP Morgan Chase;
- HBOS – acquired by Lloyds TSB in 2009;
- Lehman Brothers – bankrupt in 2008, assets sold to Barclays Capital and Nomura Holdings;
- Merrill Lynch – acquired by Bank of America in 2008.

Central Banks   A central bank (also referred to as a *reserve bank, monetary authority* or *bank of <country>* in some countries) is an institution that manages the currency, money supply and interest rates of the country in which it is located. Since 1999 in Europe, the European Central Bank has operated in addition to the various country-specific central banks.

The main functions of a central bank usually focus on the following:

- Controlling the issue of notes and coins;
- Controlling the money supply;
- Controlling non-bank financial institutions that supply credit;
- Overseeing the financial sector to prevent crises;
- Acting as lender of last resort to the banking sector;
- Acting as the government's banker;
- Acting as the government's agent in dealing with its gold and foreign exchange matters;
- Holding the government's gold and foreign exchange reserves.

Of these functions, the most important is undertaking monetary control operations, which can be sub-divided into the following three tools:

Open market operations: The money supply is increased by the central bank buying government securities (and/or using reverse repo agreements) and decreased by selling securities (and/or using repo agreements).

Discount window: The central bank can influence the amount of cash borrowed by the banks by changing its discount rate. The higher the rate, the less cash the banks will usually decide to borrow; the lower the rate, the greater amount of cash borrowed.

Reserve requirements: Banks are required to hold minimum levels of reserve. The greater the required reserves, the less lending the banks can engage in; the lower the reserve requirement, the more lending the banks can undertake.

Cooperation amongst the central banks has been centred on the Bank for International Settlements (BIS), an institution established in 1930 and, according to its website: "… the world's oldest international financial institution…". Its mission is to: "… serve central banks in their pursuit of monetary and financial stability, to foster international cooperation in those areas and to act as a bank for central banks".[17]

A list of websites for central banks and monetary authorities can be found at www.bis.org/cbanks.htm.

Quasi-Sovereigns and Supranational Agencies   In this section, we will look at a group of institutions that are neither banks nor corporations. These institutions are closely linked to governments in one way or another but are not regarded as being governments. Predominantly net borrowers, they can also be investors. Finally, they can be implicitly or explicitly guaranteed by their government and, for this reason, often attract a top-level credit rating.

The institutions fall into three categories:

- Municipalities;
- Government agencies;
- Supranational agencies.

Municipalities   Municipalities (local government, local authorities) generate revenue through local taxation and by funding themselves in several ways:

- Borrowing through central government;
- Borrowing from the banks;
- Raising capital in the bond markets by issuing bonds (known as municipal bonds or "munis").

If a municipality issues a bond to pay for general purposes, these are referred to as *general securities* and serviced out of general taxation. If the municipality wishes to fund a specific

---

[17]*Source:* BIS (online). "About BIS." Available from www.bis.org/about/index.htm?l=2. [Accessed Saturday, 31 August 2013]

project, the bonds are known as *revenue securities*. Here, it is expected that the project will generate sufficient cash to service the debt, for example, financing the construction of a toll motorway by issuing a bond and paying the interest and final redemption through the tolls levied on the motorway users.

Municipalities manage their cash and any excess liquidity in the money markets. They also use interest rate derivatives such as swaps to manage their risk. They do not tend to invest in the equity markets.

Q&A

Question

If corporate issuers can default and go bankrupt, can municipalities? What do you think?

Answer

If you think the answer is "no", then you would either expect the central government to support the issuer or the bond to be insured by one of several primary bond insurers.

If you think the answer is "yes", then you should be aware that a small percentage of issuers have defaulted. A recent example is the city of Detroit in the USA, once the "capital" of the car-making industry but now considered bankrupt, with the state of Michigan having taken over administrative control of the city.[18]

Municipals do tend to pay out higher recovery levels, anything from the full 100% of face value to as little as 40%.

Government Agencies   Governments establish agencies typically for a particular purpose, for example an infrastructural project such as the high-speed rail link, known as High Speed 2 (HS2) between London and the north of England. The project is being developed by High Speed Two Limited, a company limited by guarantee established by the UK Government and the projected cost is estimated to be GBP 42.6 bn, with the Institute of Economic Affairs forecasting the cost to rise to over GBP 80 bn.[19]

---

[18]The Michigan state governor, Rick Snyder, declared a financial emergency in March 2013, stating that the city had a USD 327 million budget deficit with more than USD 14 billion in long-term debt on its books. On 14 June 2013, Detroit defaulted on USD 2.5 billion of debt by withholding USD 39.7 million in interest payments. On 18 July 2013, Detroit became the largest US city to file for bankruptcy.
[19]*Source: Daily Telegraph* article 17 August 2013, by Robert Watts (online). "High Speed rail scheme cost to double to £80 bn, economists warn." Available from www.telegraph.co.uk/news/uknews/10249815/High-speed-rail-scheme-cost-to-double-to-80bn-economists-warn.html. [Accessed Thursday, 05 September 2013]

In fact, the first Eurobond was issued in 1963 by an Italian agency, the Autostrade Concessioni e Contruzioni. Bonds issued by these agencies are implicitly or explicitly guaranteed by the government.

Perhaps the most well-known agencies are the US mortgage agencies: the Federal National Mortgage Association, the Government National Mortgage Association and the Federal Home Loan Housing Corporation. All three are known in the markets by their colloquial acronyms: Fannie Mae (FNMA), Ginnie Mae (GNMA) and Freddie Mac (FHLHC). The basic details of these three agencies are shown in Table 4.17.

TABLE 4.17 US mortgage agencies

Agency	Purpose	Comments
FNMA	Its purpose is to buy mortgages from mortgage lenders. This is funded by borrowing in the capital markets.	Privately owned, government-sponsored agency. Bailed out by the US Government in 2008 and placed into government conservatorship.
GNMA	Its purpose is to enable mortgages for affordable housing and it was an innovator in the mortgage-backed security market.	A government-guaranteed agency.
FHLHC	Same business model as FNMA.	Was also placed into government conservatorship in 2008.

Supranational Agencies   These are agencies owned by more than one government, which, like the other types of agency we have looked at, borrow in the capital markets to raise capital for developing projects either in a specific region or globally. The shareholders of these agencies are countries rather than corporate/retail investors and, as such, are regarded as public bodies. These agencies provide their support to the relevant projects either by lending money or making grants.

The supranational agencies are prolific borrowers in the bond markets and significant investors, using the money markets and FX markets to manage their reserves. The major agencies are listed below, and ownership and purpose details are shown in Table 4.18.

- The World Bank;
- The European Investment Bank (EIB);
- The European Bank for Reconstruction and Development (EBRD);
- Inter-American Development Bank (IADB);
- Asian Development Bank (A_sDB);
- African Development Bank (A_fDB).

The World Bank tends to borrow in many currencies, using derivatives to turn them into US dollars, in contrast to the EBRD, which prefers to borrow in the local currencies of the

TABLE 4.18 Supranational agencies

Agency	Ownership	Purpose
World Bank/International Bank for Reconstruction and Development (IBRD)	Any country member of the International Monetary Fund, with shareholdings based on their economic status.	Supports projects in poor and medium-income countries.
World Bank/International Development Agency (IDA)		Supports the poorest countries.
EIB	Owned by the EU countries.	Supports projects mainly in the European region and other areas (to a lesser extent).
EBRD	Owned by 61 countries, mainly European but also non-European plus the EU and the EIB.	Provides loans and trade finance especially in central and eastern Europe.
IADB	Owned by 48 countries including the USA (30%), 26 borrowing Latin American and Caribbean countries (50%) and 20% by 21 non-borrowing countries, such as Germany and Japan.	Provides loans, grants and guarantees for Latin America and the Caribbean countries.
A_sDB	As with the IADB, membership comes from a group of international and local countries.	Provides loans, grants and guarantees for Asian countries.
A_fDB	As with the IADB, membership comes from a group of international and local countries.	Provides loans, grants and guarantees for African countries.

countries in which the projects are taking place. By far the biggest borrower is now the EIB (previously it was the World Bank).

4.2.4 Sell-Side Intermediaries

In market terminology, we use the term *sell side* to refer to those firms that either sell to the investor side of the industry (known as the *buy side*) and/or trade on their own behalf. This section defines the different sell-side intermediaries and briefly describes their roles in the market.

Brokers It is generally not possible for the buy side to access the markets directly. Instead, buy-side investors will make use of brokers for this purpose. Also known as stockbrokers, these agents provide a number of services to their clients, including:

- Advising clients on which investments to make;
- Executing transactions based on their clients' instructions (non-discretionary);
- Executing transactions on behalf of their clients (discretionary).

Brokers do not invest their own firm's capital; their prime role is to act on behalf of their clients. Brokers make their money by charging brokerage fees based on the market value of the transaction. The fee structure will reflect the level of service offered to their clients.

Example

A broker purchases on behalf of its client the shares shown in Table 4.19.

TABLE 4.19 Purchase of ABC shares by broker on behalf of a client

ABC Shares			
Purchase	1,500	shares	
Price (EUR)	5.50	per share	
Cost			EUR 8,250.00
If the brokerage fee is charged at:		0.25%	EUR 20.63
Total cost:			EUR 8,270.63

Please note that there might be additional fees to pay, depending on the market in which the transaction is executed. A typical additional fee might be stamp duty payable to the local tax authorities.

Dealers/Traders   Dealers and traders (the terms are synonymous) trade on behalf of their firm. They are free to trade in any markets and in any product subject to their own internal authorisations and limits. They are under no obligation to trade in any particular market or product. Dealers make their money by buying at a lower price than that at which they sell ("buy low, sell high"). The difference between the buy price and the sale price is known as the *spread* or *margin*; the wider the spread, the greater the profit (or loss). In highly competitive markets, this spread will tend to narrow.

Example

A dealer buys USD 100,000 nominal ABC bonds at a price of 99.5000 and sells them at a price of 101.0000. Has the dealer made a profit or suffered a loss? In this case, the dealer bought low and sold high, therefore, has made a profit on this deal. The amount of profit is calculated as follows:

$$USD\ 100,000 \times (101.0000 - 99.5000) = USD\ 1,500.00$$

Please note that:

- Bonds are typically priced as a percentage to par; in other words, the purchase price is more correctly stated as 99.5000/100 or 99.5000%.
- If the bonds were interest-bearing, the dealer would be required to add "accrued interest" to the market value of the transaction.

Market Makers   Market makers are similar to dealers and traders, in that they invest their firms' capital in securities. The big difference, however, is that market makers are obliged to make a market (quote a bid-offer price spread) and to execute transactions with buyers and sellers subject to price agreement.

This obligation to make a two-way price in securities in which they make markets can become quite onerous; for example, if share prices are going down, investors might wish to sell their securities. For the market makers, this means that they are buying shares and seeing the share price continuing to go down. In addition, they have to pay for the shares and that will require some form of financing. By contrast, if the market is going up, investors might wish to buy and the market maker will be obliged to sell. If they do not hold the securities, then delivery becomes impossible; in this case, the market maker needs access to securities borrowing facilities in order to complete the delivery.

For the very large issuing companies, several competing market makers will make prices in the securities; this makes it very competitive and helps to narrow the bid-offer spread. Market makers will adjust their prices to keep in step with the market and to persuade or dissuade investors seeking to execute a trade with them.

Broker/Dealers   So far we have seen brokers acting on behalf of clients (but not for their own account) and dealers who trade for their own account. There are firms which act in both capacities, as a broker and separately as a dealer. This can lead to a conflict of interest.

Example

A client approaches a firm in a broker capacity and wishes to buy some securities. As the broker does not hold any inventory, he is obliged to go to a dealer to obtain the securities. If the broker goes to his own dealer, there is a danger that the dealer might go into the markets and buy the securities for his own account, known as "front running". That might lead to an increase in the market price and if the broker then purchases the securities from his dealer, the purchase will be executed at a higher price in this case. To avoid the risk of a broker getting an unfair price from his dealer, the broker is obliged to seek the best price in the market. This could mean that in order to get the best price, the broker might have to purchase the securities from another dealer, perhaps a competitor.

In any event it is expected that there is a clear separation between the broker side of the business and the dealer side. We can refer to this "separation" as a *Chinese Wall*.

Inter-Dealer Brokers   We have seen that it is quite possible to have several competing market makers for any one particular security. If one of these market makers were to attempt to cover a short position (because somebody wanted to buy from a market maker that had insufficient securities) and was unable to borrow the securities, then the only option would be to go into the market and buy the securities from another market maker. This would make it obvious what the former market maker's situation was and the latter market maker would certainly seek to benefit from this by quoting a high price. To avoid such a situation, the market maker would wish to remain anonymous to its competitors but still obtain the securities needed. What they require is an intermediary that can act as a broker to the market makers, and this intermediary is known as an *inter-dealer broker* (IDB). Trading through an IDB enables the market maker to fill its position without the rest of the market knowing who is doing this.

4.2.5 Market Regulators and Market Associations

With the markets becoming more globalised, it has become necessary to regulate and supervise financial institutions of all types and sizes by means of certain requirements, restrictions and guidelines.

You will have noticed that, in recent years, there have been many examples of problems in the industry. Examples include the mis-selling of financial products, dealers exceeding their internal limits, and a decreasing confidence in the banking industry as a whole, to name but a few.

The financial regulators, usually either a government or non-government organisation, have a difficult task in ensuring that problems like these do not re-occur.

Listed in Table 4.20 are some of the more usual objectives of the regulators.

TABLE 4.20 Regulatory objectives

Regulatory Objectives	
Market confidence	Maintaining confidence in the financial system.
Financial stability	Contributing to the protection and enhancement of stability in the financial system.
Consumer protection	Securing an appropriate degree of protection for consumers.
Financial crime reduction	Reducing the possibilities for a regulated business to be used for financial criminal purposes.

Supervision of the financial markets tends to cover the initial authorisation of firms to conduct business and the ongoing monitoring of their activities. Failure to comply with any rules and regulations can lead to substantial fines and even loss of authorisation. Added to this, details of fines and censures will almost certainly be reported in the press and this adds to the reputational risk for firms.

Regulation tends to be enforced on a country-by-country basis; however, regions such as Europe are becoming more regulated from the centre (i.e. Brussels). Whether local or regional, the following organisation types are supervised:

- Stock exchanges;
- Listed companies;
- Investment managers;
- Banks and other financial service providers.

There are many regulatory authorities located across the world, but listed below is just a small selection of these:

United States
- Securities and Exchange Commission (SEC);
- Federal Reserve System (the "Fed");
- Office of the Comptroller of the Currency (OCC).

United Kingdom
- Financial Conduct Authority (FCA).

Continental Europe
- Federal Financial Supervisory Authority (BaFin), Germany;
- Autorité des Marchés Financiers (AMF), France;
- Autoriteit Financiële Markten (AFM), Netherlands;
- Commissione Nazionale per le Società e la Borsa (CONSOB), Italy;
- Swiss Financial Market Supervisory Authority (FINMA), Switzerland.

China
- China Securities Regulatory Commission (CSRC).

Japan
- Financial Services Agency (FSA).

Singapore
- Monetary Authority of Singapore (MAS).

For a complete list of regulators, please go to the website of The International Organization of Securities Commissions (IOSCO) at www.iosco.org/lists. IOSCO was established in 1983 and: "... is the acknowledged international body that brings together the world's securities regulators and is recognised as the global standard setter for the security sector".[20]

There are various agencies that have been established for a particular product or products and that span a more global point of view. Indeed, products such as Eurobonds and OTC derivatives have no domicile. In these cases, whilst individual firms are authorised and monitored by their local regulator, the products themselves are regulated by a third-party organisation. Examples of these and other associations are noted in Table 4.21 together with the headline product type they have responsibility for. For more details, you can visit the websites listed in the table.

TABLE 4.21   Regulators' and trade associations' websites

Regulator/Association	Product(s)/Industry	Website
International Capital Market Association (ICMA)	International securities (e.g. Eurobonds) and repo agreements	www.icmagroup.org
International Swaps and Derivatives Association (ISDA)	OTC derivatives	www2.isda.org
The Financial Markets Association (ACI)	Foreign exchange, interest rate products and other securities, banknotes and bullion, precious metals and commodities and their various derivatives	www.aciforex.org

---

[20]A fact sheet dated July 2013 can be found on their website at www.iosco.org/about/pdf/IOSCO-Fact-Sheet.pdf.

TABLE 4.21 (*Continued*)

Regulator/Association	Product(s)/Industry	Website
Various central securities depositories associations (CSDAs)	World Forum of CSDs European CSDA Asia-Pacific CSD Group Association of Eurasian CSDs Americas' CSDA Africa and Middle East Depositories Association	www.worldcsds.wordpress.com www.ecsda.eu www.acgcsd.org www.aecsd.com www.acsda.org www.ameda.org.eg
International Securities Lending Association (ISLA)	Securities lending and borrowing	www.isla.co.uk

4.3 MARKET STRUCTURE

4.3.1 Introduction

This section on market infrastructure considers the organisation types that take responsibility for the trading, clearing, settlement and custody of securities. In terms of the trading of securities, these can either be traded on a regulated market (e.g. a recognised stock exchange) or between two trading counterparties away from a market (i.e. "off exchange") in what we refer to as the *over-the-counter market* (OTC).

Figure 4.2 distinguishes between the regulated and OTC market structures.

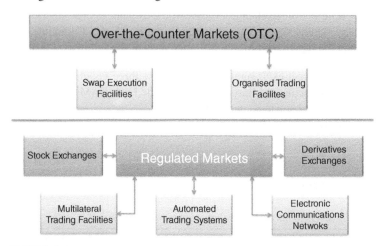

FIGURE 4.2 Market structure

4.3.2 Regulated Markets

Stock Exchanges   It is difficult to judge when the first stock exchange was formed. In fact there is little consensus on this point; however, it is true to say that stock exchanges have been around for many centuries. Some say they originated in ancient Rome; others will disagree. What is true, however, is that stock exchanges provide services for certain market participants (e.g. market makers, brokers and traders) that enable securities such as equities and bonds to be issued and subsequently traded. Traditionally, the stock exchange would have been a physical building and the trading would have taken place on the floor of the stock exchange. Furthermore, trading would not have been allowed anywhere other than the floor of the stock exchange.

Companies that wish to issue shares and raise debt through bond issues will have the securities listed on the stock exchange. Again, traditionally a security would have been listed on one particular stock exchange, more often than not in the country of the issuer. Once the securities had been issued in the so-called primary markets, then subsequent trading, known as secondary market trading, would also take place on the exchange. In today's world, there is sometimes no compulsion to have to trade listed securities on the exchange. Instead, buyers and sellers can come together away from the exchange; we refer to this as being "off exchange" (otherwise known as "over-the-counter" or OTC).

In recent times, many of the traditional stock exchanges have moved away from being a physical location to becoming computer or telephone-based. Indeed, more recently established exchanges have tended to dispense with a floor and have gone straight into trading using computers, telephones, etc.

Q&A

Question

The World Federation of Exchanges (www.world-exchanges.org/statistics/monthly-reports) produces regular reports including the Domestic Market Capitalisation report. Please download the report as at March 2014 and answer the following questions:

1. Which are the largest exchanges in each of these three geographical regions: the Americas, Asia-Pacific and Europe-Africa-Middle East (EAME)?
2. Which is the largest stock exchange in the world?
3. Which is the smallest stock exchange in the world?

Answers

Table 4.22 gives the answers.

TABLE 4.22   Answers to the three questions on stock exchanges

Region	Stock Exchange	Market Capitalisation (USD millions)
Americas	NYSE Euronext (USA)	18,306,138.70
Asia-Pacific	Japan Exchange Group, Tokyo	4,316,490.50
Europe-Africa-Middle East	Euronext	3,734,829.11
Largest	NYSE Euronext (USA)	18,306,138.70
Smallest	Bermuda SE	1,639.28

Source: World Federation Exchange members.

Whilst there is no reason why any trading in today's environment should be on the floor of an exchange, there are still a few exchanges where trading continues to take place on the floor. One example where floor trading still takes place is the New York Stock Exchange. Here, specialist brokers execute trades on behalf of buyers and sellers through a process of *open outcry*. Floor trading takes place alongside computerised trading, which was introduced in the early 1970s. The exchanges system was known as the *Designated order turnaround* system (DOT).

Derivatives Exchanges Derivatives exchanges can either be part of a stock exchange (e.g. Singapore Exchange) or a separate entity in their own right (e.g. Shanghai Futures Exchange). A selection of derivatives exchanges is listed in Table 4.23.

TABLE 4.23   Selection of derivatives exchanges

Exchange/URL	Derivatives Products	Securities Products
ASX (Australia) (www.asx.com.au)	Equity options Index Interest rates Agricultural Energy	Yes
Shanghai Futures Exchange (China) (www.shfe.com.cn/en)	Commodity futures: Non-ferrous metals Precious metals Ferrous metals Energy Natural rubber	No
SGX (Singapore) (www.sgx.com)	Equity index Foreign exchange Interest rates Dividend index	Yes
EUREX (Germany) (www.eurexchange.com)	Interest rate derivatives Equity derivatives Equity index derivatives Dividend derivatives Volatility index derivatives Exchange-traded funds Derivatives Inflation derivatives Commodity derivatives Weather derivatives Property derivatives	No
ICE (USA) (www.theice.com)	Futures and options: Energy Agriculture Financials Ferrous metals Freight Environmental OTC: ICE swap trade Physical energy Credit default swaps	No

(*continued*)

TABLE 4.23 (*Continued*)

Exchange/URL	Derivatives Products	Securities Products
Osaka Exchange (Japan) (www.ose.or.jp)	Index futures JGB futures Options on JGB futures TOPIX options Single stock options	Yes
NYSE LIFFE (part of the NYSE Euronext Group, USA) (globalderivatives.nyx.com)	Interest rates Equity derivatives Commodity derivatives	No
CME Group (USA) (www.cmegroup.com)	Agriculture Energy Equity index FX Interest rates Metals Options OTC Real estate	No

Unlike securities, which are issued by the organisation that raises equity and/or debt capital, derivative products that are traded on an exchange are created by the exchange. The derivative products have nothing to do with the underlying asset (e.g. equities, bonds, commodities), although they are priced according to the price movements of the underlying assets.

These derivative products are standardised by the exchange in terms of the criteria (referred to as contract specifications) shown in Table 4.24.

TABLE 4.24 Contract specifications

Contract Specification	Description	Example
Underlying	The asset that the contract is deliverable into/exercised into.	A government security or single shares or an index, etc.
Contract currency	The currency that the contract is traded and delivered in.	USD, EUR, JPY, etc.
Unit of trading	The size of each contract.	100,000 nominal value, 1,000 shares in ABC, etc.
Quotation	The way the contract is priced.	per GBP 100 nominal, per share, etc.
Minimum price movement	The minimum amount that the price can move.	(Also known as *tick size*) 0.01, 0.25, etc.
Expiry or delivery month	The month in which the contract is deliverable/exercisable.	Quarterly – March, June, September and December.
Trading details	Trading dates and times.	Last trading date: two business days prior to the last business day in the delivery month. Trading hours: 08:00 to 18:00.
Trading platform(s)	The methods for trading the contracts.	Open outcry and/or electronic platform.

4.3.3 Alternative Trading Venues

There are several non-exchange trading venues that compete with the traditional stock exchange model.

Multilateral Trading Facilities (MTFs)   MTFs provide similar trading services, rules and market surveillance to the regulated markets. However, MTFs do not have a listing process and cannot change the regulatory status of a security.

Under new European rules (MiFID II), investment firms will have to be authorised as an MTF if they wish to operate internal matching or crossing systems in order to execute client orders.

MTFs are also obliged to make prices on existing orders available on market data feeds (pre-trade transparency) and publish trades in real time (post-trade transparency). Furthermore, there must be a consistent application of pricing and charges to all Facility members, a system rulebook and the means by which to apply for membership of the Facility.

In 2011, two pan-European MTFs, BATS Europe and Chi-X Europe, merged to form BATS Chi-X Europe. The merged entity became a Recognised Investment Exchange in 2013. According to its press release dated 4 December 2013, BATS Chi-X Europe had 23% overall market share in Europe.[21]

Alternative Trading Systems (ATSs)   An ATS is the US equivalent of an MTF in Europe. They are similar in concept to MTFs, in that they provide a marketplace for buyers and sellers to trade in securities. There are, however, some differences between an ATS and an MTF, for example:

- They do not perform self-regulation;
- They do not necessarily provide public information on prices;
- They do not set rules governing the conduct of ATS subscribers.

In the USA, ATSs are regulated as broker/dealers and are regulated differently than traditional stock exchanges.

According to a paper prepared by the SEC's Division of Economic and Risk Analysis (DERA),[22] there are 35 broker/dealers operating 44 ATSs, and trading on the systems comprises 10–15% of US equity trading volume. Lists of current ATS operators (including ECNs – see below) can be found on the SEC website at www.sec.gov/foia/docs/atslist.htm.

Electronic Communication Networks (ECNs)   An ECN is a type of ATS that enables traders and institutional investors to deal directly amongst themselves without the need to go through an exchange/OTC market maker.

---

[21]*Source:* BATS Global Markets (online) "BATS GLOBAL MARKETS IN NOVEMBER". Available from http://cdn.batstrading.com/resources/press_releases/BATS_November2013_FINAL.pdf. [Accessed Wednesday, 22 January 2014]

[22]Tuttle, Laura – October 2013 (online) "Alternative Trading Systems: Description of ATS Trading in National Market System Stocks". Available from www.sec.gov/marketstructure/research/ats_data_paper_october_2013.pdf. [Accessed Wednesday, 22 January 2014]

ECNs include Instinet (Institutional Network), which was established in 1969 and enables US institutions to trade directly with each other. The system was opened to broker/dealers and NASDAQ market makers in 1983.

4.3.4 Over-the-Counter Market

By contrast to the stock exchange trading system, the over-the-counter (OTC) market is an off-exchange system where trading is carried out directly between the buyer and the seller. There is no stock exchange involvement with this. As with exchange trading, OTC trading occurs with financial instruments such as derivatives and Eurobonds.

OTC Derivatives In the OTC derivatives market, transactions in financial instruments such as interest rate swaps are tailored by the counterparties themselves rather than a derivatives exchange. Whilst this leads to innovation and bespoke products, there is a high degree of opacity due to the fact that there is no centralisation of the products; in other words, the only counterparties who know about the product, and the transaction, will be the buyer and the seller. This can lead to a variety of risks, including, for example, counterparty risk. In recent years, the global regulators have been concerned with this risk (and other types of risk as well) and have taken steps to introduce what is known as *centralised clearing* into the system. We will come across central counterparties (CCPs) in Chapter 5: Clearing Houses and CCPs.

A second major reform is the formation of new platforms for trading OTC derivatives electronically. In the USA, these new platforms are known as *swap execution facilities* (SEFs), and an SEF is defined as "… a facility, trading system or platform in which multiple participants have the ability to execute or trade swaps by accepting bids and offers made by other participants that are open to multiple participants in the facility or system, through any means of interstate commerce".[23]

In Europe, the EU has proposed a similar approach by means of the establishment of *organised trading facilities* (OTFs) defined as "… any system or facility, which is not a regulated market or MTF, operated by an investment firm or a market operator, in which multiple third-party buying and selling interests in financial instruments are able to interact in the system".[24]

Whilst there are some key differences in these definitions, the overall objective is to move OTC derivative instruments and trading onto an exchange-type environment (i.e. an SEF or an OTF) with increased transparency and regulatory oversight. Differences include:

- OTFs are designed to trade equities, commodities and other derivatives rather than just swaps (as under SEFs).
- The OTF model includes the ability to use execution models that include voice brokerage as well as electronic trading.

---

[23] *Source:* Futures & Options World (11 November 2011) (online). "From OTC to OTF: SEFs, OTFs and the new world of trading." Available from www.fow.com/Article/2934329/From-OTC-to-OTF-SEFs-OTFs-and-the-new-world-of-trading.html. [Accessed Wednesday, 22 January 2014]
[24] See footnote 22.

Eurobonds   The Eurobond market is a variation on the OTC theme. Whilst many Eurobond issues are listed in Luxembourg and London, none are domiciled in any country. This means that as there are no domestic exchanges on which to trade, trading takes place "off exchange". The Eurobond industry is regulated by the International Capital Market Association as a Self-Regulated Organisation and its Rule Book covers the trading and settlements of this product type.

4.4   SUMMARY

In this chapter we have seen how the buy-side and sell-side institutions participate in the markets. We examined how investors can access the markets and the intermediaries who assist in this. There are different types of investor, from private investors (retail) to institutional investors such as pension funds and insurance companies that can either invest their own assets or appoint fund managers to do this for them on a discretionary basis.

Banks play a vital intermediary role whether on a commercial, investment, private or central banking basis.

The financial markets should be regulated in order to provide investors with a transparent and fair means to invest. We therefore have domestic regulators that consider local requirements and regional regulators for a broader geographical/political region such as Europe.

There are trade associations that focus on specific markets (e.g. the FSA in Japan), products (e.g. the ISDA for derivatives) and intermediaries (e.g. the various central securities depositories associations).

Finally, we looked at regulated and OTC markets where the transactions are executed. We have seen that the traditional Stock Exchanges (where securities are listed, derivatives created and both are traded) are being challenged by alternative platforms such as Multilateral Trading Facilities, Alternative Trading Systems and Electronic Communications Networks. Furthermore, additional platforms are being introduced as a result of regulatory changes in the USA and Europe (i.e. Organised Trading Facilities and Swap Execution Facilities) in order to transition OTC derivatives onto more transparent, regulated platforms.

CHAPTER **5**

Clearing Houses and CCPs

5.1 INTRODUCTION

Part Two of this book will take you through the post-trade processing of the financial instruments that you looked at in Chapter 2: Financial Instruments. We will do this by considering market infrastructures and trade lifecycles in the ways outlined in Table 5.1.

TABLE 5.1 Market infrastructures and trade lifecycles

Market Infrastructure	Trade Lifecycle
(a) Clearing houses and CCPs	Clearing
(b) Central securities depositories	Settlement and settlement fails management
(c) Custody intermediaries	The role of the custodians

It is not possible to cover every financial product in every market; this would indeed be a very large book! Instead, we will look at the major types of financial product with a brief description of the appropriate clearing system, depository and custody intermediaries; in particular, we will look at:

- Equities;
- Government bonds;
- Eurobonds;
- Exchange-traded derivatives (futures and options);
- Centrally cleared OTC derivatives (interest rate swaps);
- Non-cleared OTC derivatives (forward rate agreements).

In Section 5.5 at the end of this chapter you will find some useful information sources for infrastructural organisations such as the clearing houses, depositories and custodians together with statistical information. You might like to bookmark these organisations' URLs so that you can access their websites without too much trouble.

5.2 OVERVIEW OF CLEARING AND SETTLEMENT

For many people, the terms *clearing* and *settlement* are synonymous. This is not strictly true; clearing is the first step in the post-trade process that leads to settlement.

Q&A

Question

What is the process that you would need to go through in order to take possession of a residential property that you wanted to purchase for you and your family?

Answer

There are five main steps for the process of purchasing a property – see Table 5.2.

TABLE 5.2   The five main steps in purchasing a property

Step	Action Taken
1. Find the property	▪ Decide what type of property you want (a house or an apartment) ▪ Decide the location of the property (country, city, urban or rural) ▪ Spend time visiting estate agents/realtors and viewing potential properties
2. Make an offer on your chosen property	▪ Offer a price for the property (hoping this will be acceptable to the vendor) ▪ Offer is either accepted or rejected ▪ Assuming offer is eventually accepted …
3. Preliminary activities	▪ Appoint a surveyor to conduct a survey on the property ▪ Appoint a legal adviser to conduct legal searches on the property ▪ Arrange finance through a bank or mortgage company ▪ Pay a deposit to the vendor's legal adviser to initiate the first step in acquiring ownership of the property ▪ Sign legal contracts (these will be held temporarily by your legal adviser)
4. Contract exchange date	▪ At a pre-specified date, your legal adviser exchanges contracts with the vendor's legal adviser ▪ You arrange for the financing to be paid to the vendor via your legal adviser's bank ▪ You are advised that payment has been made and legal documentation received
5. Obtain ownership	▪ You receive the door keys to the property and you move into your new home ▪ Details of the change of ownership are recorded on an appropriate property register

If only buying a new property was this straightforward! It does, however, make a good analogy to our world of equities, bonds and derivatives, as shown in Table 5.3.

TABLE 5.3   Property and securities analogy

Step	Analogy
1. Find the property	Price discovery (Front Office)
2. Make an offer on your chosen property	Transaction execution (Front Office)
3. Preliminary activities	Clearing (Operations)
4. Contract exchange date	Settlement (Operations)
5. Obtain ownership	Registration of a change of legal and beneficial ownership (Safekeeping)

Let us define what we mean by the terms *clearing* and *settlement*, according to the Committee on Payment and Settlement Systems (CPSS):[1]

Clearing/clearance is defined as: "The process of transmitting, reconciling and, in some cases, confirming payment orders or security transfer instructions prior to settlement, possibly including the netting of instructions and the establishment of final positions for settlement. Sometimes the term is used (imprecisely) to include settlement."

Settlement is defined as: "The completion of a transaction, wherein the seller transfers … securities or financial instruments to the buyer and the buyer transfers money to the seller. A settlement may be final or provisional."

In Chapters 7 to 9, we will explore clearing and settlement both in terms of structure and how these two overall processes work.

5.3   THE CLEARING HOUSE MODEL

The CPSS defines a clearing house as:

"A central location or central processing mechanism through which financial institutions agree to exchange payment instructions or other financial obligations. The institutions settle for items exchanged at a designated time based on the rules and procedures of the clearing house. In some cases, the clearing house may assume significant counterparty, financial or risk management responsibilities for the clearing system."

---

[1]Source: CPSS Glossary (online). "A glossary of terms used in payments and settlement systems." Available from www.bis.org/publ/cpss00b.pdf. [Accessed Friday, 24 January 2014]

The key words and phrases in this definition are shown in Table 5.4.

TABLE 5.4 Clearing house definition

Extract	Implications
Central location	There might be one clearing house per financial instrument in any one location, or
	There might be one clearing house for all financial instruments in any one location.
Institutions agree to exchange	This is an agreement rather than the actual exchange itself.
Institutions settle … at a designated time based on the rules and procedures …	The clearing house dictates how and when financial instruments are processed.
The clearing house may assume significant counterparty, financial or risk management responsibilities	This is very true; we will explore this in more detail when we consider central counterparties (CCPs).

Details of executed transactions in financial instruments are passed down from the relevant securities/derivatives exchange to the appropriate clearing house, and typically both the buyer and seller will confirm these transactions by submitting receive and delivery instructions respectively.

The clearing house will then take the necessary actions in order to make the transactions available for eventual settlement. In accordance with local practice, settlement is intended to take place at some predefined time after the trade date. Depending on the financial instrument and the location in which it was traded, typically settlement can take place from the trade date itself to one or more business days after the trade date. Settlement on the trade date is referred to as trade date T+0. Settlement three business days after the trade date is referred to as T+3.

In the clearing house model (see Figure 5.1), the clearing house will perform the following activities:

1. Validate incoming instructions from the buyer and seller (or their agents). The validation process ensures that the instructions are potentially correct (e.g. that the board lot size matches with the reference database, the price is within a prespecified tolerance and the correct amount of accrued interest accounted for).
2. Match the buyer's receive instructions to the seller's delivery instructions. If the details in both instructions agree, then the clearing house can assume that these instructions refer to the same underlying transaction and that both parties agreed to the economic terms. Where instructions do not agree, the clearing house will mark these with the status "Unmatched". The clearing house will not allow any unmatched transactions to go forward for settlement and both the buyer and the seller will be required to investigate the reasons why their instructions do not match.
3. The clearing house will judge whether there are sufficient assets to enable settlement to take place. This includes sufficient cash (or credit or access to financing) for the buyer and asset availability for the seller.
4. On the intended settlement date the clearing house will allow the transaction to settle, subject to availability, and will pass details of this to a third party where the transaction will actually settle. This third-party entity is known as a *central securities depository*.

Please note that in this model the clearing house is acting as a facilitator and does not assume any credit risk in terms of the buyer and the seller. We refer to this type of credit risk as *counterparty risk* and it is the risk that one counterparty or another will not be in a position to honour its obligations concerning the transaction or transactions executed between the two counterparties. The counterparty risk remains with both counterparties until such time as the transaction is finally settled.

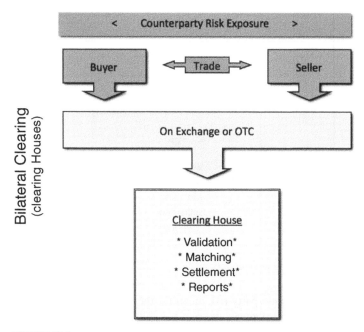

FIGURE 5.1   Clearing house model

The following organisations are examples of this particular model:

- CETIP (Brazil);
- CCASS (for exchange trades executed on the Isolated Trade System and non-exchange trades) (Hong Kong);
- Saudi Arabian Clearing House;
- Strate (South Africa);
- Fixed Income Clearing Corporation: Mortgage-Backed Securities Division (USA).

5.4   THE CENTRAL COUNTERPARTY MODEL

The CPSS defines a central counterparty (CCP) as:

> "An entity that is the buyer to every seller and seller to every buyer of a specified set of contracts, e.g. those executed on a particular exchange or exchanges."

We saw above the role the clearing house plays. It is similar to that of a CCP with one key difference: the CCP novates the transactions and assumes the counterparty risk of the buyer and, separately, the seller. Once a transaction is novated, the original counterparty risk exposure between the buyer and seller is eliminated.

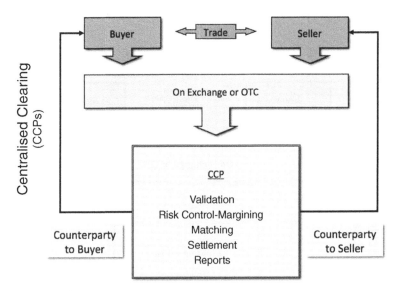

FIGURE 5.2 Central counterparty model

What does this change in counterparty risk mean for the CCP? In the clearing house model, if one party defaults before settlement, the risk lies with the counterparty to that trade. By contrast, in the CCP model (Figure 5.2), that risk exposure now rests with the CCP itself. The CCP, therefore, must have very robust risk-mitigation procedures in place otherwise there is the risk that a default, or a series of defaults by more than one party, might cause the CCP to default.

On 15 September 2008, the American investment bank, Lehman Brothers, failed.[2] The reasons why are outside the scope of this book. However, for our purposes, one of the key issues that arose from this failure concerned the bank's OTC interest rate swap positions with a notional value of USD 9 trillion. This portfolio consisted of 66,390 trades across five major currencies.[3]

LCH.Clearnet, together with member firm participation, had, by 3 October 2008, successfully auctioned off the portfolio without any damage to the CCP.

---

[2] The Report of the Examiner in the Chapter 11 proceedings of Lehman Brothers Holdings Inc. was published in March 2010. The 2,200-page report was produced by the Examiner, Anton Valukas, chairman of Jenner & Block, a Chicago law firm. The Examiner's Report can be found on Jenner & Block's website at http://jenner.com/lehman.

[3] Refer to: LCH.Clearnet press release 8 October 2008 (online). "$9 trillion Lehman OTC interest rate swap default successfully resolved." Available from www.lchclearnet.com/media_centre/press_releases/ 2008-10-08.asp. [Accessed Monday, 27 January 2014]

5.4.1 Risk Management

CCPs manage their risk mitigation by:

- Maintaining policies on the many different types of risk, e.g. counterparty credit risk, business risk, operational risk, regulatory and compliance risk;
- Applying a margin to CCP member firms' transactions;
- Maintaining default funds which are sufficient to withstand the default of one or more members;
- Protecting client positions by transferring them to another clearing member if a clearing member firm defaults;
- Collecting eligible/acceptable collateral to which appropriate haircuts have been applied;
- Covering the relationship between CCP and member firms through a rule book.

All of the above should be regularly stress-tested and updated as market conditions change.

In the event that a member firm defaults, its CCP should apply a "waterfall" line of financial defence, as shown in Table 5.5.

TABLE 5.5 CCP – line of financial defence

Defaulting member's margin (e.g. initial margin, variation margin, etc.), then, if insufficient …
Defaulting member's contribution to a default fund, then …
The CCP's reserve fund, then …
Clearing fund contribution of other members, and finally …
Equity of the CCP.

We can observe that the first line of defence is the defaulting member's own financial resources followed by the CCP's and other members' reserve funds. Finally, the CCP's equity acts as the last line of defence.

The following are examples of the CCP model:

- ASX Clear (Australia);
- CDS Clearing & Depository Services (Canada);
- China Securities Depository and Clearing Corporation[4] (China);
- Eurex Clearing (Germany);
- LCH.Clearnet (France, Belgium, Italy, Netherlands and UK);
- CCASS (for trades executed on the Exchange Trades-Continuous Net Settlement System) (Hong Kong);
- Japan Securities Clearing Corporation (Japan);
- National Securities Depository (Russia);
- SGX-Central Depository (Singapore);
- OMX Derivatives Markets (Sweden);

---

[4]Listed as the SD&C in the Comparative Table for CCPs (look out for details of the CPSS statistics below).

- SIX x-clear (Switzerland);
- National Securities Clearing Corporation (USA).

5.5 FEATURES OF CCPs AND CLEARING HOUSES

5.5.1 The Committee for Payment and Settlement Systems' Statistics

The Committee for Payment and Settlement Systems (CPSS) annually produces statistics on payment, clearing and settlement systems for a selection of countries (the so-called CPSS countries). The most recent publication can be found on the BIS/CPSS website at www.bis.org/list/cpss/index.htm.

In the section on comparative tables, you will find features on the following infrastructural systems (shown in Table 5.6):

- Interbank funds transfer systems (PS);
- Exchanges and trading systems (TRS);
- Central counterparties and clearing houses (CCP);
- Central securities depositories (CSD).

TABLE 5.6 Features of selected central counterparties and clearing houses

Category	Meaning	Comments
CCP or clearing house	The entity is a central counterparty (CCP) or a clearing house (CH).	
Owner/manager	Central bank (CB), commercial banks (B), a stock exchange (SE), another CCP (CCP)/clearing house (CH) or other type (O).	If owner and manager differ, both are provided. If (fully or partially) owned by an exchange, a CCP or a clearing house, the name of that entity is provided as well as the share of its ownership rights.
Relationship with exchange	- Internal (int) - Parental (par) - Independent from the exchange (indep).	- The CCP belongs to the same entity as the exchange, or - The CCP is a subsidiary of the exchange, or - The CCP is independent from the exchange.
Relationship with CSD	- Internal (int) - Parental (par) - Independent from the CSD (indep).	- The CCP belongs to the same entity as the CSD, or - The CCP is a subsidiary of the CSD, or - The CCP is independent from the CSD.
Intra-day margining	Routine and/or event-driven.	When event-driven, price-driven (P) or size-driven (S).
Products/markets cleared	Securities (SEC), derivatives (DER) and/or repos (REP).	
Currencies	ISO code of the cleared currencies.	

TABLE 5.6 *(Continued)*

Category	Meaning	Comments
Securities settlement agent	Agent that settles the securities leg of the transaction: ■ CSD ■ Central bank (CB) ■ Commercial banks (B) ■ Other (O).	The information is given per product and per currency.
Cash settlement agent	Agent that settles the cash leg of the securities transaction: ■ Central bank (CB) ■ Commercial banks (B) ■ Other (O).	The information is given per product and per currency.
Links to other CCPs	Such links can be based on cross-participation (cross) or on common systems.	The number of links is provided per currency area.

Source: CPSS/BIS (online). CPSS 116. Available from www.bis.org/list/cpss/index.htm. [Accessed Monday, 27 January 2014]

Q&A

You will need to download the latest annual publication (CPSS 116 dated December 2013 available from www.bis.org/publ/cpss116.htm) and find the Comparative Table for CCPs and Clearing Houses (Table CCP1) on pages 512 to 515. You will see that the majority of systems are CCPs rather than clearing houses.

Questions

Using Table CCP1, please answer the following questions:

1. Do CCPs and clearing houses clear one product type or more than one?
2. Is it true that most CCPs have links with other CCPs?
3. In Turkey, who owns the clearing system?
4. In Eurex Clearing, which two currencies are settled in commercial bank money?
5. Which country(ies) has (have) the most CCPs/CHs?

Answers

1. It varies from CCP to CCP. In China, for example, all three product types are cleared by the CSDCC, whilst the Saudi Clearing House only clears securities.
2. No, only a few have links based on cross-participation. Belgium, France, Italy, the Netherlands and the UK have the LCH.Clearnet linkage, and Japan's TFX, Switzerland's SIX x-clear and the USA's FICC/GSD maintain cross-participation links.

3. The Borsa İstanbul (formerly the Istanbul Stock Exchange) and Takasbank.
4. GBP and USD (NB: The other currencies, e.g. EUR and CHF, are settled in central bank money).
5. India and Japan, with five CCPs each.

5.6 SUMMARY

Transactions executed on-exchange and off-exchange (for products that are centrally cleared) must be cleared and settled. Clearance is the preparation for settlement and takes place in a central system known as either a clearing house or a central counterparty.

Both systems receive instructions from both counterparties to a transaction (i.e. the buyer and the seller) and will attempt to validate the information, check asset availability (cash and securities/derivatives) and match the buyer's information to the seller's. Only once these processes have been completed successfully can the transaction be settled. Settlement information is then passed on to another entity, a central securities depository, where ownership records are updated.

A clearing house does not assume any counterparty risk in the process; if one party fails before settlement, the risk lies with the counterparty.

As soon as a central counterparty validates and matches the buyer's and seller's information, it novates the transaction and becomes the counterparty to the buyer and, separately, the counterparty to the seller. This protects the buyer from the seller and vice versa. However, the CCP now has counterparty risk exposure to all its participants – a potentially huge risk.

To mitigate the counterparty risk, CCPs operate a risk-management system whereby participants contribute to a default fund, post collateral and pay margin, with the CCP itself maintaining a reserve fund and holding equity. In the event that a counterparty defaults, the CCP attempts to cover any losses using a waterfall-based line of defence that starts by netting the defaulting party's positions and ends by using its equity.

We saw the example of how LCH.Clearnet was able to deal successfully with the Lehman Brothers' default in 2008 without having to go down the waterfall too far. Nevertheless, there is the risk that a CCP could default as a result of one or more of its participants defaulting and, for this reason, the CCPs must establish robust risk-management practices, making changes where necessary.

CHAPTER 6

Securities Depositories (CSDs and ICSDs)

6.1 INTRODUCTION

We have seen in previous chapters the roles of the exchanges and trading platforms together with the clearing houses and central counterparties. We have also seen the relationships between both types of infrastructure in terms of management and ownership.

The asset types that are traded and cleared include bonds, equities, exchange-traded derivatives and centrally cleared OTC derivatives.

We are now at the stage where a third type of infrastructure plays an active role: the local (or national) and international central securities depository (CSD). As with the clearing houses and CCPs, CSDs can share certain characteristics with other CSDs but can also differ.

Please note that CSDs play no part in derivatives other than when contracts with securities as the underlying assets are exercised.

This chapter will help you to:

- Understand the purpose of the CSDs and ICSDs;
- Take a detailed look at a selection of these depositories;
- Appreciate the bilateral links between CSDs and ICSDs as well as mergers and acquisitions;
- Consider the different types of customer of the depositories and the services offered to them.

6.2 HISTORICAL CONTEXT

Until the late 20th century, securities were represented in certificated form, i.e. investors would hold physical share and bond certificates. These certificates could be held in one of several ways:

1. By the investor.
2. By a legal representative of the investor (e.g. a solicitor).

3. By the investor's stockbroker.
4. By the investor's bank (and deposited in the bank's vault or in a safety deposit box).

Securities could either be in registered form or in bearer form. For registered securities, the investor's name would be recorded on the issuer's register and noted on the certificate. For bearer securities, the investor's name would not be recorded on either the certificate or the issuer's register.

Q&A

Question

What do you think are the problems associated with physical certificates?

Answer

Physical certificates present a number of problems, including:

- **Physical documentation:** Paper is bulky and expensive to store. A private investor's portfolio might consist of several hundred certificates; an institutional investor might have several thousand.
- **Loss/theft:** Certificates can be lost in transit from seller to buyer. Whilst registered securities can be replaced (for a small fee), bearer securities cannot. Imagine you lost a bank note, i.e. cash. Would you be able to get a replacement? No!
- **Physical damage:** In November 2012, New York was hit by superstorm Sandy. The Depository Trust & Clearing Corporation's underground vaults were flooded and 1.3 million securities certificates were ruined by a tidal surge.* The DTCC was quoted as saying that it was: "… engaged in discussions with transfer agents to establish procedures for issuing replacement certificates from its computer records".
- **Delivery delays:** The process of withdrawing certificates from a vault (safe custody) for delivery to the Market can take several days. Furthermore, registered securities would also require a transfer deed to effect good delivery (bearer securities require no such additional documentation).

*Refer to Finextra (online 15 November 2012). "DTCC starts sorting through Sandy-flooded securities vault." Available from www.finextra.com/News/FullStory.aspx?newsitemid=24284. [Accessed Friday, 16 November 2012]

We can perhaps conclude that the safekeeping of securities was decentralised, with the physical certificates held either by the investor or by the investor's agent. It wasn't until the late 1960s and early 1970s that this situation changed.

In addition to the form of securities, there were other factors to be considered. For example:

- Clients, stockbrokers and banks communicated with each other by telephone, mail or telex. Furthermore, instructions to make payments and deliveries were sent by authenticated/tested telex and, on occasion, by authenticated telephone calls.

- Investment in overseas markets tended to be confined to the major markets (e.g. New York, Tokyo and the various European financial centres).
- Securities settlement was a manual process by which stockbrokers' messengers would deliver parcels of certificates to their purchasing counterparties and collect certificates from their selling counterparties, both in exchange for cheques by way of payment.

As more markets opened and investment activity (both domestically and cross-border) increased, this situation was not sustainable and something had to be done to enable securities to be held securely and for settlements to become more efficient.

Evidence of this could be found in the new Eurobond market that had been established in the early 1960s. Whilst new issuance and secondary market trading occurred in the United Kingdom and continental Europe, the physical bonds were held in New York. Indeed, the majority of deliveries and payments were made there too. By 1967, things had become so bad that deliveries were being delayed by months, resulting in a large number of settlement fails. One trading house based in London had settlement fails that amounted to three times its capital. This situation had the potential to destroy the market.

As a consequence of this paper logjam,

> *"... three enduring institutions emerged. Between them, they provided a framework in which the business could survive and progress. In the Association of International Bond Dealers (AIBD), the market forged a mechanism for self-regulation and collective expression. In Euroclear, and later Cedel, it developed mechanisms that spanned primary and secondary markets, combined depository, clearing and settlement operations in one, and worked hand-in-hand with the banking system to provide settlement-related liquidity."*[1]

You will notice that these two organisations were clearing mechanisms as well as depositories for the one particular type of security that had no domicile (i.e. a Eurobond).

Euroclear and Cedel (now known as Clearstream Banking Luxembourg) were not the only organisations that were established to handle the depository business. Depositories began to spring up in markets that would handle either a single asset type (e.g. equities only) or a range of asset types (e.g. equities, bonds and money market instruments). The key feature was that the security types that these new depositories were looking after were domestic in nature.

Examples of countries where depositories were being established around this time included the following:

- Canada – 1970;
- USA – 1973;
- Japan – 1984;
- Singapore – 1987.

---

[1] Source: Shearlock, P. and Ellington, W. (1994) "The Eurobond Diaries." Published privately by Euroclear Clearance System Société Coopérative. pp. 33–36.

Plus:

- Euroclear – 1968;
- Cedel – 1970.

Today we refer to the domestic depositories as *central securities depositories* (CSDs) and the two Eurobond depositories as *international central securities depositories* (ICSDs).

6.3 DEFINITIONS

6.3.1 Domestic (Local/National) CSDs

A CSD is either the physical entity or the system that facilitates the settlement and safekeeping of securities and ensures the reconciliation of participant accounts. Securities can be kept safe in immobilised or dematerialised form.

Settlement generally occurs in book-entry form.

6.3.2 International CSDs

An ICSD is a depository that settles trades in international and various domestic securities, usually through direct and indirect links with agents in the domestic markets. The best-known ICSDs are Euroclear Bank and Clearstream Banking Luxembourg. The Eurobond market developed partly in response to operational and regulatory inefficiencies in domestic bond markets.

There is some terminology contained within the definitions that requires some explanation:

- **Securities in immobilised form:** The physical certificates are represented by electronic records against which purchases are credited and sales debited. The physical certificates are not used for settlement purposes (i.e. they are immobilised).
- **Securities in dematerialised form:** The physical certificates are represented by electronic records (as with immobilisation above) and subsequently destroyed.
- **Book-entry settlement:** This is the settlement and movement of securities and/or cash by electronic debits and credits rather than the physical movement from seller to buyer (or payer to payee).

6.4 CENTRAL SECURITIES DEPOSITORIES

6.4.1 Features of CSDs and ICSDs

The main features of these organisations can be found in Table 6.1.

A selection of CSDs together with the features highlighted in Table 6.1 can be found on pages 524 to 527 in CPSS 116 (you downloaded this previously).

A full list of CSDs can be found on the websites of the five regional associations; we look at these later in this chapter.

TABLE 6.1 Features of selected central securities depositories

Features	Meaning		Comments
Types of securities held		(DOM)	▪ Domestic securities
		(INT)	▪ International securities
		(B)	▪ Bonds
		(C)	▪ Certificates of deposit
		(G)	▪ Government securities
		(E)	▪ Equities
		(O)	▪ Other types of securities
Owner/manager		(CB)	▪ Central bank
		(B)	▪ Commercial banks
		(SE)	▪ Stock exchange
		(O)	▪ Other type of owner
Securities settlement system	Name of the settlement system(s) with which the CSD is associated.		
Closing time for same-day transactions	Latest time of the day at which transactions can be sent to the system for settlement on the same day.		
Links to other CSDs	Direct links		▪ Based on cross-participation
	Indirect links		▪ Through local agents
Delivery lag (T+*n*)	Time lag between entering into a trade and its settlement.		
Intra-day finality		Yes	▪ System offers intra-day finality
		No	▪ System does not offer intra-day finality
DVP mechanism	The link between a securities transfer system and a funds transfer system which ensures that delivery occurs if payment occurs.		
Currencies	ISO codes of currencies in which settlement can be made.		
The cash settlement agent that settles the cash leg of the securities transactions		(CB)	▪ Central bank
		(B)	▪ Commercial banks
		(SE)	▪ Stock exchange
		(O)	▪ Other type of agent

Source: CPSS/BIS (online). CPSS 116. Available from www.bis.org/list/cpss/index.htm. [Accessed Monday, 27 January 2014]

6.4.2 Functions of CSDs

You will now be able to appreciate that the safekeeping of securities has predominantly changed from being fragmented (i.e. held by investors and/or their agents) to being centralised through the introduction of the CSDs.

Safekeeping The prime function of a CSD, therefore, is the safekeeping of securities. This might include all types of security (money markets, equities and bonds) or only one type (e.g. equities only).

When a security is issued, the issuer arranges for 100% of the bond or shares to be delivered to the appropriate CSD. Depending on the local market convention, the issue may be in any of the formats mentioned earlier:

1. **Immobilised:** The whole issue might ideally be represented by one certificate or by many certificates. For example, ABC issues USD 1 billion of bonds. There may be one

certificate with a face amount[2] of USD 1 billion or 1 million certificates each with a face amount of USD 1,000 or 200,000 certificates each with a face amount of USD 5,000. The optimal situation would be safekeeping just a single certificate per issue.

2. **Dematerialised:** The whole issue would be represented by either one certificate or some form of receipt from the issuer.
3. **Definitive certificates:** The whole issue would be fully certificated, for example, ABC issues 50 million shares that would be deliverable to buyers in one of the following ways:

An investor buys 5,000 shares and receives:

1 certificate for 5,000 shares, or

5,000 certificates for 1 share each, or

100 certificates for 50 shares each, or

any other combination.

Please note that Option 3 (definitive certificates) would result in the CSD delivering the physical certificates to the purchaser or its agent.

In Options 1 and 2, there is no need to deliver physical certificates as the deliveries and receipts of securities are recorded by book entry only, as the example in Table 6.2 shows.

TABLE 6.2 Transaction example

Transaction	Securities Settlement Account	Cash Account
Investor buys 5,000 shares against payment of EUR 20,000.00	5,000	EUR (20,000.00)
Investor's securities settled position	5,000	
Broker's position pre-trade	7,500	
Broker sells 5,000 shares against payment of EUR 20,000.00	(5,000)	EUR 20,000.00
Broker's position post-settlement	2,500	

The CSD reports to both buyer and seller that their transactions have settled and that:

The investor now holds 5,000 shares (plus cash debit);

The broker now holds 2,500 shares (plus cash credit);

The CSD is now safekeeping 7,500 shares, as shown in Table 6.3.

TABLE 6.3 Settled safekeeping positions at the CSD

Entity	Number of Shares
Investor	5,000 shares
Broker	2,500 shares
Total	7,500 shares

---

[2] Also known as the *nominal amount* or *principal amount* or *board lot size*.

In this example, the investor and the broker are participants of the CSD. The CSD regards the investor and the broker as being the owners of these shares. This might suggest that any type of entity can be a participant of a CSD. Whilst there are exceptions, the general rule is that participants tend to be locally based sell-side institutions such as broker/dealers, local banks and non-bank financial institutions. This would suggest that the following entity types are excluded for direct participation in a CSD:

- Private investors (retail), both local and foreign;
- Foreign banks;
- Foreign sell-side institutions;
- Foreign non-bank institutions.

For this group, the only way to access the CSD will be indirectly through local entities that are participants in the CSD (as shown in Figure 6.1).

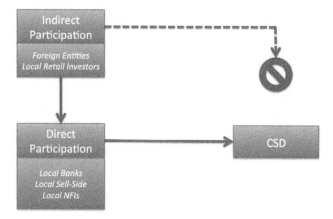

FIGURE 6.1   CSD participation

There are exceptions to this general rule; for example, there are CSDs that allow the private investor direct access (e.g. Finland, Sweden, UK and Ireland and Singapore). As with any "system", such as a payment system or clearing/settlement/safekeeping system, CSDs are exposed to systemic risk[3] and must exercise caution in terms of who they accept as participants.

Settlement   Settlement is the final step in a securities transaction, and the transfer of ownership takes place within the CSD. The CSD will receive the results of the clearing from the CCP or clearing house and pass appropriate entries over the securities accounts held by the CSD. This includes:

- Primary market activities: Receiving new securities from the issuers and their issuing agents;
- Secondary market activities: Settlement of transactions (trading, repo, securities lending, free deliveries, etc.).

---

[3] Systemic risk – the risk that the default of one or more participant(s) in a system might cause the default of the system itself (a "domino effect").

Income Collection   Dividends and interest payments (coupons) are paid by the issuers' paying agents, who, in turn, pay the CSDs. The CSDs then credit their participants with the income.

Corporate Actions   Again, the issuing and paying agents are involved on behalf of the issuers. We cover corporate actions plus proxy voting in Chapter 11.

These services can be regarded as being "core" or "basic". They are essential in the over-all safekeeping and administration of the securities. However, CSDs might offer additional services.

Securities Financing   This includes securities lending, repo and sell/buy-backs.

Collateral Management   Participants (and their clients) can use their securities to finance their daily activities by pledging securities as collateral. The CSD manages the benefits (income and corporate actions) and provides assurance to lenders that they have control over the pledged securities.

Data and Repository Services   CSDs hold vast amounts of data which can be used to deliver other services, for example, the USA's Depository Trust & Clearing Corporation (DTCC) also provides:

- The DTCC General Collateral Finance Repo benchmark index which tracks the average daily interest rate paid for repo contracts;
- Reference data services that help to standardise legal entity identifiers;
- A global trade repository service which acts as a single transaction-reporting interface between the participants that execute derivatives transactions and the regulators that need access to the positions information.

More information can be found on the DTCC website: www.dtcc.com/data-and-repository-services.aspx.

6.4.3   The Changing World of CSDs

In 1989 following its landmark study on clearance and settlement problems, the Group of Thirty (G30) published nine recommendations[4] that resulted in numerous industry reforms across the globe. In particular, Recommendation 3 made reference to CSDs:

---

[4]The Group of Thirty, established in 1978, is a private, nonprofit, international body composed of very senior representatives of the private and public sectors and academia. It aims to deepen understanding of international economic and financial issues, to explore the international repercussions of decisions taken in the public and private sectors and to examine the choices available to market practitioners and policymakers. (Quote from G30 website www.group30.org/about.htm) [Accessed Monday, 3 February 2014]

G30 RECOMMENDATION §3 – CSDs

(a) Each country should have in place an effective and fully developed central securities depository, organised and managed to encourage the broadest possible direct and indirect market participation.
(b) The range of depository eligible instruments should be as wide as possible.
(c) Immobilisation or dematerialisation of financial instruments should be achieved to the utmost extent possible.
(d) If several CSDs exist in the same market, they should operate under compatible rules and practices, with the aim of reducing settlement risk and enabling efficient use of funds and available cross-collateral.

Source: G30 Working Group (1988) "Clearance and Settlement Systems in the World's Securities Markets" Recommendation §3.

In retrospect, G30's Recommendation §3 assumed that each country/market would support between one and three CSDs. On the whole, whilst this has been the situation in the majority of markets, in one particular region there has been a consolidation in the ownership of local CSDs. This region is Europe and the consolidation has been driven largely by the two ICSDs, Euroclear Bank and Clearstream Banking Luxembourg.

Table 6.4 shows the local CSDs that are owned by Euroclear SA/NV.

TABLE 6.4   Euroclear ownership of CSDs

Country	Status	Formerly Known As … (Year Taken Over by Euroclear)
Euroclear Bank	ICSD	Transferred from Morgan Guaranty in 2000
France	CSD (1949)	SICOVAM (Euroclear France – 2001)
UK and Ireland	CSD (1996)	CrestCo (Euroclear UK and Ireland – 2002)
Netherlands	CSD (1977)	NECIGEF (Nederlands Centraal Instituut voor Giraal Effectenverkeer) (Euroclear Netherlands – 2001)
Belgium	CSD (1967)	CIK (Caisse Interprofessionnelle de Dépôts et de Virements de Titres) (Euroclear Belgium – 2002)
Finland	CSD (1997)	APK (Suomen Arvopaperikeskus Oy) (Euroclear Finland – 2008)
Sweden	CSD (1971)	VPC (Vardepappercentralen) (Euroclear Sweden – 2008)

Table 6.5 shows the local CSDs that are owned by Clearstream International, part of the Deutsche Börse Group.

TABLE 6.5   Clearstream ownership of CSDs

Country	Status	Formerly Known As …
Clearstream Banking Luxembourg	ICSD	Centrale de Livraison de Valeurs Mobilières – Cedel
Clearstream Banking Frankfurt	CSD	Deutsche Börse Clearing (formerly Deutsche Kassenverein – DKV)
Luxembourg	CSD (2011)	–

In addition, ten CSDs launched Link Up Markets in March 2009 – a joint venture to establish a common infrastructure allowing for interoperability between CSDs and introducing efficient cross-border processing capabilities (see Table 6.6).

TABLE 6.6   Link Up Markets

Clearstream Banking Frankfurt	Oesterreichische Kontrollbank AG (Austria)
Cyprus Stock Exchange	SIX SIS AG (Switzerland)
Hellenic Exchanges (Greece)	STRATE (South Africa)
IBERCLEAR (Spain)	VP Lux
MCDR (Egypt)	VPS (Norway)

Source: Link Up Markets (online) "The joint venture partners of Link Up Markets". Available from www.linkupmarkets.com/home.asp?Page=Organization. [Accessed Monday, 3 February 2014]

Elsewhere around the world, a network of bilateral relationships amongst the CSDs has arisen (see Figure 6.2). These inter-CSD links enable participants of a CSD in one country to indirectly access the CSD of another country, making it more straightforward to hold foreign securities without the need to open a participant account directly with the foreign CSD.

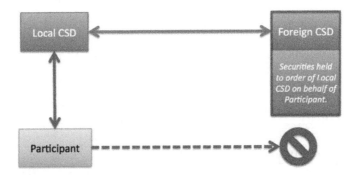

FIGURE 6.2   Inter-CSD links

One example of a CSD in country "A" offering its clients direct access to the exchange and OTC markets of country "B" relates to the Austrian CSD, CSD.Austria. It was announced in September 2013 that CSD Austria and the Russian National Settlement Depository (NSD) had launched an international direct link to the Russian securities market.[5] This link was made possible as foreign CSDs are allowed to open foreign nominee accounts with the NSD.

Since then the NSD has established further links with the Central Depository of Armenia and opened the Russian corporate bond market to international investors through links with Clearstream Banking Luxembourg and Euroclear Bank.

---

[5]*Source*: National Settlement Depository (online dated 2013-09-17). "CSD.Austria and NSD launch direct link to Russian Securities Market." Available from www.nsd.ru/en/press/ndcnews/index.php?&id36=217730. [Accessed Tuesday, 4 February 2014]

6.4.4   CSD Links and Interoperability

Background   It is usually the case that if an investor (or its agent) wishes to invest in foreign securities, it is not possible to directly access the relevant CSD. There are two options available to the investor/agent:

1. Use a custodian bank that has access to the foreign CSD (see Figure 6.3).

Interoperability §1

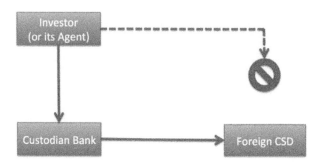

FIGURE 6.3   Custodian bank's access to foreign CSD

2. Use the local CSD's links with the foreign CSD (see Figure 6.4).

Interoperability §2

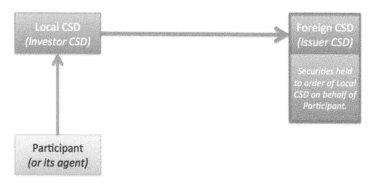

FIGURE 6.4   Local CSD's access to foreign CSD

We will look at Option 1 in Chapter 10: Custody and the Custodians. With Option 2, the link between the local CSD and the foreign CSD enables securities held in the latter to become available in the records of the former.

The local CSD (also referred to as the investor CSD) becomes a customer or participant of the foreign CSD (the issuer CSD). This would be regarded as a unilateral link. If there was a reciprocal arrangement (i.e. the issuer CSD became an investor CSD for its local investors with the original investor CSD becoming an issuer CSD), this would be a bilateral link (see Figure 6.5). In either event, both bilateral and unilateral links are regarded as *direct links*.

Interoperability §3

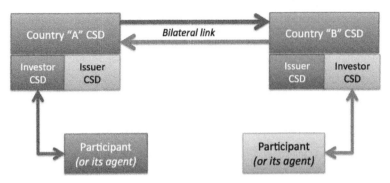

FIGURE 6.5 Direct links

Table 6.7 shows some examples of direct links.

TABLE 6.7 Direct links

Type of Link	CSDs	Countries
Bilateral	▪ MaltaClear with Clearstream Banking AG	Malta/Germany
Bilateral	▪ Monte Titoli with Iberclear-CADE	Italy/Spain
Bilateral	▪ LuxCSD with Clearstream Banking Luxembourg	Luxembourg/Luxembourg
Unilateral	▪ Monte Titoli to Iberclear-SCLV	Italy/Spain
Unilateral	▪ BOGS (Greece) to Clearstream Banking AG	Greece/Germany
Unilateral	▪ Clearstream Banking Luxembourg to CDCP	Luxembourg/Slovakia

Source: European Central Bank (online) "Eligible Links as at 20 Dec 2013". Available from www.ecb.europa.eu/paym/coll/coll/ssslinks/html/index.en.html. [Accessed Monday, 10 February 2014]

There is a fourth variation, known as *relayed links*, whereby two CSDs are linked using a third as an intermediary CSD (see Figure 6.6).

Interoperability §4

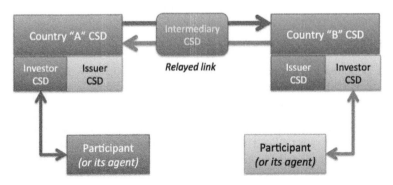

FIGURE 6.6 Relayed links

Examples of relayed links include the following:[6]

- Germany: Clearstream Banking AG via Clearstream Banking Luxembourg to Monte Titoli (Italy);
- France: Euroclear France via Euroclear Bank (Belgium) to Clearstream Banking AG (Germany);
- Luxembourg: LuxCSD via Clearstream Banking Luxembourg to KDD (Slovenia).

These links would allow securities to be delivered on a free of payment (FoP) and/or a delivery/receive against payment (DVP/RVP) basis.

Euroclear Bank and Clearstream Banking Luxembourg, the two international CSDs, are regarded as fully interoperable with their use of the bridge (see the next section).

6.5 INTERNATIONAL CENTRAL SECURITIES DEPOSITORIES

6.5.1 Background

In Section 6.2 of this chapter, we gave a brief overview of the events that led to the creation of the two international central securities depositories (ICSDs). The formation of Euroclear and Cedel occurred against the background of the issuance of physical Eurobond certificates and the problems associated with the delivery of the certificates to the various European centres where the underwriters, dealers and investors were located.

Morgan Guaranty's Brussels office was used to host the issuers' closing ceremonies that included the handing over of the new bonds to the lead underwriter. It was decided to launch a system whereby the physical certificates were replaced by a book-entry system and where receipts and deliveries against payment could occur once participants had opened securities accounts and cash accounts with the system. That system became Euroclear and it was founded in December 1968.

Whilst bond closings took place in Brussels, most Eurobonds were listed in Luxembourg. Luxembourg was also experiencing operational logjams in New York. Luxembourg-based banks, both local and foreign, decided to investigate the establishment of a rival system to Euroclear. By September 1970, the Centrale de Livraison de Valeurs Mobilières, better known as Cedel, was launched by 71 banks from 11 countries with the motto: "By the market, for the market".

So we can see that in a very short period of time, one particular product type with no national domicile, the Eurobond, could be held and processed out of two systems, both based in continental Europe. The history of these two organisations makes for interesting reading and their fierce competitiveness over the years has been good for the industry across a wide range of areas, including:

- Communication;
- New products;
- Services (both core and value-added).

---

[6]ibid.

6.5.2   Features of the ICSDs

The ICSDs are similar to the basic concept of a CSD but differ in one important respect: Euroclear and Clearstream are banks and this enables them to offer credit and certain other banking activities related to security settlement.

It can be argued that the ICSDs are as much a part of the post-trade market infrastructure as the CSDs except that the ICSDs are commercial in nature; in other words, they not only look after their customers but also their shareholders.

Whilst both ICSDs are similar to a clearing house and CSD combination, it should be noted that the ICSDs do not act as central counterparties. Their services cover the entire spectrum from new issuance to redemption.

6.5.3   Clearstream Banking Luxembourg (CBL)

Asset Classes   CBL settles a wide range of securities including:

- International debt securities, including global bonds and Eurobonds (straight, floating-rate, convertible etc.);
- Foreign bonds;
- Money market instruments, including short- and medium-term notes, commercial paper and certificates of deposit;
- Domestic bonds (government and corporate);
- Equities;
- Depository receipts;
- Investment funds;
- Warrants;
- Asset-backed securities and other collateralised debt securities.

New Issuance   CBL offers a full range of services from advice to primary distribution using its Global Issuer Hub:

- **Advisory services:** Supporting lead managers, lawyers, issuers and their agents;
- **Securities admission:** Eligibility checks and compliance checks prior to admission to the Global Issuer Hub;
- **Code allocation:** CBL is the numbering agent for international ISIN codes;
- **Electronic document transfer:** This enables the securities to be delivered electronically, rather than physically;
- **Primary market distribution:** Supports issuers and their agents in distributing the securities to investors.

Settlement   CBL has three types of settlement:

1. Internal settlement for transactions between two CBL participants.
2. External settlement for transactions with non-ICSD participants.
3. Bridge settlement for transactions between CBL and Euroclear participants.

Transactions can be settled on either a DVP/RVP or free of payment (FoP) basis.

Asset Servicing CBL processes income and corporate actions activities together with reports that include income pre-advices, corporate action notifications and market claims.

Global Securities Financing CBL provides a full range of securities financing services through its Global Liquidity Hub, including:

- Triparty collateral management and general collateral (GC) pooling;
- Automated securities lending and borrowing for fails management and strategic lending.

Investment Funds Services CBL's Vestima Funds Hub provides the link between investor, fund distributor, transfer agent and trading platform. The Vestima Funds Hub enables:

- Order routing to funds (or their agents) or to trading platforms;
- Post-trade settlement by DVP in commercial bank money;
- Collateral using investment funds as an eligible asset class in the triparty repo service;
- Value-added services including funds reference data and real-time reporting.

Inter-CSD Linkages We have seen in the previous section that there are direct links between the ICSDs and a selection of local CSDs. These links can either be unilateral or bilateral in nature.

Connectivity Participants can input instructions, access information, manage corporate action activities, send queries and handle exceptions using one or more connectivity products offered under the CreationConnect service. The three products are:

- **CreationOnline:** Via the Internet or a virtual private network (VPN);
- **CreationDirect:** By file transfer using the Internet, the Clearstream VPN, Lima or SWIFTNet FileAct;
- **Creation via the SWIFT network:** Link through SWIFTNet FIN.

In September 2013, CBL launched ClearstreamXact, an Internet-based system that initially offers participants access to CBL's collateral management service. (Settlement and asset management are planned additional services.)

6.5.4 Euroclear Bank (EB)

Asset Classes EB processes a wide range of securities including:

- International bonds, including foreign bonds, global bonds and Eurobonds;
- Domestic debt;
- Convertible bonds;
- Warrants;
- Equities;
- Depository receipts;
- Investment funds.

New Issuance   EB helps issuers, lead managers and issuing agents by:

- Helping to identify new issue structures;
- Allocating identification codes to new securities (EB is a numbering agency);
- Providing DVP issuance of the securities;
- Providing relevant administrative services.

Settlement   EB, as with CBL above, has three types of settlement:

1. Internal settlement for transactions between two Euroclear participants.
2. External settlement for transactions with non-ICSD participants.
3. Bridge settlement for transactions between EB and CBL participants.

Transactions can be settled on either a DVP/RVP or free of payment (FoP) basis.

Custody Services   These services include:

- Corporate action notifications;
- Real-time processing and reporting;
- Income and redemption processing;
- Withholding tax assistance;
- Proxy voting market claims management.

Asset Optimisation   This includes collateral management and securities lending and borrowing.

Money Transfer   Money transfer facilities include:

- Book transfers: Internal payments between participants within the EB system;
- Wire transfers: External payments made by participants outside the EB system;
- Pre-advices: Incoming payments for EB participants from outside the EB system;
- Foreign exchange services.

Credit Facilities   EB provides credit facilities to enable participants to manage their operations, especially settlements, borrowing and money transfer. Credit facilities are provided on a secured basis.

Investment Funds Services   EB's investment fund platform is FundSettlement International, which provides a single access point for fund management companies, fund distributors and transfer agents. Users have access to:

- Order validation;
- Funds settlement;
- Corporate actions processing;
- Real-time reporting;
- Client support.

Inter-CSD Linkages   We have seen in the previous section that there are direct links between the ICSDs and a selection of local CSDs. These links can either be unilateral or bilateral in nature.

Connectivity   Participants can access Euroclear through the following Internet Protocol-based networks:

- Radianz
- Infonet
- SWIFTNet
- The Internet.

Applications are either screen-based or computer-to-computer – see Table 6.8.

TABLE 6.8   Screen-based or computer-to-computer connectivity

Screen-Based	Computer-to-Computer
EUCLID PC – settlement instruction/validation plus reporting	EUCLID server
FundSettle – access to FundSettle International service	EUCLID file transfer
Triweb and Biweb – collateral management reporting	FundSettle file transfer
	SWIFT

Instructions can also be submitted by tested telex, post and, exceptionally, fax (with telephone call-back).

6.6   LINKAGES – EXCHANGES, CLEARING SYSTEMS AND CSDs

We have now examined the three main elements to the infrastructure of the industry:

- Stock exchanges;
- Clearing systems; and
- Central securities depositories.

We can add two more elements – the international CSDs and cash payment. The two ICSDs are banks and payment occurs through "commercial bank money". The national CSDs are linked to their national central banks and payment here is said to be in "central bank money".

Let us compare the linkages from three points of view:

1. The USA.
2. The European region.
3. The rest of the world, including the Asia-Pacific, Africa/Middle East and the Americas regions.

This comparison will illustrate that the USA is centralised, Europe is fragmented and Asia-Pacific is domestically focused. We will see in the next section that several CSD associations have been formed in order to introduce regional cooperation if not actual consolidation.

The European Central Bank published a brochure in November 2009[7] which summarised the linkages that existed in Europe and the USA. Reading this will give you an idea of just how complex the situation is in Europe.

6.6.1   United States of America

In the USA, corporate bonds and equities are cleared through the Depository Trust & Clearing Corporation (DTCC) and government securities, federal agencies and government-sponsored entities are processed through the Federal Reserve System (the "Fed").

In Figure 6.7, you can see just how centralised the USA landscape is.

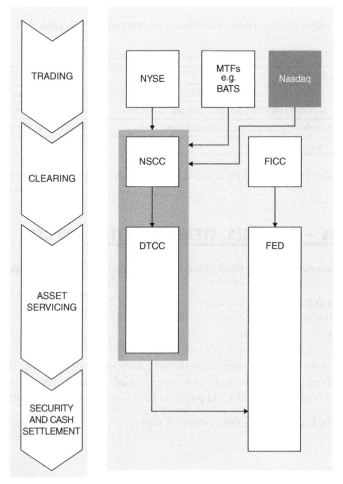

FIGURE 6.7   Linkages in the USA
Source: ECB 2009 "Settling without Borders".

---

[7]European Central Bank (online) November 2009. "Settling without Borders." Available from www.ecb.europa.eu/pub/pdf/other/settlingwithoutborders_t2sbrochure112009en.pdf?def30081f800715129a6 57731011243b. [Accessed Wednesday, 5 February 2014]

6.6.2 Europe

By comparison, Europe is very much more fragmented and complex (see Figure 6.8).

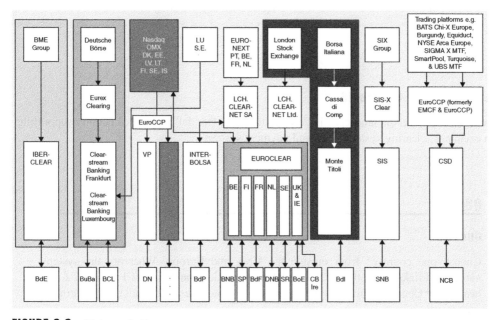

FIGURE 6.8 Linkages in Europe
Source: ECB 2009 "Settling without Borders" plus updates by author.

As we can see from Figure 6.8, the situation in Europe is that of a highly fragmented clearing, settlement, custody and payment environment.

- The shaded boxes indicate groups of companies resulting from mergers and acquisitions, including:
  - In Spain, Germany, countries in the Nasdaq OMX group and Italy, there is a vertical silo approach (*vertical integration*) whereby the stock exchange, clearing system and CSD are part of the same national group.
  - The UK and Italian stock exchanges are also part of the same group, albeit with different clearing systems and CSDs.
  - The Euroclear group includes the national CSDs of six countries. This is known as *horizontal integration*.
  - EuroCCP sends transactions to the appropriate local CSD for settlement.

Q&A

Question

How many countries are noted in the European landscape, according to ECB 2009?

Answer

Seventeen countries (i.e. 17 stock exchanges) plus eight trading platforms.

6.6.3 Rest of the World

Outside of Europe, the landscape is closer to the USA "model", with each country supporting an exchange, clearing system, CSD and payment system.

Q&A

Question

Choose one country* from outside the USA and Europe. What are the systems' names and links using the ECB template (see the left-hand side of Figure 6.7 for the headings)? Consider only corporate securities (i.e. equities and bonds) and government securities.

Answer

We have chosen Australia as an example – see Table 6.9.

TABLE 6.9

Region/Country	Australia	
	Corporate Securities	**Government Securities**
Trading	Australian Stock Exchange (ASX)	ASX
Clearing	ASX Clear	ASX Clear
Asset servicing	■ Austraclear for fixed income securities ■ ASX Settlement (via CHESS) for equities	Austraclear
Cash settlement	Reserve Bank of Australia's RITS (RTGS) system	Reserve Bank of Australia's RITS (RTGS) system

*Suggestion: For information, go to the members' section of the World Federation of Exchanges' website at www.world-exchanges.org/member-exchanges/key-information.

6.7 CSD ASSOCIATIONS

6.7.1 Introduction

There are five CSD associations based regionally:

1. Americas' Central Securities Depositories Association (ACSDA).
2. Asia-Pacific CSD Group (ACG).
3. Association of Eurasian Central Securities Depositories (AECSD).
4. European Central Securities Depositories Association (ECSDA).
5. Africa and Middle East Depositories Association (AMEDA).

In 2011 the five associations formed the World Forum of CSDs to enhance communication between the associations.

6.7.2 Americas' Central Securities Depositories Association (ACSDA)

This is a non-profit organization comprised of Central Securities Depositories and Clearing Houses of the Americas, headquartered in Lima, Peru. Its by-laws were established at the first General Assembly held in the city of Lima, Peru on August 10, 1999.

ACSDA's main purpose is to be a forum for the exchange of information and experiences among its members in a spirit of mutual cooperation and to promote best practice recommendations in services such as securities depository, clearance, settlement, and risk management. ACSDA's goal is also to support local markets in their efforts to adopt securities market regulations, while considering their specific circumstances and to serve as a channel for dialogue with other organizations worldwide.

Source: www.acsda.org

There are 18 member CSDs including Strate (South Africa)!

6.7.3 Asia-Pacific CSD Group (ACG)

The Asia-Pacific Central Securities Depository Group (ACG) was formed in November 1997 as an informal international organization with the objective to facilitate the exchange of information and to promote mutual assistance among member securities depositories and clearing organizations in the Asia-Pacific region.

Source: www.acgcsd.org/acg_01.aspx

There are 32 member CSDs from 22 countries.

6.7.4 Association of Eurasian Central Securities Depositories (AECSD)

The Association, founded in 2004 with the aim being: "… the formation of a common 'depository environment', including harmonization of the regulatory and legal framework, development of an optimal recordkeeping system for the securities market and the organization of effective interaction among the member organizations to ensure efficient cross-border securities transfers. Moreover, the question of standardization of depository technologies, development of the electronic document exchange and adoption of international messaging standards for depository transactions are high on the agenda."

Source: www.acde.ru/about_eng.php

The founding membership consisted of 11 entities from 10 countries.

6.7.5 European Central Securities Depositories Association (ECSDA)

ECSDA's objective is to offer solutions and provide advice at international level on technical, economic, financial and regulatory matters to reduce risk and increase efficiency in custody, pre-settlement and settlement arrangements for securities and related payments across Europe for the benefit of issuers, investors and market participants.

Source: www.ecsda.eu

There are 41 member national and international CSDs from 37 countries. Russia and Ukraine are also represented on the AECSD.

6.7.6 Africa and Middle East Depositories Association (AMEDA)

Established in 2005, AMEDA's main purpose is to be: "… a forum for the exchange of information and experiences among its members in a spirit of mutual cooperation and to promote best practice recommendations in services such as securities depository, clearance, settlement, and risk management.

Its goal is also to support local markets in their efforts to adopt securities market regulations, while considering their specific circumstances and to serve as a dialogue channel with other organizations worldwide."

Source: www.ameda.org.eg/what_about.aspx

There are 25 member CSDs from 24 countries.

Q&A

Question

What is unusual about South Africa, Russia and the Ukraine?

Answer

All three countries are members of two CSD associations:

- South Africa – This country is a member of AMEDA and ACSDA.
- Russia – This country is a member of AECSD and ECSDA.
- Ukraine – This country is a member of AECSD and ECSDA.

6.8 SUMMARY

The safekeeping of securities has evolved from being fragmented to being centralised. Fragmented safekeeping includes situations where securities are held in one of the following ways:

- By the investor;
- By the investor's agent (e.g. bank, legal representative);
- By the investor's bank/custodian.

Centralised safekeeping is where the issuer deposits the entire issue with a central securities depository (CSD). The securities are either in physical form or book-entry form. Securities that were originally issued in physical form can be processed through book entries across participants' securities accounts.

CSDs provide services that range from basic safekeeping and settlement to asset optimisation and securities financing. Whilst CSDs are local, i.e. they handle securities issued in their local markets, they can link to other CSDs.

The two international CSDs, Euroclear Bank and Clearstream Banking Luxembourg, were originally established to handle Eurobonds – securities that have no domicile. The services offered range from new issuance to settlement and safekeeping, money transfer, securities optimisation, income collection and bond redemptions, i.e. from the start of a bond to the finish. The ICSDs are now able to handle a wide range of asset types due to their links with several local CSDs.

Post-trade processing is generally centralised in most regions (e.g. USA) except for Europe where it is very fragmented.

There are five regional CSD associations covering the Americas, Asia-Pacific, Africa and the Middle East, Eurasia and Europe. These associations look after the interests of their CSD members.

CHAPTER 7

Securities Clearing

7.1   INTRODUCTION

In Chapter 5: Clearing Houses and CCPs, we defined clearing as: "The process of transmitting, reconciling and, in some cases, confirming payment orders or security transfer instructions prior to settlement, possibly including the netting of instructions and the establishment of final positions for settlement. Sometimes the term is used (imprecisely) to include settlement."

Clearing, therefore, is the post-trade preparation for settlement, i.e. the completion of the trade. This preparatory phase should be completed shortly after the trade has been executed; how long afterwards depends on the market convention and type of asset.

By the end of this chapter, you will be able to:

- Follow the stages within the clearing cycle;
- Differentiate between securities and derivatives clearing;
- Forecast cash requirements and securities availability.

We have seen that a clearing house differs from a central counterparty (CCP) in one fundamental way.

Q&A

Question

What is the difference between a clearing house and a CCP?

Answer

A CCP novates the buyer's and seller's transactions and becomes the counterparty to the buyer and, separately, the seller. By contrast, a clearing house is not exposed to the counterparty risk.

In this chapter, we will look at clearing from the points of view shown in Table 7.1.

TABLE 7.1   Clearing House and CCP clearing

Asset Type	Clearing Method	Example
Equities	Central counterparty	LCH.Clearnet
Eurobonds	Clearing house	International CSDs: Clearstream Banking Luxembourg and Euroclear Bank

7.2   GENERIC CLEARING CYCLE

The objective of the clearing cycle is to enable all transactions to be settled according to market convention. The macro operation is the transformation of trade details received from the Front Office through a series of micro operations into a completed (i.e. settled) transaction. These micro operations include the following:

1. Trade capture.
2. Trade enrichment and validation.
3. Trade reporting.
4. Confirmation/affirmation.
5. Clearing instructions.
6. Forecasting – cash.
7. Forecasting – securities.

We will look at these micro operations in more detail; in the meantime, here are some brief summaries.

7.2.1   Trade Capture

All transactions executed by the Front Office will be entered onto a trade/dealer's blotter. The blotter can either be electronic or spreadsheet-based, depending on the product traded and the organisational structure of the Front Office (as shown in Figure 7.1).

Generic Micro Operation §1

FIGURE 7.1   Trade capture

Summary: the Front Office books trades and corrects errors.

7.2.2 Trade Enrichment and Validation

Trade data are fed into applications that:

- Hold trade details;
- Calculate Profit & Loss;
- Calculate risk.

The trades should be validated to ensure that limits and authorities have not been exceeded.

Trade information will be basic and will need to be enriched (see Figure 7.2) with reference to the appropriate databases (e.g. securities, counterparty, etc.) and calculations made (e.g. accrued interest, total settlement amounts, brokerage, etc.).

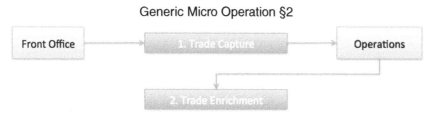

Generic Micro Operation §2

FIGURE 7.2 Trade enrichment

Summary: Operations should ensure that trades are executed correctly and additional information is added to the basic trade details.

7.2.3 Trade Reporting

Exchange-traded transactions are transparent and can be seen by the regulatory authorities. This is not the case for OTC transactions which tend to be opaque in nature. All transactions should be reported (see Figure 7.3) either to a trade repository or an authorised reporting mechanism (ARM).

Generic Micro Operation §3

FIGURE 7.3 Trade reporting

Summary: transactions should be reported to the appropriate authorities.

7.2.4 Confirmation and Affirmation

It is quite possible for transaction details to differ in one or more respects from those of the counterparty. To ensure that both the buyer and the seller have the same transaction details, both parties will confirm transaction details with each other (see Figure 7.4). This usually happens on the trade date.

Where a broker, for example, has traded on behalf of a client, two-way confirmation is not appropriate. Instead, the broker alleges the transaction against its client and the client either affirms the trade (i.e. agrees the details) or rejects/queries the trade. Trade affirmation should be completed no later than the day after the trade date (T+1).

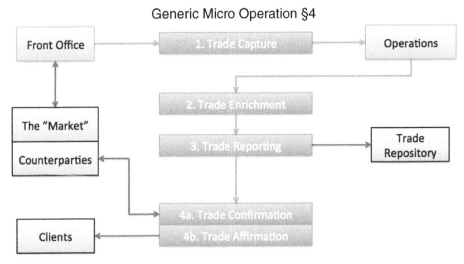

FIGURE 7.4   Trade confirmation/affirmation

Summary: confirmation and affirmation ensure that both parties to a transaction are in agreement with the contract details.

7.2.5 Clearing Instructions

At this stage, both counterparties have captured transaction details from the Front Office and confirmed those details with each other. At this point, both counterparties submit clearing instructions to the appropriate clearing system (see Figure 7.5).

The buyer will instruct the clearing system to receive securities against payment of cash and the seller to deliver securities against payment of cash. The clearing system will validate any incoming instructions to ensure that the transaction has the potential to be correct and is, therefore, settleable.

This is followed by a matching process in which the clearing system attempts to pair off one counterparty's delivery instruction with another counterparty's receipt instruction. Successful pairings are known as *matched instructions*; unsuccessful pairings are *unmatched instructions* and these will have to be investigated and corrected by the relevant counterparties.

Matched instructions can now be forwarded for settlement; however, unmatched instructions can never settle.

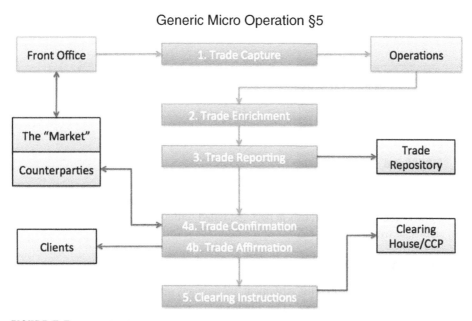

FIGURE 7.5   Clearing instructions

Summary: the clearing system will attempt to match the buyer's instructions with the seller's. Subject to further clearing phases, matched instructions can settle, whilst unmatched instructions can never settle.

7.2.6   Forecasting – Cash

Rather than borrow cash for each purchase and lend cash from each sale, market participants tend to net their cash exposures on a currency-by-currency basis. Participants will make cash forecasts in advance (or on the day itself) of when the cash is due to be debited or credited.

Efficient cash forecasting helps to make the best use of cash and in so doing reduces financing costs (see Figure 7.6). The challenge for Operations is to estimate the odds of expected cash movements actually taking place on the intended dates. Techniques such as *fund to fail* and *fund to settle* can certainly help in the forecasting process.

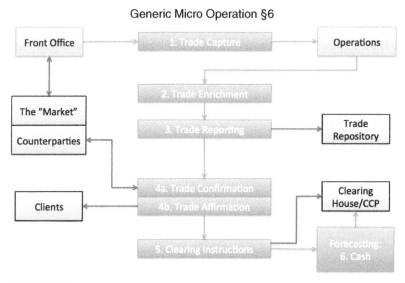

FIGURE 7.6   Cash forecasting

Summary: correct cash forecasting helps to ensure efficient settlement; conversely, poor cash forecasting will lead to financing costs at best and failed settlements, together with associated interest claims, at worst.

7.2.7 Forecasting – Securities

Where sales of securities are due for settlement, participants need to ensure that the securities are available ("available for delivery") (see Figure 7.7).

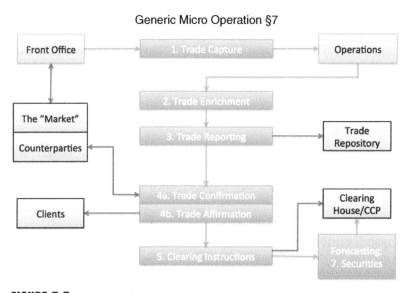

FIGURE 7.7   Securities forecasting

There could be good reasons why securities are not available, for example, the participant might be waiting for a previously traded purchase to settle. Whatever the reason, Operations need to take appropriate action to reduce the impact of a failed settlement.

Sales that failed to settle have a knock-on effect on the associated cash pay proceeds, resulting in an inability to reinvest cash and an impact on the overall cash-forecasting process.

Summary: in the same way that cash must be actively managed (see above), so should the availability or otherwise of securities. Again, as with cash, Operations need to be proactive in how they predict securities' movements and balances.

In conceptual terms, these seven generic micro operations represent very much the same transformation of an executed transaction into a completed contract. Each market will maintain different practices in detail for each and every asset class traded in that market. At the end of the clearing phase, transactions can be moved into the settlement phase, as shown in Figure 7.8. We will cover settlements in the next chapter.

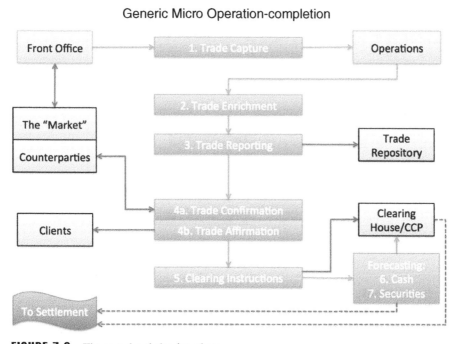

FIGURE 7.8 The completed clearing phase

We will now look at these phases in more detail using a small equities portfolio as an example. This portfolio is managed by a trading organisation known as T01 and consists of 14 holdings of UK equities. The securities are valued at approximately GBP 3 million using last night's closing prices and there is a cash balance of approximately GBP 150,000.

This example portfolio is based on one of a selection of settlement simulations that the author uses in his training courses. By necessity, it is spreadsheet-based and delivered in paper format. This enables students to appreciate the underlying process that might otherwise be disguised in an automated, electronic operational environment.

7.3   TRADE CAPTURE

7.3.1   Dealer's Blotter

The dealer's blotter is a record of the assets that the dealer is responsible for, and is updated whenever assets are bought or sold. T01's blotter (see Figure 7.9) is a simplified version that lists all 14 holdings and includes last night's closing prices,[1] the dealer's opening positions plus their market values. In our example, the shares are worth GBP 2,970,444.78 and there is a cash balance of GBP 148,522.24.

Dealer Name:	T01									
Issue	Short Code	Closing Price (GBX)	Opening Position	Opening Mkt Value	Net Buys & Sells	Sub-Total	Corporate Actions	Total Holding	Closing Px (GBX)	Market Value
BAE Systems	BA	417.50	50,000	£ 208,750.00						
Barclays Bank	BARC	259.00	35,000	£ 90,650.00						
BP	BP	505.95	75,000	£ 379,462.50						
BT Group	BT-A	413.94	10,000	£ 41,394.00						
Costain Group	COST	315.00	30,000	£ 94,500.00						
Glencore Xstrata	GLEN	336.53	50,000	£ 168,265.00						
HSBC Holdings	HSBA	635.70	40,000	£ 254,280.00						
Int'l Airlines Group	IAG	445.50	20,000	£ 89,100.00						
National Express	NEX	301.90	60,000	£ 181,140.00						
Rolls Royce	RR	990.00	50,000	£ 494,999.95						
Schroders	SDR	2,681.00	24,000	£ 643,440.00						
Tesco	TSCO	333.40	10,000	£ 33,340.00						
Vodafone	VOD	250.71	30,000	£ 75,213.33						
Wm Morrison S/Mkts	MRW	239.90	90,000	£ 215,910.00						
		TOTAL SHARES (GBP):		£ 2,970,444.78			SECURITIES VALUE (GBP):			
				Opening Position	Trading	C/Actions	Income			
Cash Balance		TOTAL CASH (GBP):		£ 148,522.24				TOTAL CASH (GBP):		
		TOTAL VALUE (GBP):		£ 3,118,967.02				TOTAL VALUE (GBP):		

FIGURE 7.9   Dealer's blotter

7.3.2   Trade Input

In our settlement simulation, the dealer executes six transactions against various counterparties and these transactions are entered either in an electronic trade capture system or manually on trade tickets.

These six transactions are shown on the dealing sheet (see Figure 7.10); note that whilst the information provided is minimal, it is sufficient for Operations to perform the necessary clearing and settlement activities.

---

[1]Note that UK equities are priced in pence (GBX) and valued in sterling (GBP). GBX is not an official ISO code; however, it is generally recognised in the markets.

Your Team Name		T01				Trade Date		25-Feb-14	
Your Reference	Trading Venue	Purchase or Sale	Quantity	Security Description	Price	Counterparty	Time of Trade	Trader ID
T01/1	London (LSE)	Pur	5,000	IAG	445.20	T02	09:15	AKD12
T01/2	London (LSE)	Pur	5,000	BARC	257.45	T03	10:23	AKD12
T01/3	London (LSE)	Sale	2,500	HSBA	630.50	T02	10:26	AKD12
T01/4	London (LSE)	Pur	10,000	TSCO	331.65	T04	12:40	AKD12
T01/5	London (LSE)	Sale	15,000	MRW	239.60	T04	14:55	AKD12
T01/6	London (LSE)	Pur	10,000	BARC	256.65	T03	14:56	AKD12
				.				
				.				
				.				
				.				
				.				
				.				
				.				
				.				

FIGURE 7.10 Dealing sheet

Q&A

Question

For whom have these transactions been dealt? Is it for the dealer's proprietary book or for clients?

Answer

This information is not stated on the dealing sheet. As there are no clients' names noted, let us assume that these are proprietary transactions.

From the dealing sheet we can see not only the various transactions but also the trading venue on which the transactions were executed, the times the transactions were executed and the trader's identification.

7.3.3 Trade Output

The information contained in the dealing sheet will be submitted to the Middle Office either electronically or manually using a trade ticket. Figure 7.11 illustrates an example of a trade ticket.

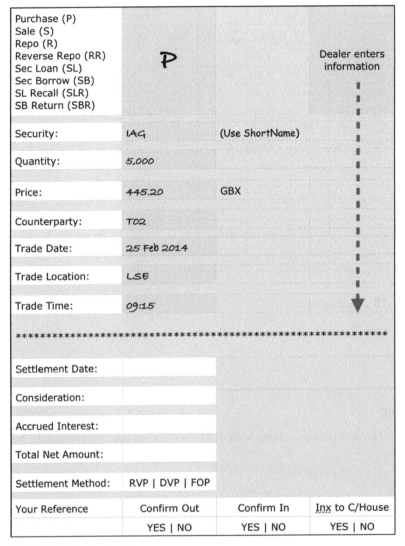

FIGURE 7.11   Trade ticket

Copying information from the blotter to a trade ticket is not ideal as it takes time and there is the risk of incorrectly rekeying information. For example, a sale might be incorrectly entered as a purchase.

7.4 TRADE ENRICHMENT AND VALIDATION

The Middle Office will start the process of making each transaction ready for clearing. This involves the following activities:

- Ensuring that the dealer has entered all the required information on the trade ticket.
- Calculating the purchase costs or sale proceeds. This will include accrued interest for bonds, stamp duty for equities (where appropriate) and brokerage fees for client

transactions. For simplicity, we will not consider stamp duty for our settlement simulation example.

- Updating the company's risk profiles. This includes ensuring that the individual dealer is authorised to trade these particular assets and whether or not the dealer has exceeded trading limits. With equities in particular, it is also important to ensure that any post-trade positions do not breach disclosure levels (in the event that they do, these positions need to be disclosed to the appropriate authorities).
- Ensuring that the quantity of securities traded is an exact multiple of that security's board lot size.

For our purposes, the Middle Office will add the settlement date, consideration and total net amount to the trade ticket and will identify the correct settlement method (shown in Figure 7.12).

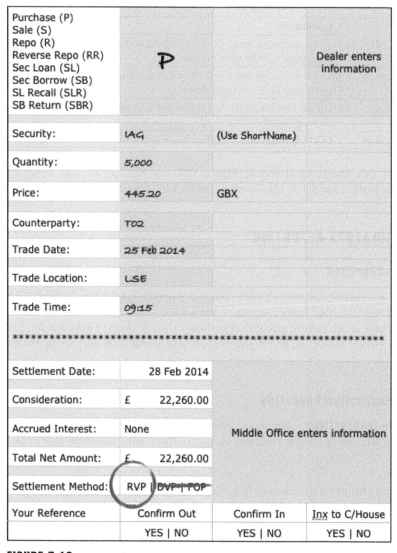

FIGURE 7.12   Transaction ticket

We can see that we now have almost the full details of this particular transaction, as follows:

- The settlement date for this particular asset type is T+3, making it 28 February 2014.
- The consideration is the quantity of shares multiplied by the price (remembering that, as these are UK equities, they have been priced in pence and should be converted into pounds sterling).
- There is no accrued interest and we are disregarding stamp duty in our example.
- As this transaction is a purchase, the regular settlement method will be receive versus payment (RVP).

There are two pieces of information missing at this stage: the account numbers of both trading counterparties and the name of the clearing system. In an automated environment, this information would be picked up from the appropriate databases, as shown in Table 7.2.

TABLE 7.2   Counterparties and clearing system

Database	Comments
Company T01	T01 is a clearing member of the clearing house and will have an associated participant account number/code.
Counterparty	T02 is a clearing member of the clearing house and will have an associated participant account number/code.
Asset type	UK equities traded on the London Stock Exchange clear through a specified clearing system.
Clearing system	LCH.Clearnet.

By contrast, in a manual environment, Middle Office or Settlements staff would add these extra details to the trade ticket, confirmation and clearing house instructions.

7.5   REGULATORY REPORTING

7.5.1   Background

As part of a regulatory authority's obligations to maintain confidence in the financial markets and reduce financial crime, regulated firms have to send reports of their transactions to the regulator at the earliest possible opportunity (i.e. by close of business on T+1). This helps the regulator detect and investigate suspected incidents of market abuse and/or market manipulation.

7.5.2   Transaction Reporting

Reportable Transactions   Regulated firms must report all purchases and sales of financial instruments whether acting as principal or agent. There are transaction types that are not reportable:

1. Securities financing transactions (e.g. securities lending/borrowing).
2. The exercise of options and covered warrants.
3. Primary market transactions in equities and bonds (including depository receipts on these).

Reportable Instruments Regulated firms have to report transactions that have been executed:

(a) In any financial instrument (e.g. equities, bonds, derivatives, etc.) that has been admitted to trading on a regulated market;[2] or
(b) In any OTC derivative where the underlying asset is either an equity or debt-related financial instrument, as noted in (1) above.

There are exceptions; the following need not be reported:

(c) Transactions in any OTC derivative where the underlying asset is either a multiple equity or multiple debt-related financial instrument (e.g. a stock index);
(d) Transactions in commodity, interest rate and foreign-exchange OTC/listed derivatives (e.g. a commodity futures contract).

Content of a Transaction Report A transaction report contains information regarding an individual transaction executed on a financial market and contains 21 separate fields, including:

- The financial instrument identifiers;
- The firm that executed the transaction;
- The counterparty to the transaction;
- The buy/sell identifier;
- The price;
- The quantity, etc.

The regulators regard transaction reporting as being so important in their role of ensuring that the markets function well that they will heavily fine firms which either mis-report transactions or fail to report them altogether.

7.5.3 Transaction-Reporting Mechanism

Transactions can be reported to the regulator by firms using systems known as *approved reporting mechanisms* (ARMs). Table 7.3 lists ARMs approved by the UK's Financial Conduct Authority.

TABLE 7.3   List of approved ARMs

ARM	System	ISIN	OTC	AII
Credit Suisse Securities (Europe) Limited	DARE	Yes	Yes	Yes
Euroclear UK and Ireland	CREST	Yes	No	No
Xtrakter	TRAX	Yes	Yes	Yes
London Stock Exchange	UniVista	Yes	Yes	Yes
Getco Europe Ltd	GETCO	Yes	Yes	Yes
Abide Financial Ltd	TransacPort	Yes	Yes	Yes

AII – Alternative Instrument Identifier

---

[2] A list of regulated markets covered by MiFID in Europe can be found in the Regulated Markets section of the ESMA database (http://mifiddatabase.esma.europa.eu/Index.aspx?sectionlinks_id=4&language=0& pageName=Home).

7.5.4 Trade Repositories

The over-the-counter (OTC) derivatives markets are inherently opaque because trading takes place away from an exchange in products that are formulated to suit the buyer and seller. Globally, regulators have become concerned that this opacity prevents them from monitoring the build-up and distribution of exposures in the relevant markets. To overcome this problem, regulators have introduced the requirement that trade repositories (TRs) capture and retain key information regarding open (OTC) derivative trades.

The information held by the TRs is then disseminated to the appropriate regulators. This not only enhances market transparency but also helps public authorities and market participants to monitor OTC derivative exposures. The overall objectives for the TRs are to support sound risk management, market discipline and effective oversight, regulation and supervision of the markets.

Examples of Trade Repositories　In Europe, several TRs have been registered by the European Securities Markets Association (ESMA) in accordance with the European Market Infrastructure Regulation (EMIR). These are shown in Table 7.4.

TABLE 7.4　European trade repositories

Trade Repository	Derivative Asset Class
DTCC Derivatives Repository Ltd	All asset classes
Krajowy Depozyt Papierów Wartosciowych S.A.	All asset classes
Regis-TR S.A.	All asset classes
UnaVista Limited	All asset classes
CME Trade Repository Ltd	All asset classes
ICE Trade Vault Europe Ltd	Commodities, credit, equities and interest rates

7.6 CONFIRMATION AND AFFIRMATION

At the moment that a transaction is executed, both counterparties enter into a legally-binding contract to either deliver an asset against cash or pay cash against receipt of an asset. It is therefore imperative that both counterparties recognise their transactions not only from their point of view but also from their counterparty's point of view.

How might these points of view differ? Here are some possible examples:

- One or both of the counterparties might make a mistake when entering the transaction details either into their automated systems or onto a manual dealing sheet.
- Both counterparties might assume that they have purchased securities when, of course, one counterparty will purchase and the other will sell.
- The price may have been misheard or miskeyed; this can happen especially when trading takes place by open outcry or over the telephone.

It is therefore quite possible to get any of the transaction details incorrect for one reason or another. For this reason, counterparties will confirm their transaction details with each other at the earliest possible opportunity. Counterparties must ensure that:

* They send a confirmation to their counterparty; and
* Make sure they receive their counterparty's confirmation and check it for accuracy. Where there are inconsistencies, staff should check their own records and contact their counterparty.

7.6.1 Confirmations

Where direct market participants (e.g. market makers, dealers, traders and brokers) have traded with each other, it is normal market practice for both participants to exchange confirmations with each other. Furthermore, it is expected that this process should be completed by close of business on the trade date.

There are two main ways of constructing a confirmation:

1. Sending a SWIFT message using a Message Type 517: Trade Confirmation Affirmation (MT517) or Message Type 518: Market-Side Securities Trade Confirmation (MT518). In the settlement simulation we use a slimmed-down version of the MT518 to confirm trades; see Figure 7.13 for the purchase of 5,000 IAG shares.
2. Using an electronic trade confirmation system (ETC) as provided by companies such as Omgeo (www.omgeo.com), SmartStream (www.smartstream-stp.com) and Traiana (www.traiana.com).

Once you have sent the MT518, you can tick the "Yes" box on the [Confirm Out] box located at the bottom of the trade ticket (see Figure 7.11) or flag the system that this has been done.

The incoming MT518 from counterparty T02 for its sale of 5,000 IAG shares is shown in Figure 7.14.

Q&A

Question

Please compare T02's details with T01's; what conclusion do you come to?

Answer

The trade details in T02's confirmation agree with those in T01's trade ticket and confirmation.

Once you have received and checked the incoming MT518, you can tick the "Yes" box on the [Confirm In] box on the trade ticket (see Figure 7.11) or flag the system that this has been done.

Message sent by:	Team: T01

We confirm that we have:

purchased from you/sold to you *

MT 518	Market-Side Trade Confirmation

Delete as necessary

(This message should be handed to your counterparty)

Data Elements	Details
Transaction Ref. Nbr.	T01/1
Trade Date	25 February 2014
Place of Trade	LSE (London Stock Exchange)
Time of Trade	09:15
Settlement Date	28 February 2014
Quantity of Securities	5,000
Securities ShortName	IAG
Counterparty	T02
Receiver (Buyer)	T01 Account 12345
Deliverer (Seller)	T02 Account 98765
Deal Price (GBX)	445.20
Settlement Amount (GBP)	£ 22,260.00
Settlement Method	[RVP]

FIGURE 7.13 Outgoing trade confirmation

7.6.2 Affirmation

Until 1992 the only way to legally agree trade details was by using paper confirmations. On many occasions these paper confirmations either arrived late or not at all. A group of brokers and buy-side institutional investors came together to develop a system that would enable firms to accurately agree confirmation details on the trade date. This system was called *electronic trade confirmation* (ETC).

As we saw above, confirmations are exchanged for trades executed between two market participants. The situation is slightly different where a market participant (e.g. a broker) has dealt on behalf of a buy-side financial institution such as an investment management company.

Message sent by:	Team: T02

We confirm that we have:

purchased from you/**sold to you** *

MT 518	Market-Side Trade Confirmation

* Delete as necessary

(This message should be handed to your counterparty)

Data Elements	Details
Transaction Ref. Nbr.	T02/1
Trade Date	25 February 2014
Place of Trade	LSE (London Stock Exchange)
Time of Trade	09:15
Settlement Date	28 February 2014
Quantity of Securities	5,000
Securities ShortName	IAG
Counterparty	T01
Receiver (Buyer)	T01 Account 12345
Deliverer (Seller)	T02 Account 98765
Deal Price (GBX)	445.20
Settlement Amount (GBP)	£ 22,260.00
Settlement Method	[DVP]

FIGURE 7.14   Incoming trade confirmation

As the investment management company is regarded as a client, it is not appropriate for it to generate a trade confirmation. This results in a one-way situation where the broker sends a confirmation note to the investment management company.

Q&A

Question

What are the potential problems with a one-way confirmation?

Answer

The potential problems for the broker are:

- They cannot be sure that their confirmation note has been received by the investment management company.
- If there is a problem with the confirmation, the broker may not be informed, or may be informed too late to enable good settlement to take place.

The principles of trade affirmation are straightforward and involve the following steps:

- The broker alleges transaction details electronically using an ETC system;
- The investment management company's system automatically compares the affirmation details with its own records; and
- Either agrees (i.e. affirms) electronically with the broker or rejects the message and both parties investigate the discrepancy.

The target date for affirmation completion is typically by T+1 at the latest; this extra day is to enable the investment management company to calculate trade allocation numbers and to advise its broker accordingly. Best practice encourages affirmation on T+0, i.e. on the trade date itself. This is known as *same-day affirmation* (SDA).

Trade Allocation   Trade allocation is required when an investment management company places a bulk order with a broker on behalf of several underlying clients. The broker will execute the bulk order and advise the investment management company of the transaction details. The investment manager (IM) must then let its broker (B) have a breakdown of the bulk order into its component parts client by client. In the example shown in Table 7.5, a bulk order for 5 million ABC shares is sent to the broker.

TABLE 7.5   Bulk order and trade allocation

	ABC Shares	**Client**	**From**	**To**
Bulk order	5,000,000	–	IM	B
Execution	Purchase 5,000,000	–	B	IM
Allocation	500,000	Client 01	IM	B
Allocation	1,000,000	Client 02	IM	B
Allocation	1,500,000	Client 03	IM	B
Allocation	2,000,000	Client 04	IM	B

We can see that a bulk order of 5 million shares is allocated to four clients in the proportions noted in the table. There are two points to note here:

1. If the broker is not able to execute the bulk order at one price, it might need to make a series of transactions at different prices. From this, an average price will be calculated.

2. In our example, there are four clients; in reality there could be many clients to whom the bulk order will be allocated.

In Figure 7.15, we can see a graphical representation of the trade confirmation/affirmation process.

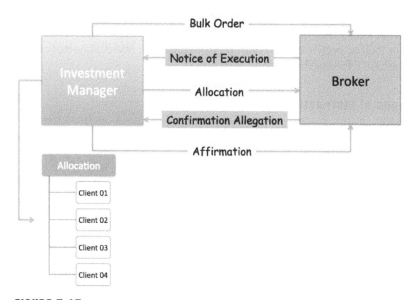

FIGURE 7.15 Trade affirmation/confirmation

In summary, the bulk order is executed in the market and transformed through the allocation process into four separate transactions, each with its own clearing and settlement processes.

Same-Day Affirmation (SDA) In markets where there is a short settlement cycle (e.g. $T+2$), the idea of trade affirmation happening on $T+1$ potentially becomes unworkable, as this leaves very little time for the remaining clearing and settlement processes to take place. SDA has been defined[3] as: "The agreement of all trade details on the trade date between a broker/dealer and an investment manager (or their agent)". Omgeo also stated that there was a direct correlation between high SDA rates and high settlement rates.

As the markets, and Europe in particular, move towards shorter settlement cycles, SDA will become a necessity.

Benefits of SDA Not only does SDA enable shorter settlement cycles to occur but there are also direct benefits including risk reduction (e.g. reduced settlement fails) and cost efficiencies

---

[3]See Omgeo's white paper, October 2010 "Mitigating Operational Risk and Increasing Settlement Efficiency through Same Day Affirmation."

(e.g. reduced operating costs). In addition, SDA can be seen as an enabler in the move to harmonise settlement practices, straight-through processing and information flows.

7.7 CLEARING INSTRUCTIONS

We have now reached the stage where trades have been executed and either confirmed or affirmed so that both buyer and seller are legally aware of the contract details.

At this stage, a clearing house or central counterparty (CCP) becomes involved. Both the buyer and seller (or their respective agents) must prepare settlement instructions that are sent to the clearing house/CCP for matching.

7.7.1 Types of Instruction

There are four types of settlement instruction (see Table 7.6).

TABLE 7.6   Settlement instruction types

Instruction	Description	SWIFT Message Type
Receive versus payment (RVP)	Buyer's instruction to settle its purchase of securities against simultaneous payment of cash.	MT541
Delivery versus payment (DVP)	Seller's instruction to settle its sale of securities against simultaneous receipt of cash.	MT543
Receive free of payment (FoP)	Buyer's instruction to settle its purchase of securities or inbound transfer of securities. Cash paid separately.	MT540
Deliver free of payment (FoP)	Seller's instruction to settle its sale of securities or outbound transfer of securities. Cash received separately.	MT542

Most purchases and sales require RVP and DVP instructions. Free of payment instructions are used in situations such as:

1. When the movement of securities occurs separately from the movement of cash. An example would be an investor who buys securities and arranges for them to be delivered to his custodian but makes a payment from another bank.
2. When the movement of securities is not associated with a cash counter-value. An example would be where an investor requests his custodian to transfer securities from one of his portfolios to another (where both portfolios are held by the same custodian).

Examples of DVP and RVP Instructions   Returning to our settlement simulation example, trading company T01 had executed six transactions, of which four were purchases and two were sales. We should therefore prepare four MT541s and two MT543s. As before, we have prepared basic versions of these two SWIFT message types and entered them on to separate spreadsheets (see Figures 7.16 and 7.17).

SWIFT Instruction - Receipt against Payment		MT541	T01

(This message should be handed to the Clearing House)

Field Description	1	2	3	4
Settlement Date	28 February 2014	28 February 2014	28 February 2014	28 February 2014
Your Ref Number	T01/1	T01/2	T01/4	T01/6
Date of Trade	25 February 2014	25 February 2014	25 February 2014	25 February 2014
Place of Trade	London (LSE)	London (LSE)	London (LSE)	London (LSE)
Securities ID	IAG	BARC	TSCO	BARC
Quantity	5,000	5,000	10,000	10,000
Safekeeping Account	T01	T01	T01	T01
Deliverer of Securities	T02	T03	T04	T03
Settlement Amount	£22,260.00	£12,872.50	£33,165.00	£25,665.00

FIGURE 7.16 Receive versus payment

SWIFT Instruction - Deliver against Payment		MT543	T01

(This message should be handed to the Clearing House)

Field Description	1	2	3	4
Settlement Date	28-Feb-14	28-Feb-14		
Your Ref Number	T01/3	T01/5		
Date of Trade	25-Feb-14	25-Feb-14		
Place of Trade	London (LSE)	London (LSE)		
Securities ID	HSBA	MRW		
Quantity	2,500	15,000		
Safekeeping Account	T01	T01		
Receiver of Securities	T02	T04		
Settlement Amount	15,762.50	35,940.00		

FIGURE 7.17 Delivery versus payment

The six instructions noted above will be submitted by T01 to the appropriate clearing house. For their part, the three counterparties alleged in T01's instructions will submit their instructions.

7.7.2 Instruction Validation

The object of instruction matching by the clearing house is to ensure that any one transaction is represented by two instructions – one for delivery and one for receipt.

On receipt of any instruction, the clearing house will validate the instruction message to ensure that the information is potentially correct. Validation might include:

- Checking that the quantity meets the board lot size characteristics for that particular security. For example, an instruction for USD 1,000 of a bond will be rejected if the board lot size is USD 10,000.
- Checking that the settlement amount looks reasonable. If not, there is the possibility that an incorrect price has been used in the calculation. For example, if the settlement amount for the purchase of 5,000 IAG shares (reference T01/1 above) was GBP 24,000.00, that would suggest a price of GBX 480.00 was used. As the market was GBX 445.20 at the time of the trade, the difference of GBX 34.80 is 7.82% above the market price and above an acceptable tolerance of, say, ±3.00%.

7.7.3 Instruction Matching

The clearing house will attempt to match receipt instructions with delivery instructions either in real time or on a batch process. The matching process will result in two outcomes:

1. Instructions that match, i.e. the clearing house identifies RVP and DVP instructions that relate to the same transaction.
2. Instructions that do not match, i.e. the clearing house is unable to match an RVP with a corresponding DVP.

In Figure 7.18 you will see that all the counterparties have submitted their instructions and the clearing house has attempted to match these instructions one against another.

CH Ref	STO Ref	STO	Trade	Quantity	Issuer	Settlement Amount	Cpty	S/D Date
2	T01/2	T01	Purchase	5,000	BARC	£ 12,872.50	T03	28-Feb-2014
9	T03/1	T03	Sale	5,000	BARC	£ 12,872.50	T01	28-Feb-2014
4	T01/3	T01	Sale	2,500	HSBA	£ 15,762.50	T02	28-Feb-2014
12	T02/2	T02	Purchase	2,500	HSBA	£ 15,762.50	T01	28-Feb-2014
1	T01/1	T01	Purchase	5,000	IAG	£ 22,260.00	T02	28-Feb-2014
11	T02/1	T02	Sale	5,000	IAG	£ 22,260.00	T01	28-Feb-2014
6	T01/6	T01	Purchase	10,000	BARC	£ 25,665.00	T03	28-Feb-2014
10	T03/2	T03	Sale	10,000	BARC	£ 25,665.00	T01	28-Feb-2014
5	T01/4	T01	Purchase	10,000	TSCO	£ 33,165.00	T04	28-Feb-2014
7	T04/1	T04	Sale	10,000	TSCO	£ 33,165.00	T01	28-Feb-2014
3	T01/5	T01	Sale	15,000	MRW	£ 35,940.00	T04	28-Feb-2014
8	T04/2	T04	Purchase	15,000	MRW	£ 35,940.00	T01	28-Feb-2014

FIGURE 7.18 Clearing house instructions v1

Q&A

Question

Do the instructions in Figure 7.18 match?

Answer

Yes. All six transactions are correctly matched.

As all the instructions for the six transactions match, the clearing house will be in a position to allow the transactions to settle subject to there being sufficient cash for the purchases and availability of the securities for the sales.

In Figure 7.19, you will find a second version of the clearing house's instruction capture system.

CH Ref	STO Ref	STO	Trade	Quantity	Issuer	Settlement Amount	Cpty	S/D Date
2	T01/2	T01	Purchase	5,000	BARC	£ 12,872.50	T03	28-Feb-2014
9	T03/1	T03	Sale	5,000	BARC	£ 12,872.50	T01	1-Mar-2014
4	T01/3	T01	Sale	2,500	HSBA	£ 15,762.50	T02	28-Feb-2014
12	T02/2	T02	Sale	2,500	HSBA	£ 15,762.50	T01	28-Feb-2014
1	T01/1	T01	Purchase	5,000	IAG	£ 22,260.00	T02	28-Feb-2014
11	T02/1	T02	Sale	5,000	IAG	£ 22,400.00	T01	28-Feb-2014
6	T01/6	T01	Purchase	10,000	BARC	£ 25,665.00	T03	28-Feb-2014
10	T03/2	T03	Sale	10,000	BARC	£ 25,665.00	T01	28-Feb-2014
5	T01/4	T01	Purchase	10,000	TSCO	£ 33,165.00	T04	28-Feb-2014
7	T04/1	T04	Sale	10,000	TSCO	£ 33,165.00	T02	28-Feb-2014
3	T01/5	T01	Sale	15,000	MRW	£ 35,940.00	T04	28-Feb-2014
8	T04/2	T04	Purchase	15,000	MRW	£ 35,940.00	T01	28-Feb-2014

FIGURE 7.19 Clearing house instructions v2

Q&A

Question

In the version shown in Figure 7.19, do the instructions match? Please suggest reasons for any unmatched instructions.

Answer

We have some unmatched as well as some matched instructions – see Table 7.7.

TABLE 7.7 Matched and unmatched instructions

CH Ref:	Matched?	Reason
2/9	No	Settlement dates differ.
4/12	No	Both counterparties have DVP instructions.
1/11	No	Settlement amounts differ.
6/10	Yes	OK
5/7	No	T01 alleges RVP against T04, and T04 alleges DVP against T02.
3/8	Yes	OK

For each of the four unmatched instructions, the clearing house is not able to choose which instruction is actually correct. In fact, they all appear feasible! To resolve the problems, the clearing house will send a report to each counterparty listing both the matched and the unmatched instructions.

In addition, with the unmatched instructions, the clearing house will report to both the instructing counterparty and the alleged counterparty. Examples for counterparties T01 and T02 are shown in Figures 7.20 and 7.21.

CH Ref	STO Ref	STO	Trade	Quantity	Issuer	Settlement Amount		Cpty	Settlement Date	Instruction Status
6	T01/6	T01	Purchase	10,000	BARC	£	25,665.00	T03	28-Feb-2014	MATCHED
3	T01/5	T01	Sale	15,000	MRW	£	35,940.00	T04	28-Feb-2014	MATCHED
2	T01/2	T01	Purchase	5,000	BARC	£	12,872.50	T03	28-Feb-2014	UNM-CPTY
4	T01/3	T01	Sale	2,500	HSBA	£	15,762.50	T02	28-Feb-2014	UNM-CPTY
1	T01/1	T01	Purchase	5,000	IAG	£	22,260.00	T02	28-Feb-2014	UNM-CPTY
5	T01/4	T01	Purchase	10,000	TSCO	£	33,165.00	T04	28-Feb-2014	UNM-CPTY
12	T02/2	T02	Sale	2,500	HSBA	£	15,762.50	T01	28-Feb-2014	UNM-YOUR
11	T02/1	T02	Sale	5,000	IAG	£	22,400.00	T01	28-Feb-2014	UNM-YOUR

FIGURE 7.20 Clearing house matched report to T01

CH Ref	STO Ref	STO	Trade	Quantity	Issuer	Settlement Amount		Cpty	Settlement Date	Instruction Status
12	T02/2	T02	Sale	2,500	HSBA	£	15,762.50	T01	28-Feb-2014	UNM-CPTY
11	T02/1	T02	Sale	5,000	IAG	£	22,400.00	T01	28-Feb-2014	UNM-CPTY
4	T01/3	T01	Sale	2,500	HSBA	£	15,762.50	T02	28-Feb-2014	UNM-YOUR
1	T01/1	T01	Purchase	5,000	IAG	£	22,260.00	T02	28-Feb-2014	UNM-YOUR

FIGURE 7.21 Clearing house matched report to T02

Please note that there are three possible outcomes under instruction status:

1. MATCHED: Both halves of the transaction have been matched by the clearing house.
2. UNM-CPTY: This is your instruction that has not been matched by your counterparty.
3. UNM-YOUR: This is your counterparty's instruction that you have not matched.

The counterparties concerned will need to investigate the unmatched items and contact their counterparties. Whoever was at fault will need to correct their instruction(s) so that we end up with the situation in Figure 7.18 "Clearing house instructions v1".

In an ideal situation, all counterparties should be able to submit their instructions to the clearing house on T+1 at the latest, especially if this is via an automated STP system. Otherwise, instructions that are manually re-keyed might struggle to be submitted by T+1, with T+2 being more realistic. Manual re-keying on this basis will be impractical when settlement cycles contract to T+2.

Unmatched instructions can never settle, and in circumstances where instructions are unmatched on the settlement date, the party at fault can expect to receive an interest claim from their counterparty.

Let us assume that the clearing house has received and matched all the instructions. The clearing house now makes a judgement as to which transactions will settle or fail to settle. We will cover the topic of settlements in the next chapter, but in the meantime, the clearing house needs to verify that there are sufficient cash funds and securities balances to enable the transactions to settle.

7.8 FORECASTING – CASH

7.8.1 Introduction

Before we look at the topic of cash forecasting, here is an imaginary situation in our private lives. You believe that you have a balance of Hong Kong dollars 13,000 in your bank account and you go online to check the balance, only to discover that you have an overdrawn position of Hong Kong dollars 7,000. Furthermore, you went overdrawn one week ago and have been incurring overdraft interest at a rate of 500 basis points over the Hong Kong interest rate of, say, 0.02%, i.e. 5.02% per annum.

What has possibly gone wrong? Firstly, it would appear that you have made a payment of Hong Kong dollars 20,000 and omitted to record the entry in your records. Secondly, having forgotten to record the payment, you failed to cover the overdraft. Even if you had had sufficient funds on a deposit account at your bank, the bank would not automatically transfer funds from your deposit to your current account to cover the payment. The net result would be that overdraft charges would accrue at approximately one Hong Kong dollar per day until the overdraft was repaid.

We can apply the same idea in our clearing activities. Firstly, we need to know what cash is available now, secondly, which transactions that should have settled have not and, finally, which cash payments and receipts are to be expected. All three points of view need to be considered from one particular day.

7.8.2 Timing Issues

The first question we need to ask ourselves is what value date do we need to consider in order to cover our cash forecast? We can consider this from three angles:

 1. The time zones in which we are based and in which the currencies are based.

2. The external payment system's payment deadlines.
3. Internal deadlines to meet our Treasury Department's funding requirements.

Time Zones   Where we are dealing in the currencies of countries located to the east of us, we have less time available. This might result in performing our cash forecasting today for a value date tomorrow.

Where we are dealing in the currencies of countries close to our time zone, our respective business days will open and close at much the same time. This should result in us being able to forecast today for a value date today.

Where we are dealing in the currencies of countries located to the west of us, we have more time available. Not only can we forecast today for a value date today, but we will have more time to make the necessary funding arrangements.

Payment System Deadlines   These tend to be in the late afternoon, towards the market's close of business.

Internal Treasury Deadlines   The Treasury Department requires sufficient time for its funding requirements, allowing it to meet its bank's deadlines as well as the payment system's deadlines.

For the purposes of the settlement simulation example, we are able to fund today for a value date today (same-day value) and there is a 12:00 deadline for funding instructions to be received by the Treasury Department.

7.8.3 Cash Forecasting Methodology

We can forecast our funding requirements in four phases (see Figure 7.22).

Transaction Date:	28-Feb-14		Value Date:	28-Feb-14
Funding Deadline. Instructions to Treasury by:	12:00	latest		
		Cash	Cash	Running
Phase A		DR	CR	Balance
Bank Balance	Brought Down	£ 0.00	£ 148,522.24	£ 148,522.24
Phase B				
increased by	Unsettled Sales Proceeds		£ 0.00	£ 148,522.24
reduced by	Unsettled Purchase Costs	£ 140,000.00		£ 8,522.24
		Start-of-Day Adjusted Cash Position :	£ 8,522.24
Phase C				
reduce by	Pending Purchase Costs	£ 93,962.50		£ (85,440.26)
increase by	Pending Sale Proceeds		£ 51,702.50	£ (33,737.76)
increase by	Income Collection		£ 14,948.00	£ (18,789.76)
reduce by	Corporation Action Payables	£ 76,250.00		£ (95,039.76)
increase by	Corporation Action Receivables		£ 0.00	£ (95,039.76)
		Expected Future Cash Balance :	£ (95,039.76)
		Borrow cash	£ 100,000.00
			£ 4,960.24
Phase D	Funding Action required:	Borrow cash from Treasury		

FIGURE 7.22   Cash forecasting

Phase A: Bank Balance   We have a balance on the bank account of GBP 148,522.24 and this agrees with the dealer's blotter. A cash reconciliation shows that there are payments and/or receipts that were expected but not debited/credited.

Phase B: Unsettled Items   One or more purchases that should have settled have failed. The cash total amounts to GBP 140,000.00. We therefore need to reduce the balance in Phase A by this amount to leave us with a start-of-day adjusted position of GBP 8,522.24.

Phase C: Pending Items   These are the items that are due to be settled on the value date (i.e. 28 February 2014 – the intended settlement date for the six transactions executed on the 25 February). We have also included other types of transaction such as income collection and corporate actions receivable/payable. In reality, you consider all items that fall due on the value date.

The total of Phases B and C amounts to an expected future cash balance of GBP (95,039.76). In other words, if all the items were cleared, your account would be overdrawn and incurring interest charges. Furthermore, if your credit limit were GBP 50,000.00, then some of the payments might be blocked and not clear.

Phase D: Action Required   You have an expected cash shortfall of GBP 95,039.76 and you can cover this by borrowing from your Treasury Department. You could borrow the exact amount, but it might be preferable to borrow a "round amount" of, say, GBP 100,000.00. As your deadline for this transaction is 12:00, it would be a good idea to start preparing your funding requirements as early as possible.

7.8.4   Funding Uncertainties

You have now completed your cash funding for value date 28 February 2014. You are sure that Phases A and B are correct, but how certain can you be that the items in Phase C will actually settle as expected?

Q&A

Question

What would be the impact if the sale(s) failed to settle?

Answer

With the non-receipt of GBP 51,702.50, your expected future cash balance would be a debit of GBP 146,742.26. As you have only borrowed GBP 100,000.00, you will still be approximately GBP 47,000 overdrawn.

The challenge is, wherever possible, to predict which items are unlikely to settle. For your purchases, you will have no forewarning that they are about to settle. However, for your sales, you are in control of your inventory and should know in advance what securities are available for delivery.

This challenge can be overcome by adopting one of two approaches:

1. Fund to settle.
2. Fund to fail.

"Fund-to-Settle" Approach   This approach is subject to the following caveats:

1. That your sales will settle. This requires a high degree of confidence that you have sufficient inventory.
2. That your purchases might settle. As you cannot be sure, it is prudent to ensure that there is sufficient cash available.
3. Where you know that payment has to be made on the value date, for example a corporate action payable.

In conclusion, this is an optimistic approach.

"Fund-to-Fail" Approach   This approach is subject to the following caveats:

1. That your sales will not (or probably will not) settle and that you will fund the proceeds only on receipt.
2. That your purchases will not (or probably will not) settle and that you will fund the costs only on the date payment is to be made. This particular approach may not leave you enough time to fund the position.
3. Where you suspect that payment will not be made to you on the value date, for example, a late dividend or coupon payment.

In conclusion, this is more of a pessimistic approach.

The reality is that the funding officer has to weigh up the chances that an item may or may not settle as expected. Reference to internal records of historic settlement activity and, where available, market information can help the funding officer be more accurate in anticipating cash-funding requirements.

7.8.5 Benefits of Predictive Forecasting

The main object of predictive forecasting is to make sure that there is sufficient cash to cover all activities. Performed well, the cost of funding can be reduced; indeed, it is quite possible to make a positive return, especially when interest rates are reasonably high. Errors in cash forecasting can be expensive and will add to the overall cost of providing an operational service to the Front Office. At worst, there is a reputational risk should counterparties become aware of funding issues in your organisation.

7.9 FORECASTING – SECURITIES

7.9.1 Introduction

Q&A

Questions

Here are some questions regarding the selling of securities for you to think about:

1. Can you sell securities that you have previously purchased?
2. Can you sell securities that you have previously purchased but not yet received?
3. Can you deliver securities that you have purchased but not yet received?
4. Can you sell securities you do not own?
5. Can you deliver securities that you do not hold in custody?

Answers

Here are some answers:

1. Yes. You are free to sell any security that you legally own.
2. Yes. In most markets, you can sell securities even though a previous purchase has not settled. However, in some markets and with some retail investors, the broker might insist that it receives the securities from the client before executing a sale.
3. No. Even though you are the legal owner, you are unable to deliver as you do not have the securities "available for delivery". In this case, you can only deliver once the purchase has settled.
4. It depends on the situation. For market participants (e.g. market makers), the answer is "yes", as they sell in response to market situations. This often requires the market makers to sell securities they do not own, i.e. they sell "short". On the other hand, institutional investors (except hedge funds) and retail investors are not permitted to sell short.
5. No. If your securities are not held in custody, they are not "available for delivery".

These questions are posed to make the distinction between securities that you legally own (or not) and the availability of securities for delivery. Forecasting for securities is similar in concept to cash forecasting (e.g. we are looking at one particular date – the settlement date). The main difference is that we are focusing on our sales rather than our total trading activities.

The situation is different regarding derivatives contracts. Market participants and investors can buy "long" and sell "short". Unlike securities, derivatives contracts cannot be delivered and received in the same way that equities, bonds, etc. are delivered. In fact, the only delivery we have to worry about is when contracts are exercised into the underlying asset.

7.9.2 Securities that are Available for Delivery

Please refer back to the settlement simulation and in particular to the following documents:

- Dealer's blotter (see Figure 7.9): This lists the securities that have been previously purchased.
- Dealing sheet (see Figure 7.10): There are six transactions, two of which are sales.

Are you able to deliver the 2,500 HSBA shares and 15,000 MRW shares? According to the dealer's blotter, there are sufficient securities (40,000 HSBA shares and 90,000 MRW shares); however, are they available for delivery (AFD)?

You reconcile both positions with the results shown in Table 7.8 and Table 7.9.

TABLE 7.8   Reconciliation of HSBA shares

HSBA Shares			
Ownership	Balance	Balance	Location
Trading book	40,000	−40,000	Custodian
Totals:	**40,000**	**−40,000**	

TABLE 7.9   Reconciliation of MRW shares

MRW Shares			
Ownership	Balance	Balance	Location
Trading book	90,000	−90,000	Custodian
Totals:	**90,000**	**−90,000**	

Both positions reconcile and, as the shares are located at the custodian, they are available for delivery. You can now be confident that if your delivery instructions are matched at the clearing house, you will settle both sales and receive the cash proceeds.

7.9.3 Securities that are Not Available for Delivery

We can change the scenario by altering the location of both holdings. The reconciliations now look like those shown in Table 7.10 and Table 7.11.

TABLE 7.10   Reconciliation of HSBA shares – second version

HSBA Shares			
Ownership	Balance	Balance	Location
Trading book	40,000	−25,000	Custodian
		−15,000	Counterparty 01
Totals:	40,000	−40,000	

TABLE 7.11 Reconciliation of MRW shares – second version

MRW Shares			
Ownership	**Balance**	**Balance**	**Location**
Trading book	90,000	−10,000	Custodian
		−25,000	Counterparty 02
		−35,000	Counterparty 03
		−20,000	Counterparty 04
Totals:	**90,000**	**−90,000**	

As before, both positions reconcile; however, there are only 25,000 HSBA shares and 10,000 MRW shares that are AFD. Whilst the sale of 2,500 HSBA shares can settle, the sale of 15,000 MRW shares cannot.

There are various options available:

1. Do nothing. Allow the sale to fail and wait until one of the outstanding purchases settles.
2. Borrow 5,000 MRW shares. This will provide the availability to settle the trade.
3. Offer a partial delivery of 10,000 shares to your counterparty T04.

We will take a more detailed look at the management of settlement fails in the next chapter.

7.10 SUMMARY

Clearing is a set of post-trade activities and is the process of transmitting, reconciling and, in some cases, confirming payment orders or security transfer instructions prior to settlement, possibly including the netting of instructions and the establishment of final positions for settlement.

As soon as the trade is captured from the Front Office systems, it goes through the following stages:

- Trade validation and enrichment – this takes the basic trade details and adds extra information such as the settlement date, cash amounts, accrued interest, fees and commissions, etc.;
- Trade confirmation – exchanging confirmations between market participants or affirming trade details with customers/clients;
- Transmitting delivery/receipt instructions to a clearing system;
- Responding to unmatched reports from the clearing systems;
- Forecasting cash requirements and securities availability.

On the satisfactory completion of the clearing process, the transactions can go forward to settlement. This is the topic of the next chapter.

CHAPTER 8

Settlement and Fails Management

8.1   INTRODUCTION

In the previous chapter we followed a typical transaction from the Front Office through to clearing. In this chapter we will cover the final phase in the transaction lifecycle, in which the liabilities of both the buyer and the seller are completed. We refer to this as *settlement*.

The term "settlement" can be defined as:

> "The completion of a transaction, wherein the seller transfers delivery versus payment (DVP) securities or financial instruments to the buyer and the buyer transfers money to the seller."[1]

This definition is valid for securities and other cash market financial instruments, but what about derivatives? "Open" derivatives contracts can be open for months, if not years, and the concept of settlement is only truly valid when derivatives contracts are exercised, i.e. in instances where the underlying asset is delivered or received. You will recall from the previous chapter that open derivatives contracts are either margined (for open exchange-traded and cleared OTC derivatives transactions) or collateralised (for non-cleared OTC derivatives).

In this chapter you will learn about the following topics:

- The different types of settlement;
- The concept of delivery versus payment and the three BIS DVP models;
- The locations in which settlement takes place;
- The reasons why transactions fail to settle;
- The ways in which settlement fails are managed.

---

[1]*Source:* BIS/Committee on Payment and Settlement Systems (March 2003) (online). "A glossary of terms used in payments and settlement systems". Available from www.bis.org/publ/cpss00b.pdf. [Accessed Monday, 10 March 2014]

8.2   THE DIFFERENT TYPES OF SETTLEMENT

In the BIS/CPSS definition of settlement above, you will have noticed the term "DVP". We will discuss this in Section 8.3.

Whilst it would appear from the definition that the seller delivers securities direct to the buyer (and the buyer pays the seller), in reality most settlements take place by a process known as *book-entry transfer*; in other words, electronic transfers rather than physical transfers.

In the days when securities were certificated (i.e. held in physical form) investors would typically arrange for their banks to hold their share and bond certificates in the banks' own vaults. In order to settle their sales, the investors would instruct their banks to withdraw the appropriate certificates from the vaults. Having done this, the banks would arrange for the buyers' brokers to collect the certificates, together with any transfer documentation, and in exchange hand a cheque or bank draft to the bank by way of payment.

This activity required a small army of bank and broker messengers who would spend their day delivering payments in exchange for securities and delivering securities in exchange for payment. We could describe this as an extreme example of a decentralised settlement system (see Figure 8.1). Today, not only is the clearing process centralised but also the settlement process. This makes settlement much more efficient and cost-effective and enables the settlement cycle to be shortened from trade date plus many days to trade date plus three days or less.

One further consequence is that we do not see many messengers.

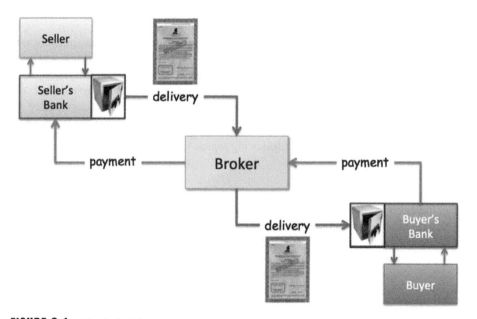

FIGURE 8.1   Physical settlement

Today, in the 21st century, securities are delivered electronically by book-entry transfer. Delivery can be made either on a transaction-by-transaction basis or on a collective basis. The former is known as *gross settlement* and the latter as *net settlement*.

8.2.1 Gross Settlement

Consider the example shown in Table 8.1, in which an investor has an inventory position of 1,000,000 ABC shares, all of which are available for delivery, and has executed a number of transactions (see Table 8.1). (We can ignore the cash counter values for the purposes of this example.)

TABLE 8.1 Gross settlement – total 1 million shares

Direction	Quantity of Shares	Counterparty
Sale	(150,000)	Broker "A"
Sale	(500,000)	Broker "B"
Sale	(350,000)	Broker "C"
Total:	(1,000,000)	

Q&A

Question

Can we settle all three transactions shown in Table 8.1?

Answer

Yes we can. There are 1 million shares available for delivery (AFD) and there will be three separate deliveries made (each delivery will incur a transaction charge levied by the settlement system).

In terms of timing, the settlement system can settle these trades in one of two ways:

Settlement in real time: As soon as the securities are available, the transaction(s) will be settled. This is a continuous process with no waiting involved. We refer to this version as *real time gross settlement* (RTGS).

In our example above, all three transactions would settle as soon as the settlement system opened for business (at, say, 08:30).

Settlement at a designated time: The settlement system will defer the actual settlement to a predetermined time during the settlement day, for example, at the close of business. Although the securities are available, there is an intra-day delay until the actual settlement happens. We refer to this version as a single *batch* process.

There is no reason why a settlement system could not operate a multi-batch process with settlement taking place at, say, 10:30, 13:00, 15:00 and 17:00 (local time). The multi-batch process now begins to resemble RTGS.

In our example above, all three transactions would settle at 10:30 (two hours later).

If we add two more transactions to our example and add the settlement times (see Table 8.2), you can see that all the transactions have settled on the same day albeit at different times. Even if Broker D's 200,000 shares were available from 13:01, settlement would only have been completed in the next batch at 15:00.

TABLE 8.2   Gross settlement – timing issues

Direction	Quantity of Shares	Counterparty	Settlement Time
Sale	(150,000)	Broker "A"	10:30
Sale	(500,000)	Broker "B"	10:30
Sale	(350,000)	Broker "C"	10:30
Purchase	200,000	Broker "D"	15:00
Sale	(200,000)	Broker "E"	15:00
Total:	(1,000,000)		

8.2.2   Net Settlement

By contrast, a net settlement system would be able to reduce overall exposures by off-setting deliveries and receipts, leaving a smaller net obligation. In net settlement, all the inter-institution transactions in the same security and all due for settlement on one particular day are accumulated. At the end of the day, the settlement accounts of the institutions are adjusted to reflect either one debit/delivery or one credit/receipt in that security, as shown in the example in Table 8.3.

TABLE 8.3   Net settlement

Direction	Shares	Counterparty	Net Position	Delivery
Sale	(150,000)	Broker "A"		
Sale	(500,000)	Broker "A"	(650,000)	To Broker "A"
Sale	(350,000)	Broker "B"		
Purchase	200,000	Broker "B"		
Sale	(200,000)	Broker "B"	(350,000)	To Broker "B"
Total:	(1,000,000)		(1,000,000)	

In this example, there will be two deliveries rather than the five that would have happened in the previous gross settlement example.

Q&A

Question

What would be the netting results for the transactions noted in Table 8.4?

TABLE 8.4 Transactions for net settlement

Ref:	Counterparty	Buy/Sell	Quantity	Counterparty
1	A	Buys	10,000	B
2	A	Sells	(50,000)	C
3	A	Buys	40,000	D
4	B	Sells	(15,000)	C
5	C	Sells	(45,000)	D
6	E	Buys	5,000	D

Answers

Table 8.5 gives the answers.

TABLE 8.5 Netting results for the transactions shown in Table 8.4

Counterparty	Opening Position	Net Debit/Credit	Closing Position
A	15,000	0	15,000
B	30,000	(25,000)	5,000
C	25,000	20,000	45,000
D	10,000	0	10,000
E	20,000	5,000	25,000
Totals:	100,000	0	100,000

For the six transactions, there were only three actual credits/debits plus two zero movements, with an overall net movement of zero. In other words:

- The net debits and credits total zero, and
- The closing position total is the same as the opening position total.

The question above requires the central counterparty/clearing house to monitor the incoming settlement instructions so that it can perform the settlement netting exercise. This could not be done by the participants themselves as, for example, counterparty "A" is only aware of its three transactions (Refs 1 to 3) and cannot know what transactions the other counterparties have executed amongst themselves (Refs 4 to 6).

8.3 DELIVERY VERSUS PAYMENT

Q&A

Question

What, in your opinion, are the risks or problems in the following scenarios?

1. You purchase some securities and the seller asks you to pay before it delivers the securities to your account.
2. You sell some securities and the buyer asks you to deliver the securities to its account before making payment to you.
3. You purchase some securities and you agree with the seller that, on the settlement date it will deliver the securities to your account at Bank A and that you will pay the seller through its account at Bank B.
4. You sell some securities and you agree with the buyer that, on the settlement date you will deliver the securities to the buyer's account at Bank C and it will pay into your account at Bank D.

Answers

Table 8.6 gives the answers.

TABLE 8.6 Problems and risks for the four scenarios

Scenario	Problems/Risks
1	You run the risk that, having paid the seller, you do not receive the securities either because the seller is unwilling or unable to deliver. The seller is not at risk as it has been paid.
2	You run the risk that, having delivered securities to the buyer, you do not get paid either because the buyer is unwilling or unable to pay. The buyer is not at risk as it has received the securities.
3	Your risk is much the same as in Scenario 1, with the added potential problem that either or both halves of the settlement are delayed for one reason or another. In addition, delivery of securities and payment of cash might be made to the incorrect locations.
4	Your risk is the same as in Scenario 3.

The common theme in all four scenarios is the separation of the securities transfer and the corresponding payment of cash. In order to overcome the separation, it is good market practice to ensure that delivery and payment occur at the same time and in the same place. Furthermore, if the seller does not have availability for delivery and/or the buyer does not have sufficient cash, then the transaction will not settle.

From the seller's point of view, we refer to this connection of securities and cash as *delivery versus payment* or DVP. Conversely, from the buyer's point of view, we have *receipt versus payment* or RVP. Irrespective of whether we are discussing a sale or a purchase, we tend to use the term DVP in both instances.

8.3.1 Definition of DVP

In 1989, the Group of Thirty (G30) published a document entitled *Clearance and Settlement Systems in the World's Securities Markets* which addressed the issues and challenges of clearing and settlement. From the workings of the G30's Steering Committee, nine recommendations were made.

Recommendation 5 stated that: "Delivery versus payment should be employed as the method for settling all securities transactions." Commenting on this recommendation, the G30 noted that:

> *"An area of substantial risk in the settlement of securities transactions occurs when securities are delivered without the simultaneous receipt of value by the delivering party. Simultaneous exchange of value is important to eliminate the risk of ... failure to perform according to contract. DVP effectively eliminates any exposure due to delivery delay by a counterparty."*[2]

The G30 subsequently defined DVP as the:

> "Simultaneous, final, irrevocable and immediately available exchange of securities and cash on a continuous basis throughout the day."

On this basis, not one of the four scenarios noted above would be regarded as settlement on a DVP basis.

In summary, a DVP system is a securities settlement system that provides a mechanism to ensure that delivery occurs if (and only if) payment occurs. Furthermore, the mechanism ensures that payment occurs if (and only if) delivery occurs.

8.3.2 DVP Models

Three broad structural approaches (shown in Table 8.7) to achieving DVP were identified by the Committee on Payment and Settlement Systems (CPSS) and these approaches are referred to as *models*.

TABLE 8.7 DVP models

Model	Definition
1	Systems that settle transfer instructions for both securities and funds on a trade-by-trade (gross) basis, with final (unconditional) transfer of securities from the seller to the buyer (delivery) occurring at the same time as final transfer of funds from the buyer to the seller (payment).
Summary:	Gross, simultaneous settlements of securities and funds transfers.
Example:	See the example that we used earlier for gross settlement.

(continued)

---

[2]*Source:* Group of Thirty (1988) "Clearance and Settlement Systems in the World's Securities Markets". Apdf version of this publication is available by email request www.group30.org [ISBN: 1-56708-076-6].

TABLE 8.7   (*Continued*)

Model	Definition
2	Systems that settle securities transfer instructions on a gross basis, with final transfer of securities from the seller to the buyer (delivery) occurring throughout the processing cycle, but that settle funds transfer instructions on a net basis, with final transfer of funds from the buyer to the seller (payment) occurring at the end of the processing cycle.
Summary:	Gross settlement of securities transfers followed by net settlement of EOC of funds transfers.
Example:	Consider the following three transactions: 1. You sell 10,000 ABC shares against EUR 40,000.00 2. You buy 15,000 RST shares against EUR 45,000.00 3. You sell 25,000 XYZ shares against EUR 60,000.00 Settlement using Model 2 would be: 1. Delivery of 10,000 ABC shares, and 2. Receipt of 15,000 RST shares, and 3. Delivery of 25,000 XYZ shares, followed by 4. Net receipt of EUR 55,000.00.
3	Systems that settle transfer instructions for both securities and funds on a net basis, with final transfers of both securities and funds occurring at the end of the processing cycle.
Summary:	Simultaneous net settlement of securities and funds transfers.
Example:	Consider the following three transactions: 1. You sell 10,000 ABC shares against EUR 40,000.00 2. You buy 15,000 ABC shares against EUR 60,000.00 3. You sell 25,000 ABC shares against EUR 100,000.00 Settlement using Model 3 would be: 1. Delivery of 20,000 ABC shares, together with 2. Simultaneous net receipt of EUR 80,000.00.

Refer to Committee on Payment and Settlement Systems (online). "Delivery versus payment in securities settlement systems". Available from www.bis.org/publ/cpss06.htm. [Accessed Tuesday, 11 March 2014]

8.3.3   Settlement Instructions for DVP

Institutions that are participants of the SWIFT messaging system will use the standardised RVP/DVP message types. In addition, clearing systems will offer their own proprietary communication system. For example, both ICSDs, Euroclear (EOC) and Clearstream Banking Luxembourg (CBL) use their proprietary systems and SWIFT, as shown in Table 8.8.

TABLE 8.8 Selection of DVP/RVP message types

	RVP	DVP	Comments
SWIFT message	MT541	MT543	
Euroclear Bank (EOC)			**EOC's system: EUCLID**
	01 P	02 P	EOC-EOC trade
	03 P	07 P	EOC-domestic trade outside EOC
	03C P	07C P	EOC-CBL bridge trade
Clearstream Banking Luxembourg (CBL)	41: RVP	51: DVP	**CBL's system: Creation** CBL-CBL trade
	61: RVP	8M/8A: DVP	CBL-domestic trade outside CBL
	41CE: RVP	51CE: DVP	CBL-EOC bridge trade

8.4 FREE OF PAYMENT SETTLEMENT

Whilst the majority of purchase and sale transactions are settled on a DVP basis, there will be circumstances when DVP is not appropriate. These can include the following:

1. Transfers of securities from one custodian to another on behalf of the same investor. In this case, as the investor has neither sold nor purchased the securities, there is no cash counter value.
2. Purchases and sales for which the settlement of the securities occurs in a different location to that of the cash. An example could be where your purchased securities are delivered to your custodian, but payment is made separately to the seller.

In the first example, the delivering custodian will send an MT542 instruction (delivery free of payment – DFoP) to the clearing system and the receiving custodian will similarly send an MT540 instruction (receive free of payment – RFoP). A payment instruction is not required as there is no countervalue.

In the second example, your custodian will send an MT542 and you will make a separate payment to the seller.

8.4.1 Settlement Instructions for Free of Payment

For comparison purposes, the free of payment instruction types for SWIFT, EB and CBL are shown in Table 8.9.

TABLE 8.9 Selection of FoP message types

	RFoP	DFoP	Comments
SWIFT message	MT540	MT542	
Euroclear Bank (EOC)			**EOC's system: EUCLID**
	01 F	02 F	EOC–EOC trade
	03 F	07 F	EOC–outside EOC
	03C F	07C F	EOC–CBL bridge trade
Clearstream Banking Luxembourg (CBL)	4F: RFP	5F: DFP	**CBL's system: Creation** CBL–CBL trade
	6F: RF	8D/81: DF	CBL–outside CBL
	4FCE:RF	5FCE: DF	CBL–EOC bridge trade

8.4.2 Where Settlement Takes Place

We saw in Chapter 6 that the securities are held centrally within a Central Securities Depository (CSD). The CSD holds and maintains records of ownership including changes in ownership. It is therefore within the CSD that settlement takes place, based on clearing information passed down from the associated clearing system (clearing house or CCP).

8.4.3 Settlement Conventions

Securities are expected to settle in full and straight away after the trade date. In reality, an amount of time is required for clearing and funding activities which results in a short time lag. On-exchange settlement conventions tend to be fixed, whilst off-exchange conventions can be more flexible (e.g. in Germany, on-exchange is T+2 and off-exchange can range from T+0 to T+40).

In general, the conventions are:

Eurobonds – T+3 (changed on October 2014 to T+2)

Equities – T+2

Government – T+1

Q&A

Questions

Please refer to the comparative tables for CSDs (Table CSD1,[3] pages 524–527) and answer the following questions:

1. Which of the three DVP models is most widely used?
2. What is the delivery lag (i.e. settlement convention) for the five Euroclear-owned domestic CSDs?
3. What is the delivery lag for government securities and equities in the USA?
4. Which markets have a T+2 delivery lag?

Answers

Table 8.10 provides the answers.

TABLE 8.10 Answers to the four questions regarding the comparative tables for CSDs

Question	Answer	Comments
1	There are 26 examples of DVP1	Plus 16 of DVP3 and 9 of DVP2
2	T+3	Sweden is T+3 for EUR and T+2 for SEK. UK's Crest is owned by Euroclear UK and Ireland

---

[3]BIS (online) "CPSS – Red Book statistical update" CPSS 116. Available from www.bis.org/publ/cpss116p2.pdf [Published December 2013, accessed Friday, 24 January 2014]

TABLE 8.10 *(Continued)*

Question	Answer	Comments
3	Government securities (NBES) T+1 Equities (DTC) T+3	Both can also settle on T+0
4	Belgium Canada Germany Hong Kong India Japan Korea Saudi Arabia Sweden Turkey	(NBB) (CDS) (CBF) (CCASS and CMU) (NSDL and CDSL) (JASDEC – DVP3 model) (KSD for equities traded on-exchange) (For bonds) (SEK) (Takasbank and MKK)

8.5 SETTLEMENT FAILS

8.5.1 Overview of Settlement Failure

Logically, there is no reason why transactions should fail, especially in an era when securities are generally:

- Fungible;
- Deeply liquid;
- Held centrally within a CSD/ICSD environment;
- Easily and electronically transferable.

However, in the pre-settlement, clearing phase of a transaction, any unmatched transactions will not and cannot settle. In addition, taking the four bullet points in turn, there can be exceptions, such as:

- It is possible to hold bearer securities in non-fungible form. This can slow the delivery process as specific certificates need to be identified before delivery can occur.
- Many markets insist on minimum amounts of issued securities to be made available. This helps to reduce the risk of illiquidity on any one issue of securities. A problem arises when securities are sold to investors who either are unable or unwilling to make their positions available for securities lending purposes. This reduces the liquidity.
- Centrally-held securities have been a long-held objective for the market; however, it is possible in some markets for securities to be held outside the CSD/ICSD infrastructure (e.g. physical certificates held by investors themselves).
- We will discuss how securities are held in Chapter 10 and we will see that some securities still require re-registration of ownership either before settlement can occur or at some time shortly afterwards.

Whilst these exceptional situations will rarely prevent a transaction from failing outright, they can add delays and costs to the process.

8.5.2 Why Transactions Fail to Settle

Settlement fails are considered to be inevitable in many markets and almost impossible to eliminate totally. According to the European CSD Association[4]:

- In March 2012, the settlement efficiency rate in Europe was 98.9% in value terms and 97.4% in volume terms.
- Among the 1.1% of transactions (by value) that fail to settle on time, most will settle the following day, with a settlement fail rate of less than 0.5% on the intended SD+1.

The ECSDA also noted that three markets (Greece, Romania and Slovenia) demonstrated a 100% efficiency rate. Three factors explained this rate:

1. The CSDs mostly settled on-exchange transactions that were pre-matched and directly input into the settlement system in full straight-through-processing mode.
2. Buy-ins are automatically triggered if a trade fails to settle (on SD in Slovenia and SD+1 in Greece and Romania). In addition, in Slovenia, OTC trades either settle on SD or are cancelled before the end of SD.
3. It was noted that Greece had 2.6% of the weighted average volume, Slovenia 0.09% and Romania 0.39%.

We will examine why transactions can fail to settle on the intended settlement date and what actions can be taken to resolve the problems.

Here is a list of possible reasons why transactions might fail:

- Processing problems – unmatched transactions;
- Sales – insufficient securities, inability to borrow or reverse repurchase;
- Purchases – insufficient cash, collateral or credit;
- Systemic issues.

We will consider these in turn.

Processing Problems   Operations staff should ensure that any unmatched instructions are investigated and resolved at the earliest opportunity, and certainly before the settlement date. The institution that is found to be at fault can expect an interest claim from its counterparty, as shown in the example below.

---

[4]*Source:* ECSDA (online) "2012 Statistical Exercise on Matching and Settlement Efficiency" dated 18 September 2012. Available from www.ecsda.eu/uploads/tx_doclibrary/2012_09_18_ECSDA_ Statistical_Exercise.pdf. [Accessed Thursday, 1 May 2014]

Example

Broker-dealer "A" (BD-A) purchased USD 5,000,000 BHP 2.125% bonds due in 2018 against payment of USD 4,934,236.11 from Broker-dealer "B" (BD-B) with intended settlement date today.

BD-A matched the instructions one day after the settlement date, when the transaction also settled. As BD-A caused the delay, it received an interest claim from BD-B.

Q&A

Question

If the interest claim was charged at 5.00%, how much interest would BD-B claim from BD-A?

Answer

The claim would be USD 685.31 (USD 4,934,236.11 × 5/100 × 1/360).

Sales/Deliveries   Settlement fails can occur if there are insufficient securities with which to make a delivery. Let's look at some examples.

Partial Settlement   BD-A has the following positions with GSK 1.5000% bonds due in 2017 (GSK):

- A depot position of USD 3,000,000 GSK that is AFD;
- A purchase of USD 2,000,000 GSK against payment of USD 2,050,576.00 from BD-B, intended settlement date today (RVP); and
- A sale of USD 5,000,000 GSK against payment of USD 5,130,040.00 to BD-C, intended settlement date today (DVP).

   Situation: We are informed that the purchase has failed and, as a result, the sale has also failed.

   Problem: Neither the sale proceeds nor the purchase costs have been credited/debited, leaving a net outstanding credit cash amount of USD 3,079,464.00. If the cash funding had been calculated on a fund-to-settle basis, this cash difference could have been allocated to another investment or been placed into the money market.

   Solution: The reactive solution would be to wait until the purchase settles to provide sufficient bonds to settle the sale. In any case, Operations should chase the seller, who might be waiting to receive the bonds from one of its purchases. The proactive approach would be for BD-A to contact BD-C and offer a partial delivery of the USD 3,000,000 bonds already held in depot.

BD-C is under no obligation to agree to this, but might do so if they require the bonds for another delivery and/or wish to maintain a good working relationship with BD-A.

Actions required: Assuming BD-C agrees to accept a partial delivery, the following actions should take place:

- Both counterparties cancel the original instructions for USD 5,000,000 GSK.
- Both counterparties agree with the new amounts and then input instructions for new, re-shaped instructions:
  - USD 3,000,000 GSK vs USD 3,078,024.00 cash, and
  - USD 2,000,000 GSK vs USD 2,052,016.00 cash.
- Both sets of re-shaped instructions will be matched.
- The USD 3,000,000 shape will settle, leaving the balance of USD 2,000,000 outstanding.
- There should be a full audit trail which tracks the re-shaping of the original USD 5,000,000 transaction into the two re-shapes (this helps the accounts and reconciliation functions to identify the new cash debit and credit amounts to be tracked).

It is quite possible for there to be more than one partial delivery, in which case the same re-shaping exercise must be completed. For example, BD-B might offer, say, USD 1,000,000 of the balance of USD 2,000,000 GSK to BD-A.

If BD-C does not agree to a partial delivery, BD-A might be able to borrow or "reverse repo" USD 2,000,000 GSK, for a fee, and fully settle the sale of USD 5,000,000 GSK bonds. We cover the topic of securities lending and borrowing and repo/reverse repo in Chapter 12: Securities Financing.

Bilateral Netting BD-A has the following positions with EDF 4.6000% Bonds due 2020 (EDF):

- A zero depot position of EDF;
- A purchase of USD 5,000,000 EDF against payment of USD 5,605,350.00 from BD-B, intended settlement date today (RVP); and
- A sale of USD 5,000,000 EDF against payment of USD 5,615,350.00 to BD-B, intended settlement date today (DVP).

Situation: We are informed that the purchase has failed and, as a result, the sale has also failed.

Problem: Neither the sale proceeds nor the purchase costs have been credited/debited, leaving a net outstanding credit cash amount of USD 10,000.00. This situation is not as serious as in the example regarding partial settlement above.

Solution: The reactive solution would be to wait until the purchase settles to provide sufficient bonds to settle the sale. In any case, Operations should chase the seller, who might be waiting to receive the bonds from one of its purchases. The proactive approach would be for BD-A and BD-B to agree to net out the bond positions and cash amounts.

Actions required: The following actions should take place:

Both counterparties cancel the original instructions for USD 5,000,000 EDF.

BD-B pays USD 10,000.00 cash to BD-A's bank account.

There should be a full audit trail which tracks the changes to the bond and cash delivery/payment amounts.

Please note that this bilateral netting refers to the same pair of counterparties and the same security.

Gridlock Scenario

Situation: One particular security, for example ABC securities, has been traded amongst several broker/dealers, as noted in Figure 8.2.

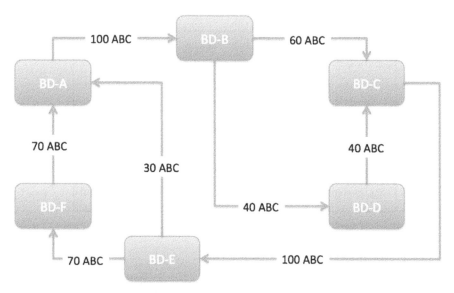

FIGURE 8.2 Gridlock with ABC securities transactions

Problem: If we assume that not one of the counterparties has any ABC securities in depot, then all of the transactions in Figure 8.2 will fail. When BD-C chases BD-B and BD-D, the responses will be the same, i.e. the counterparties are waiting to receive ABC from elsewhere. The same will happen when BD-B chases BD-A, and so on. Furthermore, the counterparties are only aware of the transaction they are involved with (so BD-E is only aware of its purchase of 100 ABC from BD-C and its sales of 70 ABC to BD-F and 30 ABC to BD-A).

Solution (A): This situation presents a problem in a gross settlement environment unless all the counterparties can somehow ascertain each other's situations. One counterparty might attempt to borrow from another institution that is unconnected with this gridlock. For example, if BD-A could borrow 100 ABC from an institutional investor or other broker/dealer, then the gridlock would unravel thus:

(a) BD-A delivers 100 ABC to BD-B;

(b) BD-B now has 100 ABC and delivers 60 ABC to BD-C and 40 ABC to BD-D;

(c) BD-D now has 40 ABC and delivers 40 ABC to BD-C;

(d) BD-C now has 100 ABC and delivers 100 ABC to BD-E;

(e) BD-E now has 100 ABC and delivers 70 ABC to BD-F and 30 ABC to BD-A;

(f) BD-F now has 70 ABC and delivers 70 ABC to BD-A;

(g) BD-A now has 100 ABC and returns 100 to the institutional investor or other broker/dealer.

Solution (B): In a multilateral netting system where the clearing system novates the transactions, the system has oversight of each and every participant's depot balance, credit situation and outstanding transactions. If the situation was appropriate, the clearing system would mark each transaction as settled, passing debits and credits to the securities and cash accounts for each participant. See Figure 8.3 for a simplified solution.

You Buy	Cash	You Sell	Cash
100	(300.00)	(400)	1,280.00
200	(640.00)	(500)	1,550.00
300	(930.00)		
You deliver	300 ABC	You receive	960.00 Cash

Your Counterparty is the CCP (through novation)

FIGURE 8.3   Multilateral netting

Purchases/Receipts   We have concentrated on the seller's lack of securities as being the prime cause of settlement fails. Even if the seller does have availability, if the buyer has insufficient cash or access to credit or financing, the settlement could still fail. Problems with cash are generally due to funding mistakes and are resolved quickly.

The purchaser's cash-related problems will result in interest claims from the seller, with the interest rate charged being close to the typical overdraft rate for the currency at the time of the claim.

Example

If your sale of USD 10,000,000 France Telecom 2.500% bonds due in 2015 against payment of USD 10,886,500.00 failed to settle due to the purchaser's cash problem, you would claim interest from the intended settlement date up to the date the transaction actually settles.

Q&A

Question

How much would you claim if the interest rate was 9.5% p.a. for 1 day (actual/360)?

Answer

The claim would be USD 2,872.83 (USD 10,886,500.00 × 0.095 × 1/360).

We have seen that settlements might fail for a variety of reasons, either due to the lack of availability of an asset or an operational error. Fails are usually corrected within a day or so.

Failed sales or deliveries can be managed by borrowing securities or using "reverse repo"; we cover the topic of securities financing in Chapter 12. In the sequence shown in Figures 8.4, 8.5 and 8.6, we see how a failed or failing transaction can be completed.

Fails management (a)   Suppose investor A sells bonds to a broker/dealer, who then resells the bonds to investor B. The delivery and payment obligations of the three parties on the morning of the settlement date are shown with dotted lines in Figure 8.4.

FIGURE 8.4   Fails management (a)

Fails management (b)   If A fails to deliver the securities to the broker/dealer, this will cause the broker/dealer to fail B. To cure its fail to B, the broker/dealer can either borrow or "reverse repo" the securities from investor C and deliver the borrowed/reversed securities. Actual settlement of securities and cash are shown with solid lines in Figure 8.5. The original failed transaction between A and the broker/dealer is shown with dotted lines.

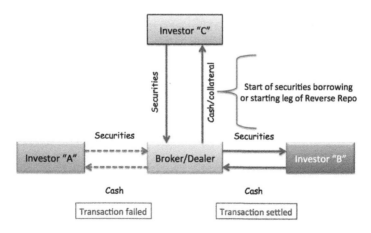

FIGURE 8.5   Fails management (b)

Fails management (c)   Investor A finally delivers the securities to the broker/dealer who can now terminate the securities borrowing/reverse repurchase agreement with investor C (Figure 8.6).

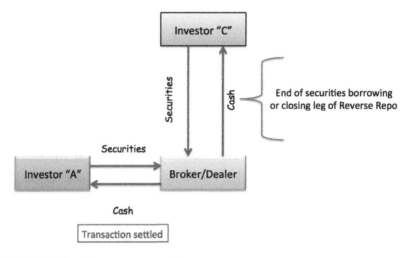

FIGURE 8.6   Fails management (c)

We have seen that settlement fails can be resolved without too much trouble; they are not deliberate and usually occur because the seller does not have the securities available for delivery. Alternatively, the purchaser may not have sufficient cash or available credit. There are means by which counterparties can work around fails (e.g. through partial settlement or by using bilateral letting).

From time to time, however, it may not be possible to resolve settlement fails other than by enforcing a chain of events that will enable the transactions to settle not with the original counterparty but through a third party. These events are known as *buy-ins* and *sell-outs* and can either be invoked at the discretion of the affected counterparty or compulsorily by the relevant stock exchange.

Buy-Ins   A buy-in occurs when a seller is unable to deliver securities (see Figure 8.7). The buyer needs to find a market participant who not only has the required inventory but is also willing to sell the securities to the buyer. This market participant can be, for example, another dealer that ordinarily would be a competitor to the buyer, but in this instance is willing to act as a buy-in agent.

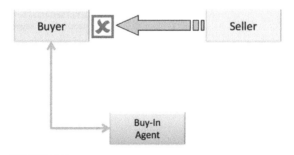

FIGURE 8.7   Buy-in

The buyer will be expected to warn the seller of its intention to buy the securities in and, after a predetermined amount of time, will execute the buy-in. If the reason for the settlement failure was that the seller was also awaiting securities from a previous purchase, then it might appear that the seller also has to arrange for a separate buy-in.

Indeed, there could be a longer chain of failed transactions, and to overcome the requirement for multiple buy-ins, the original buy-in is "passed on" from the first seller's counterparty along the chain to the counterparty that effectively caused the problem.

In Figure 8.8 you can see that counterparty "A" (the original buyer) has bought in securities against counterparty "B" using an appropriate buy-in agent. For its part, counterparty "B" has passed the buy-in notice on to its counterparty "C", who, in turn, has passed it on to the final failing seller, counterparty "*n*".

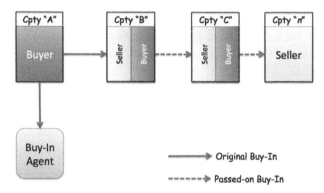

FIGURE 8.8   Buy-in pass on

Let us consider two examples of a buy-in; in the first of these we will see how the Eurobond market handles a buy-in and in the second, we'll see how a buy-in is automatically initiated in the Singapore market.

Eurobonds   For member firms of the International Capital Market Association (ICMA), the decision to apply a buy-in rests with the buyer (and with the seller for a sell-out). If the buyer is in no particular rush to receive the securities, it might take the decision to wait until the seller is able to deliver. Under ICMA's rules, Section 450: Buy-In,[5] member firms have the right to issue the seller with a buy-in notice. The notice warns the seller that if it fails to deliver the securities within five business days, the buy-in will be executed. The buy-in agent must be an ICMA reporting dealer but must not be affiliated with the buyer.

In the event that the original transaction fails to settle, the buy-in is executed at the best market price for guaranteed delivery on the normal settlement date convention (i.e. T+3). The original buyer is entitled to claim the difference between the original purchase price and the bought-in price from the original seller (as shown in Table 8.11).

---

[5]Refer to the ICMA Rule Book at http://icmagroup.org/Regulatory-Policy-and-Market-Practice/Secondary-Markets/ICMA-Rule-Book (available to ICMA members and subscribers only).

TABLE 8.11   Buy-in price difference

	Price	Counterparty
Original purchase	101.6875	Seller
Bought-in price	101.8125	Buy-in agent
Difference	*0.1250*	*Charged to the seller*

Singapore   In Singapore, we have an example of a buy-in process that is automatically initiated by the local clearing system. For transactions executed on the Singapore Stock Exchange (SGX), the local clearing system (central depository)[6] will automatically execute a buy-in if the seller has insufficient securities available for delivery by noon on the intended settlement date (T+3).

The buy-in price starts at the higher of two minimum bids above the previous day's closing price or any of the transacted/bid prices available one hour before the buy-in commences. In addition, the CDP charges a processing fee and brokerage on each buy-in contract.

Sell-Outs

Q&A

Question

If a seller has sufficient securities to deliver, why might that transaction fail?

Answer

The only possible answer is that the buyer does not have the cash or credit to pay for the securities. Ordinarily, the buyer would correct that situation at the earliest possible opportunity.

But what if the buyer is unable to arrange suitable financing? In this case, there might be a strong possibility that the buyer is close to defaulting. Were this to be the case, the transaction would remain unsettled and the seller would not receive the cash proceeds from its sale. The ICMA rules make provision for this situation in Section 480: Sell-out. Section 480 is essentially a mirror of Section 450 except that partial deliveries are not acceptable and there is no provision for a pass-on (see Figure 8.9).

---

[6]The CDP is a wholly owned subsidiary of the SGX (www.sgx.com) and is also a central counterparty (CCP).

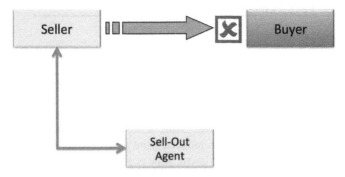

FIGURE 8.9   Sell-out

Systemic Issues   The majority of transactions that fail on the intended settlement date will eventually settle within a day or two, whether it takes the trading counterparties to intervene (e.g. arrange a partial settlement) or the clearing system to automatically initiate a buy-in.

Situations can arise, however, which have led to chronic fails, as the following two examples demonstrate (one involved government securities and the other foreign exchange).

SITUATION 1

In 1974 the German central bank, the Bundesbank, placed Bank Herstatt into liquidation just after several banks had released payments of the Deutschmark side of approximately USD 1 billion of USD/DEM foreign-exchange transactions. By the time New York opened, Bank Herstatt had ceased operations and the US dollar side of the transactions had failed to settle. It was to be another thirty years before payment-versus-payment was introduced through the establishment of CLS Bank, the "continuous link settlement" system.

SITUATION 2

By the time the two World Trade Center buildings had been destroyed on 11 September 2001, trading in government securities was already well under way. As a result of the destruction of trading records and connectivity problems in the Manhattan district, there was almost USD 440 billion worth of government security settlement fails within the Fixed Income Clearing Corporation's records.

Although the outstanding sales balance reduced to USD 90 billion by the end of the first week, it took several more weeks for the market to reconcile the positions. The US Treasury increased an existing issue by 50% to USD 12 billion to help ease the situation.

8.6   THE MOVE TO SHORTER SETTLEMENT CYCLES

8.6.1   Background

We saw that settlement efficiency is mostly very high, especially in Europe according to the ECSDA research noted above. This, together with the removal of physical certificates and the settlement of most asset classes by book-entry transfer, begs the question as to why we need several days to process transactions when, in theory, it should be possible to settle any transaction on the trade date. This "trade date settlement" idea has one big advantage: counterparty risk exposure is reduced from several days (e.g. T+3) to intra-day and consequently the need for margin/collateral to be posted for the duration of the open trade status is reduced. Systemic risk is also reduced, with fewer open trades waiting for SD in a pending queue.

There are some challenges, however:

- The institutional client part of the industry may not be willing or able to replace legacy systems with state-of-the art, fully automated STP systems that can cope with shorter processing cycles.
- As we will see in Chapter 10: Custody and the Custodians, there are long, time-consuming communication chains from the client to the foreign CSD.

Although not announced as such, the "compromise" option is to reduce the settlement cycle across the globe to T+2. This provides sufficient time for processing (with the timing and communication issues noted above) and reduces the counterparty risk exposure to a more acceptable level.

8.6.2   Project Status

Europe   The European Commission announced its intention to introduce T+2 settlement in all 27 Member States with effect from 1 January 2015. Germany already operates under T+2, with other markets typically under T+3. Government securities tend to be under T+0 or T+1.

Asia   Like Europe, the settlement is fragmented. Unlike Europe, there is no regulatory driver for harmonisation; nevertheless, there is a reasonable degree of harmonisation with markets such as India, Hong Kong, Korea and Taiwan already operating under T+2 and other markets such as Australia, China, Singapore and Japan under T+3. As other regions and markets migrate to T+2, it is probable that T+3 markets will follow.

USA   In 1995, the USA shortened its settlement cycle from T+5 to T+3, with plans for a further move to T+1 shelved in the early 2000s. In April 2014, the DTCC announced that it would support a move to T+2 with a three-year implementation timescale.

Canada   Currently on a T+3 cycle, Canada has no immediate plans other than to observe what the USA does.

International Securities   The international bond business is OTC and, as such, does not directly come under the European Commission's requirements to move to T+2. One of the key provisions of the new regulations is the requirement: "… that the intended settlement date for transactions in transferable securities which are executed on regulated markets, MTFs or OTFs shall be (T+2). But this does not apply to transactions which are negotiated privately but executed on trading venues, nor to transactions which are executed bilaterally but reported to a trading venue."[7]

To overcome the potential dual settlement date convention, ICMA's John Serocold stated that: "The emerging conclusion is that ICMA's Secondary Market Rules and Recommendations should be amended to provide for T+2 settlement in the absence of agreement to the contrary."[8] This moved occurred on 6 October 2014.

8.7 SUMMARY

In this chapter we have seen that settlement is the completion of any transaction. There are two types of settlement:

- Gross settlement, where individual transactions settle on a one-by-one basis. Whilst this means that transactions settle in the shape and size that they were executed, it does allow settlement to occur in real time.
- Net settlement, where a clearing system will net out deliveries and receipts, debits and credits across its clearing members' securities and cash accounts. In order for this to happen, the clearing system has to accumulate the deliveries and receipts over a period of time before netting can take place. This netting might only occur once in a day or several times throughout the day. The more frequently netting can occur, the more similar it becomes to real-time settlement.

One of the operational risks that can occur is *settlement risk*, where one half of the transaction settles (e.g. securities are delivered) and the other half of the transaction fails (e.g. payment is not made). To mitigate this risk, it is normal market practice for settlement to take place on a delivery versus payment (DVP) basis.

There are three so-called DVP models, as defined by the Bank for International Settlements' Committee on Payment and Settlement Systems:

- Model 1: Gross, simultaneous settlements of securities and funds transfers.
- Model 2: Gross settlement of securities transfers followed by net settlement of funds transfers.
- Model 3: Simultaneous net settlement of securities and funds transfers.

---

[7]*Source:* ICMA Quarterly Report §33 (2Q 2014) (online). Available from "Previous versions" tab at www.icmagroup.org/Regulatory-Policy-and-Market-Practice/Regulatory-Policy-Newsletter. [Accessed Wednesday, 9 April 2014]
[8]ibid.

Although DVP is the preferred method of settlement, there are occasions when this may not be appropriate (e.g. an investor is transferring his assets from one custodian to another without there being any change of beneficial owner). In this situation, the transfer will be made without any counter value, i.e. on a free-of-payment basis. FoP deliveries require greater operational oversight than DVP, because if the free deliveries are made to the wrong recipient, there is the risk that the deliverer may not get the assets back.

With securities it is expected that settlement is made in full shortly after the trade is executed. As a certain amount of time is required for the clearance and funding processing to take place, it is appropriate that the intended settlement date should be between one and three days after the trade date. In general terms, government securities tend to settle on T+1, Eurobonds on T+3 and equities around the T+2 to T+3 timespan.

Most transactions do settle on the intended settlement date, although for liquidity-related reasons some do fail to settle on time. Participants can either wait or make arrangements to manage the settlement fails through one or more of the following techniques:

- Partial settlement;
- Bilateral netting;
- Multilateral netting through a securities settlement system;
- Invoking buy-ins or sell-outs, as appropriate.

Fails can occur on rare occasions through systemic problems and these can require intervention from a central authority (e.g. a government issuing a new tranche of securities) or the introduction of a new centralised system (e.g. the foundation of CLS Bank in the foreign exchange industry).

Finally, the move to universal T+2 settlement is gaining momentum, especially in Europe, with the USA and Canada some way behind and the rest of the world somewhere in between.

CHAPTER 9

Derivatives Clearing and Settlement

9.1 INTRODUCTION

We described some of the derivative products in Chapter 2: Financial Instruments and noted that these products can be subdivided into two types:

- Exchange-traded derivatives (ETDs)
- Over-the-counter derivatives (OTCDs).

This distinction guides us in terms of the post-transaction processing. Until recently, ETD transactions were cleared through a central counterparty (CCP) and OTCD transactions were processed between the trading counterparties. Today, it is expected that OTCD transactions are also cleared centrally; a change that has come about through regulatory pressure.

Central counterparties (CCPs) support trade and position management across a wide range of asset types including securities and derivatives. The concepts for derivatives clearing are similar to those for securities; however, there are some significant differences, including:

- After securities transactions have been cleared, settlement occurs in the appropriate central securities depository. There is no such concept of a CSD for derivatives. Cleared derivatives positions are managed by the CCP and non-cleared positions by the two counterparties involved.
- Securities are settled in full shortly after trade execution. This means that the counterparty risk between buyer and seller (in a clearing house context) is extinguished on settlement and, likewise, between buyer and CCP together with seller and CCP.
- Derivatives contracts remain open until they are either closed out or are exercised. This results in a credit exposure for the duration of the open status of the contract. This risk is mitigated in part by the use of margin (cleared derivatives) and collateral (non-cleared).

The purpose of this chapter is to show you the ways in which ETDs and OTCDs are cleared. By the end of this chapter you will:

- Understand how cleared and non-cleared derivatives are processed;
- Be able to calculate margin calls for cleared derivatives;
- Be able to calculate collateral requirements for non-cleared derivatives;
- Understand why the regulators introduced changes to the post-trade processing of OTCDs.

9.2 REGULATORY CHANGES

9.2.1 Background

For some time before the 2007/2008 financial crisis, large volumes of bilateral OTC derivatives transactions: " … had created a complex and deeply interdependent network of exposures that ultimately contributed to a build-up of systemic risk. The stresses of the (2007/2008 financial) crisis exposed these risks: insufficient transparency regarding counterparty exposures; inadequate collateralisation practices; cumbersome operational processes; uncoordinated default management; and market misconduct concerns."[1]

In September 2009, the G20 heads of state, together with other invited heads of state and international organisations, held the third "Summit on Financial Markets and the World Economy" in Pittsburgh, Pennsylvania.

From this Summit, the G20 agreed to reform the OTC derivatives markets with the objectives of improving transparency, mitigating systemic risk and protecting against market abuse. The key elements in achieving this reform were that:

1. All standardised OTC derivatives should be traded on exchanges or electronic platforms, where appropriate.
2. All standardised contracts should be cleared through central counterparties (CCPs).
3. OTC derivatives contracts should be reported to trade repositories.
4. Non-centrally cleared contracts should be subject to higher capital requirements.[2]

Margin requirements were added to the reform programme by the G20 in 2011.

We will address these four elements in Section 9.4 on cleared derivatives.

9.2.2 Financial Stability Board (FSB)

The FSB has assumed responsibility for the oversight of this project and collates information from its member countries regarding progress made.

---

[1]Quote from the Financial Stability Board (online) "OTC Derivatives Reforms Progress" dated 2 September 2013. Available from www.financialstabilityboard.org/publications/r_130902a.pdf. [Accessed Tuesday, 22 April 2014]

[2]As note 1.

The FSB publishes regular progress reports on its website (www.financialstability-board
.org). In its summary of the 7th Progress Report, dated 8 April 2014, the FSB noted that:

- There has been continued progress in the implementation of OTC derivatives market
reforms.
- Market participants' use of centralised infrastructure continues to increase.
- Overall, there are clear signs of progress in the implementation of trade reporting, capital
requirements and central clearing.
- Implementation of reforms to promote trading on exchanges or electronic trading platforms, however, is taking longer.[3]

9.2.3 Reform Requirements

There are five areas that require market reforms. These are:

1. Trade reporting;
2. Central clearing;
3. Capital requirements;
4. Margin requirements;
5. Exchange and electronic platform trading.

In order to meet these reform objectives a number of practical issues have emerged, including
the concern that: " … regulatory requirements are implemented in a consistent and coordinated
fashion across jurisdictions, given the highly cross-border nature of OTC derivatives markets".[4]

As you will have observed in the FSB's summary (see above), progress has been taking place
across all five areas. As at the end of March 2014, progress could be summarised as follows:

1. **Trade reporting:** The majority of FSB member jurisdictions have trade reporting requirements either partially or fully in effect. Full implementation for all jurisdictions is expected
by the end of 2014.
2. **Central clearing:** China, Japan and the USA have implemented clearing mandates. Other
jurisdictions have adopted regulation (Korea and India), proposed regulation (Mexico
and Russia), published assessments (Australia), commenced authorising CCPs (EU) or
adopted legislative framework for further reforms (Hong Kong).
3. **Capital requirements:** Capital requirements are now effective in more than half the
member jurisdictions, with only Indonesia yet to make any preliminary studies (although
this is anticipated during 2014). Almost all other jurisdictions should have requirements
in effect by the end of 2014.[5]

---

[3]*Source:* FSB (online). "OTC Derivatives Market Reforms – Seventh Progress Report on Implementation" dated 8 April 2014. Available from www.financialstabilityboard.org/publications/r_140408.pdf.
[Accessed Wednesday, 23 April 2014]
[4]ibid.
[5]For detailed information on capital requirements, see Basel Committee on Banking Supervision (online)
"Basel III: A global regulatory framework for more resilient banks and banking systems." (December

4. **Margin requirements:** The framework for non-centrally cleared derivatives was finalised by the BCBS-IOSCO[6] in September 2013, but only the EU and the US have taken any regulatory steps towards implementation. Several jurisdictions anticipate taking steps toward implementation closer to 2015.
5. **Exchange and electronic platform trading:** China, Indonesia and the US now have regulations requiring organised platform trading, with other jurisdictions having the legislative frameworks in place.

9.3 EXCHANGE-TRADED DERIVATIVES CONTRACTS

9.3.1 Introduction

Unlike securities transactions where settlement occurs shortly after the trade date, derivatives transactions can remain open for much longer periods of time, ranging from a few months to many years. This time delay exposes participants to credit risk and this can include "counterparty-to-counterparty" and "clearing system-to-counterparty" exposures.

There are two generally accepted methods of mitigating this credit risk exposure depending on whether the derivatives transaction was exchange-traded (ETD) or OTC (OTCD). ETD transactions are typically margin-based and OTCD transactions tend to be collateralised. Now that there is the regulatory requirement to centrally clear OTCD transactions, it is perhaps more correct to refer to derivatives transactions that are either cleared through a CCP or non-cleared. Figure 9.1 shows the situation before the enactment of Dodd–Frank (USA) and EMIR (European Union) and Figure 9.2 shows the situation afterwards.

FIGURE 9.1   Clearing before regulatory intervention

2010, revised June 2011). Available from www.bis.org/publ/bcbs189.pdf. [Accessed Wednesday, 5 February 2014]

[6]Basel Committee on Banking Supervision/International Organization of Securities Commissions (2013) (online) "Margin requirements for non-centrally cleared derivatives". Available from http://www.bis.org/publ/bcbs261.pdf. [Accessed Tuesday, 22 April 2014]

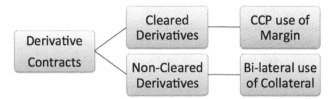

FIGURE 9.2 Clearing after regulatory intervention

Please note that some standardised OTCDs such as some interest rate swap products have been centrally cleared for a number of years.

9.3.2 Derivatives Exchange and Clearing System

For exchange-traded contracts such as futures and options, the derivatives exchange and the clearing system may be either part of the same organisational structure or separate organisations. In either event, there will be good links between the exchange and the clearing system.

Members of an exchange may also be members of the clearing system. If not, they must have a non-clearing agreement with a clearing member. Figure 9.3 shows the relationships between the exchange, the clearing system and their respective members.

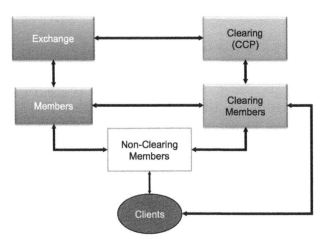

FIGURE 9.3 Exchange-traded derivatives

Members of an exchange can also be members of a clearing system and they submit trade details to the clearing system for clearance. If they only clear transactions for their own business, they are known as *clearing members* (or *individual clearing members*). If they also clear the business of non-clearing members (see below), they are known as *general clearing members* (GCMs).

9.3.3 Give-Up Agreements

Certain exchange members may choose not to be either CMs or GCMs. These organisations are known as *non-clearing members* (NCMs) and will either clear through a GCM or "give-up" the trade to a CM or GCM.

Where a client, its executing-only broker (the NCM) and CM/GCM have entered into a tri-party Give-Up Agreement, trades executed by the NCM are transferred (or given up) to the client's CM/GCM. In this way, the client is free to use multiple execution-only brokers but consolidate all the trades with the single CM/GCM, as shown in Figure 9.4.

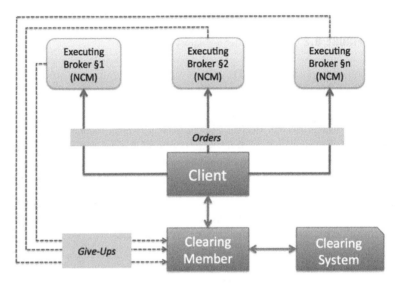

FIGURE 9.4   Give-Up Agreements

The Give-Up Agreement (its full name is the International Uniform Brokerage Execution Services Agreement) was developed by the Futures Industry Association (www.futuresindustry .org) in 1995. Later, in 2007, the FIA implemented the Electronic Give-Up Agreement System (EGUS) which: "decreased the time (taken) to execute ... (a Give-Up) Agreement from an average of 39 days to 2 days".[7]

9.3.4   Clearing Process

As soon as a CCP has registered a transaction, novation occurs and the CCP becomes the counterparty to the buyer and to the seller. To limit and protect itself from the default risk of a clearing member, the CCP collects margin on all open positions. Clearing members' margin positions are calculated either once a day or several times intra-day.

There are two types of margin: initial margin and variation margin.

1. **Initial margin (IM):** A deposit called by a CCP on all net open positions and returned when the positions are closed. Assets used for IM delivery can be eligible securities and cash.
2. **Variation margin (VM):** A member's profit or loss on open positions calculated daily using closing mark-to-market prices. VM is treated either as realised (cash amounts are credited/debited to members' accounts) or unrealised profits or losses.

---

[7]*Source:* Futures Industry Association (online) "Give-Up Projects/EGUS". Available from www.futures-industry.org/egus.asp. [Accessed Thursday, 27 February 2014]

9.3.5 Margin Calculations

There are two approaches that can be taken: we can calculate margin for a single position or for a collection (or portfolio) of positions in similar classes of derivatives.

The *single position approach* is straightforward and should help you to understand the basic principles involved. Let us consider a fictitious futures contract with the contract specifications given in Table 9.1.

TABLE 9.1 Interest rates future – contract specifications

Contract size	USD 100,000	Nominal value of the underlying asset (e.g. a government security)
Tick size	USD 10.00	Minimum price movement of 0.01% of the contract size
Initial margin	USD 2,000.00	per contract

The initial margin is the number of contracts multiplied by the IM amount per contract.

The variation margin is the difference in contract price multiplied by the tick size multiplied by the number of contracts.

Example

You open a futures position of ten contracts at a price of 138.00. The price of the contract closes on the trade day at 138.20. Using the contract specifications shown in Table 9.1, we can calculate the margin amounts shown in Tables 9.2 and 9.3.

TABLE 9.2 Initial margin

Number of Contracts	Initial Margin per Contract	Initial Margin	Debit/Credit to IM Account
10	USD 2,000.00	USD 20,000.00	Debit

TABLE 9.3 Variation margin

Number of Contracts	Opening Price	Closing Price	Tick Size	Variation Margin	Debit/Credit to VM Account
10	138.00	138.20	USD 10.00	USD 2,000.00	Credit

The total margin amount will be USD 18,000.00, as analysed in Table 9.4.

TABLE 9.4 Margin analysis

	Debit	Credit	
IM account	USD 20,000.00	USD 2,000.00	VM account
		USD 18,000.00	Bank account
	USD 20,000.00	USD 20,000.00	

Q&A

Question

Using the information in Table 9.1, what are the daily IM and VM balances for the following trades opened on Day 1 and closed out on Day 3?

Day 1

Opening purchase of 200 contracts @ 138.00

Closing price @ 138.07

Day 2

Sale of 150 contracts @ 138.12

Closing price @ 138.15

Day 3

Purchase 150 contracts @ 138.20

Closing sale of 200 contracts @ 138.18

Answer

By the close of Day 3, the initial margin account balance is zero and the variation margin account is USD 24,000.00 in credit. This credit balance represents the overall profit on the trades (see Figure 9.5).

Date	Direction	Contracts	Price	Closing Price	Initial Margin	Debit/ Credit	Variation Margin	Debit/ Credit
Day 1	Opening	0						
	Buy	200	138.00		$ (400,000.00)	Debit		
	Mark-to-Market	200		138.07			$ 14,000.00	Credit
	C/fwd	200			$ (400,000.00)	Debit	$ 14,000.00	Credit
Day 2	B/dwn	200	138.07		$ (400,000.00)	Debit	$ 14,000.00	Credit
	Sell	150	138.12		$ 300,000.00	Credit	$ 7,500.00	Credit
	Mark-to-Market	50		138.15			$ 4,000.00	Credit
	C/fwd	50			$ (100,000.00)	Debit	$ 25,500.00	Credit
Day 3	B/dwn	50	138.15		$ (100,000.00)	Debit	$ 25,500.00	Credit
	Buy	150	138.20		$ (300,000.00)			
	Sell (p/o 200)	50	138.18		$ 100,000.00		$ 1,500.00	Credit
	Sell (p/o 200)	150	138.18		$ 300,000.00	$ 100,000.00	$ (3,000.00)	Debit
	Closing	0			$ 0.00		$ 24,000.00	Credit
				Final Balances:	$ 0.00		$ 24,000.00	Credit

FIGURE 9.5 Answer to margin question

Here is an explanation of what happened throughout the three days:

Day 1: The IM calculation is 200 contracts × USD 2,000.00 = USD 400,000.00.
The position was opened at 138.00 and, at the close of business, revalued at 138.07. If the tick size is 0.01, there has been a gain of 7 ticks and the VM calculation is 200 contracts × 7 × USD 10.00 = USD 14,000.00.

Day 2: 150 contracts have been sold at 138.12. The profit is 5 ticks (138.12 − 138.07), amounting to USD 7,500.00, and USD 300,000.00 of the IM are credited (150 contracts × USD 2,000.00). Finally, the close of business price is 138.15, resulting in a profit of 8 ticks and a VM credit amounting to USD 4,000.00 (50 contracts × 8 ticks × USD 10.00).

Day 3: 150 contracts are purchased at 138.20 and the total position of 200 contracts then closed out at 138.18. Overall, on the IM account there will be a net credit of USD 100,000.00 [8] resulting in a final balance of zero. To calculate the VM on the closing trade of 200 contracts, you should compare the prices as follows:

(a) 50 (part of sale of 200) @ 138.18 against the brought-down balance of 50 @ 138.15 (profit of 3 ticks).

(b) 150 (balance of sale of 200) @ 138.18 against the purchase of 150 @ 138.20 (loss of 2 ticks).

The *portfolio position approach* considers the overall risk to a portfolio of derivative and/or securities and calculates a "worst case" loss that the portfolio might experience under different market conditions. These market conditions are altered by inputting changes to futures prices and, for options, implied volatility shift. The system used for this is the Standard Portfolio Analysis of Risk (SPAN) system, developed by the Chicago Mercantile Exchange[9] in 1988.

SPAN is widely used by many exchanges around the world, including Tokyo, London and Singapore.

9.3.6 Initial Margin – Eligible Assets

CCPs will accept suitable assets with an appropriate haircut to cover initial margin calls. The Chicago Mercantile Exchange's clearing system (CME Clearing) will accept a variety of assets, known as Acceptable Performance Bond Collateral, including those shown in Table 9.5.

---

[8] Refer to the last three entries in the Initial Margin column and the last entry in the Debit/Credit column of Figure 9.5.

[9] Regarding terminology, the CME refers to "performance bond" for initial margin and "settlement variation" for variation margin.

TABLE 9.5   CME – acceptable performance bond collateral

Asset Class	Description	Haircut Applied
Cash	USD	0%
Cash	AUD, GBP, CAD, CHF, EUR, JPY, NZD, NOK and SEK	5%
Letters of credit (LCs)	LCs for performance bond (capped at 40% of core requirement)	0%
US Treasuries	T-bills, T-FRNs, T-notes, T-bonds TIPS and T-strips	Depends on time to maturity, T-bonds: 0–1y @ 1% 1–3y @ 2% 3–5y @ 3% 5–10y @ 4.5% 10–30y @ 6%
Foreign sovereign debt	Canada, France, Germany, Japan, Sweden and UK	Depends on time to maturity, notes and bonds: 0–5y @ 6% 5–10y @ 7.5% 10–30y @ 9% >30y @ 10.5%
Foreign sovereign debt	Canada, France, Germany, Japan, Sweden and UK	Discount bills: 0–5y @ 5%
US equities	Shares from S&P 500 Index	30%
Gold	Physical	15%

Source: CME Group (online) "Acceptable Performance Bond Collateral for Futures, Options, Forwards, OTC FX and Commodity Swaps". Available from www.cmegroup.com/clearing/files/acceptable-collateral-futures-options-select-forwards.pdf. [Accessed Thursday, 17 April 2014]

9.4   CLEARED OTC DERIVATIVES CONTRACTS

Following on from the requirement to report OTC derivatives contracts to a trade repository, there is the requirement to clear these contracts through a CCP. Clearing through a CCP is not a new concept; for example, LCH.Clearnet's SwapClear has been clearing OTC interest rate swaps since 1999.[10]

Figure 9.6 illustrates the relationships in the trade and post-trade OTCD environment.

---

[10]*Source:* LCH.Clearnet (online) Swapclear: "… clears swaps in 17 currencies: USD, EUR and GBP out to 50 years, JPY to 40 years, AUD, CAD, CHF and SEK to 30 years, NZD out to 15 years and the remaining 8 currencies out to 10 years. It also clears Overnight Indexed Swaps (OIS) out to 30 years in EUR, GBP and USD and out to 2 years in CHF and CAD." Available from www.lchclearnet.com/swaps/swapclear_for_clearing_members. [Accessed Thursday, 17 April 2014]

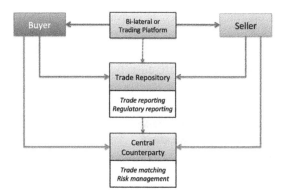

FIGURE 9.6   Trade and post-trade OTCD environment

9.4.1   Types of OTC Derivative that are Cleared Centrally

Although the expectation is that all types of OTCD are cleared centrally, the reality is that the more complex and complicated types are not currently offered for clearing. According to the FSB's April 2014 OTC derivatives markets reform progress report[11], certain types such as swaptions and caps/floors are not offered for clearing whilst other types such as interest rate swaps have a high proportion that are cleared centrally (see Figure 9.7).

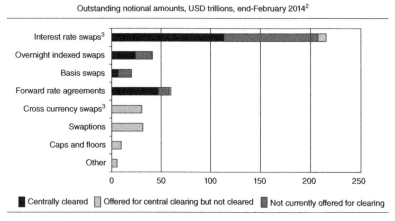

FIGURE 9.7   Central clearing of interest rate OTCDs
Sources: DTCC; various CCPs; FSB calculations.
[1]Estimate based on public trade repository information and present central clearing offerings of ASX, BM&F BOVESPA, CCIL, CME, Eurex, HKEx, JSCC, KDPW, LCH.Clearnet, Nasdaq OMX, SCH and SGX. Amounts cleared include transactions subject to mandatory clearing requirements in certain jurisdictions and those cleared voluntarily. [2]Adjusted for double-counting of dealers centrally cleared trades amounts reported to DICC by 16 large dealers. [3]Includes vanilla (>98% of total) and exotic (<2% of total) products as classified by DTCC.

---

[11]*Source:* Financial Stability Board (online) "OTC Derivatives Market Reforms – 7th Progress Report on Implementation". Available from www.financialstabilityboard.org/list/fsb_publications/page_1.htm. [Accessed Tuesday, 22 April 2014]

Furthermore, a higher proportion of OTC credit derivatives are not currently cleared centrally (see Figure 9.8).

Central Clearing of OTC Credit Derivatives[1]

Outstanding notional amounts, USD trillions, end-February 2014[2]

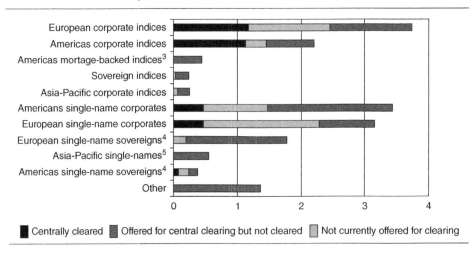

FIGURE 9.8   Central clearing of credit OTCDs

Sources: DTCC; various CCPs; FSB calculations.
[1]Estimates based on public trade reapository information and present central clearing offerings of CME, Eurex, ICE Clear Credit, ICE Clear Europe, JSCC and LCH Clearnet. Amounts cleared include transctions subject to mandatory clearing requirements in certain jurisdictions and those cleared voluntarily. [2]Adjusted for doublecounting of dealers' centrally cleared trades and triple-counting of clients' centrally cleared trades; amounts reported to DTCC for all counterparties. [3]Includes both residential and commercial mortage-backed indices. [4]Includes sovereigns, sub-sovereign states and state-owned enterprises. [5]Includes corporates, sovereigns and state-owned enterprises for Japan, Asia ex-Japan and Australia/NZ.

9.4.2   Trading Platforms

In Section 9.2, we saw that one of the key market reforms was the trading of OTCDs on exchanges or electronic trading platforms, and that China, Indonesia and the USA have regulations in place that require organised platform trading. There are several types of trading platform, as defined by IOSCO,[12] and these are shown in Table 9.6.

---

[12]*Source:* IOSCO (online) "Report on Trading of OTC Derivatives" dated February 2011. Available from www.iosco.org/library/pubdocs/pdf/IOSCOPD345.pdf. [Accessed Wednesday, 23 April 2014]

TABLE 9.6 Trading platforms

Platform Type	Definition	Definition Proposed By:
Broker crossing system (BCS)	A facility to assist the execution of client orders against other client orders and/or house orders.	European Commission
Designated contract markets (DCM)	DCMs are boards of trade (or exchanges) that operate under the regulatory oversight of the CTFC (USA).	CTFC (USA)
Multilateral trading facility (MTF)	An MTF is a multilateral system, operated by an investment firm or a market operator, which brings together multiple third-party buying and selling interests in financial instruments in a way that results in a contract.	MiFID (EU)
National securities exchange (NSE)	An NSE is a securities exchange that has registered with the US Securities and Exchange Commission under Section 6 of the Securities Exchange Act of 1934.	SEC (USA)
Organised trading facility (OTF)	An OTF is a facility or system operated by an investment firm or a market operator which, on an organised basis, brings together buying and selling interests or orders relating to financial instruments, whether discretionary or non-discretionary, excluding facilities or systems already regulated as a regulated market, MTF or systematic internaliser.	MiFID (EU)
Regulated market (RM)	An RM is a multilateral system operated and/or managed by a market operator, which brings together or facilitates the bringing together of multiple third-party buying and selling interests in financial instruments – in the system and in accordance with its non-discretionary rules – in a way that results in a contract, in respect of the financial instruments admitted to trading under its rules and/or systems, and which is authorised and functions regularly and in accordance with further provisions outlined in MiFID.	MiFID (EU)
Swap execution facility (SEF) or security-based SEF (SB-SEF)	An SEF (or SB-SEF) is a trading system or platform in which multiple participants have the ability to execute or trade swaps (or security-based swaps) by accepting bids and offers made by multiple participants in the facility or system, through any means of interstate commerce.	Dodd–Frank Act (USA)
Systematic internaliser (SI)	An SI is an investment firm which, on an organised, frequent and systematic basis, deals on its own account by executing client orders outside a regulated market or a multilateral trading facility.	MiFID (EU)

Source: IOSCO (February 2011).

9.4.3   Trade Repositories

We have seen that all OTCD contracts should be reported to a trade repository (TR). This is the means through which regulators can access trade information as part of their management of systemic risk. The result is that reported trades will become as transparent as ETD transactions.

According to the FSB's 7th Progress Report, most of the member jurisdictions have operational TRs, with only a few not yet operational, as shown in Table 9.7.

TABLE 9.7   Operational trade repositories

OTCD Type	Commodity	Credit	Equity	Foreign Exchange	Interest Rate
Operational	18	18	17	20	22
Not yet operational	1	2	1	2	1
Total:	**19**	**20**	**18**	**22**	**23**

Source: FSB (April 2014).

Most TRs are unique to one particular market (e.g. SAMA in Saudi Arabia) and others are more global. An example of this is the DTCC Global Trade Repository (USA), which has a presence in six markets (see Table 9.8).[13]

TABLE 9.8   DTCC Global Trade Repository

Name of Trade Repository	Market
DTCC Data Repository (U.S.) LLC	USA
DTCC Derivatives Repository Ltd., London	Europe
DTCC Data Repository (Japan) KK	Japan
DTCC Derivatives Repository Ltd., London	Hong Kong
DTCC Data Repository (Singapore) PTE Ltd	Singapore
DTCC Data Repository (Singapore) PTE Ltd	Australia

9.4.4   Central Counterparties

Trade matching and risk management take place at the appropriate CCP, in much the same way as with ETDs above.

According to the FSB's 7th Progress Report, operational CCPs are as shown in Table 9.9.

TABLE 9.9   Operational CCPs

OTCD Type	Commodity	Credit	Equity	Foreign Exchange	Interest Rate
Operational	12	6	7	9	16
Not yet operational	0	1	0	4	0
Total:	**12**	**7**	**7**	**13**	**16**

Source: FSB (April 2014).

---

[13]*Source:* DTCC (online) Data and Repository Services. Available from www.dtcc.com/en/data-and-repository-services.aspx. [Accessed Thursday, 1 May 2014]

No single CCP clears all five types of OTCD; some clear only one type and others clear up to four (see Table 9.10 for examples).

TABLE 9.10 Types of OTCD cleared by CCPs

OTCD Type	Commodity	Credit	Equity	Foreign Exchange	Interest Rate
Cantor Clearinghouse (US)				Yes	
ICE Clear Credit (US)		Yes			
BM&F BOVESPA (Brazil)	Yes		Yes	Yes	Yes
Nasdaq OMX Stockholm (Sweden)	Yes		Yes	Yes *(not yet operational)*	Yes

Source: FSB (April 2014).

All the CCPs are licensed in their own jurisdiction, with some being licensed, registered or holding an exemption in foreign jurisdictions (see Table 9.11 for examples).

TABLE 9.11 Local/foreign registered CCPs

CCP	Location	Authorities With Which CCP is Licensed
ASX Clear (Futures)	Australia	Local: ASIC and RBA Foreign: None
CME Clearing Europe	UK	Local: BoE Foreign: None
Eurex Clearing	Germany	Local: BaFIN and Bundesbank Foreign: BoE (UK) and pending with CFTC (US)
LCH.Clearnet Limited	UK	Local: FCA and BoE Foreign: CFTC (US), ASIC and RBA (both Australia) plus exemptions in Canada, Germany and Switzerland.

Source: FSB (April 2014).

9.5 NON-CLEARED OTC DERIVATIVES CONTRACTS

Non-centrally cleared (also known as bilaterally cleared) OTC derivatives transactions are executed either between buyer and seller or on a trading platform. The main difference from cleared OTCD transactions is that these OTCD contracts are processed and risk managed between the two trading counterparties. These are legally binding contracts that need to be fully documented.

9.5.1 Documentation

Trading between any two parties is covered under a set of documents, as shown in Table 9.12.

TABLE 9.12 Documentation

Document	Description
Master Agreement	Published by the International Swaps and Derivatives Association (ISDA). The current version is the 2002 edition and it defines the terms and conditions under which both parties deal with each other. All transactions between the two parties are covered by this single agreement.
Schedule	Used to customise the Master Agreement including amendments and additional terms.
Confirmation	Confirmations are exchanged for each transaction and include relevant terms of the transaction.
Definitions	ISDA publishes a series of booklets, defining each type of derivative transaction, and user guides.
Credit Support Annex	An optional document, the CSA is used when both parties agree to use collateral to cover risk exposures.

Within the set of documents shown in Table 9.12 there are many variations, depending on the asset class of the derivative, the year the document was published and in which country the document applies. The International Swaps and Derivatives Association (ISDA), founded in 1985, has over 800 member institutions from 64 countries and has done much to improve the industry's operational structure, reduce counterparty credit risk and increase transparency.

There are six asset classes listed on the ISDA website:

- Credit derivatives/credit default swaps;
- Equity derivatives;
- Interest rate derivatives;
- FX derivatives;
- Energy, commodities, developing products;
- Structured products and others.

A variety of publications including definitions, confirmation templates, etc. can be found for each of these six classes. Please go to the Asset Classes section of the ISDA website (www2.isda.org/asset-classes) and familiarise yourself with some of the documentation available.

There is an extensive library and bookstore available on the ISDA website, parts of which are available for members only. The remaining parts are open for general inspection and are categorised as shown in Table 9.13.

Please go back to the Bookstore section of the ISDA website (www.isda.org/publications/pubguide.aspx) and familiarise yourself with some of the documentation contained within the nine categories noted in Table 9.13.

TABLE 9.13 ISDA publications

Category	Examples of Documents
ISDA Master Agreement	Master Agreements (2002, 1992) plus MA user guides and MA translations.
ISDA credit support documentation	Credit Support Annexes (CSAs) in English and New York law versions, user guides, amendments to CSAs, the 2001 ISDA margin provisions and collateral documentation.
Cleared swap documentation	FIA-ISDA Cleared Derivatives Execution Agreement plus various addenda.
ISDA definitions and confirmations	Sub-categorised by product type: commodity/energy, equity, inflation, property index, credit, FX, interest rate and currency and miscellaneous documents.
ISDA operations and novation material	Novation definitions, best practice statements and user guides.
ISDA protocols/EMU and Euro material	Documentation relevant to the economic and monetary union in Europe (1997), Euro definitions (1998) and the introduction of the Euro (2001 Euro Protocol).
Regulatory documentation	Initiative documents relevant to Dodd–Frank (USA) and EMIR (EU).
Disclosure documents	Annexes from 2012 (plus 2013 updates) regarding disclosure relating to certain CTFC requirements.
FpML and miscellaneous ISDA documents	FpML user guides, index of terms, terms for escrow float transactions and a pre-confirmation trade notification template (2001).

It will be apparent from your review of the ISDA website just how much documentation is required in the OTC derivatives business. There is a high degree of focus in terms of product type, so organisations will only require the relevant documentation for their own business.

Q&A

Question

Now that you have examined the ISDA website, why do you think there is so much documentation?

Answer

Think back to what you know about financial instruments such as equities, bonds and exchange-traded derivatives. These instruments are all highly standardised, for example, shares can be transferable in lots of one share and bonds in lots of USD 1,000. Derivatives exchanges determine the contract specifications so that users of ETDs will know exactly

FINANCIAL MARKETS OPERATIONS MANAGEMENT

what the economic consequences of trading in, for example, 100 contracts of the Long Gilt Future (March 2015) at a price of 123.45 are.

With OTCDs there is not the same degree of standardisation and therefore there is a greater risk that transaction details might be omitted or mistaken. Traditionally, each OTCD transaction was bilaterally agreed between the buyer and the seller and processed/risk managed by them for the term of the contract. This resulted in the need for confirmations to state the exact terms of the trade down to the level of stating the day-count convention applicable to the trade.

It is relevant to note that many of the so-called "vanilla" OTCDs do have a degree of standardisation and this provides a good opportunity to move away from bilaterally cleared to centrally cleared processing.

9.5.2 Non-Cleared OTCD Processing

Due to the numerous types of OTCD and their complexities, space does not permit us to look at each of them in turn from an operational point of view. Rather, we will go through the overall process flows from trade capture to maturity, giving some examples along the way. Many of these processes are quite similar across the whole financial operations spectrum and we will concentrate on those that are particularly relevant to OTCD transactions.

9.5.3 Trade Capture

As soon as the trades are entered into the trade capture system (either automatically or manually), the details of each trade should be verified. This can be complicated, depending on the type of derivative being entered, and every detail from the trade ticket (term sheet) should be carefully checked. Remember that these are bespoke transactions and not standardised like ETD or cash market products.

If we compare the trade details of a forward rate agreement (FRA) with an option (Table 9.14), we can see that the terminology can differ.

TABLE 9.14 Options vs FRAs

	Option	FRA
Trade direction	Hold (buy) or write (sell)	Buy or sell
Quantity	Number of contracts	Notional amount
Asset	Underlying single name or basket or index	Currency of the notional amount
Key dates	Trade date Expiry date(s)	Trade date Effective date Settlement date FRA period (term)

TABLE 9.14 *(Continued)*

	Option	FRA
Option style	European American Asian Bermudan Knock-in and Knock-out Quanto Composite Digital	N/A
Option type	Call or put	N/A
Cost/price	Premium	Interest rate (fixed)
Settlement	Cash settled or physical delivery of the underlying	Discounted difference between fixed interest rate and reference rate (floating) calculated on the notional amount

In its annual Operations Benchmarking Survey 2013,[14] ISDA noted that the most common errors across the five product categories[15] were caused by:

1. Payment date(s)/termination date.
2. Miscellaneous fees.
3. Counterparty names.

9.5.4 Confirmation

Counterparties can initially affirm the key economic details of their trades with each other before sending outgoing confirmations, chasing and reviewing incoming confirmations or investigating and reconciling confirmation discrepancies. A confirmation provides a more detailed view of a transaction at one point in time and should be sent as soon as possible.

In order to standardise the confirmation format, the ISDA has prepared a set of templates. Examples available on the ISDA's Bookstore include an eight-page confirmation of a non-deliverable cross-currency interest rate swap transaction and eighteen forms, of similar length, covering confirmations for the various types of equity-based transaction.

---

[14]*Source:* ISDA (online) "ISDA Operations Benchmarking Survey 2013" published April 2013. Available from www2.isda.org and search "surveys". [Accessed Friday, 26 April 2013]
[15]Interest rate, Credit, Equity, Currency options and Commodity.

With the notable exception of equity derivatives, confirmations are sent electronically (see Table 9.15).

TABLE 9.15   Confirmations

Derivative Type	Electronically Eligible		Not Electronically Eligible
	Electronically Confirmed	Not Electronically Confirmed	
Interest rate	86%	7%	7%
Credit	98%	0%	1%
Equity	30%	10%	60%
Currency options	69%	15%	16%
Commodity	66%	20%	13%

Source: ISDA Operations Benchmark Survey 2013.

Electronically transmitted confirmations are usually all sent by T+1, with non-electronically transmitted confirmations all sent by T+6 to T+10. The average number of business days for which confirmations are outstanding tends to be in the region of 0.3 to 1.6 days late, with the notable exception of equity-based (6.1 days).

9.5.5 Settlement

Depending on the derivatives contract, a settlement action may or may not take place. Some examples are shown in Tables 9.16, 9.17 and 9.18.

TABLE 9.16   Settlement actions for an FRA

Forward Rate Agreement	Term Sheet	Action Required
Notional amount	USD 10,000,000	
Deal type	Dealer buys 3 × 9 FRA	
Trade date	Today	Book trade and confirm details with counterparty
Settlement date	In three months' time	*Two days prior to SD, observe reference rate, calculate discounted amount of interest receivable or payable. Prepare payment or pre-advice instructions*
Maturity date	In nine months' time	
Contract period	A six-month period starting in three months' time	
Reference rate	Six-month BBA USD LIBOR	

TABLE 9.17 Settlement actions for an OTC option

OTC Options	Term Sheet	Action Required
Trade date	Today	Book trade and confirm details with counterparty
Option type	Call	
Option style	Bermudan with exercise opportunity every Wednesday by close of business. Holder's choice to exercise; physical delivery.	*Every Wednesday, observe share price. If price is > break-even (USD 10.00), your dealer can exercise the option. Settlement will be for regular settlement: 10,000 shares DVP USD 90,000.00.*
Expiry	10 weeks' time	
Deal type	You hold 100 contracts of a single name equity (each contract = 100 shares)	
Premium	USD 1.00 per share	On T+1, pay premium of USD 10,000 to writer.
Strike price	USD 9.00 per share	

TABLE 9.18 Settlement actions for a bi-laterally cleared interest rate swap

IRS Bilaterally Cleared	Term Sheet	Action Required
Notional	CCY 10,000,000	
Term	5 years	
Fixed	5% p.a. payable annually	
Floating	Six-month benchmark rate + 50 bp receivable semi-annually (Act/365)	
Trade date	Today	Book trade and confirm details with counterparty. Observe 6m interest rate.
Effective date	T+2	
Reset dates	Every six months – 2 days	*Observe 6m interest rate for next reset period.*
Payment dates (fixed)	Every 12 months	*Pay interest of 500,000.00*
Payment dates (floating)	Every six months	*Receive interest at previous reset rate plus 50 bp*

9.5.6 Collateral

Unlike ETDs and cleared OTCDs, where a CCP assumes the credit risk through novation and calls initial margin plus variation margin as appropriate, bilaterally cleared OTCDs expose both buyer and seller to credit risk throughout the duration of the contract. A 30-year, bilaterally cleared interest rate swap (IRS) would have a 30-year credit exposure.

If we consider a single IRS transaction, on the trade date the value of the floating leg would equal the value of the fixed leg. Thereafter, one leg would be worth more or less than the other, thus creating an exposure for one of the counterparties. Consider a seven-year interest rate swap on a notional amount of GBP 20 million, as shown in Table 9.19. You will observe that the NPVs differ.

TABLE 9.19   Interest rate swap

Interest Rate Swap	Terms	
Notional amount	GBP 20,000,000	
Duration	7 years	
Fixed rate payer	Client	@ 1.5% payable annually
Floating rate receiver	Big Bank	6-month LIBOR
Net present value of fixed interest payments	GBP 1,946,691	
Net present value of floating interest receipts	GBP 2,124.937	

Q&A

Question

Which counterparty has the exposure in Table 9.19?

Answer

Big Bank has the exposure and is therefore at risk if the client defaults. Why? It is because the client owes this difference to Big Bank (see Table 9.20).

TABLE 9.20   Big Bank's exposure to its client

NPV of client's payments	GBP (1,946,691.00)
NPV of Big Bank's receipts	GBP 2,124,937.00
Difference	GBP 178,246.00
In favour of:	Big Bank

In the example above, if the client paid/delivered assets to Big Bank with a value of GBP 178,246, then there would be no exposure from one party to the other. We refer to this payment or delivery as *collateral*, and collateral is used as a risk-management tool in order to reduce counterparty risk across many different activities, including the non-centrally cleared OTC derivatives business.

According to the ISDA Margin Survey 2014,[16] 90.2% of all non-centrally cleared (i.e. bilateral) transactions were subjected to collateral agreements of one form or another (Credit Support Annexes, margin provisions or other types of agreement). Just 9.8% were not subjected to any agreement of any type.

Collateral consists of cash and securities, with cash being the largest proportion. The breakdown of collateral received and delivered, as noted in the ISDA Margin Survey 2014, was as shown in Table 9.21.

TABLE 9.21   ISDA Margin Survey 2014

Collateral Type	Received 2014 (2013)	Delivered 2014 (2013)
Cash	74.9% (79.5%)	78.3% (78.7%)
Government securities	14.8% (11.6%)	18.2% (18.4%)
Other securities	10.3% (8.9%)	3.4% (2.9%)

At any moment in time, any two counterparties will have an exposure to each other, with the exposed party calling for collateral to mitigate any credit risk. Whilst it might be prudent to move collateral on a daily basis, it will certainly be an operational burden to do so. In order to overcome this, arrangements can be made so that collateral is only moved under pre-specified conditions.

Initial Margin/Independent Amount   When two parties enter into an agreement (Credit Support Annex), they will agree either that one party deposits an initial margin with the other party or assigns a percentage of the total trade notional to the other party. This is known as an *independent amount*.

For example, Party "A" might deliver USD 5 million of collateral to Party "B" (initial margin). Alternatively, Party "A" might assign, say, 8% of the total trade notional amount to Party "B". If the amount was USD 50 million, then the IA would be USD 4 million.

How would both parties decide who had to pay the IM or IA to whom? Credit analysis will reveal which party is the most credit risky in relation to its counterparty. If Party "A" was rated BB+ and Party "B" AAA, the latter would be more likely to be exposed and would call for IM or an IA to be assigned.

Threshold   A threshold is one example of a collateral parameter and represents the amount of unsecured exposure that is allowed by either party before collateral is called. The amount of threshold would be agreed based on credit exposure analysis by both parties.

Minimum Transfer Amount (MTA)   An MTA is the amount of collateral that is required before any collateral is delivered. For example, if the MTA is USD 1 million and the required collateral is, say, USD 800,000, then no delivery will be made. However, should the required collateral increase to USD 1,240,000, then a delivery would take place.

---

[16]*Source:* ISDA (online) "ISDA Margin Survey 2014" published April 2014. Available from www2.isda.org and search "surveys". [Accessed Monday, 14 April 2014]

Rounding Convention   To avoid making payments for odd amounts, both parties can agree to round amounts up or down to, say, the nearest USD 100,000. If we take the example in the Minimum Transfer Amount section above, the required collateral delivery of USD 1,240,000 would be rounded down to USD 1,200,000.

In September 2013, the Basel Committee on Banking Supervision (BCBS) and the Board of the International Organization of Securities Commissioner (IOSCO) jointly published a policy framework that established minimum standards for margin requirements for non-centrally cleared OTCDs.

The requirement to exchange initial margin with a threshold of up to EUR 50 million will commence from 1 December 2015 and the requirement to exchange variation margin will become effective on the same date.

9.5.7   Event Monitoring

If you refer back to Tables 9.16, 9.17 and 9.18 in Section 9.5.5, you will have noticed that some of the items listed in the "Action Required" column were in italic typeface. This was to denote that these actions should occur once or several times throughout the term of the transaction. Operations staff must be constantly aware of the possibility that external events can and do have an impact on open transactions. These include:

- Interest rate resets on interest rate swaps;
- Corporate action events on underlying assets such as equities and bonds;
- Exercise events on futures and options (exercise might be optional or automatic);
- Foreign exchange rates;
- Public holidays and non-business days (a working day in one market might be a non-working day in another);
- Trigger events, such as bankruptcy, that might result in an obligation with predefined characteristics being delivered against a credit default swap contract.

9.5.8   Reconciliation

Reconciliation covers two areas:

1. **Cash (nostro) reconciliation:** We cover this topic in Chapter 14.
2. **Portfolio reconciliation:** Matching all trades (and resolving reconciliation breaks) between two separate counterparties.

Portfolio Reconciliation   Organisations are expected to reconcile their portfolios of bilateral OTCD transactions with each of their counterparties. The objective is to make sure that the portfolio contents of both counterparties agree as of any particular date. Furthermore, portfolio reconciliation helps to ensure that collateral disputes do not occur and, if they do, to allow the collateral function to investigate.

Due to the non-standardised nature of OTCD transaction details, both counterparties need to establish reconciliation procedures to ensure that they have a consistent set of information on which to perform a reconciliation. The ISDA published the minimum field requirements in its *Minimum Market Standards for Collateralised Portfolio Reconciliation* in January 2010.[17]

The minimum fields contained in a data file should include those shown in Table 9.22.

TABLE 9.22 Portfolio reconciliation minimum data requirements

Field	Description
Your legal entity name	Your name (and legal entity identifier – LEI).
Counterparty legal entity name	Counterparty's name (and LEI).
Your trade ID	Your trade ID should be recognisable by your counterparty.
Counterparty trade ID	Counterparty's trade ID should be recognisable by you.
Group IDs (if multi-leg)	Common ID that enables a counterparty to relate a set of multiple bookings back to a single trade ID.
External match ID	An externally applied ID for trades confirmed electronically.
Product ID/name	This includes an asset class and product, e.g. – Interest rate derivatives/FRA; – Equities/options; – Credit derivatives/single name; – Foreign exchange/forward; – Commodities/energy natural gas swap.
Dates	Trade date/start date/end date/exercise date.
Mark-to-market (MTM)	Revaluation price and currency.
Current notional/quantity	Original and current notional amount or quantity.
Trade currency	Initial currency of the transaction and settlement currency if applicable.

Source: ISDA Minimum Market Standards (2010).

Reconciliation breaks might be due to timing issues (one party transmits its portfolio before its counterparty has a chance to transmit its own) or there might be genuine breaks where there are trade booking differences or valuation differences.

9.6 SUMMARY

There are two main types of derivative: exchange-traded derivatives and OTC derivatives. We can subdivide derivatives into their underlying asset classes:

- Credit derivatives;
- Equity derivatives;
- Interest rate derivatives;
- FX derivatives;

---

[17]Refer to ISDA (online) Excel spreadsheet. Available from www2.isda.org/functional-areas/ infrastructure-management/collateral and selecting "January 20, 2010 Portfolio Reconciliation Minimum Market Standards". [Accessed Monday, 28 April 2014]

 ▪ Energy, commodities and developing products;
 ▪ Structured products and others.

ETD products are transparent to the industry, highly standardised and designed by the appropriate exchange. ETD transactions are dealt on-exchange and cleared through a central counterparty (CCP) which novates each transaction. This novation replaces the original counterparty risk exposures with bilateral exposures between the CCP and each counterparty. In order to manage this risk, CCPs charge their clearing members initial and variation margin (in addition to other financial buffers).

By contrast, OTCD products were tailored to suit the counterparties, traditionally opaque, complex and often complicated. Transactions were executed off-exchange by bilateral agreements between buyer and seller. Transactions were processed/managed by the two counterparties to any transaction and may or may not have been collateralised.

OTCDs were therefore regarded by the regulators as being highly risky, especially as transactions were not usually reported to the regulators. This situation has been changing over recent years and especially after the 2007 global financial crisis and the collapse of several market participants, most notably Lehman Brothers. We now have a situation where the OTCD is changing:

 ▪ Transactions should be dealt on a trading platform (bilateral negotiation still occurs). This is making the OTCD look like an ETD.
 ▪ All transactions must be reported to a trade repository which holds the "golden copy" of each transaction.
 ▪ All OTCD transactions should be cleared centrally. This works well for the more standardised type of OTCD – types that the CCPs are comfortable handling. The more complex, complicated OTCDs are still processed by the counterparties concerned. This is making the OTCD look like an ETD.
 ▪ OTCD transactions that are non-centrally cleared (i.e. bilaterally cleared) are mostly collateralised, with cash and government securities being the predominant class of collateral.
 ▪ Counterparties are expected to reconcile their portfolios with each other on a regular basis.

The changes in the OTC derivatives business are very much "work in progress" and regular progress reports are published by the Financial Stability Board on its website (www.financialstabilityboard.org/list/fsb_publications/index.htm). The latest progress report § 7 was published on 8 April 2014.

Custody and the Custodians

10.1 INTRODUCTION

Part Three of the book will take you through the post-settlement environment of safekeeping, asset servicing and asset optimisation.

We have seen in previous chapters that securities are generally no longer certificated; previously certificated securities tend to be either dematerialised or immobilised and newly issued securities might be represented by a single (global) certificate. This move has certainly helped to ensure that clearing and settlement are straightforward, as sales and purchases are represented by debits and credits across a securities account. We have also noticed that clearing systems, whether in the form of a clearing house or a central counterparty, play an important role. This leaves us with the question of how the securities are held in a safe and secure environment.

In much the same way that clearing and settlement take place centrally, so does the safekeeping (or custody) of securities. Securities issued in one particular domestic market will be held by the relevant local central securities depository. In this chapter we will therefore look at the relationship between the investor (i.e. the beneficial owner), the CSD and the intermediaries that sit between the investor and the CSD.

By the end of this chapter you will:

- Be able to define "custody";
- Understand the forms in which securities are issued and the impact on their safekeeping;
- Know what a nominee is and how it can be used by the custodians;
- Appreciate the relationships between the beneficial owner, a local custodian, a global custodian and the CSD/ICSD;
- Understand the relationship between beneficial owner and custodian together with the products and services that are available.

10.2 CUSTODY

10.2.1 What is Custody?

Q&A

Question

How would you define "custody"?

Answer

At its basic level, custody is the safekeeping of securities and other asset classes. An example of this might be a legal representative keeping his client's physical certificates in the office safe.

At the other extreme, a bank can offer additional services over and above safekeeping. This would include asset servicing (e.g. corporate actions), asset optimisation (e.g. securities lending) and offering typical banking-related services such as foreign exchange and cash management.

A beneficial owner that only invests in his own market will use a locally based custodian; if he invests globally, he might use either a number of local custodians (one in each market) or a global custodian.

10.2.2 Forms of Securities

There are two forms of securities. From a securities issuer's point of view, it either has to know or wishes to know who the owners of the securities are. In this case, the issuer (or more likely a third party appointed by the issuer) records the owners' details on a register. We refer to these asset types as *registered securities*.

By contrast, if the issuer is not obliged to know who the owners are, then it might issue securities that are in bearer form. In this case, ownership details are not required and will therefore not need to be recorded on a register. We refer to these asset types as *bearer securities*.

Registered and bearer securities display certain characteristics that need to be considered from an operational point of view. Table 10.1 shows the characteristics of registered securities and Table 10.2 those of bearer securities.

TABLE 10.1 Registered securities

Registered Securities	Certificated	Non-Certificated
Ownership	Ownership evidenced by "name-on-register" (held by issuer's agent) plus the name is noted on the certificate.	Ownership is only evidenced by "name-on-register" (held by issuer's agent).

TABLE 10.1 (*Continued*)

Registered Securities	Certificated	Non-Certificated
Issuer's agent	Known as a registrar or transfer agent.	
Change of ownership	Change of ownership is recorded by the registrar/transfer agent. Certificates are issued for increases in ownership (e.g. purchases) and cancelled for decreases (e.g. sales).	Change of ownership is recorded by the registrar/transfer agent.
Loss of certificate	A replacement can be obtained from the registrar for a fee plus a letter of indemnity.	Not applicable.
Communication from issuer to investor	Through registrar who maintains the list of investors (information "pushed" to investor).	

TABLE 10.2 Bearer securities

Bearer Securities	Certificated	Non-Certificated
Ownership	No evidence of ownership on certificate. Ownership is evidenced by investor (or his agent) holding the certificate. Alternatively, a depository can hold 100% of an issue on behalf of its participants.	CSD maintains records of participants' holding as a result of settlement results received via the clearing process.
Change of ownership	Seller delivering certificate to buyer.	CSD amends records to reflect change.
Loss of certificate	Not possible to obtain a replacement.	Not applicable
Communication from issuer to investor	Issuer does not know its investors. It must therefore publish any communication and rely on the investor seeing it (information "pulled" by investor).	

10.2.3 Ownership Transfer – Bearer Securities

In any securities transaction, ownership is transferred from the seller to the buyer. If we use a shopping analogy, the goods that you purchase belong to you and the cash that you pay belongs to the shopkeeper. I hope that you will agree that this is the case; but what makes it so? What evidence is there to prove that you do own the goods that you have purchased (and the shopkeeper owns the cash)?

As your name will not be noted on the goods, the only evidence that you are the owner is that these goods are under your control, i.e. in your shopping bag. If questioned by a third party (e.g. a security guard), you can demonstrate that you have purchased the goods by showing the till receipt. Your purchased goods are analogous to securities that are in bearer form. You will have noticed that the transfer of ownership was straightforward and only required the shopkeeper to hand over the goods to you.

It is no different for the cash side of the transaction. The cash has been placed in the till and a receipt issued to the purchaser. Neither you nor the shopkeeper will have written your names on the cash; again, cash is a bearer asset and is also fungible in nature. Fungibility occurs when one unit of an asset is exactly the same as another unit of the same asset, e.g. a one euro coin is the same as any other one euro coin. Indeed, a EUR10 note is the same as ten one euro coins.

For bearer securities, transfer of ownership in a certificated environment is the delivery by the seller to the purchaser. In an un-certificated environment, transfer of ownership is achieved by debiting the seller's securities account and crediting the buyer's securities account.

10.2.4 Ownership Transfer – Registered Securities

The situation is slightly different for registered securities, as evidence of legal ownership rests with the issuer (or its registrar/transfer agent) and any change of ownership must be advised to the issuer. So, whilst a transaction for a registered security is no different from that for a bearer security, there is an extra step in the process that needs to be considered.

If we continue with our shopping analogy, say you had purchased some computer software and had paid for it in the expected manner. Once you have loaded the software onto your computer, you might be expected to register the software with the publisher. This usually involves entering your personal details and an activation code containing an alphanumeric character sequence. In effect, you have told the software publisher that you are the licensed owner/user of that software. In a registered securities context, you have told the issuer of the securities that you are now the owner of the securities. Unlike the software analogy, in order for the buyer to take ownership, the seller has to surrender ownership. This is done through a legal document known as a *stock transfer form* (STF). The STF authorises the issuer's registrar to reflect the change of ownership on the share register. The seller completes the top half of the form and the buyer the bottom half.

On the share register, the entries shown in Table 10.3 would be made for a sale of 500 shares.

TABLE 10.3 Share register entries

Owner	Existing Holding	Increase	Decrease	New Holding
Seller	1,500		−500	1,000
Buyer	2,000	500		2,500
Totals:	3,500	500	−500	3,500

The same principle applies for un-certificated registered securities; entries over the share register remain the same. The main difference is that there is no requirement to surrender share certificates and complete the stock transfer form as above. Instead, once the transaction has been settled, the securities settlement system electronically informs the registrar of the change of ownership. This electronic advice replaces the stock transfer form.

To summarise, depending on market practice, owners of registered securities can either hold physical securities with their names recorded on the issuer's share register or statements from the issuer denoting the quantity of securities owned.

Investors with securities registered in their own names have a direct stake (share) in the issuer. This type of ownership enables the issuer to communicate directly with the investors.

Operational complications can arise if the owner decides to ask a third-party custodian to hold their securities on their behalf. This will not be a problem for bearer securities but will be for registered securities, as the following examples illustrate:

- The owner wishes to sell some or all of his holding. The owner will request his broker to execute the sale and request his custodian either to deliver the physical securities or electronically transfer the securities to the broker. If the securities are in physical form, this will require a stock transfer form to be completed by the owner and delivered to his custodian. This can take time and might lead to a delay in the settlement process.
- The issuer sends a communication to the owner and requires a response. This communication will be sent to the owner at the address recorded on the register. The custodian will not be aware of this and may not be in a position to help the owner if a problem arises.
- If the owner has a problem (e.g. a dividend has not been received), he has to contact the issuer. His custodian may not be able to investigate on his behalf, as the issuer would only recognise the owner and not the custodian.

From these three examples you might correctly assume that the custodian will have operational issues when holding securities for owners that are registered in the owners' own names. There are alternative ways that owners can hold their securities:

1. Re-register the securities in the name of the custodian.
2. Re-register the securities in the name of a nominee managed by the custodian.

We will look at these in turn below.

10.3 HOLDING SECURITIES

10.3.1 Register in the Custodian's Name

If the owner decides to re-register his securities in the name of his custodian, legally he is surrendering ownership to that custodian. Now the issuer communicates directly with the custodian and no longer with the original owner. From an operational point of view, this change would enable the custodian to settle and administer the securities. It only requires a single instruction/communication with the owner rather than potentially several which the above examples might require.

The biggest risk for the owner, however, is that the custodian is now the legal owner of the securities and if the custodian were to default, it might be difficult or impossible to demonstrate that the custodian's customer was, in fact, the legal owner.

What is required is the separation of legal ownership from beneficial ownership. Where the owner's name is on the shareholder register, both types of ownership are combined. The objective is to enable the owner to retain beneficial ownership and the custodian to obtain legal ownership. This is where the concept of a nominee account comes in.

Having stocks recorded in the investor's own name at the central securities depository is uncommon, but not impossible, in most countries. There are some exceptions, such as in Singapore, where most local brokerage accounts require investors to have their own account at the central depository (CDP), or in the UK, where the process of having a personal account at CREST is straightforward, if rarely done by most investors.

10.3.2 Nominee Account

A nominee company is a legal entity in its own right, with its own share capital, Memorandum and Articles of Association together with a Company Secretary. In essence, a nominee company is no different from any other type of company and is legally separate from the custodian. This distinction is important because, in the event of the custodian defaulting, the nominee company remains as a going concern.

The Company Secretary and the authorised signatories will be members of staff of the custodian. The nominee company cannot itself default because it does nothing: it does not lend money, it does not invest, it does not take risk, etc. All that a nominee company is established to do is to act as a "flag of convenience", which, in this context, means that it acts as the legal owner of securities with its name recorded on the shareholder register.

In terms of legal ownership, therefore, securities registered in the custodian's name have the same legal status as securities registered in the name of the nominee company. The big difference is the separation of the custodian's risk of default.

Using a nominee company enables the custodian to keep safe and administer its customers' securities to its maximum efficiency. The custodian's customer retains beneficial ownership and therefore receives dividends in the usual way, albeit paid by his custodian rather than the issuer. The customer does, however, lose the direct relationship with the issuer that they would have had had their own name been recorded on the shareholder register.

What name should the custodian give its nominee company? To avoid any potential legal confusion, it is usually not a good idea to have the name of the custodian contained within the name of the nominee company. For example, when the author worked for Barclays Bank International in the 1970s, the branch address was 29 Gracechurch Street, London EC3. The branch operated a nominee company: "29 Gracechurch Street Nominees Limited" and customers' registered securities would have been registered in this name.

There are two ways in which a nominee company's name can be used:

1. Omnibus (pooled) account.
2. Segregated (designated) account.

Omnibus (Pooled) Account   In an omnibus account structure, all the customers' securities are registered in the name of the custodian's nominee company, for example, Wharfedale Nominees Limited, as listed in Table 10.4.

TABLE 10.4   Omnibus nominee account

ABC, Ordinary Shares (registered in a single nominee name)		
Customer	**Customer Holding**	**Registrar Holding**
Customer 1	10,000	
Customer 2	15,000	
Customer 3	20,000	
Customer 4	25,000	
Customer 5	30,000	
Total:	100,000	100,000

The following points should be noted:

- All five customers beneficially own a total of 100,000 shares, with each customer's shares commingled within the omnibus account.
- The registrar has 100,000 shares recorded on its shareholder register, with the legal owner being the nominee company.
- If a dividend is paid by ABC of GBP 1 per share, the issuer's paying agent will pay the nominee company GBP 100,000 and the nominee company will apportion that single dividend payment across each of the customers' cash accounts in proportion to their holdings.
- If, for example, Customer 4 sells its holding of 25,000 shares, there will be sufficient shares in the account from which to make a delivery.

Q&A

Question

As a custodian, what action would you take if (a) Customer 3 purchased 30,000 ABC shares and sold 100,000 ABC shares, and if (b) on the settlement date the purchase did not settle?

Answer

It would be technically possible to make a delivery of 100,000 ABC shares, as there are 100,000 shares recorded on the shareholder register. However, only 20,000 shares in this account are held to the order of Customer 3 and therefore the custodian's choices are either to wait until the purchase settles or to offer a partial delivery (20,000 shares) to the buyer.

It would therefore be wrong to deliver the 100,000 shares, as you do not have the authority from the other customers to deliver their shares. If the custodian did deliver the 100,000 shares and any one of the other customers decided to sell, then you certainly would not be able to make the delivery on behalf of the other customers on the intended settlement date.

The only exception to this would be if all the customers had agreed in writing to make their securities available for securities lending and borrowing purposes. In this case, the custodian would make the full delivery of 100,000 shares and pay a lending fee to the customers who have collectively loaned 80,000 shares.

Segregated (Designated) Account   As an alternative to the omnibus account structure, customers can request that their securities are held separately from other customers. In this case, the securities will be registered in several nominee names; the name of the nominee company remains the same, but a designation is added to that name. In this case, there will be many accounts held by the registrar (as opposed to a single account in the omnibus structure).

If we consider the five customers above, we might have the situation shown in Table 10.5.

TABLE 10.5   Designated nominee account

ABC, Ordinary Shares (registered in multiple nominee names)			
Customer	**Customer Holding**	**Name on Register**	**Registrar Holding**
Customer 1	10,000	Wharfedale Nominees Limited sub account: A01	10,000
Customer 2	15,000	Wharfedale Nominees Limited sub account: A02	15,000
Customer 3	20,000	Wharfedale Nominees Limited sub account: A03	20,000
Customer 4	25,000	Wharfedale Nominees Limited sub account: A04	25,000
Customer 5	30,000	Wharfedale Nominees Limited sub account: A05	30,000
Total:	100,000		100,000

The following points should be noted:

- All five customers beneficially own a total of 100,000 shares, with each customer's shares registered in the same nominee name but with a unique designated sub account.
- The registrar has five separate accounts holding each customer's shares and totalling 100,000 shares.
- If a dividend is paid by ABC of GBP 1 per share, the issuer's paying agent will pay the nominee company five amounts of GBP 10,000, GBP 15,000, GBP 20,000, GBP 25,000 and GBP 30,000 respectively and the nominee company will credit the dividend payments across each of the customers' cash accounts.
- If, for example, Customer 4 sells its holding of 25,000 shares, there will be sufficient shares in its designated account from which to make a delivery.

10.3.3   CSD Nominee

So far, we have considered the nominee concept from the point of view of the custodian (or indeed any firm such as a broker that might act in the capacity of a custodian). From the issuer's point of view, there will be many different names of nominee companies in both omnibus and designated forms.

There are markets where the CSD maintains a nominee name and registers securities in this name.

Street Names   In the USA, the CSD operates street name securities. In principle, street names are similar to nominee names, in that the street name is recorded on the share register and is the legal owner (with the investor as the beneficial owner). The name used by the Depository Trust & Clearing Company is "Cede and Co."

In countries where it is not possible to use a nominee account structure, investors might only be able to register their securities in either their own name or in the name of their custodian.

10.3.4 Safekeeping Methods – Summary

Figure 10.1 summarises the ways in which an owner/investor might hold their securities.

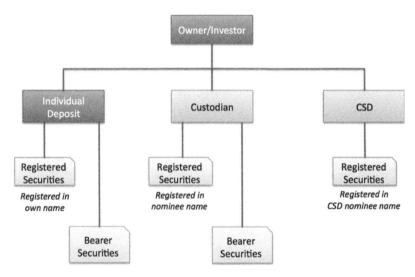

FIGURE 10.1 Holding securities – summary

10.4 THE CUSTODIANS

We have seen in a previous chapter that most markets support one or more central securities depositories. We therefore have a situation where the investor that owns securities has them ultimately held by a local/domestic CSD. In this section we will look at the intermediaries that stand between the investor and the CSD and explore the interrelationships between them in the following three circumstances:

1. Custody in a local market.
2. Custody in the global markets.
3. Custody in the EuroMarkets.

10.4.1 Custody in a Local Market

This custody model can be applied when the investor owns securities issued in his own market. The investor has three possible choices, he can:

(a) Appoint a custodian to act on his behalf regardless of how many brokers he chooses to use; or
(b) Hold his securities in his broker's participant account at the CSD; or
(c) It might be possible for the investor to open a direct securities account with the local CSD.

In the majority of cases, the custodian is likely to be a bank. If we take Canada as an example, a Canadian-based investor might use CIBC Mellon or RBC as their custodian bank. Figure 10.2 illustrates the investor–custodian–CSD links.

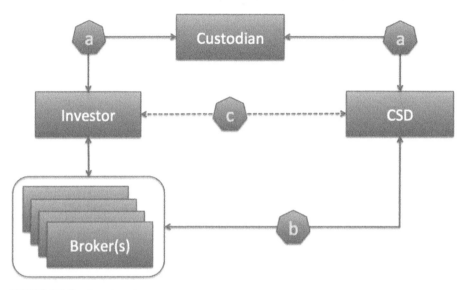

FIGURE 10.2   Local market

TABLE 10.6 (*Continued*)

	Advantages	Disadvantages
(b)	▪ The investor does not select or manage the custodian. ▪ The investor's broker(s) will send instructions to the CSD and receive reports from the CSD. ▪ The investor is free to purchase additional services from other providers.	▪ Problems might arise if the investor buys through one broker and sells the same securities through another. ▪ The investor will receive reports from multiple sources (if using more than one broker). ▪ The broker may not be willing to offer additional services.
(c)	▪ The investor has a direct relationship with the CSD. ▪ The investor uses the CSD for all transactions executed in the local market (regardless of the number of brokers used). ▪ The investor is free to purchase additional services from other providers.	▪ The investor will have to send delivery/payment instructions to the CSD. ▪ The CSD may only offer the basic custody service including income collection and corporate actions.

Although each of these three choices has its own advantages and disadvantages, it makes sense to make use of a local custodian and/or local brokers and/or the local CSD. These arrangements certainly work well when most, if not all, of the investor's securities are locally based.

What might the situation be if the investor has securities held, say, in two or three different markets? The investor could very well apply the same "local" model in each of the markets. The same advantages and disadvantages would apply but the time and effort required to manage these relationships would be more demanding. For example, there would be additional considerations, including:

- The need for appropriate legal agreements in each of the markets;
- The need to understand the workings of the markets (whilst similar, there will be technical differences);
- The potential difficulties in collating information from more than one market;
- Time zone problems and different deadlines;
- Possible language issues.

All of these will require the investor to actively manage different relationships. If these markets are located in the same region, there is an opportunity to consolidate the custodian situation, as shown in Table 10.7. Conversely, if these markets are located in different regions, then the local market model might be the most appropriate.

TABLE 10.7   Regional custody

Region	Countries
North America and the Caribbean	Bermuda, Canada, Mexico and USA
Latin America	Argentina, Brazil, Chile, Colombia, Costa Rica, Ecuador, Peru, Uruguay and Venezuela
Europe, Middle East and Africa (EMEA)	Countries on and close to the Greenwich Meridian, i.e. from Iceland to the UAE to South Africa
Asia-Pacific	From Russia and India to the west of the region through China, Indonesia, Malaysia, Singapore, etc. to Japan and South Korea to the east of the region. This region might also include Australia and New Zealand; if not, see below.
Australasia	Australia and New Zealand

In the situation where the investor happens to be based, for example, in Brazil and chooses to invest in a few of the other Latin American countries, he might choose a Brazilian custodian that has links to the custodians in the other countries, as shown in Figure 10.3.

FIGURE 10.3   Local markets in the same region (the brokers have been removed for reasons of clarity)

In this scenario, the investor maintains a single relationship with his local custodian. The Brazilian custodian, in the role as a regional custodian, maintains links with the local CSD in Brazil and the foreign CSDs in Chile and Ecuador.

10.4.2   Custody in Global Markets

Now we can consider an institutional investor that is globally invested. Its choices, as we have seen above, might be to:

- Appoint a local custodian in each and every market that it invests in. This could be in the region of 100+ markets; or
- Appoint regional custodians in North and Latin America, EMEA, Asia-Pacific and Australasia (i.e. five custodians).

Either way, the investor has a challenging set of relationships to manage. One solution is to appoint a single custodian that manages a network of local custodians located in the countries in which most investors choose to invest.

Global Custody   The single custodian is known as a *global custodian* and the individual local custodians are known as *sub-custodians* (or *agent banks*). Collectively, we refer to this as *global custody*.

A global custodian was defined by the International Securities Services Association (ISSA)[1] in 1990, as follows:

> "A global custodian provides clients with multi-currency custody, settlement and reporting services which extend beyond the global custodian's and client's base region and currency; and encompass all classes of financial instruments."

It should be noted that the client and its global custodian do not have to be in the same country.

The Global Custodians   The global custodians are typically banks that offer a range of services including securities services. For example, Northern Trust's Asset Servicing includes the following headline services:[2]

- Collateral and liquidity management;
- Cross-border pooling;
- Execution services;
- Fund services;
- Global custody;
- Investment operations outsourcing;
- Securities lending;
- Transition management;
- Treasury services.

---

[1] *Source:* International Symposium of Securities Administrators (since renamed International Securities Services Association). "Global custodian" was defined at the 5th Symposium in May 1990. ISSA 5 Symposium Report not available online – www.issanet.org.
[2] *Source:* Northern Trust (online) Asset Servicing. Information available from www.northerntrust.com/asset-servicing/europe/services/investment-risk-and-analytical-services. [Accessed Thursday, 3 April 2014]

Gauging the size of the business is difficult, but it is estimated that the key figure, assets under custody (AUC), exceeds USD 140 trillion, with the top ten global custodians holding around 80% of this. The top five global custodians are shown in Table 10.8.

TABLE 10.8   Assets under custody

Rank	Provider	AUC (USD Billions)
1	BNY Mellon	27,900
2	J.P. Morgan	21,000
3	State Street	20,996
4	Citi	14,500
5	BNP Paribas	8,986

Source: © 2014 globalcustody.net. Reproduced with consent. Extract from: www.globalcustody .net as at Wednesday, 16 July 2014.

Global Custody Structure   As you will observe in Figure 10.4, the client has one relationship to manage; this is with the global custodian. For the global custodian, in addition to its clients, it has to manage its network of sub-custodians, each of which represents the entry point into the relevant market (e.g. clearing systems and CSDs).

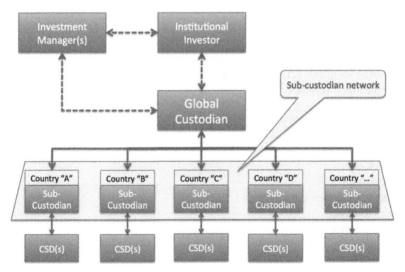

FIGURE 10.4   Global custody structure: sub-custodian network

The network consists of banks that operate in a particular market and whose clients are the global custodians. Please note that the same banks can act as local custodians, as explained above.

An example of a sub-custodian network is that of HSBC Securities Services[3] in Table 10.9.

TABLE 10.9 HSBC Securities Services acting as a local custodian

Region	Countries
Asia-Pacific (in 16 countries)	Australia, Bangladesh, China (Shanghai and Shenzhen), Hong Kong SAR, India, Indonesia, Japan, Malaysia, New Zealand, Philippines, Singapore, Sri Lanka, South Korea, Taiwan, Thailand and Vietnam.
Europe (in 7 countries)	Cyprus, Germany, Greece, Kazakhstan, Malta, Turkey and United Kingdom.
Americas (in 4 countries)	Argentina, Bermuda, Brazil and Mexico.
Middle East and North Africa (in 11 countries)	Bahrain, Egypt, Jordan, Kuwait, Lebanon, Mauritius, Oman, Palestine, Qatar, Saudi Arabia and United Arab Emirates.

In addition to HSBC Securities Services, other banks that act as sub-custodians in multiple locations include:

- Citi
- BNP Paribas
- Deutsche Bank
- Standard Chartered Bank.

The Clients   The main types of institutional investor that purchase global custody services tend to be:

- Investment managers (including sovereign wealth funds and hedge funds), who use external custodians to handle their client business across the globe.
- Institutional investors (e.g. pension funds, insurance companies and charities):
  - Pension funds can be self-invested but are more likely to use investment managers. Using a global custodian can ensure that information is consolidated by the custodian on behalf of the pension fund.
  - Insurance companies use external custodians to handle their client business across the globe.
- Institutional funds (e.g. mutual funds, sicavs, hedge funds, private equity funds, etc.), which use external custodians to handle their business across the globe.
- Custodian banks looking to appoint sub-custodian agents in those markets where the global custodian does not have suitable branches. It is therefore likely that some global custodians will choose to use competitor banks as sub-custodians.

---

[3]*Source:* HSBC Securities Services (online) "Sub-Custody & Clearing – Markets". Available from www.hsbcnet.com/gbm/products-services/securities-services/sub-custody-clearing/markets#null. [Accessed Thursday, 3 April 2014]

It is possible to consider the relationships between institutional clients, investment managers and the global custodian banks from two points of view. In both cases, information (e.g. transaction instructions submitted to the custodian and reports submitted by the custodian) is exchanged between the investment manager and the custodian. The question remains as to who is the actual client of the custodian: is it the investment manager or is it the institutional client?

Institutional Client appoints Custodian   The institutional client appoints one or more investment managers (at "A") and the custodian (at "C"); it can arrange for its investment manager(s) to communicate with the single custodian (at "B"), as shown in Figure 10.5. This has the advantage that the custodian is totally involved with all the investment managers and can report on a consolidated basis back to the institutional client.

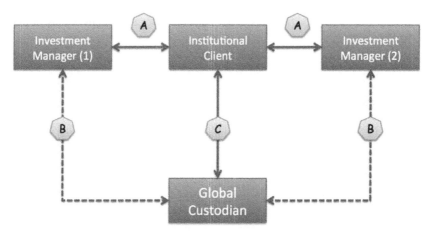

FIGURE 10.5   Institutional client appoints global custodian

In terms of a day-to-day operational relationship, the investment managers are quasi-clients of the custodian, although the latter's fees are charged back to the institutional client.

For any investment manager involved in this type of arrangement, there is one disadvantage and that is the likelihood that the investment manager will be dealing with several global custodians, each one having been appointed by the investment manager's client. That can make it challenging for the investment manager to manage so many relationships.

Investment Manager appoints Custodian   The investment client appoints the investment manager, as above (at "A"). However, as an alternative to the above arrangement, it is possible for the investment manager to appoint its own choice of global custodian (at "B") and thus the institutional client just has a single relationship to manage, i.e. with its investment manager. The choice of global custodian remains solely with the investment manager, as shown in Figure 10.6.

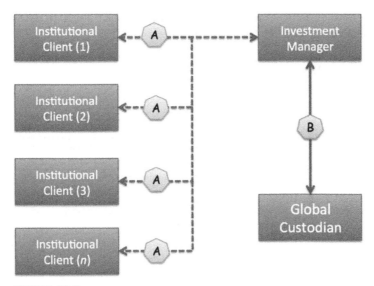

FIGURE 10.6 Investment manager appoints global custodian

The advantage for the investment manager is perhaps clear to see; it is able to deal with the global custodian of its choice and not have to be concerned with managing a network of global custodial relationships. The disadvantage for the institutional clients is that they cannot benefit from some of the compliance-related services offered by the global custodian.

Global Custody Services   If we can regard the services offered by the clearing systems and CSDs (and to a lesser extent by the sub-custodians) as being wholesale-based, we can think of the services offered by the global custodians as being more retail-based. Let us take settlements as an example; for a CSD, a transaction will settle when both the asset and cash are available. This can be regarded as wholesale. The global custodian will attempt to make the settlement look better than it really is; it will attempt to add value to the client. We will see how this can be achieved below.

The global custodian is therefore acting as an intermediary between the owner and the market infrastructure and, at the same time, adding a degree of value for the benefit of the owner.

The types of service offered by the global custodians can be divided into two groups:

1. Basic services.
2. Value-added services.

Not every client will want or need all of the services on offer, but it is generally the case that most clients will require the basic services. Clients may not need or may not be permitted to take some of the value-added and related services; it depends entirely on each client's situation.

Nevertheless, global custodians are innovators and will constantly seek to develop services and products that clients might be interested in taking.

1. Basic services (see Table 10.10).

TABLE 10.10 Basic services

Basic Services	Comments
Client service	The day-to-day servicing of a client's accounts, including the resolution of problems and queries as they arise.
Relationship management	The overall custodian/client working relationship, including decisions on product development, policies and agreements.
Clearing and settlement	Ensuring timely settlement of securities transactions, chasing fails and managing outstanding items.
Securities safekeeping	Provision of pooled and/or segregated custody accounts, reconciling clients' positions.
Income collection	Collecting dividends and coupons and ensuring that the correct amounts are received. Claiming entitlements on failed cum-dividend transactions.
Corporate actions	Taking responsibility for the completeness, accuracy and timeliness of pre-advice corporate action data that are available in local markets and submitting instructions for voluntary events.
Proxy voting/class actions	Notification of meeting types, dates, resolutions and some information on votes and results, in the appropriate language. Arranging for clients' voting decisions to be relayed to the issuer and handling class actions where appropriate.
Cash management	Sweeping and pooling of cash balances. Management of cash surpluses through either investment in liquid funds using the custodians' own products or via a third party.
Foreign exchange	Quoting competitive exchange rates and enabling clients to execute trades on-screen in all tradable currencies, 24 hours a day.
Withholding tax services	Reclaims in markets that have tax treaties and exemptions.
Recordkeeping and reporting	Providing multi-currency reporting on clients' securities and cash positions, along with transaction status. Includes regulatory and specialist reporting.
Technology	Communications via SWIFT, custodians' proprietary systems and web-based information delivery.
Network management	Access to (and management of) global network of sub-custodians in anywhere from 70 to more than 100 markets. Adding new markets and evaluating and providing information about the risks involved are important to both fund managers and institutional investors.
Market information	Financial market profiles (operating regulations, systems and procedures in local markets, etc.). Commenting on infrastructure risks in capital markets, evaluating CSD risk. Market surveillance and risk monitoring.

2. Value-added services (see Table 10.11).

TABLE 10.11 Value-added services

Value-Added Services	Comments
Securities lending	Enhancing overall portfolio performance by offering a managed, fully collateralised securities lending programme.
Investment accounting	Accounting and reporting for investment funds. Includes preparing financial statements (balance sheet, changes in equity, income statements and cash flows), earnings per share, NAV per share, financial instrument disclosures, etc.
Pricing and valuation	Obtaining and verifying local market prices, revaluing securities and translating into clients' base currencies. Includes listed and unlisted securities.
Performance measurement	Monitoring funds' performance against benchmarks and providing insights into that performance. Analytics include investment strategy performance by geography, investment type and industry, as well as benchmarking against other managers and market indices.
Derivatives clearing	Transaction processing for both ETD and OTC derivatives through the custodians' global clearing member status. This includes the centralisation of clients' positions and margin payments. Custodians manage collateral and provide an independent pricing service for non-cleared OTC derivatives.
Fund administration	Accounting and administration for onshore and offshore collective investment programmes.
Transition management	Minimise the costs and risks associated with asset reallocation.
Commission management	Help to reduce commission exposure through effective transaction cost control.
Compliance management	Monitor compliance with clients' investment guidelines. Provide an independent check of clients' compliance with market regulations and investment guidelines.

10.4.3 Custody in the EuroMarkets

In Chapter 6: Securities Depositories (CSDs and ICSDs), we looked at the two organisations that were established to look after the Eurobond market. The fact that Euroclear Bank (EB) and Clearstream Banking Luxembourg (CBL) were located in Brussels, Belgium and Luxembourg respectively was, in some ways, irrelevant, as the Eurobond was not a type of security domiciled in either country.

CBL's and EB's typical types of client have always included sell-side organisations (e.g. member firms of the International Capital Market Association – dealers, market makers, broker/dealers, investment banks, etc.) together with investment fund distributors and providers. It is not the usual practice for an institutional client to be a direct participant of the ICSDs.

Both expanded into equity and domestic bond markets through a network of depositories, custodian banks and local CSDs. In Figure 10.7 we can see that there are two options available. The investment manager and sell-side firms can either:

- Have indirect links to the ICSD (B) by using the global custodian (A), or
- Have direct links to the ICSD (C).

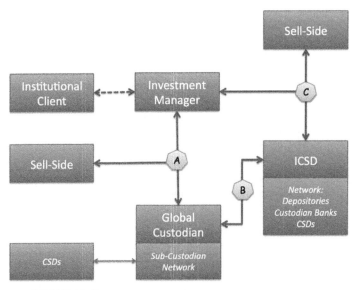

FIGURE 10.7   Links with the ICSDs

It is possible to appreciate that there is a blurring of the distinction between a global custodian (and its links to the local CSDs through its network of sub-custodians) and an ICSD (which traditionally handled Eurobonds, foreign bonds and global bonds).

However, differences do remain:

- Whilst both ICSDs have become banks (as are the majority of global custodians), they are still regarded as being part of the market infrastructure (similar to the CSDs).
- Institutional clients can appoint a global custodian, as we have seen already, but would not be a direct participant of an ICSD.
- A global custodian is effectively an intermediary that provides a wider range of services to its clients than provided by the ICSDs.
- The ICSDs' payment and settlement instruction deadlines are absolute whilst the global custodians' deadlines can be more flexible. (This is mainly because the global custodians have to allow themselves more time to meet their sub-custodians' internal deadlines and those of the CSDs.)

Furthermore, both ICSDs differ in the way they use CSDs. As shown in Table 10.12, the Euroclear group controls a number of European CSDs, with Clearstream controlling just two (again, in Europe) – see Table 10.13.

TABLE 10.12 Euroclear group

Group Member	Market
Euroclear Bank	ICSD services offering a single entry point for more than 40 securities markets
Euroclear Belgium	Domestic CSD in Belgium (formerly CIK)
Euroclear Finland	Domestic CSD in Finland (formerly APK)
Euroclear France	Domestic CSD in France (formerly SICOVAM)
Euroclear Nederland	Domestic CSD in the Netherlands (formerly NECIGEF)
Euroclear Sweden	Domestic CSD in Sweden (formerly VPC)
Euroclear UK & Ireland	Domestic CSD in the United Kingdom (formerly CREST Co)
Euroclear UK & Ireland	Domestic CSD in Ireland (formerly CREST Co)

TABLE 10.13 Clearstream

Group Member	Market
Clearstream Banking Luxembourg	ICSD services offering a single entry point for more than 50 securities markets
LuxClear	Domestic CSD in Luxembourg
Clearstream Banking Frankfurt	Domestic CSD in Germany (formerly Deutsche Börse Clearing)

Third-Party Providers Both ICSDs look to the following third parties for services:

- Securities information vendors for pricing, income, corporate actions, etc.;
- Depository services such as custody, settlement in local markets, income and corporate actions processing;
- Cash correspondent banks for payment instructions and links to national cash-clearing systems;
- Fund transfer agents who process fund orders;
- Communication networks that support the ICSDs' processing services.

10.5 TARGET2SECURITIES (T2S)

10.5.1 Introduction

We have seen before that the European landscape is fragmented (see Figure 10.8)[4] compared with the USA where the clearing and settlement infrastructure is centred on the DTCC (equities and corporate bonds) and Federal Reserve System (US government securities).

---

[4]*Source:* European Central Bank (November 2009). "Target2Securities – Settling without Borders". Available from www.ecb.europa.eu. [Accessed Monday, 6 September 2010]

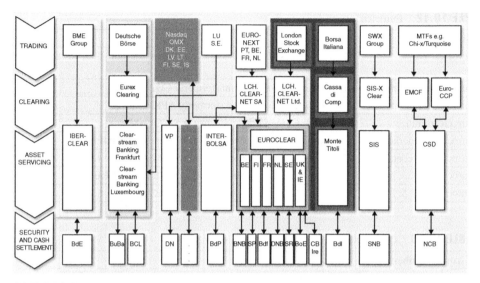

FIGURE 10.8   Fragmented European landscape

With the merger of some European CSDs into the Euroclear group (see above) and Link Up Markets (the joint venture to facilitate message exchange amongst several other CSDs – Austria, Cyprus, Denmark, Germany, Greece, Norway, Spain, Switzerland and South Africa in March 2009), it does not seem possible to harmonise clearing and settlement across Europe.

In 2001 the Giovannini Group[5] identified 15 barriers that prevented efficient cross-border clearing and settlement within the European Union. The T2S project will help remove six of these barriers:

1. National differences in information technology and interfaces.
2. National clearing and settlement restrictions that require the use of multiple systems.
3. Differences in national rules relating to corporate actions, beneficial ownership and custody.
4. The absence of intra-day settlement finality.
5. Practical impediments to remote access to national clearing and settlement systems.
6. National differences in operating hours/settlement deadlines.

10.5.2 Eurosystem

Target2Securities (T2S) is the project owned and managed by the Eurosystem[6] with the objective of removing the barriers, inefficiencies and costs found in the current fragmented landscape and replacing them with a single system.

---

[5]Refer to The Giovannini Group (2001) "Cross-Border Clearing and Settlement Arrangements in the European Union" pp. 44–59. Available online from http://ec.europa.eu/internal_market/financial-markets/docs/clearing/first_giovannini_report_en.pdf [Accessed Monday, 7 April 2014]

[6]The Eurosystem is the central banking system of the Euro area, comprising the ECB and the national central banks of the 18 EU Member States whose common currency is the Euro.

T2S will neither become a CSD nor replace the existing CSD arrangements. Instead, T2S will be integrated with the Eurozone payment system (Target2) using a single IT system with a single set of standards and a single operational framework. T2S will provide DVP through real-time gross settlement in central bank money.

The general objectives of T2S are:

- To reduce risk in the European post-trade environment;
- To streamline the European settlement process;
- To enhance freedom of choice in the European securities settlement industry;
- To reduce the cost of settling securities transactions in Europe.

10.5.3   How T2S Will Work

As shown in Figure 10.9, the T2S system will integrate: "… both securities accounts and cash accounts on a single IT platform, so that only one interface will be necessary between the CSDs and the T2S platform. T2S will accommodate both the market participants' securities accounts, held at either one or multiple CSDs, and their dedicated central bank cash accounts, held with their respective national central bank. The dedicated cash accounts will be used exclusively for settlement purposes in T2S and will be linked to the participants' cash accounts held in TARGET2 or another non-euro central bank RTGS account."[7]

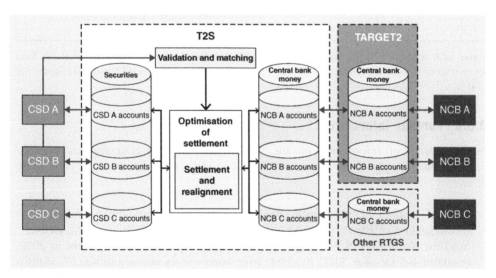

FIGURE 10.9   Integrated model – T2S and Target2

[7]*Source:* European Central Bank (online) "About T2S/What is T2S?". Available from www.ecb. europa.eu/paym/t2s/about/about/html/index.en.html. [Accessed Monday, 7 April 2014]

10.5.4 Migration Plan

The first migration wave of CSDs is scheduled to start in June 2015, as noted in Table 10.14.

TABLE 10.14 T2S migration waves

First Wave 22 June 2015	Second Wave 28 March 2016	Third Wave 12 September 2016	Fourth Wave 6 February 2017
Bank of Greece Securities Settlement System (BOGS)	Euroclear Belgium	Clearstream Banking (Germany)	Centrálny depozitár cenných papierov SR (CDCP) (Slovakia)
Depozitarul Central (Romania)	Euroclear France	KELER (Hungary)	Eesti Väärtpaberikeskus (Estonia)
Malta Stock Exchange	Euroclear Nederland	LuxCSD (Luxembourg)	Euroclear Finland
Monte Titoli (Italy)	Interbolsa (Portugal)	Oesterreichische Kontrollbank (Austria)	Iberclear (Spain)
SIX SIS (Switzerland)	National Bank of Belgium Securities Settlement Systems (NBB-SSS)	VP Lux (Luxembourg)	KDD – Centralna klirinško depotna družba (Slovenia)
		VP Securities (Denmark)	Lietuvos centrinis vertybinių popierių depozitoriumas (Lithuania)

Source: ECB (online) T2S Spotlight. "When will T2S be available to the market?" Available from http://www.ecb.europa.eu/paym/t2s/about/press/html/index.en.html. [Accessed Thursday, 11 September 2014]

10.5.5 Further Information

There is plenty of information on the ECB's website (www.ecb.europa.eu/paym/t2s/html/index.en.html) plus there are several YouTube videos, of which three are particularly useful:

- YouTube (online) "T2S Benefits". Available from http://www.youtube.com/watch?v=wPmeHjA1VeQ&list=PL347E929CBF4A76F7. Published by ECB Euro 8 May 2012.
- YouTube (online) "T2S and Beyond" (Conference on securities settlement in 2020) Frankfurt 4–5 October 2011. Available from http://www.youtube.com/watch?v=ORCuKWh21JY&list=PL347E929CBF4A76F7. Published by ECB Euro 8 May 2012.
- YouTube (online) "How is the T2S Community preparing for wave 1?" (Panel Session) 25 June 2014. Available from http://www.youtube.com/watch?v=AVF2BaWGv81&index=8&list=PL347E929CBF4A76F7. Published by ECB Euro 25 June 2014.

10.6 SUMMARY

In this chapter we have looked at custody in terms of the forms of securities (registered and bearer) and what that means in terms of the safekeeping of securities.

We saw that ownership of registered securities is reflected on the issuer's register, which is maintained by a registrar or transfer agent. Securities can be registered in the name of one of the following entities:

- The actual beneficial owner;
- The custodian bank;
- A nominee name.

Remember that whoever's name is in the register is the legal owner; using a nominee or a custodian bank transfers legal ownership to that entity. The investor, as the beneficial owner, must trust the nominee/custodian bank to pass the benefits of ownership on to the investor as and when received from the issuer.

We then considered the three ways in which securities can be held in custody:

1. Custody in a local market – suitable for those investors that tend to invest in their local markets and perhaps a few cross-border markets as well.
2. Custody in the global markets – for globally invested institutions that might choose to use a single global custodian to handle their assets.
3. Custody in the Euro markets – for institutions that are focused on the international bond markets.

Not only do the global custodians have access to many markets through their network of sub-custodians, but they also offer a wide range of services. These include the basic services, such as settlement, safekeeping and reporting, and value-added services, such as investment accounting, derivatives clearing and securities lending.

In the Euro markets, the two international central securities depositories (Clearstream Banking Luxembourg and Euroclear Bank) have serviced their participants' requirements for new issuance, settlement, safekeeping and credit-related (securities and cash financing) services. Both ICSDs have expanded their services to include equities through their links to local CSDs and investment funds.

Finally, we explained how the Eurozone is harmonising the fragmented settlement situation in Europe by developing T2S. T2S is an integrated model that will enable participants to settle trades in central bank money on a DVP basis across the participating CSDs and the Target2 payment system.

CHAPTER 11

Corporate Actions

11.1 INTRODUCTION

A corporate action is an event usually initiated by the issuer of the securities (mainly equities but also, to a lesser extent, bonds) and sometimes by a third party. A corporate action can result either in a financial impact on the shareholders or bondholders or on the capital structure of the issuer itself.

There are many different types of corporate action event; the exact number is difficult to calculate. Nevertheless, corporate actions can be grouped into nine event-type categories with numerous sub-types. You will find a list of these categories in Appendix 11.1 at the end of this chapter.

The key relationship has always been between the issuer and the investor. This was certainly true in the days when investors owning registered securities (typically equities) would have their names recorded on the issuer's shareholder register. In today's world, and especially where investors own international securities, this one-on-one relationship is less frequent, as there are a number of intermediaries acting on behalf of both issuer and investor. We will identify these intermediaries and examine their roles and responsibilities in this chapter.

Each and every type of corporate action event requires one or more actions to be taken. For the purposes of this book, we will concentrate on only a few of the more usual types of event. Depending on the type of event, the actions required can and do differ in detail; however, we can summarise the actions that are required into the following types:

1. Information from issuer;
2. Communication to investor;
3. Decision to be made/no decision required by investor;
4. Conclusion with results debited or credited to the investor's account.

These four actions apply in the vast majority of events.

In November 2001, the Giovannini Group published a report entitled *Cross-Border Clearing and Settlement Arrangements in the European Union* in which a number of barriers to efficient cross-border clearing and settlement were noted.[1] In particular, corporate actions were discussed in Barrier 3: "Differences in national rules relating to corporate actions, beneficial ownership and custody" (see below).

GIOVANNINI BARRIER 3

National differences in the rules governing corporate actions… can be a barrier to efficient cross-border clearing and settlement. As corporate actions often require a response from the securities owner, national differences in how they are managed may require specialised local knowledge and/or the lodgement of physical documents locally, and so inhibit the centralisation of securities settlement and custody. Particular difficulties in respect of corporate actions arise from the inconsistent treatment of compensation and cash accruals and from the differing practices used to apply the effects of corporate actions to open transactions, e.g. different countries apply different treatments to the payment of a dividend on a security involved in an open transaction. Efforts to improve consistency in the rules governing corporate actions are essential if the integration of EU equity markets is to proceed. More specifically, implementation (as planned through ECSDA) of ISO 15022 message standards for communication between CSDs on corporate actions would help to speed up information dissemination across systems.

The Giovannini Group (November 2001), "Cross-Border Clearing and Settlement Arrangements in the European Union" (report updated in 2003)

By the end of this chapter you will:

- Understand the complexities of corporate action events;
- Understand the event processing and information flows;
- Know the operational risks involved;
- Appreciate the changes within the industry;
- Understand the impact of corporate actions on other departments.

11.2   TYPES OF CORPORATE ACTION EVENT

We can consider corporate action events from two perspectives: those that are voluntary or mandatory and those that are predictable or unpredictable (announced).

11.2.1   Voluntary or Mandatory Events

Corporate action events can either be voluntary or mandatory. From the shareholder's point of view, a voluntary event is where the shareholder has the option to participate in the event.

---

[1]The Giovannini Group (October 2001) (online) "Cross-Border Clearing and Settlement Arrangements in the European Union". Available from http://ec.europa.eu/internal_market/financial-markets/docs/clearing/first_giovannini_report_en.pdf. [Accessed Tuesday, 26 February 2002]

By contrast, a mandatory event is where the shareholder has no option but to participate in the event. Please note that a voluntary event for the issuer could very well be a mandatory event for the investor.

11.2.2 Predictable or Announced Events

A predictable event is one where the security has one or more events that will be known from the time that security is first issued. An announced event is one where, in most circumstances, the issuer decides to take action in some form or another.

All events will be a combination of both of the above perspectives; so, for example, a redemption on a state bond will be mandatory and predictable. A bonus issue, on the other hand, will be mandatory and announced. For corporate actions staff, the most risky combination will usually be announced and voluntary, mainly because someone, either the investor or its intermediary, has to make a decision as to what action to take. A decision that is either missed or submitted late will not be executed by the issuer's agent.

In Appendix 11.2, you will find a list of voluntary and mandatory events for both equities and bonds.

11.3 PARTICIPATION IN CORPORATE ACTIONS

The two key participants in any corporate action event are the issuer and the investor (or the investor's agent, such as a fund manager). As we have seen above, it is unlikely, although not impossible, that the issuer will communicate directly with the investor. Instead, the issuer communicates via a chain of intermediaries. These intermediaries include the following:

- Fund manager;
- Global custodian;
- Local/sub-custodian;
- Local central securities depository;
- International central securities depository;
- Data vendors;
- Receiving/paying agent.

11.3.1 Fund Manager

Fund managers act on behalf of their clients as regards corporate action events as well as managing their assets. It is the fund manager, rather than the client, who decides what action to take where the event is voluntary in nature (e.g. where an issuer announces a rights issue).

11.3.2 Global Custodian

Whether the global custodian's client is the institutional investor or the fund manager, its role is to act as an information taker (from the sub-custodian) and information giver (to the fund manager) plus decision taker (from the fund manager) and decision giver (to the sub-custodian). The global custodian has the responsibility of ensuring that the results of any corporate action event (whether voluntary or mandatory) are correctly actioned and recorded. The global custodian is very dependent on its sub-custodian for much of the information/decisions/results flows and, as a control, will verify any corporate actions information that has been published.

11.3.3 Local/Sub-Custodian

Typically, a local bank can act in both capacities depending on the type of client. The roles and responsibilities mirror those of the global custodian (i.e. information/decisions/results flows), with the difference being that the custodian is located in the market where the issuer's securities are listed. This makes the local/sub-custodian much closer to the market than the global custodian would be.

11.3.4 Local Central Securities Depository

It is usual for the local CSD to hold the entire issue of any eligible security on behalf of the beneficial owner. (Remember that there will be a local sub-custodian/global custodian chain or a local custodian as intermediary between the CSD and beneficial owner.) The issuer's agent will communicate with the CSD.

11.3.5 International Central Securities Depository

The ICSDs, Euroclear Bank (EB) and Clearstream Banking Luxembourg (CBL), hold their participants' securities in one of three ways, depending on the type of security:

1. Each ICSD will have appointed a specialised depository that holds securities for one or other of the ICSDs. There are, therefore, two SDs in this case.
2. Both ICSDs jointly appoint a common depository that holds the entire issue to the order of EB and CBL. The CD therefore has only two clients for each issue held.
3. Each ICSD has a participant custody account with some, but not all, local CSDs.

11.3.6 Data Vendors

Data vendors will also be recipients of information broadcast by the issuers. In addition to corporate actions information, the data vendors provide pricing information and information on companies and securities.

Examples of data vendors include Bloomberg, Markit, Morningstar, SIX Financial Information, Sungard and Thomson Reuters. You can find more details on the Software and Information Industry Association's Financial Information Services Division at www.siia.net.

11.3.7 Receiving/Paying Agent

Typically a bank, a receiving/paying agent is appointed by an issuer to make periodic cash payments (dividends, coupons and bond redemption proceeds) to the issuer's investors and receive payments for relevant corporate action events such as rights issues.

Depending on the exact types of relationships, the chains of communication can best be described in the manner shown in Figure 11.1.

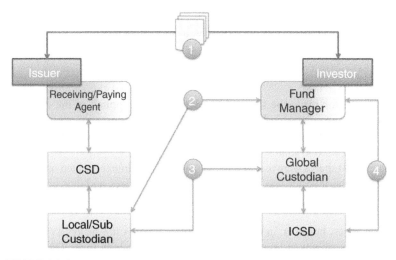

FIGURE 11.1 Communication chains between issuer and investor

1. This represents the origin of any corporate action where the issuer communicates directly with the investor. The investor submits its decisions, where required, direct to the issuer.

   It is more usual in today's environment for intermediaries to act on behalf of the issuer and investor; in which case:
2. In a domestic situation, the issuer communicates through its agent to the local central securities depository, from there to a local custodian and finally to the investor's fund manager.
3. In a foreign situation, the issuer communicates in much the same way as in 2 above, except that the local custodian now acts as the global custodian's sub-custodian. The global custodian communicates with its client's fund manager.
4. If the fund manager is a direct participant in one of the two international central securities depositories, communication takes place between the fund manager and the ICSDs. If not, it is the global custodian that is the participant in one of the ICSDs and communication flows accordingly.

We will look at information flows in more detail in Section 11.6.

11.4 ENTITLEMENTS, KEY DATES AND CLAIMS

11.4.1 Entitlement

With any corporate action event, one of the first tasks is to establish who is entitled to benefit from the event. If we consider an asset class such as equity/shares, this will not normally be a problem, as the following example demonstrates.

An investor purchased 50,000 registered shares several weeks ago and the purchase settled on the intended settlement date. Within a very short period of time these shares would have been registered in either the investor's name or in the name of the appropriate nominee. The issuer will know that this investor's name will be on its shareholder register. Today, the issuer announces a corporate action event, for example, a cash dividend.

Who, then, is entitled to receive this cash dividend? It will be the investor for the following two reasons:

1. When the investor made the original purchase, it was implied in the contract that the purchase was made cum-dividend ("cum" is from the Latin "with"). On the assumption that the investor was still the owner of the shares, then he would be fully entitled to the dividend on the 50,000 shares.
2. Once the 50,000 shares were registered in the investor's name (i.e. noted on the shareholder register) then the investor was the legal owner of the shares and thus entitled to receive the cash dividend.

A complication arises, however, in the situation where the investor makes a purchase and, for whatever reason, the shares are not on the shareholder register in time. The issuer will pay the dividend to whoever's name is on the shareholder register; in this case, the purchaser will not receive the dividend even though the purchase was made cum-dividend. Who, then, will receive this dividend? As the dividend is paid to whoever's name is on the register, the dividend will actually be paid to the seller of the shares rather than the purchaser (the investor).

11.4.2 Record Date

For this reason there needs to be a mechanism by which the correct entity is not only entitled to receive the benefit but receives the benefit in actuality. This is how it works. The shareholder register is a dynamic document, in that buyers and sellers are continuously having their names added to and removed from the register. As the issuer can only pay a dividend to those named on the register, you can perhaps appreciate that on a very busy register it becomes very difficult to identify the true beneficiaries. For this reason, the issuer will close the register on one particular date. This date is known as the *record date* (also known as the *books close date*). Once the register has been closed, the dividend is paid to the name(s) on the register at that time. As before, this will correctly identify the beneficiaries.

11.4.3 Ex-Dividend Date

But we still have a problem. An investor may have purchased shares only a few days before the record date. In this situation it is unlikely that the transaction would even have settled, let alone have the purchaser's name added to the register. To overcome this problem, the local stock exchange will declare an *ex-dividend date* that occurs shortly before the record date ("ex" from the Latin "without"). How many days before depends on the local settlement convention. It is usually one day less than the number of days between the trade date and the intended settlement date. If the settlement convention is $T+3$, then the number of days between the ex-dividend date and the record date is two.

We can look at this another way – the investor needs to purchase shares just before the record date to be sure of qualifying for the dividend payment. In the above example of a $T+3$ settlement cycle, three days are needed before the shareholder's name goes on the register (i.e. the day before the ex-dividend date).

What, then, happens on the ex-dividend date? Firstly, on the ex-dividend date, the share price will drop by the amount of the dividend compared with the previous day (*ceteris paribus*). Secondly, the shares will trade ex-dividend and published price lists and broker contract notes will be flagged with an "xd" tag after the price. This emphasises that the shares are being bought without any entitlement to the next dividend payment.

GlaxoSmithKline (GSK:L) paid a dividend of GBX 18.00 per ordinary share on 3 October 2013. The shares went ex-dividend on 7 August and the record date was two days later, on 9 August. For the week commencing 5 August, the share price fluctuated as shown in Table 11.1.

TABLE 11.1   GlaxoSmithKline share price fluctuation

Date	Price (GBX)	Price± (GBX)
Monday, 5 August 2013	1,705.00	
Tuesday, 6 August 2013	1,694.00	(11.00)
Wednesday, 7 August 2013	1,670.00	(24.00)
Thursday, 8 August 2013	1,659.50	(10.50)
Friday, 9 August 2013	1,663.00	3.50

Sources: Yahoo! Finance (online) GSK:L share prices, available from http://finance.yahoo.com. [Accessed Wednesday, 9 October 2013]

Note that the share price dropped GBX 24.00 on the ex-dividend date; some of this drop can be explained by the removal of the dividend (GBX 18.00 per share) from the share price.

Figure 11.2 shows the timeline from the original announcement of the dividend through to the payment date.

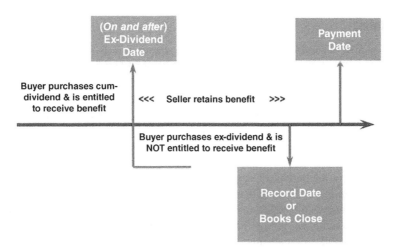

FIGURE 11.2   Cum- and ex-dividend timeline

11.4.4 Payment Date

The third key date is the *payment date*. This can occur weeks, if not months, after the record date and is not governed by either the record date or the ex-dividend date. For example, Vodafone (VOD:L) paid its final dividend for 2013 on 7 August 2013, almost two months after the record date (14 June) and the ex-dividend date (12 June).

We now have three key dates to be concerned with, and each of these should be diarised and checks made to ensure that any investors holding the shares receive the correct amount of dividend and on the correct date. Furthermore, we can now identify two trading periods:

- **Cum-entitlement period:** Where the investor executes a purchase trade and is entitled to receive the benefit (the dividend in this case) and the seller loses this entitlement.
- **Ex-entitlement period:** Where the investor executes a purchase trade and is not entitled to receive the benefit and the seller retains the benefit. This is shown in Figure 11.3.

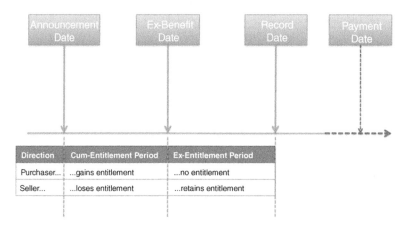

FIGURE 11.3   Normal cum-benefit and normal ex-benefit trading

11.4.5 Claims

A situation can arise whereby an investor purchased shares cum-dividend but settlement was delayed (e.g. the seller did not have sufficient securities to enable the settlement to take place). In this situation, who do you think will receive the dividend? Remember, to receive a dividend, the investor's name must be on the shareholder register. In this case, it is the seller whose name is on the shareholder register and who will receive the dividend. However, as the purchase was traded cum-dividend, it should be the purchaser who is entitled to receive the dividend. There are two solutions to this problem:

1. The purchaser (or the purchaser's agent) must claim the dividend from the seller, remembering that there might be more than one seller involved.
2. The clearing house would be aware that, although the transaction was dealt cum-dividend, the purchaser's name was not on the shareholder register in time for the record date. The clearing house will automatically "compensate" the purchaser by debiting the seller's cash account and crediting the purchaser's cash account.

This compensation process is very much more efficient and timely compared with market claims; nevertheless, corporate action staff will need to monitor the situation carefully.

Q&A

Question

What action would you take if your client had an existing position together with a failed purchase? Using the example of Vodafone, noted above, the dividend was paid at a rate of 6.92p per ordinary share.

Answer

The investor's traded position on the ex-dividend date was 15,000 shares and the investor was therefore entitled to receive a dividend of GBP 1,038.00. Of this total, 10,000 shares would have been registered on time and the remaining 5,000 shares would still be registered in the name of the seller (see Table 11.2a). In this case, the investor would receive the dividend in two parts (see Table 11.2b).

TABLE 11.2a Status of transactions

Transaction Date	Transaction	Status
8 May 2013	Purchase 10,000 shares	Settled 10 May 2013
10 June 2013	Purchase 5,000 shares	Delayed – settled 17 June 2013

TABLE 11.2b Dividend receipts

Payment Date (2013)	Shares on Register	Dividend Rate (pence per share)	Dividend Amount (GBP)	Received From:
7 August	10,000	6.92	GBP 692.00	Issuer
7 August	5,000	6.92	GBP 346.00	Market compensation or claim
Totals:	**15,000**	**Ordinary shares**	**GBP 1,038.00**	

One final point to be aware of: the Reconciliations Section would be expecting to receive GBP 1,038.00 on the bank account; instead, there will be two amounts to look out for – GBP 692.00 from the issuer and GBP 346.00 through the compensation mechanism. (Please note that we have not yet discussed the topic of withholding tax. This will be covered later in Section 11.10.)

11.4.6 Key Dates for Bonds

The situation with bonds is rather less complicated than with shares for the following reasons.

Firstly, coupon payment dates for fixed-income bonds are known in advance (i.e. from the date the bonds are issued) and can therefore be diarised. This also applies for bonds with variable coupon amounts, even though the actual coupon amount is not known until the coupon rate is fixed with reference to a specified benchmark interbank offered rate such as LIBOR, EURIBOR, etc.

Secondly, as the issuers of bearer bonds do not know who their bondholders are, the issuers have to rely on the bondholders to claim their coupons from the issuer's paying agent. Traditionally, this involved removing (known as *clipping*) the coupon from the host bond and presenting it to the issuer's paying agent. This coupon clipping had to be done some time in advance of the coupon payment date so that there was sufficient time for the coupon to be presented to the paying agent. Exactly how long was governed by the type of bond.

Thirdly, issuers of registered bonds would maintain a bondholder register similar to equities and could therefore make the coupon payment to whoever's name was on the register.

11.5 CORPORATE ACTION EVENT PROCESSING

11.5.1 Introduction

In this section we will cover the general principles that govern the processing of all corporate action events, whether they involve cash only, securities only or some combination of both. You will then see how certain corporate action events are processed and the challenges they present to the operational staff.

We will examine the corporate action event types shown in Table 11.3.

TABLE 11.3 Corporate action types

Voluntary or Mandatory	Predictable or Unpredictable	Corporate Action Event
Mandatory	Unpredictable	Cash dividend
Mandatory with option	Unpredictable	Optional stock dividend
Mandatory	Predictable	Fixed-income bond coupon
Mandatory	Predictable	Floating-rate bond coupon and rate fixing
Mandatory	Predictable	Bond redemption
Voluntary or Mandatory	Predictable	Bond conversion
Mandatory	Unpredictable	Capitalisation issue (bonus issue)
Voluntary	Unpredictable	Rights issue

In general, the processing of corporate action events typically involves the following nine processes:

1. Communicating the event/event announcement
   Once the issuer has decided to initiate a corporate action event, it will have to pass on full event-related information to all market participants and CSDs, who, in turn, will notify their customers (i.e. participant local custodians). The local custodians will notify their

customers (i.e. the global custodians), who will notify their customers/fund managers, etc. Every organisation must be able to gather the information and verify its accuracy. It is important that the underlying beneficial owners are notified as quickly and accurately as possible.

2. Reconciliation – ante event
   Positions should be reconciled to ensure that the correct entitlements are either received in full or claimed where necessary.

3. Event creation
   Having notified their clients about the upcoming event, the custodians will create an "event" in their in-house systems. All relevant dates like deadlines, pay dates, ex dates and record dates need to be correctly diarised to ensure that important actions are taken at the right moment and are not forgotten. If necessary, the information published by the agent should be translated before it can be sent to the customers. Any unclear information will need to be investigated by contacting the information provider and/or the issuer's agent.

4. Claims processing
   Positions that are entitled to benefit from an event but have been delayed (e.g. failed settlement) should be identified and claims processed.

5. Instructions processing
   Voluntary/optional events are operationally the most risky. The issuer's agent will have a timetable for decisions and appropriate actions. Failure to meet these deadlines will usually result in the customer missing the opportunity to participate in the event.

   In order to meet the issuer's deadline, every participant in the communication chain will need to allow time to pass the information on and receive any instructions. It may be the case that the beneficial owner has to make a decision several days ahead of the issuer's deadline.

6. Entitlement calculation
   Once information has been received and verified by the custodians, they must first calculate the securities amounts and/or cash that the beneficial owners are entitled to. Secondly, the custodians must advise their customers of the full terms of any event, what the options are and what results can be expected.

7. Payment/delivery
   Once the lead agent releases the results of the event (cash, securities or both) the custodians should update their internal books and records under advice to their customers.

8. Reconciliation – post event
   Every event needs to be reconciled after completion to ensure that every aspect of the event has been processed correctly.

9. Reporting
   Reporting on the progress of the event takes place throughout the event.

Whilst every corporate action event is different, the above processes can act as a template for processing corporate actions. We will now look at a number of different events to see what happens, to understand the operational risks and the types of controls that will mitigate these risks.

11.5.2   Cash Dividend

Shareholders usually invest in shares in order to benefit from either capital growth or income. Here, we are concerned with income and this is the result of when a company chooses to distribute any profits. This distribution is made by way of a cash payment to those shareholders who are entitled. Companies are not obliged to pay cash dividends even if there are sufficient profits. They might argue that it is better to reinvest any profits in the business (and in so doing hope to grow the business and increase the share price).

The company's board of directors will publish its half-year or full-year results and announce its intention to pay a dividend. This publication is made on a declaration date. For example, Barclays Bank declared its second interim dividend for the year ending 31 December 2013 on 30 July 2013 together with the rate and other relevant dates (see Table 11.4).

TABLE 11.4   Barclays Bank dividend

Date (2013)	Action
30 July	Declaration date
Dividend rate	GBX 1.00 per share (i.e. GBP 0.01 per share)
7 August	Ex-dividend date
9 August	Record date
13 September	Payment date

Source: Barclays (online) Dividends. Available from http://group .barclays.com/about-barclays/investor-relations/private-shareholders/ dividends. [Accessed Thursday, 10 October 2013]

In addition to the Barclays ordinary shares listed in London, there are American depository receipts (ADRs) traded and held in the USA. As the ADR ratio is 1:4 (one ADR:four ordinary shares), a dividend of 1p per ordinary share would equate to a dividend of 4p per ADR. The GBP/USD exchange rate was set by Barclays at 1.569273, resulting in a cash payment rate of USD 0.062770 per ADR.[2]

The second stage is to reconcile the investor's position in order to establish how many shares are traded cum-entitlement and of these, how many shares are outstanding due to a delayed settlement.

The third stage is to create the event in the books and records, including diarising the key dates, advising clients and passing cash entries over the accounts. The accounting entries have to achieve two objectives:

1. To accrue the dividend amount on the ex-dividend date (whilst we know how much the dividend will be at this point, the dividend has not yet been paid).
2. On the payment date, the accrual will be reversed and replaced by an actual payment, as listed in Table 11.5.

---

[2]*Source:* J.P. Morgan DR Market Announcement (online) "Cash Dividend Announcement for Barclays PLC". Available from www.adr.com/Home/LoadPDF?CMSID=c32e3edb707a46bbbebb2d56aa454986. [Accessed Thursday, 10 October 2013]

TABLE 11.5 Event creation in books and records

When	Action Required	Account Debit	Account Credit
On ex-dividend date	Accrue the dividend	Outstanding dividends *(Balance Sheet debtor)*	Equity dividends *(Profit & Loss account)*
On payment date	Reverse the accrual and …		Outstanding dividends
On payment date	… book the receipt	Bank	
This has the overall effect of:			
		Debit to the bank	
		Credit to the	Equity dividends

We have ignored the impact of taxation on the dividend; we will return to this topic later in Section 11.10.

As a cash dividend is regarded as a mandatory event, there is no requirement to send any instructions to the issuer. We can therefore move to stage 5 and calculate the entitlements. Taking the Barclays dividend above as an example, the entitlement calculations and corresponding accounting entries are shown in Tables 11.6 and 11.7 respectively.

TABLE 11.6 Entitlement calculations

Holding	500,000	Ordinary shares
Dividend Rate	1.00	GBX per share
Ex-Dividend Date	Wednesday, 7 August 2013	
Payment Date	Friday, 13 September 2013	
Dividend Amount	GBP 5,000.00	Gross amount

TABLE 11.7 Accounting entries

Date	DR/CR	Account	Amount
7 August 2013	DR	Outstanding dividends	GBP (5,000.00)
	CR	Equity dividend	GBP 5,000.00
13 September 2013	CR	Outstanding dividends	GBP 5,000.00
	DR	Bank	GBP (5,000.00)

Q&A

Question

What would the situation be if 200,000 ordinary shares had been purchased cum-dividend but not settled on time?

Answer

You would receive the dividend in two amounts: one amount on 300,000 shares direct from the issuer and a second amount on 200,000 shares by way of a claim. You would need to post separate accounting entries for each amount over both days, as per Table 11.8.

TABLE 11.8 Accounting entries

Date	DR/CR	Account	Amount
On ex-dividend date			
7 Aug 2013	DR	Outstanding dividends (depot)	GBP (3,000.00)
7 Aug 2013	DR	Outstanding dividends (claim)	GBP (2,000.00)
7 Aug 2013	CR	Equity dividend	GBP 5,000.00
On payment date			
13 Sep 2013	CR	Outstanding dividends (depot)	GBP 3,000.00
13 Sep 2013	CR	Outstanding dividends (claim)	GBP 2,000.00
13 Sep 2013	DR	Bank (dividend from issuer)	GBP (3,000.00)
13 Sep 2013	DR	Bank (dividend from claim)	GBP (2,000.00)

11.5.3 Optional Stock Dividend

If the issuer wishes to retain cash in the business it can give the shareholder the option of taking either cash or shares to the value of the cash dividend. So whilst the sharing of the profits, once approved, can be regarded as a mandatory event, we now have the situation where a choice has to be made. The convention in most markets is that shareholders will accept the dividend in cash rather than opting to take shares. (Accepting cash gives the shareholder reinvestment choices; taking shares does not.).

In order to cultivate the number of shares allotted, we have to be informed of two pieces of information:

1. **The amount of cash per share:** This will be straightforward and will be announced by the company in the usual way.
2. **The cash value of each new share:** In order to do this, the company needs to know the market price of each share. The problem is that the share price changes all the time, making it difficult to inform the shareholder how many shares they will receive. To overcome this problem, the company will fix a price based, for example, on the average closing price of the shares over the last several days or so. The exact basis on which this consolidation is made will be contained in the original event announcement.

An example of this type of corporate action involves the final dividend of 59.0p per share for the year ended 31 March 2013 by ABC plc. (see Table 11.9).

TABLE 11.9 Event timetable

Date (2013)	Event
31 July	Shares in the company quoted ex-dividend
2 August	Record date
31 July to 6 August	Stock reference pricing days (i.e. five dealing days)
7 August	Stock reference share price confirmed as 1,575p per share
30 August	Last day for receipt of decision
27 September	Cash dividend paid/first day of dealing in new shares

Q&A

Questions

The shareholder owns 250,000 shares. Using the above information, answer the following questions:

1. If the shareholder requires cash, how much will he receive on 27 September?
2. If the shareholder requires the alternative of shares, how many shares will he receive on 27 September?

Answers

1. If the shareholder requires cash then the gross amount of dividend will be GBP 147,500.00 (see Table 11.10).

TABLE 11.10 Cash option

Position	Dividend per Share (GBX)	Total Dividend (GBP)
250,000	59.00	GBP 147,500.00

2. If the shareholder requires new shares, the quantity is calculated by multiplying the number of shares held on the record date by the cash dividend rate and then dividing by the reference share price (see Table 11.11).

TABLE 11.11 Stock/scrip option

Dividend Equivalent	Reference Price (GBX)	Number of New Shares
GBP 147,500.00	1,575.00	9,365.08

This calculation results in a fraction of a share (0.08), which, as this is a non-board lot size, cannot be issued. The cash value of this fractional share amounts to GBP 1.25,[3]

---

[3]This is the difference between the dividend equivalent (GBP 147,500.00) and the value of the new shares (9,365 shares x 1,575p = GBP 147,498.75).

and this is held over until the next dividend payment and used together with the next dividend to buy more shares. An alternative description would be that the shareholder has the option to receive one new share for every 26.6949 existing shares (i.e. 250,000/9, 365.08).

As you will have noticed, there is a decision that needs to be made in terms of whether to take shares or receive cash. In most cases, the default option is to take cash; in other words, if the shareholder wishes to take cash then he need take no action. If, however, he requires new shares, then he must make this decision within the deadline specified by the company.

11.5.4 Fixed-Income Bond Coupon

Bond issuers have an obligation to service their debts on a predefined basis. In the case of a fixed-income bond, the amount of coupon and the payment date of the coupons are known in advance. As a consequence, there is no need for the bond issuer to make an announcement of this event. Depending on whether the bonds are in bearer form or in registered form, the bondholder will either have to claim the coupon (bonds in bearer form) or will automatically be paid by the issuer (bonds in registered form).

Bonds in Bearer Form   Traditionally, the custodian bank that held the bond certificates on behalf of the bondholder (the investor) would separate the appropriate coupon (known as *coupon clipping*) from the host bond and present it to the bond issuer's paying agent. The paying agent would pay the amount of coupon noted on the coupon itself to the custodian (and the custodian would credit the funds to the investor's cash account).

Interest on bonds accrues on a daily basis and the corresponding accounting entries are posted to match. On the coupon payment date, the accrued interest account is debited and the bond interest account credited with the full amount.

Most bonds today are held centrally by a central securities depository and this makes the collection of coupon payments much more efficient. However, in situations where the bonds are held by the investor (or his custodian), it is possible to present the coupons to the paying agent after the coupon payment date. In this situation, the paying agent will pay the coupon but will not pay any interest on the coupon itself; in other words, there is a funding implication through the late presentation of the coupon to the paying agent. There is a time limit for presenting coupons and this is usually in terms of a number of years; time enough for even the most inefficient custodian or forgetful investor to claim the dividend. This time limit is referred to as a *prescription period*.

Depending on the market convention for any particular bond, coupons are paid annually, semi-annually or quarterly. Therefore, the first coupon will be paid twelve months, six months or three months after the date on which the bond was issued. There are occasionally exceptions when the first coupon is paid either before or after the expected first coupon date. We refer to these as either a *first short coupon* or a *first long coupon*. Whether short or long, once the first coupon has been paid, the normal payment frequency follows.

First Long Coupon   On 21 November 2011, GDF Suez issued a EUR 1 billion note due on 21 January 2020.[4] The main provisions relating to interest payable are shown in Table 11.12.

TABLE 11.12   GDF Suez note

Issue Date	21 November 2011
Coupon Rate	3.125% p.a.
Payment Dates	21 January each year from and including 21 January 2013 to and including the maturity date
First Coupon Payment Date	21 January 2013
Day-Count Convention	Actual/Actual (ICMA)
Fixed Coupon Amount	EUR 3,125.00 per EUR 100,000 nominal amount subject to the "broken amount"
Broken Amount	EUR 3,647.26 per EUR 100,000 falling on 21 January 2013

The *broken amount* represents the coupon from the issue date, 21 November 2011, up to 21 January 2013; a period of approximately one year and two months.

Q&A

Question

Does the broken amount calculation (using the above information and your knowledge of accrued interest) reconcile?

Answer

Using the date function on your Texas Instruments BAII Plus calculator, on an Actual/Actual (ICMA) day-count basis, there are 61 days from 21 November 2011 to 21 January 2012. On the nominal amount of EUR 100,000, 61 days represents EUR 522.26 of coupon. The full coupon for the year ending 21 January 2013 we know is EUR 3,125.00, which, when added to the first amount, comes to a total coupon amount of EUR 3,647.26.

This reconciles with the provisions noted above.

First Short Coupon   An issuer might wish to issue a bond in September 2013 with interest paid semi-annually, for example, in June and December. Within the provisions of the issue terms and conditions, the first coupon would be paid in December 2013 – approximately three months after the bond was issued. Thereafter, subsequent coupons would be paid in June 2014, December 2014, etc.

---

[4]*Source:* www.gdfsuez.com/wp-content/uploads/2012/05/gdfs-jan2020-fr0011147305.pdf. [Accessed Friday, 11 October 2013]

11.5.5   Floating-Rate Note (FRN) Coupon and Rate Reset

FRNs are medium- to long-term debt obligations with variable interest rates that are adjusted periodically (typically every one, three or six months). The interest rate is usually fixed at a specified spread (margin) quoted in basis points over a specified money market reference rate such as:

- London Interbank Offered Rate (LIBOR): LIBOR is the average interbank interest rate at which a selection of banks on the London money market are prepared to lend to one another. LIBOR comes in 15 different maturities and in 10 different currencies. LIBOR is regarded as one of the benchmark rates.
- Euro Interbank Offered Rate (Euribor): Euribor is the average interbank interest rate at which European banks are prepared to lend Euros to one another. Euribor, like LIBOR, comes in 15 different maturities. Euribor is also regarded as a benchmark rate.
- 13-week US Treasury bill:[5] Short-term debt issued by a government's Treasury department.

Examples of FRNs include the issuance on 26 September 2013 by the Swedish Internet-based bank, Skandiabanken, of two FRNs raising Norwegian Kroner 3 billion:[6]

- NKR 2 billion FRNs (3-month Nibor + 49bp) due September 2018;
- NKR 1 billion FRNs (3-month Nibor + 30bp) due September 2016.

With FRNs, there are two aspects to be concerned with: firstly, there is the coupon for the period about to end and, secondly, there is the fixing of the interest rate for the period about to start. Although the coupon rate does change (floats) from one period to another, the coupon is reset ("fixed") for one particular coupon period.

Coupon Payment   This is a straightforward process that we covered in Section 11.5.4 above.

Consider the security shown in Table 11.13.

TABLE 11.13   ABC Bank plc FRN due January 2022

Aggregate Nominal Amount	EUR 1.5 billion
Issue Date	17 January 2012
Interest Commencement Date	17 January 2012
Board Lot Size:	EUR 1,000
Interest Basis	3-month Euribor + margin of 1.55% per annum (155 basis points)
Reference Rate	3-month Euribor

[5]The US Treasury commenced issuing US Treasury FRNs with effect from January 2014.
[6]*Source:* Nordic FIs & Covered (online) "Skandiabanken in Norwegian debut with NKR3bn FRNs". Available from http://nordic-fi.com/skandiabanken-in-norwegian-debut-with-nkr3bn-frns. [Accessed Saturday, 12 October 2013]

TABLE 11.13 (*Continued*)

Interest Determination date(s)	Two TARGET settlement days prior to the commencement of each interest period
First Interest Payment Date	17 April 2012
Day-Count Convention	Actual/360
Business Day Convention	Modified following business day convention
Interest Rate Determination	Screen rate determination

Let us assume that today is the coupon payment date and that it is 17 October 2013. We are holding a position of EUR 1 million nominal amount of this FRN. What will be the coupon payment amount? To answer this we need to know the coupon rate from our securities database. For today's coupon payment, the coupon rate would have been fixed three months ago, i.e. commencing 17 July 2013. Taking the three-month Euribor rate in July of 0.222% plus the margin, the interest rate for the period ending 17 October 2013 would have been 1.7720% per annum. In this case, the coupon on our holding of EUR 1 million would be EUR 4,528.44 (see Table 11.14).

TABLE 11.14 ABC FRN coupon payment

Nominal Amount	Coupon Rate	Days in Coupon Period (Actual)	Coupon Payment
EUR 1,000,000	1.772%	92	EUR 4,528.44

For value date 17 October 2013 we will receive EUR 4,528.44 (ACT/360 day convention) and this will be credited to our income account.

Reset of FRN Coupon   In addition to receiving the coupon for the previous period, we have to reset (fix) the coupon rate for the next three-month period. We have to know when to reset the coupon rate and the source of the reference rate.

It is normal business practice to reset two business days before the start of the interest period. In terms of the source of the interest rate, you have to refer to the terms and conditions contained in the issuing prospectus. Referring to the above details of ABC FRN, you will note that the interest determination date is two TARGET settlement days prior to commencement.

Q&A

Question

For the ABC Bank plc. FRN due January 2022 and using the Euribor rates in Table 11.15, what will the coupon rate for the next coupon period be, how much will the coupon be and when will the next coupon be paid?

TABLE 11.15 Euribor rates

Euribor 2013 tables and graphs for:

3 months ‡	
First 2013 Euribor rates by month	
02-01-2013	0,188 %
01-02-2013	0,234 %
01-03-2013	0,206 %
02-04-2013	0,210 %
01-05-2013	0,207 %
03-06-2013	0,200 %
01-07-2013	0,222 %
01-08-2013	0,228 %
02-09-2013	0,225 %
01-10-2013	0,225 %
01-11-2013	0,226 %
02-12-2013	0,236 %

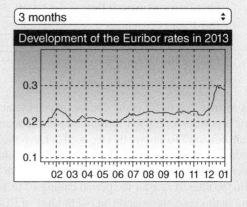

Source: http://www.euribor-rates.eu/euribor-2013.asp?i1=6&i2=6. [Accessed Thursday, 1 May 2014]

Answer

The answers can be found in Table 11.16.

TABLE 11.16 Answers to the questions on the coupon for the ABC Bank plc FRN

Board Lot Size	EUR 1,000
Interest Determination Date	Tuesday, 15 October 2013
Reference Rate	0.225% p.a. (3m Euribor rate)
Margin	155 basis points
Coupon Rate	1.775% p.a.
Commencing	Thursday, 17 October 2013
Payment Date	Friday, 17 January 2014 (92 days)

To finish off this subsection, it is worth knowing that there are variants of FRNs, some of which are noted below:

- **Drop-lock bond:** This is a bond that automatically converts to a fixed-rate bond if the interest rate used to reset the floating rate falls to a predetermined level. The new fixed rate stays in place until the bond reaches maturity.
- **Mismatch FRN:** An FRN where the coupon is based on, say, six-month LIBOR but reset every two months.

- **Capped FRN:** An FRN where the coupon cannot rise above a maximum rate.
- **Floored FRN:** An FRN where the coupon cannot fall below a minimum rate.
- **Mini-max (or collared) FRN:** An FRN where the coupon cannot rise above a maximum rate or fall below a minimum rate.
- **Flip-flop FRN:** An FRN backed by two different bonds, one with a variable interest rate and one with a fixed interest rate. The bondholder may choose which interest rate at any time, depending on which one is higher for a given period.
- **Convertible-rate FRN:** An FRN that allows issuers and bondholders to convert from a floating rate of interest to a fixed rate, or vice versa.
- **Inverse FRN:** An FRN in which the coupon moves inversely to the movement of the reference rate; if the reference rate moves down, the coupon rate increases.
- **Variable rate note:** An FRN with a spread over the reference rate which is not fixed.
- **Perpetual FRN:** An FRN that has no redemption date.

11.5.6   Bond Redemption

With the exception of bonds that have no redemption date (perpetual and un-dated bonds) the issuer is obligated to repay the bond on the predetermined date as set out in the issuing prospectus. As this is an obligation, this event type is both mandatory and predictable. Depending on the rules of the (I)CSD that is holding the bonds, the investor's holding will be frozen shortly before the redemption date. This prohibits any further deliveries of the bond.

The securities database will hold details of the redemption date and should be diarised so that the Front Office can reinvest the redemption proceeds. In the vast majority of cases, the redemption value is at par (i.e. 100% of the face value). The exceptions occur when the bond is redeemed early; see below for more details.

In the example used above, the ABC Bank FRN is due to be redeemed in full on 17 January 2022 and in the same way that the coupons on physical certificates were presented to the paying agent for the coupon payments, the host bond is likewise surrendered to the paying agent. If, for any reason, this is delayed, then the bondholder is still entitled to receive the redemption proceeds but, as before, with no extra interest. The prescription period for the bond tends to be longer than for its coupons – sometimes in the region of 20 years or so. This should never have to happen in the financial markets, but could possibly happen if a private investor were to hold the physical certificates either at home or with, say, a solicitor.

Bonds that have a single redemption date are known as *straight bonds*. There are bonds that can be repaid early either because the issuer wishes to do so or, separately, because the investor wishes. We refer to these types of bonds as having either a *call option* or a *put option* respectively.

Q&A

Question

Why would an issuer wish to repay its bonds early or an investor surrender its bonds early?

Answer

Issuer: if the interest rate in the markets is lower than the coupon rate on the bond, the issuer can reduce its cost of borrowing by repaying the bond early and borrowing money elsewhere at a lower rate of interest.

Investor: if the interest rate in the markets is higher than the coupon rate on the bond, the investor can obtain a better rate return by putting the bond back to the issuer and reinvesting the cash in another product earning a higher rate of interest.

The issuer will call a bond early if it is to the issuer's advantage; this, of course, will be to the disadvantage of the investor. For this reason, the redemption price will usually be slightly *greater* than par. For example, ABC Company, which issued a bond due for final redemption on 30 June 2020, has written into the terms and conditions that the bond can be redeemed early on any coupon payment date commencing 30 June 2016. If this bond has an annual coupon payment date, then the repayment schedule shown in Table 11.17 might be arranged.

TABLE 11.17   Bond (with call option) early redemption schedule

Possible Call Date	Redemption Price	Comment
30 June 2016	102.0000%	Early redemption opportunity §1
30 June 2017	101.5000%	Early redemption opportunity §2
30 June 2018	101.0000%	Early redemption opportunity §3
30 June 2019	100.5000%	Early redemption opportunity §4
30 June 2020	100.0000%	Final redemption date

By contrast, the investor will "put" a bond back to the issuer early if it is to the investor's advantage; this, of course, will be to the disadvantage of the issuer. For this reason, the redemption price will usually be slightly *lower* than par. For example, XYZ Company, which issued a bond due for final redemption on 30 June 2020, has written into the terms and conditions that the bond can be redeemed early on any coupon payment date commencing 30 June 2016. If this bond has an annual coupon payment date, then the repayment schedule shown in Table 11.18 might be arranged.

TABLE 11.18   Bond (with put option) early redemption schedule

Possible Call Date	Redemption Price	Comment
30 June 2016	98.0000%	Early redemption opportunity §1
30 June 2017	98.5000%	Early redemption opportunity §2
30 June 2018	99.0000%	Early redemption opportunity §3
30 June 2019	99.5000%	Early redemption opportunity §4
30 June 2020	100.0000%	Final redemption date

(Please note that the calculation of the redemption price is outside the scope of this text.)

Call Option If an issuer calls a bond early, this will be a mandatory event (although voluntary from the issuer's perspective) and the investor will have no choice in the matter. The investor's holding will be debited from his depot a few days before the bond is repaid and on the appropriate date, the redemption proceeds plus the final coupon will be credited to the investor's cash account. From an accounting entry point of view, the bond redemption proceeds are credited to a capital account and the coupon to an income account. The Corporate Actions Department needs to be aware that a bond is about to be called early and they should make sure that the Front Office is also aware.

Put Option An early redemption on a bond with a put option will be a voluntary event from the investor's perspective (and therefore mandatory for the issuer). The Corporate Actions Department will be informed by its custodian or (I)CSD of the opportunity to put the bond back to the issuer and a decision date will be advised. The Corporate Actions Department will seek a decision whether to put the bond or not, from the appropriate decision-maker (Front Office or client). If the decision is made to put the bond, then an instruction must be sent to the custodian or (I)CSD. On receipt of the instruction, the custodian will deliver the bond from the depot and present it to the issuer's paying agent, in exchange for which the redemption proceeds plus coupon will be paid.

If an instruction to put the bond is either not submitted to the custodian or submitted late, then no action will be taken by either the custodian or the paying agent. This means, of course, that the decision-maker will not receive the expected cash proceeds but will still retain the bond. The choices available to the decision-maker will be either to sell the bond in the open market or wait for the next opportunity to put the bond back to the issuer; in the case of our example, this will be in 12 months' time.

11.5.7 Bond Conversion

Convertible bonds are bonds that are issued by corporations and that can be converted to shares in the issuing company at the bondholder's discretion. Convertible bonds typically offer higher yields than ordinary shares, but lower yields than straight bonds. Most convertible bonds are callable by the bond issuer either on or before a contractual conversion date.

Otherwise, a conversion will be a voluntary event when the investor decides to convert. (In contrast, if the convertible bond was called by the issuer, then this would be a mandatory event.)

The full characteristics and features of any convertible bond will be held within the securities database. Table 11.19 shows an example of the key conversion features of a convertible bond.

TABLE 11.19 Conversion details

Issuer	The Sumitomo Bank Ltd
Issue	2.75% convertible bonds due 30 September 2000
Aggregate Principal Amount	USD 120 million
Denomination	USD 5,000
Coupon Payment Dates	30 September and 31 March *(commencing 30 September 1985)*

(continued)

TABLE 11.19 (*Continued*)

USD/JPY	244.60
Conversion Price	JPY 2,142
Conversion Right	The bondholder may convert at any time on or after 5 August 1985 and up to the close of business on 25 September 2000

The conversion right is an optional event type for the bondholder and, as you will observe, the bond may be converted at any time between the two dates mentioned. Should the investor choose to convert the bond on any day other than one of the two coupon payment dates, any accrued interest will be lost.

The terms and conditions for this bond state the means by which the bond must be presented to the conversion agent and any accompanying documentation. Any costs associated with this conversion are for the account of the bondholder.

Q&A

Questions

1. How many shares would one bond be convertible into?
2. If the bondholder chooses to convert on a coupon payment date, what will happen in terms of the coupon payment?

Answers

Each bond with a denomination of USD 5,000 will be converted into 570.96171 shares:

USD 5,000 × FX rate of 244.60 = JPY 1,223,000 divided by the conversion price of JPY 2,142 results in 570.96171 shares.

According to the terms and conditions, fractions of shares will not be issued on conversion; however, if more than one bond is deposited for conversion at any one time by the same bondholder, the calculation will be on the basis of the aggregate principal amount. However, in the above situation, the bondholder will receive 570 shares only.

If the bondholder chooses to convert on a coupon payment date, then the full coupon for the previous coupon period will be paid.

With this particular bond issue, the conversion price could have been subjected to adjustment if certain events had occurred, including:

1. A free distribution of shares (e.g. a stock dividend);
2. A subdivision or consolidation of shares;
3. An offer of rights or warrants to existing shareholders;
4. An issue of other securities convertible into shares.

Not only was this convertible bond potentially subject to adjustments, but also the convertible bond was callable by the bank on or after 30 September 1988 during the 12-month period commencing 30 September in any of the years shown in Table 11.20.

TABLE 11.20 Early redemption schedule

Year	Redemption Price
1988	104.0000
1989	103.5000
1990	103.0000
1991	102.5000
1992	102.0000
1993	101.5000
1994	101.0000
1995	100.5000
1996 to final redemption	100.0000

Related Structures In addition to convertible bonds, other related structured securities include the following:

1. **Exchangeable bonds:** These give the bondholder the right to exchange the principal of the security for a specified amount of alternative securities from a different issuer.
2. **Mandatory convertibles:** These oblige the bondholder to exchange the principal for a specified amount of alternative securities.
3. **Reverse convertibles:** The issuer (not the investor) has the right to exchange the bond for a given number of shares.

In the event that a convertible bond is not converted, the bond acts in a similar way to a straight bond, i.e. it pays a coupon and will be redeemed in due course.

11.5.8 Capitalisation (Bonus) Issue

A capitalisation issue occurs when a company wishes to convert some or all of its reserves into share capital. To do this, the company creates new shares and gives them to existing shareholders in a particular ratio. This ratio is calculated depending on the number of existing shares and the number of new shares, as the following example illustrates:

Example

In April 2007, the RBS Group's share price had been trading for some time at a price which was high relative to the average share price of companies trading on the London Stock Exchange. As a result, RBS decided to lower the share price by issuing new ordinary shares to existing shareholders. This event is known as a *bonus issue*.

The terms of the bonus issue were that for every one share held by shareholders at the close of business on 4 May 2007 (the record date), they would have received two new shares.

As such, shareholders would now hold three times the number of RBS shares they previously held. If, for example, a shareholder had held 100 shares prior to 4 May 2007, he would now hold 300 RBS shares (100 existing shares + 200 bonus issue shares).

As a result of this bonus issue, the price of each share was lowered, as expected by RBS, to reflect the allocation of the new shares. The development of the share price is shown in Table 11.21. During the week commencing 30 April 2007, the RBS share price was 965.47p per share. On 7 May 2007, it had risen to 972.98p per share, but on the effective date for the bonus issue (8 May), it had fallen to 646.00p per share by close of business.

TABLE 11.21   RBS share price development

Effective Date: 8 May 2007	Quantity	Share Price (GBX)	Value (GBP)
Existing shares	2	972.98	GBP 1,945.95
Bonus shares	1	0.00	GBP 0.00
Total shares	3	equals…	GBP 1,945.95
Post-bonus share price	3	648.65	GBP 1,945.95

You will observe that the price, in theory, should have gone down to 648.65p per share but instead fell further to 646.00p per share. This can be accounted for by dealings executed during the day together with any information that the market may have picked up.

A bonus issue is a mandatory event and is announced; it is therefore important that information about this event is received either directly from the issuer or from the investor's custodian. In the event that the Bonus Issue is not noticed, the sudden drop in share price, as we saw with the RBS group event, should certainly put the corporate action staff on alert that something has happened to the shares.

The new shares would usually rank *pari passu*[7] with the existing shares and therefore the new shares can be added to the existing position.

11.5.9   Rights Issue

When a company wishes to raise fresh capital, it has a number of choices including a secondary issue of shares (*rights issue*). With a rights issue, the company offers its current shareholders the right to buy new shares in the company at a price discounted to the market price. This corporate actions event can be classified as being "voluntary" and "optional". This makes it a particularly risky type from an operational point of view and great care must be taken to ensure that communications and processing are absolutely accurate and timely.

Some reasons as to why rights issues can be so problematic are listed in Table 11.22.

---

[7]"Pari passu" is a Latin phrase that means "ranking equal" or "equal in all respects".

TABLE 11.22 Problems with rights issues

1. Choices:	There are typically four choices available to the shareholder who can: 1. Accept the offer by paying the call amount on or before the last date for payment; 2. Sell the rights in the open market; 3. Take the zero cost option (also known as a "cashless take-up" or "tail swallowing") whereby sufficient rights are sold and the sale proceeds used to accept the offer on the remaining rights; 4. Take no action and allow the rights to lapse on the deadline date.
2. Time:	The amount of time from the initial announcement of a rights issue up to the last day for acceptance and payment tends to be around three weeks.
3. Communication:	Within this short period of time, the company making the offer must communicate the full details to the shareholder (either directly or indirectly through the custodial infrastructure).
4. Negotiable Rights:	The shareholder will initially receive a number of rights to the new shares and these rights are negotiable. As with the rights issue itself, there are deadlines in terms of when the rights can be sold.

Let us consider an example of a recent rights issue – Barclays Bank plc. In July 2013, Barclays Bank plc. announced its intention to raise around GBP 5.8 billion by way of a rights issue to be launched in September 2013. The basic terms of the issue were as follows:

- Ex-entitlement date: 18 September 2013
- Basis of entitlement: One new ordinary share (nil paid) for four existing ordinary shares held
- Cost of subscription: 185p per share

Listed in Table 11.23 are the key dates, commencing with the record date and ending with the posting of share certificates for those shareholders who preferred their shares to be in certificated form.

(It should be noted that market convention in terms of terminology can differ between markets. These differences will be annotated in the list of key dates with explanations after this.)

TABLE 11.23 Rights issue key dates

Date/Time (2013)	Details	Refer to Note:
Close of business 13 September	Record date	~
17 September	Dispatch of forms (to certificated shareholders only)	1
08:00 18 September	Dealings in new ordinary shares (nil paid) commence	2
08:00 18 September	Existing ordinary shares go ex-rights	~

(continued)

TABLE 11.23   (*Continued*)

Date/Time (2013)	Details	Refer to Note:
15:00 25 September	Latest time for receipt of instructions from certificated shareholders to sell all their nil paid rights or to effect cashless take-up	~
15:00 30 September	Last date for splitting provisional allotment letters, nil or fully paid	3
11:59 2 October	Last date for acceptance and payment of rights issue and registration of renounced provisional allotment letters	4
08:00 4 October	Results of rights issue to be announced	5
08:00 4 October	Dealings in new ordinary shares, fully paid, commence	6
By Thursday 17 October	Definitive share certificates to be posted and cheques for any lapsed rights to be posted	~

Notes:

(1) In the UK, shareholders (typically at the retail level) sometimes prefer to hold their shares in certificated form. Otherwise, shareholders' UK securities are in dematerialised form.

(2) In the UK, the basis of entitlement refers to a number of new ordinary shares (nil paid) for a number of existing ordinary shares held. Elsewhere, the basis of entitlement would be quoted in two parts:

   a number of rights for a number of existing shares, then
   a number of new shares for a number of rights (against payment).

(3) The use of the term "provisional allotment letters" (PALs) is a throwback to the time when the nil paid rights (NPRs) were in paper form and the PALs were used for payment of subscription costs and delivery purposes when the NPRs were sold.

(4) When the seller sold NPRs, he had to renounce ownership of them. This was done by signing the PAL before delivery. The buyer added their details to the PAL and submitted them for re-registration.

(5) On 4 October, the bank announced that the rights issue was 95% subscribed (with the 5% difference mostly due to shareholders based in countries where there are restrictions on rights issue subscriptions).

(6) Once the NPRs have been subscribed to, they are referred to as being *fully paid shares*. If these rank *pari passu* with the existing ordinary shares, then both lines of shares are amalgamated. However, if the new shares do not rank *pari passu,* then two separate lines of shares must be maintained for the time being until the restriction is lifted.

Theoretical ex-rights Price and Nil Paid Price   In most cases the NPRs (or rights) are negotiable. At what price could a shareholder sell or buy an NPR? To answer this, we must first calculate what the ex-rights price might, in theory, be. This price is known as the *theoretical ex-rights price* (TERP) and is calculated by taking the ratio (in this case 1:4) and adding the market value of the existing shares (four) to the subscription cost of the NPR (one). The information in Tables 11.24 and 11.25 shows how this is done.

TABLE 11.24   Barclays rights issue information

Known Information:	
Ratio:	1 new:4 existing shares
Subscription price:	GBX 185.0 per share
Current market price of existing share:	GBX 309.5 per share

TABLE 11.25 Barclays rights issue calculations

Condition	Price (GBX)	Value (GBX)
If 4 existing shares @	309.5	1,238.0
... and 1 new share @	185.0	185.0
... then 5 shares	are worth:	1,423.0
... therefore 1 share (i.e. TERP)	is worth:	284.6

We can see that one new ordinary share, in theory, is worth 284.6p – lower than the market price. To calculate the value of the NPR when the market price is 309.5p, take the TERP and subtract the subscription price to give you the NPR (284.6 − 185.0 = 99.6). A potential purchaser of the NPRs would therefore be prepared to buy them at 99.6p and pay the subscription cost of 185.0p (total 284.6p).

The various deadlines are specified in the rights issue prospectus and failure to comply will have operational implications, mainly resulting in financial and reputational costs, as the following scenario shows. Take the Barclays Bank example and assume that you are working in the Corporate Actions Department of a fund management company. Your clients have positions in the bank's shares:

Client "A"	1,000,000 ordinary shares
Client "B"	2,500,000 ordinary shares
Client "C"	1,500,000 ordinary shares
Client "D"	5,000,000 ordinary shares
Total:	10,000,000 ordinary shares

You have communicated with your Front Office colleagues and sought their decisions. They decide to accept the offer and take up their entitlement to the new ordinary shares. The last day for acceptance and payment is Wednesday, 2 October at 11:59 latest. So far, so good.

However, a simple mistake was made; the latest time was recorded as 23:59 and not 11:59. You decide to send the acceptance information at 17:00, only to be advised that you are too late and that your acceptance has been rejected.

Q&A

Question

What happens next and what are the financial consequences?

Answer

Your clients are expecting to receive more shares costing GBX 185.0 per new ordinary share. As you missed the deadline, your Front Office will have to buy the shares in the market but only charge the clients the subscription cost. Your costs will therefore be the difference between the market cost and the subscription cost plus any stamp duty, brokerage, etc. associated with the transaction, as shown in Table 11.26.

TABLE 11.26   Costs due to missed rights issue call

The total costs (excluding transaction fees) on the missed acceptance on 2,500,000 shares will amount to GBP 2,209,628.13, calculated as follows:		
Your purchase of 2,500,000 Barclays Bank ordinary shares @ 271.35p per share	=	GBP 6,783,750.00
plus brokerage (assume 0.25%)	=	GBP 16,959.38
Purchase amount	=	GBP 6,800,709.38
plus stamp duty (SDRT @ 0.5%) on consideration	=	GBP 33,918.75
less subscription costs (2.5 million shares at 185p per share) charged to client	=	GBP (4,625,000.00)
Resultant loss for your account	=	GBP 2,209,628.13

Do you inform your clients that a mistake has been made (even though they will not be any worse off financially)? Certainly, the Front Office will have to be advised, as it will be required to execute the transaction in the market. As for the actual clients, the ethical choice would be to admit the mistake and confirm that the client had not lost financially as a consequence of the mistake.

11.5.10   Other Examples of Event Types

We have covered several of the more usual types of corporate action event. There are, of course, many others and their definitions can be found in Appendix 11.1 at the end of this chapter. There can be confusion with some events that impact on the share capital, the par value of shares and the total number of shares in issue. Table 11.27 highlights some of these differences.

TABLE 11.27   Other corporate actions

Event	Capital Increase/Decrease	Par Value of Shares	Number of Issued Shares
Capital increase	Up	Up	N/A
Reduction of issued shares	Down	N/A	Down
Reduction of face value	Down	Down	N/A
Subdivision (split)	N/A	Down	Up
Consolidation (reverse split)	N/A	Up	Down

Finally, let's look at the ways in which ratios of new shares to existing shares can differ from one market to another. The classic example is comparing the USA with most other markets. For example, when we looked at the RBS group bonus issue (above), we saw that the ratio was two new shares for every one existing share, i.e. a 2:1 ratio. We also saw that, by implication, the number of shares post-event was three. Had this been a bonus issue in the USA, the ratio would have been 3:1; in other words, the shareholder would have a total of three shares post-event when he had one share ante-event.

It can therefore be seen that both these ratios are, in effect, the same – they are just quoted differently. This can make it potentially confusing for clients/shareholders when, for example, a European-based custodian passes on information to a USA-based client. One way to mitigate against any potential for confusion is to additionally state the number of shares the client owns, the number of shares the client will receive (or deliver) and the number of shares after the event has been completed.

Earlier we saw the nine processes that are required for the majority of corporate action events. To summarise, here are the nine headings:

1. Event announcement;
2. Reconciliation (ante-event);
3. Event creation;
4. Claims processing;
5. Instructions processing;
6. Entitlement calculation;
7. Payment;
8. Reconciliation (post-event);
9. Reporting.

You will not require all of these in every situation, for example, there are no payments with bonus issues or bond conversions. Claims processing may not be required and mandatory events do not require any instructions to be submitted. Nevertheless, this list acts as a good *aide memoire*.

11.6 INFORMATION FLOWS

11.6.1 Introduction

We took a quick look at the communication chain between issuer and investor in Figure 11.1. In this section we will analyse the problems of communicating and some of the solutions.

11.6.2 The Communication Problem

Unlike settlements and clearing, where there is a high degree of standardisation within different asset classes and across different markets, corporate actions are both complex and often complicated, due mainly to the non-standardised nature of a very broad range of event types. Add to this the difficulties of communicating in different languages and across time zones and country borders, and it is amazing that the industry does not experience more problems than it does.

The problem of complexity is not something that the industry has a great deal of influence over, as it is the issuer's choice as to what it wants to do and how it wishes to tailor the events in order to suit its own particular situation.

We have seen that unless there is a direct communication link between issuer and investor, there has to be a group of intermediaries between them. We will now examine the approaches taken in communicating information from issuer to investor and from investor back to the issuer. The following Figures will help you to understand the different approaches that we need to consider depending on what types of organisation are contained in the communication chain.

Q&A

Question

What do you think the communication links are between each of the main types of intermediary where there is a global custodian involved?

Answer

Some of the communication risks together with their causes and mitigations are shown in Table 11.28.

TABLE 11.28   Communication risks

Risk Type	Causes and Mitigation
Data/information capture risk	Data standards, timeliness and accuracy of the information.
Replacement risk	Financial costs associated with making mistakes.
Decision-making/election risk	Either making the wrong decision or failing to make any decision on time
Reputational risk	Making mistakes can harm an organisation's reputation in the market.
Reconciliation risk	Poor reconciliation can lead to missed opportunities to participate in a corporate action event.

There are more detailed explanations in the chapter.

11.6.3   Global Communication Chain

The various items of information transmitted from issuer to investor are highlighted in blue in Figure 11.4 and the corresponding decisions in the opposite direction are highlighted in red.

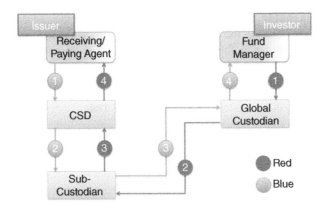

FIGURE 11.4 Communication via global custodian

Information from Issuer to Investor If we consider the more difficult scenario of an announced/voluntary event, such as a rights issue, and complicate it by placing the issuer and investor in two separate countries, then we have the potential for a difficult situation. We have seen in the section on rights issues that there is not a great deal of time from the announcement to the last day for acceptance and payment; there are also inherent dangers associated with the voluntary nature of the event.

Blue point 1 in Figure 11.4 shows the starting point for any information and announcements made by the issuer; its agent will pass the information on to the appropriate CSD and from there (blue point 2) to the sub-custodian acting on behalf of its client the global custodian (blue point 3). The information from blue points 1 to 3 has, in all probability, been sent via the standard message types developed by SWIFT. These messages are not only standardised and authenticated but also used by the four intermediary types. There is a weakness, however, in that the issuer on the one hand and the fund manager on the other may not be direct participants in the SWIFT network. If they are not direct participants, they are unable to use the appropriate message types and instead will be required to use alternative methods of communication, such as emails, faxes, hardcopy messages, etc. The disadvantages of these alternative methods include the extra time and effort required to prepare, check, transmit, receive and re-enter into SWIFT message format. There is also the risk that incoming information may be re-keyed incorrectly, resulting in inaccurate or incorrect information going from giver to taker. What might the solution be? Permit all participants involved to have direct access to the SWIFT message type. In so doing, the processing will become closer to the straight-through processing ideal.

Let us consider that the information has been received by the fund manager in a timely and accurate manner (in spite of the potential problems noted above). The information has been received by the fund manager's Corporate Actions Department, where appropriate checks have to be made to verify the information, enter the details into the systems and submit details to the Front Office staff for a decision. Remember that Operations Departments are not authorised to make decisions of this nature; it is for the Front Office to do this.

Now let us consider the amount of time required to relay the decision details from the investor's fund manager to the issuer's agent.

Information from Investor to Issuer   If we work back from the last day for acceptance and payment on a rights issue to the time when the Front Office has to make its decision, we might have the timeline shown in Table 11.29.

TABLE 11.29   Decision timeline

Process	Number of Days Lead Time	Date
Last day for acceptance and payment (from CSD)	Last day (LD)	Friday, 30 May 2014 @ 12:00
CSD to receive decisions from its clients (sub-custodians)	LD – 2	Wednesday, 28 May 2014 @ 17:00
Sub-custodians to receive decisions from their clients (global custodians)	LD – 3	Tuesday, 27 May 2014 @ 17:00
Global custodians to receive decisions from their clients' fund managers	LD – 5	Friday, 23 May 2014 @ 15:00
Fund managers to receive decision from their Front Office	LD – 5	Friday, 23 May 2014 @ 12:00

We can therefore see that the Front Office is required to make its decision as to whether to accept the rights issue one week in advance of the Last Day. How do you think the fund manager will respond to that? It would not be unreasonable for the fund manager to request that a decision is delayed until the actual Last Day, and furthermore as close as possible to the deadline time.

Why would this be the case? The answer is simple (for the fund manager) but a challenge for the Corporate Actions staff dealing with this; a lot can happen in the markets and, for this particular event, it is a question of whether the Subscription Cost is at an acceptable discount to the market price of the shares. It would be a bad investment decision to accept a Subscription Cost of, say, EUR 15 per new share if the market price of the existing shares were, say, EUR 11 per share.

The intermediaries are therefore wishing to receive a decision (blue point 4 in Figure 11.6) as early as possible whilst the decision-maker wants to delay this until the last possible moment. There is, however, a degree of flexibility within each of the individual intermediary's own internal deadlines. This is to allow as much time as possible for their clients to make a response.

A global custodian will, for example, add the following rider to its request for a decision: "If we do not hear from you by < time> on < date>, we will take no action. If, however, we do receive your instruction after this deadline but before the Last Date, we will attempt to submit your instructions on a 'best efforts' basis. If these instructions miss the issuer's own deadlines, we will not be held accountable and will not make your client(s) 'good' as a result."

11.6.4   Local Communication Chain

The communication issues in a local context are not such a problem. The global custodian, with its cross-border perspective, is now removed from the chain and the problems of language, time zones and different processing practices no longer apply. The banks that act as sub-custodians now act in a local custodian capacity, as shown in Figure 11.5.

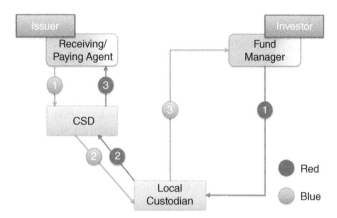

FIGURE 11.5 Communication via local custodian

11.6.5 International Central Securities Depository Chain

The previous communication chains apply predominantly to equity securities. With respect to international securities, such as Eurobonds, we bring the two ICSDs into the frame.

We can therefore see from Figure 11.6 that the global custodians and one or both of the ICSDs communicate with each other. For bond-related corporate actions, the ICSDs communicate with either a specialised or common depository (depending on the way the bonds are actually held).

In some situations, the ICSDs have bilateral links with some CSDs and can communicate on equity-related corporate actions through these.

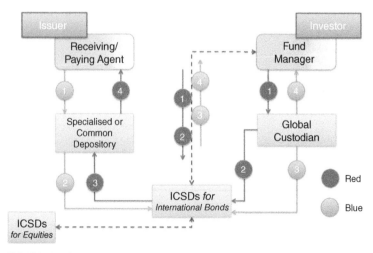

FIGURE 11.6 ICSD communication with depository, global custodian and fund manager

11.6.6 Summary

We have seen that it is rarely practical for issuer and investor to communicate directly with each other. The use of intermediaries is therefore required and, depending on the types of intermediary, there are going to be communication difficulties.

The longer the communication chain, the more time is required to make sure that the investor is informed of any corporate action details as quickly and as accurately as possible. The same is required once the investor has made a decision on an optional event, so that the investor can benefit from any choices that are available.

Having a standardised communication system, such as the message types provided by SWIFT, certainly eases many of the communication difficulties, as does the inclusion of investors and issuers on the SWIFT network.

11.7 CORPORATE ACTION RISKS

11.7.1 Introduction

A few years ago, Exchange Data International posted the following quotation on its website:

> *"In most Financial Institutions the current process for handling corporate actions is predominantly paper-based, difficult to manage, open to discrepancy, both time and labour intensive and does not form part of the Client Management process."*

This quotation is no longer on the website, but the challenges noted do still exist, even in an era where much of the operation processing is reasonably standardised and automated.

We will consider the risks brought about by a "… predominantly paper-based, difficult to manage, open to discrepancy, both time and labour intensive…" array of processes.

The main sources of risk within corporate actions can be summarised as follows:

- Data/information risk;
- Replacement risk;
- Decision-making/election risk;
- Reputational risk;
- Reconciliation risk.

Q&A

Question

From what you have learnt about corporate actions, what might cause some of the above risks and how might you mitigate against their impact?

Answer

Some possible "challenges", depending on the local market conventions, are shown in Table 11.30.

TABLE 11.30 Corporate action risks

1	If the shares are registered in the name of the investor, the investor will have to attend the AGM in person in order to vote. This is difficult if the investor has a broad range of domestic investments and has to travel to the conference centre where the AGM is being held. It is almost impossible if the investor's portfolio consists of a geographically diverse number of investments.
2	If the shares are registered in the name of a nominee, the fund manager has the same issues as in (1) but magnified to a greater degree.
3	The retail investor with a voting interest amounting to a fraction of a percent might be discouraged from voting at all due to the need to attend the AGM in person.
4	By contrast, the fund manager controlling a substantial voting interest of several percent might wish to exercise a vote, but may not be able to spare the time and cost of attending the AGM.
5	Shares located within a CSD are held to the order of the local/sub-custodian (and not to the order of the actual investor). The CSD therefore does not know the identity of the underlying investor, only that the local/sub-custodian is acting on behalf of a third party who may be the actual investor or an agent (e.g. another custodian) acting on behalf of the investor.

We set out below our thoughts on the main sources of risk.

11.7.2 Data/Information Capture Risk

There are almost as many ways in which issuers disseminate information on corporate actions as there are markets around the world. There is a varying degree of standardisation: better in the developed markets but less so in the developing/emerging markets. Lack of standardisation leads to manual interventions rather than automated information capture, with the data having to be checked to ensure accuracy (also known as *data cleansing*).

Global custodians will check the same information, as supplied by different suppliers/vendors, at least twice.

Message standards such as the introduction of ISO 15022 and latterly ISO 20022 have certainly helped the situation. So has participation by the buy-side in the SWIFT system, and more recently by non-bank financial institutions and larger corporates. This was a major change from the original policy of "banks only" participation in SWIFT.

We saw in the communication chain just how challenging it can be for the issuers to notify the investors, through many different parties, with sufficient time for the investors to understand the information and take the required action in order to settle the event.

11.7.3 Replacement Risk

This is the risk associated with the efforts, costs and embarrassment of missing an event which the investor has instructed its custodian to accept. As we saw with the missed rights issue, the financial costs can be significant.

11.7.4 Decision-Making/Election Risk

This risk applies to voluntary events, both announced and predictable. Where an election decision has been delayed or a date has been missed, financial loss is almost certain and can be very expensive depending on the circumstances. Examples are shown in Table 11.31.

TABLE 11.31   Decision-making/election risks

Corporate Action Event	Predictable/ Announced	Impact of Missed Election
Rights issue	Announced	Purchase shares in the market. Loss is the cost less subscription cost (plus any transaction costs and appropriate stamp duty fees).
Conversion	Predictable	▪ Sell bonds and buy shares in the market. ▪ Loss of accrued interest if converted earlier than, say, a coupon payment date.
Proxy vote	Announced	Failure to vote on a particular resolution might prevent the issuer from obtaining sufficient votes to pass the resolution.
Optional stock dividend	Announced	The investor might decide to accept the non-default option, but fail to submit the necessary forms on time. Therefore, the cash dividend (the usual default option) might be used to purchase shares; the investor might require extra cash to achieve this.
Early redemption on a puttable bond	Predictable	▪ Retain bond in portfolio, or ▪ Sell bond in the open market and refund any cash difference if applicable.
Market claims	Either	▪ Prompt action should be taken to ensure that the correct amount of the asset is received (or delivered). ▪ Possible funding implications through inability to deliver if new position has subsequently been sold.

Not only should corporate actions systems help in the processing of any event, but they should also provide warnings of impending dates and deadlines, with appropriate escalation as the absolute deadlines approach.

11.7.5 Reputational Risk

The reputation of the investor's agent (fund manager, custodian, etc.) can be irreparably damaged if there are frequent mistakes made. Clients might leave or seek damages through litigation, the Front Office might lose trust in its Corporate Actions Department and, if clients are constantly being disadvantaged, the regulator might fine and censure the company.

11.7.6 Reconciliation Risk

Positions that are subjected to a corporate action event of any type should be reconciled at the start of the event and at the close of the event. Some events that take a considerable amount of time (e.g. class actions and takeovers) should be reconciled on a regular basis with reference to the Front Office or investor. This ensures that the correct amounts of shares or bonds are identified, market claims initiated/responded to and received/delivered as required.

11.8 INDUSTRY INITIATIVES

11.8.1 Introduction

In spite of the risks and complexities associated with corporate actions activities, industry initiatives to improve corporate actions do not appear to have kept up with, say, clearing and settlements. The move to T+2 settlement is just one example of the drive to standardise this part of the operational function across markets.

As long ago as 1990, work by the International Securities Services Association (ISSA) identified some weaknesses in this area and since then, various associations and working groups have attempted to introduce changes to the ways in which corporate actions activities are processed.

Furthermore, in 1990, KPMG Peat Marwick McLintock[8] made several observations on the subject, including: "Problems (with decision-making/elections) normally arise when the custodian receives late notice of clients' intentions." and: "Failure to action instructions quickly will, in most cases, result in financial loss, interest claims and poor client relations."

You will see in this section which entities have been involved, what they have recommended and what still needs to be addressed.

11.8.2 The International Securities Services Association (ISSA)

ISSA was founded in 1979 in response to the need for an organisation that could: "...disseminate information in the rapidly changing securities markets...".[9] In 1990, it agreed a number of recommendations during its biennial Symposium §5 (ISSA 5), including recommendation 5:

> *"Standard messages should be used and time frames should be developed for various corporate actions. Distinctions should be made between the corporate actions requiring timely reaction by the client versus those which involve a simple notification and no response.*

---

[8]KPMG Peat Marwick McLintock (1990) "Global Custody: Solutions for the ever-changing world". Published by Euromoney Publications plc. ISBN 1 85564 042 2 (pp. 53–55).

[9]*Source:* ISSA (online) "About ISSA/History". Available from http://issanet.org/e/2/hist.html. [Accessed Tuesday, 22 October 2013]

> *The information must be provided electronically as well as in hard copy. A central body, either public or private and accessible to domestic and international bodies must be designated as the official carrier of the data in each market."*

By the time ISSA 6 was held (in 1992), many of the then current practices and shortcomings had been identified and a proposal was made for the standardisation of "Types of Corporate Actions".[10] For example, in choosing between a "capitalisation issue" and a "bonus issue", ISSA remarked that: "The designation 'bonus issue' is somewhat misleading, since a conversion of reserves into capital stock takes place, i.e. the shareholder does not receive shares as a 'bonus'".

In addition, terms of reference for a new Working Group for Corporate Actions (and Proxy Voting) were drafted. By May 2010, the Working Group had finalised its Global Corporate Actions Principles as its: "...contribution to align current industry efforts to achieve a more efficient global corporate actions processing environment".

The Working Group, by now under the chairmanship of Citibank's John Kirkpatrick, published a Progress Update Report in September 2013. In Section 2, the report highlighted the progress made since the previous update in 2012. In summary, three areas were described:

1. Efforts were largely unsuccessful in trying to persuade the issuer community to promote the Principles, as it did not regard them as being its problem.
2. As a result, the Working Group decided to approach CSDs and stock exchanges and persuade them to become the primary agencies for centralising corporate actions information in their individual markets. The CSDs have been surveyed on this matter.
3. Significant progress has been made in the paperless automation of corporate action processes once the data have been digitised. The industry take-up of the ISO 20022 standard has helped by enabling higher automation rates.

If corporate actions are of particular interest to you, the following files are available from the ISSA website (http://issanet.org):

- Global Corporate Actions Principles – Report (May 2010);
- Annexes to the May 2010 Report;
- Global Principles for Corporate Actions and Proxy Voting: Progress Update Report (September 2013).

11.8.3 Giovannini Group

Dr Alberto Giovannini, CEO of Unifortune SGR Spa, was asked by the European Commission to: "...address the most basic pillar of the infrastructure that supports financial markets: the

---

[10]*Source:* ISSA (1992) "Report on Cross-Border Proxy Voting and Corporate Actions – Appendix 4" (pp. 21–23). Report is no longer available on the ISSA website.

system that ensures that securities exchanged within the European economy are properly delivered from the seller to the buyer".

In the first of two reports published in November 2001, the Giovannini Group identified fifteen so-called *barriers* to efficient cross-border clearing and settlement in the EU. Regarding corporate actions, Barrier 3 held most relevance; it suggested that rules on corporate actions (and other areas) should be harmonised at the EU level (see below).

BARRIER 3: DIFFERENCES IN NATIONAL RULES RELATING TO CORPORATE ACTIONS, BENEFICIAL OWNERSHIP AND CUSTODY

National differences in the rules governing corporate actions ... can be a barrier to efficient cross-border clearing and settlement. As corporate actions often require a response from the securities owner, national differences in how they are managed may require specialised local knowledge and/or the lodgement of physical documents locally, and so inhibit the centralisation of securities settlement and custody.

Particular difficulties in respect of corporate actions arise from the inconsistent treatment of compensation and cash accruals and from the differing practices used to apply the effects of corporate actions to open transactions....

Efforts to improve consistency in the rules governing corporate actions are essential if the integration of EU equity markets is to proceed. More specifically, implementation ... of ISO 15022 message standards for communication between CSDs on corporate actions would help to speed up information dissemination across systems.

Source: Extracts from Barrier 3: First Report – Cross-Border Clearing and Settlement Arrangements in the European Union (November 2001) Giovannini Report.

In the second report (April 2003), the Group considered what actions should be taken in order to remove the problems identified in the first report. It identified two fundamental aspects:

1. The variety of rules, information requirements and deadlines for corporate actions, and
2. The rules and laws governing securities markets.

The report mentioned that one of the European Central Securities Depositories Association's Working Groups had looked at the use of ISO 15022 guidelines for the creation of information dissemination templates.

11.8.4 European Central Securities Depositories Association (ECSDA)

The ECSDA was formed in 1997 and provides: "a forum for CSDs to exchange views and take forward projects of mutual interest" (see below).

ECSDA represents 41 national and international central securities depositories (CSDs) across 37 European countries. The association provides a forum for European CSDs to exchange views and take forward projects of mutual interest. It aims to promote a constructive dialogue between the CSD community, European public authorities and all other stakeholders looking to achieve an optimal regulatory framework for clearing and settlement.

Source: ECSDA (online) "A Forum for European CSDs". Available from www.ecsda.eu/about.html. [Accessed Wednesday, 23 October 2013]

Working as part of the so-called Broad Stakeholder Group (BSG),[11] in February 2013 the ECSDA published its 5th Implementation Progress Report/2012 Activity Report on the dismantling of Giovannini Barrier 3.[12]

The BSG made a commitment to: "...steer, monitor and coordinate private sector actions towards a comprehensive and timely application of the Market Standards for Corporate Actions Processing...".[13]

The full text of the Standards can be found on the European Banking Federation's website.[14] This is a very detailed document, but the subject matter covers the following areas:

- The information flow throughout the chain of relevant parties;
- Key dates and their sequence;
- The operational processing of corporate actions.

And looks at:

- Information from issuer to issuer (I)CSD;
- Information from the issuer (I)CSD to its participants;
- Information flow from (I)CSD participants to end investors;
- Key dates; and
- Processing

---

[11]The BSG consists of the European issuers, the European Central Securities Depositories Association (ECSDA), the European Banking Federation (EBF), the European Association of Cooperative Banks (EACB), the European Savings Banks Group (ESBG), the Association for Financial Markets in Europe (AFME), the Federation of European Stock Exchanges (FESE) and the European Association of Clearing Houses (EACH). Euroshareholders has an observer status.

[12]*Source:* ECSDA (online) "Dismantling Giovannini Barrier 3: The Market Standards for Corporate Actions Processing and General Meetings – 5th Implementation Progress Report and 2012 Activity Report" (February 2013). Available from www.ecsda.eu/uploads/tx_doclibrary/2013_02_28_5th_BSG_Report.pdf. [Accessed Wednesday, 23 October 2013]

[13]ibid.

[14]*Source:* EBF (online) "European Industry Standards/Key Documents". Available from www.ebf-fbe.eu/index.php?page=market_standards. [Accessed Wednesday, 23 October 2013]

... for the following categories of corporate actions, as well as transaction management:

- Distributions
  - Cash distributions (e.g. cash dividend, interest payment);
  - Securities distributions (e.g. stock dividend, bonus issue);
  - Distributions with options (e.g. optional dividend).
- Reorganisations
  - Mandatory reorganisations with options (e.g. conversion);
  - Mandatory reorganisations (e.g. stock split, redemption);
  - Voluntary reorganisations (e.g. tender offer).
- Transaction management
  - Market claims (distributions);
  - Transformations (reorganisations);
  - Buyer protection (elective corporate actions).

The implementation of the Standards is being addressed by the European Market Implementation Group (E-MIG). Two of the conclusions that the E-MIG came to in a workshop held in November 2012 were that:

- Overall progress in implementing the Standards is steady but slow; however, efforts towards acceleration would most likely result in unwanted cutting of corners.
- The prioritisation of Standards is deemed helpful to applying limited resources in a focused manner; an additional prioritisation for markets with a lower level of implementation is not deemed advisable.

The reported levels of implementation are shown in Table 11.32.

TABLE 11.32   Standards implementation levels

Type of Corporate Action	8 Major Markets*	All Reporting Markets
Cash distributions	75% met 17% in progress 8% not met	69% met 19% in progress 12% not met
Securities distributions	69% met 19% in progress 12% not met	65% met 23% in progress 12% not met
Distributions with options	53% met 35% in progress 12% not met	50% met 27% in progress 23% not met
Mandatory reorganisations with options	62% met 23% in progress 15% not met	59% met 19% in progress 22% not met
Mandatory reorganisations	72% met 15% in progress 13% not met	70% met 19% in progress 11% not met
Voluntary reorganisations	67% met 18% in progress 15% not met	58% met 22% in progress 20% not met

Source: ECSDA "Implementation Status for the Corporate Action Standards – Autumn 2012".

11.9 CORPORATE GOVERNANCE AND PROXY VOTING

11.9.1 Introduction

The ways in which corporate entities are governed and controlled are known collectively as *corporate governance*. In particular, corporate governance refers to the ways in which corporations interact with their internal stakeholders (e.g. boards of directors, senior managers and employees) and external stakeholders (e.g. shareholders, bondholders, suppliers, customers, governmental agencies, etc.).

For the purposes of this book, we are only concerned with the relationship between the corporation and its shareholders and bondholders.

[The European Corporate Governance Institute has some useful information on its website (www.ecgi.org) including the full texts of Corporate Governance Codes for the United Nations and the many countries from which the membership is drawn.]

11.9.2 Relations with Shareholders

It is the responsibility of the corporation's board of directors to maintain a dialogue with its shareholders based on the mutual understanding of its objectives. This includes discussions with major shareholders on the corporation's governance and strategy and listening to its shareholders' views.

Corporations use the AGM to communicate with shareholders and to request them to vote on resolutions on issues such as:

- Electing directors;
- Appointing auditors;
- Approving by-laws and by-law changes;
- Fundamental changes, for example:
  - Amending the company's name, or
  - Amending the articles regarding such matters as the location of the registered office, restrictions on share transfers, restrictions on activities and changes involving such matters as amalgamation, dissolution and continuance;
- Selling all, or substantially all, of the company's assets.

You should be aware that shareholders are not involved in the day-to-day management of the company; this is the responsibility of the company's directors and managers.

Typically, shareholders with ordinary shares/common stock receive one vote per share. Other variations include:

- Each Class B ordinary share/common stock is entitled to ten votes;
- Each non-voting ordinary share/common stock does not carry a vote.

These proposed changes are summarised in the information circular sent to shareholders prior to the AGM. The share register is closed at least ten days before the AGM to enable the company secretary to prepare a list of shareholders and the number of shares held by each.

However, this means that, in theory, the shareholder must attend the AGM in order to exercise his/her vote.

Q&A

Question

What are some of the operational challenges for a shareholder who wishes to vote?

Answer

Challenges include:

1. If the shares are registered in the name of the investor, the investor will have to attend the AGM in person in order to vote. This is difficult if the investor has a broad range of domestic investments and has to travel to the conference centre where the AGM is being held. It is almost impossible if the investor's portfolio consists of a geographically diverse number of investments.
2. If the shares are registered in the name of a nominee, the fund manager has the same issues as in (1) but magnified to a greater degree.
3. A retail investor with a voting interest amounting to a fraction of a percent might be discouraged from voting at all due to the requirement to attend the AGM in person.

Since the early 1990s and especially since the Cadbury Report was published in the UK during 1992,[15] there has been a growing move to encourage investors of all sizes (the owners of the company) to pay more attention to corporate governance in the companies in which they have invested. Consequently, there has been an increasing need to vote one way or the other on the resolutions presented at the AGM.

With the challenges noted above, there had to be alternative solutions to enable voting to take place. Three solutions have been introduced:

- Electronic voting (i.e. there is no requirement to attend an AGM in person);
- A reduction in the costs involved;
- Allowing a third party to vote on behalf of the investor (i.e. proxy voting).

11.9.3 Proxy Voting

So, proxy voting occurs when a shareholder appoints a third party to vote on his/her behalf, usually in the absence of the shareholder. Depending on the local conventions, the investor

---

[15]The Committee on the Financial Aspects of Corporate Governance, chaired by Adrian Cadbury, and Gee & Co Ltd (1 December 1992) "Financial Aspects of Corporate Governance". Available from www.ecgi.org/codes/documents/cadbury.pdf.

can either instruct his custodian to vote or send a proxy card to the company's agent. For each resolution placed before the AGM, shareholders have the option to instruct their proxy to vote:

(a) For the resolution;
(b) Against the resolution;
(c) To withhold their vote.

We have noted above that voting was not normally an issue for the majority of shareholders unless there was some kind of conflict between shareholders and the directors of the company. In the 21st century, this attitude has changed and shareholders are more willing to express an opinion through the voting mechanism.

This presented the industry with a number of problems, not least of which was the communication chain between the company (issuer) and the shareholder. If proxy voting was to become the norm, then there had to be a degree of standardisation on timing and information issues. In its 1992 symposium, ISSA reported on cross-border proxy voting and made recommendations on improving procedures and looking at the data content of any information.

Time Schedule ISSA proposed a standardised time schedule that would enable communication between the issuer and shareholder to occur effectively (see Table 11.33).

TABLE 11.33 Voting timetable

Business Days Prior to Date of Meeting	Who Initiates	What Happens
25	Company/issuer	Announcement of meeting, agenda and resolutions
22	Company's agent banks and custodian banks	Daily consultation of a central database and/or receipt of information from nominee/CSD
22	Custodian banks	Information of clients holding shares and requesting instructions about proxy voting
17 – 12	Client holding shares	Voting instructions to custodian banks (yes/no/withheld)
7	Custodian banks	Blocking their clients' holdings until after meeting
6	Custodian banks	Requesting proxy cards from CSD or nominee
3	Custodian banks	Sending voting instructions to company or its agent

Source: Symposium Report, ISSA 6 (May 1992) "Cross Border Proxy Voting" (pp. 240–247).

Introducing this timetable (or a similar variation) helps to ensure that where a shareholder wishes to vote, it can do so in a standardised and orderly fashion.

Data Formats In the same way that settlements and, to a lesser extent, corporate actions activities can be communicated in SWIFT format, proxy voting can also adopt appropriate SWIFT message types. There are two appropriate message types:

MT560 – Notice of bond and shareholders' meeting;
MT561 – Proxy or authorisation and instructions to vote.

Proxy voting basically contains three groups of information (A–C) and flows in three steps (1–3):

> **Group A:** Basic information that includes the company's name and location, time and place of meeting, identification of securities and items on the agenda.
>
> **Group B:** Account reference that includes the quantity of securities involved, the account holder's reference and any information from custodian to beneficial owner.
>
> **Group C:** Voting instructions.

The above information is communicated in the following steps:

1. The company invites all interested parties to the meeting (containing Group A information).
2. Custodians (local/sub/global) inform the beneficial owners (Groups A and B information).
3. Beneficial owners wishing to use a proxy to vote must authorise a third party to act as proxy (Groups A, B and C information). (Otherwise, the beneficial owner deals direct with the company.)

11.9.4 Relations with Preference Shareholders

Preference shares (preferred stock) are a class of shares that contain one or more features that ordinary shares (common stock) do not. These features can include:

- **Dividends:** Most preference shares have a fixed dividend amount; either quoted as a percentage or as an amount per share. The company must pay the preference shareholders before the ordinary shareholders.
- **Liquidation:** Preference shareholders rank senior to the ordinary shareholders but junior to the remaining creditors.
- **Convertibility:** The investor has the right to exchange preference shares for ordinary shares if the preference shares have a conversion feature.
- **Voting rights:** Normally, preference shareholders do not have the right to vote. Under certain circumstances, however, shareholders may gain the right to vote should dividends not be paid.

11.9.5 Relations with Bondholders

Bondholders are creditors of the company and do not have the right to vote. By contrast, shareholders legally own a share in the issuing company. In the normal course of events, the company has a fiduciary obligation to its shareholders but not to its bondholders.

11.9.6 Company in Bankruptcy or Administration

These relationships can change in the event that the company gets into financial trouble prior to going into administration or filing for bankruptcy. In this case, a committee is appointed to look after the bondholders' interests. Should a company become bankrupt or go into administration, then the company's creditors are repaid, subject to sufficient assets being liquidated. In the meantime, bondholders will not receive any further coupon payments or shareholders any further dividends.

There is an order in which creditors are repaid, usually based on the degree of risk when issuing money to the company (see Table 11.34).

TABLE 11.34   Order of creditor repayment priority

Priority	Creditor Status	Examples
1st	Secured creditors	Loans backed by an asset – something measurable.
2nd	Unsecured creditors	Loans backed by the good name of the issuer only.
3rd	General creditors	Suppliers of goods and services.
4th	Shareholders (preference)	Preference shareholders normally have a claim on liquidation payments equal to the par value.
5th	Shareholders (ordinary)	Shareholders have a residual claim only and are last in line as they are the owners of the company.

11.9.7   Disclosure Reporting

Q&A

Question

What would you become if you held 50% of the voting shares in a company, plus one share?

Answer

You would, in effect, become the majority owner of that company: the biggest single shareholder. As you would always win any vote tabled at an AGM (or Extraordinary General Meeting), you would effectively control that company.

In all probability, this may not be a good idea from the company's point of view. With the use of nominee names, it can be possible to build a substantial holding in a company without the company knowing who the stakeholder is. For this reason, companies are entitled to know who the underlying beneficial owner is and this can be achieved by demanding that the nominee reveal who the underlying investors are. Failure to declare the information will result in the holding being frozen (e.g. no share transfers or dividend payments).

Depending on the market, investors holding less than 1% of the voting shares in a company are regarded as *minority shareholders* and more than 5% as *majority shareholders*. Reporting rules have a provision that once a shareholder becomes a majority shareholder, the shareholder (or its agent) must disclose that fact to the appropriate authorities. In addition, further disclosure is required when the holding increases past the next whole percentage point and/or decreases likewise. This enables the company's directors, employees and shareholders (together with the relevant authorities) to ascertain who is in a position to control or influence control of the company. On reaching a predefined level, the investor can be forced either to dispose of some shares or to make a formal bid to the company.

Examples of large holdings limits are shown in Table 11.35.

TABLE 11.35 Disclosure limits

Country	Large Holding	Disclosure Timing
Australia	5%	Within two business days
China	5%	Within three business days
France	5%, 10%, 20%, 33.33% or 66.66%	Within five trading days
Germany	5%, 10%, 25%, 50% or 75%	Within five business days
India	5% plus any change exceeding 2%	Within four business days
Italy	2%, 5%, 7.5%, 10% and subsequent multiples of 5%	Within five business days
Japan	5% + 1% increments	Within five business days (15th day of month following acquisition for financial institutions)
Russia	20% and subsequent multiples of 5%	Within five business days
South Africa	10%	During the month of acquisition
United Kingdom	3% + 1% increments	Within two business days (UK issuers) and four business days (non-UK issuers)

On 11 October 2013 the British Government floated the Royal Mail at an IPO price of 330p per share. The IPO proved to be such a success that by the end of the month the price had risen to 560p per share. It was reported in the *Financial Times* that the following institutional investors had acquired major shareholdings in the company:

- GIC (Singapore's sovereign wealth fund) – 4.1%;
- The Children's Investment Fund (a hedge fund) – 5.8%.

11.10 WITHHOLDING TAX

11.10.1 Introduction

Q&A

Question

In our daily lives, whether we are individual people or corporate entities, we are subject to taxation of one form or another. What forms of tax are you aware of?

Answer

Table 11.36 lists several taxes that you are probably aware of and some that you may not be.

TABLE 11.36   Taxes

Tax	Description
Capital gains tax	Based on the profits earned from the disposal of an asset.
Corporation tax	Based on the profits earned by companies.
Environmental tax	Based on financial offsetting of using carbon-based fuels (carbon tax) and greenhouse gas emissions.
Excise duty	Based on the quantity of a product such as petrol/diesel/gasoil.
Vehicle tax	An annual tax on car ownership based on the vehicle's carbon emission levels.
Financial transaction tax	Based on types of financial transaction.
Income tax	Based on personal earnings and usually paid on a "Pay As You Earn – PAYE" basis for employees.
Inheritance tax	Tax that arises on the death of an individual and usually based on the value of the deceased's possessions (property, investments, cash, etc.).
Property tax	Based on the value of a property and charged annually by a local municipality to the owner of the property.
Toll tax	Based on the use of a transport facility such as a bridge, motorway or tunnel. Usually a fixed charge dependent on the type of vehicle.
Value added tax (VAT)	Based as a fixed percentage of the sales price, charged by the seller to the buyer, and payable periodically by the seller to the tax authorities.
Dividend tax	Another form of income tax levied on dividend payments made to shareholders.

The above list of the different types of tax might give you the impression that anything and everything you have as an individual or a corporate entity is constantly subjected to taxation of one form or another. For our purposes, it is the last tax, dividend tax, with which we are concerned in this section.

It is normal market practice for the company paying a cash dividend to deduct (or withhold) the standard rate of tax and pay only the net amount to the shareholder. So, whilst this is a dividend tax, we normally refer to it as a *withholding tax* (WHT).

If a WHT rate is 10% and a company wishes to pay a (gross) dividend of 100, then the shareholder will receive 90, i.e. 100 minus 10. If the shareholder is a basic rate taxpayer, then there is no requirement to pay any further tax. However, if the shareholder is a higher rate taxpayer, then this next dividend is grossed up to 100 and the higher rate of tax applied to this gross amount.

11.10.2   The Problem of Double Taxation

This approach appears to be straightforward, as both the company paying a dividend and the shareholder receiving a dividend are located in the same country. A problem arises, however, when the shareholder is a non-resident of the country in which the company is located. It is quite possible that the dividend is initially taxed at the company's domestic rate (i.e. at 10% as quoted above) and paid to the shareholder, who is then charged tax at his domestic rate. If this domestic rate is, say, chargeable at 20%, then the shareholder will receive a net amount of 72 (i.e. 90 − 18). What we have here is an example of double taxation; in other words, the same dividend has been taxed initially in the country of the company and finally in the country of the shareholder.

On the one hand, the tax authority in the company's home country receives tax and on the other hand, the tax authority in the shareholder's home country also receives tax. Whilst good for the respective tax authorities, this situation is patently unfair on the shareholder, and it has been for global tax authorities to come up with a solution that enables the tax authorities to receive taxation and for the shareholder to pay tax at his normal domestic rate.

11.10.3   Double Taxation Treaties

To protect against the risk of double taxation where the same income is taxable in two countries, both tax authorities will enter into bilateral agreements known as *double taxation treaties* (DTTs) whereby the two tax authorities concerned agree to charge a lesser rate of tax (known as a *treaty rate*). Many, but not all, countries have DTTs in place; there are more than 3,000 DTTs worldwide.

According to Article 10: Dividends in the OECD "Model Tax Convention on Income and on Capital (2010)",[16] withholding tax charged should not exceed 15% of the gross amount and it is up to the two countries to mutually agree how they will apply this limit. The rate agreed between the two countries is known as the *treaty rate*. Where there is no DTT in existence, the full tax amount is deducted at a rate known as the *non-treaty rate*.

Shown in Table 11.37 is a fictitious example involving Country$_{(INV)}$ (the country of the investment) which has a treaty rate with Country$_{(TR)}$ and a non-treaty rate with Country$_{(NTR)}$.

TABLE 11.37   Treaty rate and non-treaty rate countries

Country$_{(INV)}$	Treaty Rate	Non-Treaty Rate
Country$_{(TR)}$	15%	–
Country$_{(NTR)}$	–	20%

Not only do we need to know the country of issue of a security and its DTT status, we also have to know the country of residence and the tax liability status of the investor/beneficial

---

[16]*Source:* OECD (online) Available from www.keepeek.com/Digital-Asset-Management/oecd/taxation/model-tax-convention-on-income-and-on-capital-condensed-version-2010_mtc_cond-2010-en. [Accessed Tuesday, 5 November 2013]

owner. This information will be held within the relevant reference information databases and will enable the correct amount of income to be received by the investor. In order to benefit from the DTT, investors will be expected to provide appropriate documentation proving their tax status and enabling their custodian to claim any over-paid taxes.

11.10.4 Tax Reclaims

The traditional means of ensuring that the correct amount of dividend was received was a method known as a *tax reclaim*. In a reclaim situation, the investor would initially be overtaxed and would subsequently reclaim the difference. This proved to be problematic for many countries and, as a result, investors would frequently not bother to make a reclaim.

In more recent years, investors were persuaded that they should expect their custodians to make these claims on their behalf; something which the custodians were not particularly able to do well. As servicing tax reclaims became more important for the investors, the custodians had to find a way to provide this service in a cost-effective manner. The custodians also lobbied tax authorities and found a way to work with them in designing a reclaim service.

A key part of this was to persuade the tax authorities to allow the custodians to certify the tax status of their clients and, in so doing, enable dividends to be paid with the correct amount of tax deducted at source rather than through a subsequent reclaim. Investors were therefore able to receive the correct amount of dividend on the payment date and not have to be concerned with subsequent reclaims.

So that the custodians could ensure that the correct amount of tax was deducted, their records needed to indicate the tax status of their clients (e.g. fully taxable, partially taxable or non-taxable) as well as the DTT status of the countries in which the investment had taken place.

Consider the following example. A custodian is holding 50 million shares in ABC Group on behalf of clients that are either fully or non-taxable and that are resident in countries which do and do not have a DTT with the country in which ABC is located. ABC announces a dividend of 0.50 per share. Table 11.38 illustrates how this position of 50 million shares can be subdivided by the investors' country of residence and its DTT status.

TABLE 11.38 Treaty rates and non-treaty rates

Custody Client	Position (m)	Tax Status	Gross Dividend (m)	Country$_{(TR)}$ @15% (m)	Country$_{(NTR)}$ @ 20% (m)
Client "A"	15	Full	7.50	6.38	
Client "B"	10	Non	5.00	5.00	
Client "C"	5	Full	2.50		2.00
Client "D"	20	Non	10.00		8.00
Totals:	50		25.00	11.38	10.00

Please note that although Client D is a non-taxpayer, the dividend has suffered a 20% deduction. This is because there is no treaty rate between the client's country of residence and the country of the investment. In this situation, the client (or its custodian) might have to reclaim this tax as a separate exercise.

11.11 IMPACT ON OTHER DEPARTMENTS

11.11.1 Introduction

As with other operational functions, Corporate Actions do not work in isolation. There are interdependencies that should be recognised and efforts made to provide information and assistance where necessary. Here are some thoughts on these interdependencies.

11.11.2 Front Office

The main issue is that it might be the responsibility of Corporate Actions Operations to update the Front Office position systems with details of an event (e.g. entering a transaction that represents a bonus issue). This activity could be described as unusual, as the Front Office normally enters transaction details into its own systems.

Trading for normal settlement ahead of a corporate action event taking place might be inappropriate if the resultant securities are received after the normal settlement date, i.e. the transaction will fail due to insufficient securities.

New securities may not rank *pari passu* with the old securities, and the Front Office might decide to sell the total position. In this situation, there should be two separate trades – one for the old shares and one for the new. If the Front Office is unaware of the *pari passu* status, it might over-sell the old shares only, causing settlement problems.

Example

You have a position of 100,000 ABC plc. ordinary shares. ABC issues one new share for every ten existing shares. The new shares will not be entitled to the next dividend (and thus do not rank *pari passu* with the old shares). The correct position is shown in Table 11.39.

TABLE 11.39 Positions post corporate action event

Old Shares	Old Shares	New Shares	Comments
ID ref:	ABC	ABCN	▪ New shares have a different ID ref until both positions are amalgamated after the next dividend.
Position:	100,000	10,000	▪ Two separate positions.
Transaction:	Sell 100,000	Sell 10,000	▪ Two transactions.
Incorrect situation:	Sell 110,000		▪ There are only 100,000 old shares available to deliver. ▪ The dealer has gone short 10,000 old and is long 10,000 new.

As the Front Office is the internal client for its proprietary positions, it is the responsibility of the Corporate Actions Operations to let it have sufficient information to make timely and accurate decisions. Other issues to be aware of include:

- ▪ Obtaining instructions from the Front Office for voluntary events;
- ▪ Executing instructions within the issuer's deadlines.

11.11.3 Clients

Clients and their agents (e.g. fund managers) are the external equivalent of the Front Office and should be treated in the same way. Again, it is the responsibility of the Corporate Actions Operations staff to let them have sufficient information to make timely and accurate decisions. Other issues to be aware of include:

- Providing sufficient information to clients so that they can make timely and accurate decisions;
- Obtaining instructions from the clients for voluntary events;
- Executing instructions on behalf of the clients within the issuer's deadlines.

11.11.4 Settlements

Settlements are responsible for ensuring that transactions settle on time and actively managing failed transactions. Corporate Actions Operations should be made aware of any fails that might affect the correct allocation of entitlements.

Example 1

Shares have been purchased cum-dividend. Due to a settlement fail, the shares are not registered in time for the record date. Corporate Actions Operations must either submit a claim to the selling broker/counterparty or check to make sure that the clearing system has correctly compensated the dividend.

Example 2

Shares have been purchased cum-rights. Due to a settlement fail, the shares are not registered in time for the record date. Corporate Actions Operations must request the selling broker/counterparty to act on behalf of the purchaser, i.e. sell any rights or accept the offer and pay the call amount. The selling broker/counterparty will expect to receive the call monies from Corporate Action Operations in order to cover the call payment.

11.11.5 Securities Lending and Borrowing

Under the terms of the Securities Lending Agreement (SLA), the securities lender is entitled to benefit from corporate action events as they occur, with the possible exception of voting. Lenders that wish to vote generally need to recall loaned securities ahead of any voting opportunities.

In much the same way that benefits are allocated to a seller in the event that a settlement fails (see above), with securities lending it is the borrower that initially receives the benefit. It is necessary for both lenders and borrowers to ensure that any corporate action events are apportioned to the correct party.

11.11.6 Reconciliations

Although cash and securities reconciliations are reactive events, nevertheless any corporate action events that have been missed or input incorrectly should be identified at this stage. Here are two examples:

1. Yell Group plc. changed its name to Hibu plc. in May 2012. You have a holding in Yell Group shares and fail to notice that the name has been changed. As a consequence, you have not made the necessary updates to your securities positions. A typical securities reconciliation is shown in Table 11.40.

TABLE 11.40 Yell Group and Hibu plc. reconciliation

Issuer	Trade Date Position (Ledger)	Custodian Position (Statement)
Hibu plc., ordinary shares	0	100,000
Yell Group plc., ordinary shares	100,000	0

Reconciliations would identify this as a reconciliation break that would be rectified by passing entries to debit Yell Group ordinary shares and credit Hibu ordinary shares. At first sight, it may not be obvious that these two positions are closely related, although either contacting the custodian or researching both companies would show the reason for the reconciliation break.

2. A more serious situation would potentially arise if a bond were to be called for early redemption. If the position records are not updated and the Front Office attempts to sell the original position, there will be no bonds with which to make a delivery. The result will be that the Front Office has sold bonds it does not own and therefore has sold short.

11.11.7 Pricing and Valuation

We have seen that share prices can change as the result of a corporate action (e.g. a 1:1 bonus issue will tend to reduce the share price by 50%). Failure to enter corporate action events into the position records could mean that the Front Office might assume that a security is either undervalued or overvalued and might be tempted to trade accordingly.

Example

You hold a position of 50,000 shares in Heineken and the share price is EUR 50.32 per share. The company announces a 1:4 bonus issue and, as a result, the share price drops to EUR 40.2560 per share, as shown in Table 11.41.

TABLE 11.41 Heineken bonus issue

Heineken Shares	Quantity	Price (EUR)	Value (EUR)
Existing holding	50,000	50.32	2,516,000.00
1:4 bonus issue	12,500	0.00	0.00
Total	62,500	40.2560	2,516,000.00

Had the bonus shares not been entered into the system, you would have shown a position of only 50,000 shares, priced at EUR 40.2560 per share and valued at only EUR 2,012,800.00 (i.e. an apparent loss of EUR 503,200.00).

11.11.8 Reference Data

The information held in the securities database must be accurate and up to date, otherwise potential opportunities for predictable/voluntary and certain mandatory events might well be missed.

Example

You are holding a position of USD 5 million Swire Pacific 1.25% bonds due in April 2018. According to your database, this is a straight bond with a single redemption date; however, this is incorrect and in fact the bond has a put option. If interest rates were at a level whereby you or your client would wish to put the bond back to the issuer, then your database would not be in a position to advise you of the terms of any potential early redemption (e.g. dates and prices).

11.12 SUMMARY

A corporate action is any situation or event that is initiated by the issuing company and which has an impact on the issuer itself and/or the issuer's shareholders or bondholders.

Corporate actions can be either benefits (e.g. a cash dividend paid to shareholders) or "situations" that impact the issuer's balance sheet (e.g. a capitalisation issue).

Some types of corporate action are known as mandatory events. These occur without any beneficial owner choice (e.g. a stock split). Other types are optional or voluntary, where the beneficial owner has a choice to make (e.g. a rights issue).

There is a large number of corporate action types, ranging in complexity from reasonably straightforward (e.g. a share consolidation) to complicated and time-consuming (e.g. a hostile, contested takeover bid).

All corporate actions are time-sensitive and care must be taken especially when handling optional events, as failure to execute a required action by a specified date can result in substantial financial losses.

APPENDIX 11.1: CORPORATE ACTION EVENT TYPE CATEGORIES

Corporate actions can be grouped into nine key event-type categories with numerous sub-types:

1. **Capital changes:** Bonus issue, consolidation, enfranchisement, distribution, forward stock split, par value change, recapitalisation, redenomination, renominalisation, reverse stock split, rights offering, unit split, spin off, scheme of arrangement.

2. **Dividends:** Cash dividend, disbursement, dividend waived, return of capital, scrip dividend, stock dividend, dividend reinvestment plan.
3. **Earnings:** Actual earnings, forecasted earnings, adjusted earnings.
4. **Payments:** Cash payment, interest payment, payment waived, return of debt, scrip payment.
5. **Mergers:** Merger, merger election, offer to buy, takeover, demerger.
6. **Redemptions:** Call, escrow to maturity, fixed redemption, full call, partial call, partial pre-refunded, pre-refunded, repayment, sinking fund redemption.
7. **Repurchases:** Buy-back, consent, consent tender, conversion, exchange, exercise, odd lot tender, partial put/retainment option, put mandatory, put optional, relinquishment option, retainment option, tender offer.
8. **Shareholder meetings:** Shareholder meeting, Annual General Meeting, Extraordinary General Meeting.
9. **Information announcements:** Bankruptcy, default, information, liquidation, name change, new offer, poison pill.

APPENDIX 11.2: VOLUNTARY AND MANDATORY EVENTS FOR EQUITIES AND BONDS

Here you will find a list of voluntary and mandatory events for both equities and bonds. This list is an extract from the Securities Market Practice Group's "SMPG CA Global Market Practice – Part 2 for Standards Release 2014" released 12 February 2014.

The EIG+ tab contains the following information:

1. Corporate action event name;
2. A definition plus any comments made by the SMPG;
3. Short name code for the event (CAEV);
4. Mandatory/voluntary/choice indicator code (CAMV);
5. Other technical information.

The SMPG Corporate Actions Global Market Practice Part 1 document, together with the Part 2 spreadsheet, is updated fairly often. It is, therefore, a good idea to visit the website frequently.

The full list is available to guest visitors and can be obtained from http://smpg.webexone .com.

Click through to Documents>Public Documents>2. Corporate Actions>A. Final Global Documents>2. CA Global Market Practice – Part 2 – SR2014 V1.1.xlsm (last updated 1 August 2014).

CHAPTER 12

Securities Financing

12.1 INTRODUCTION

In Chapter 7: Securities Clearing, we saw that forecasting was an important part of the clearing process. We require sufficient cash to pay for our purchases and securities availability to ensure delivery of our sales.

Recall our choices in Table 12.1.

TABLE 12.1 Financing choices

Transaction	Comments	Financing Choices
Our purchases	Our funding costs increase if we are unable to pay for our purchases. The trades might settle (incurring overdraft charges) or might be blocked by the clearing house (resulting in interest charges from our counterparties).	▪ Rely on credit line/overdraft ▪ Sell assets ▪ Use securities financing
Our sales	We will not receive the cash proceeds as expected. We will lose re-investment opportunities and the lack of cash might also result in failed purchases.	▪ Use securities financing

We can conclude that securities financing allows us to borrow cash for our purchases (and other funding requirements) and borrow securities to facilitate our sales (and other securities deliveries).

There are three types of securities financing:

1. Securities lending and borrowing;
2. Repurchase agreements;
3. Sell/buy-backs.

By the end of this chapter, you will be able to:

- ▪ Understand the different types of securities financing;
- ▪ Follow the lifecycle of a securities financing transaction;
- ▪ Appreciate the risks involved and how they can be mitigated;
- ▪ Understand the roles of the participants and intermediaries.

12.2 TYPES OF SECURITIES FINANCING

Securities financing is the temporary lending of assets to a borrower in exchange for a fee. Asset types include:

- Cash
- Securities
  - Equities
  - Bonds

We will see that cash is lent and borrowed predominantly through repurchase agreements and, to a much lesser extent, sell/buy-backs and securities through securities lending and borrowing.

12.2.1 Securities Lending and Borrowing

Securities lending and borrowing ("securities lending") involves a transfer of securities (such as shares or bonds) from a "lender" to a third party (the "borrower"), who provides the lender with collateral in the form of shares, bonds or cash.[1]

Legally, a securities loan is the transfer of title against an irrevocable undertaking to return equivalent securities. This means that registered securities such as shares will be transferred out of the lender's name into that of the borrower and registered back in the lender's name when they are returned.

When we look at the motivations for securities lending, we will see that the borrower will sell, lend-on or otherwise dispose of the securities. In order to do this, the borrower must have legal ownership of the securities. The lender therefore surrenders legal ownership, implying a disposal rather than a temporary loan of the securities.

A securities lending agreement will bridge the gap between the legal and economic nuances of this business. For securities lending, the Global Master Securities Lending Agreement (GMSLA), published by the International Securities Lending Association (ISLA), is used.

12.2.2 Repurchase Agreements

A repurchase agreement (*repo*) is the sale of securities together with an agreement for the seller to buy back the securities at a later date. The primary purpose of a repo is to enable the seller to borrow cash using the securities as collateral.

If the above definition of a repo is stated from the seller's point of view, what is the buyer's?

For the buyer, there is an agreement to purchase securities together with an agreement to sell them back to the seller. The primary purpose is to enable the buyer to lend cash, taking the securities as collateral. We refer to this agreement as a *reverse repo*.

In any particular transaction, there will be a repo (seller) and a reverse repo (buyer).

---

[1]*Source:* ISLA (online) "Securities Lending – A Guide for Policymakers". Available from www.isla.co.uk/images/PDF/Publications/sl_aGuide_for_Policy_makers.pdf. [Accessed Saturday, 28 December 2013]

A repo is generally used to raise cash, i.e. for financing purposes. A repo can also be securities-driven, i.e. the "buyer" is borrowing securities and using cash as collateral.

The legal agreement is the Global Master Repurchase Agreement (GMRA), published jointly by the Securities Industry and Financial Markets Association (SIFMA) and the International Capital Market Association (ICMA).

12.2.3 Sell/Buy-Backs

In contrast to securities lending and repo activities, which are covered by the various editions of the GMSLA and GMRA respectively, sell/buy-back transactions were traditionally a sale of and a subsequent re-purchase of securities. These were undocumented and treated as two separate transactions. Today, sell/buy-backs are documented and covered by the GMRA supported by a sell/buy-back annex.

Apart from some operational differences, a documented sell/buy-back is similar to a repo and a buy/sell-back to a reverse repo.

Undocumented sell/buy-back transactions are riskier than those covered by the appropriate documentation.

12.2.4 Summary of Securities Financing Transactions

The three types of securities financing transaction are summarised in Figure 12.1.

Characteristic	Securities Lending	Repo Agreements & Documented Sell/Buy-Back	Undocumented Sell/Buy-Back
Motivation	Security specific	Financing or Security specific	Financing
Maturity	Open (Call) or Term	Open (Call) or Term	Open (Call) or Term
Method of exchange	Sale with agreement to purchase equivalent securities	Sale with agreement to purchase equivalent securities	Sale and repurchase
How exchanged	▪ Securities vs. Cash ▪ Securities vs. Non-cash Collateral	▪ Securities vs. Cash (if securities specific) ▪ Cash vs. Securities (if financing)	Cash vs. Securities
Collateral type	▪ Cash ▪ Non-cash (bonds, CDs, LCs, equities, etc.)	▪ Cash (if securities specific) ▪ General collateral (e.g. bonds)	Usually bonds
Collateral substitution	Borrower's choice	▪ No (if securities specific) ▪ Original seller's choice (if financing)	No

FIGURE 12.1 Summary of securities financing transactions

Characteristic	Securities Lending	Repo Agreements & Documented Sell/Buy-Back	Undocumented Sell/Buy-Back
Return paid to giver of:	▪ Cash (*) ▪ Securities lent	Cash	Cash
Form of return	▪ Rebate rate (if cash) ▪ Lending fee (if non-cash)	Interest rate quoted as a repo rate (paid as interest on the cash)	Interest rate quoted as a repo rate (paid through the difference between sale price and buy-back price)
Income (coupons & dividends)	Manufactured and paid to the lender	Paid to original seller	Normally factored into the buy-back price
(*) The cash giver receives interest on the cash (rebate rate) and the cash taker reinvests the cash (reinvestment rate) at a higher interest rate. The difference between the reinvestment and rebate rates represents the return to the securities lender.			

FIGURE 12.1   (*Continued*)

12.3 THE PLAYERS AND THEIR MOTIVATIONS

12.3.1 Introduction

We have seen that securities financing is driven by the need for either cash or securities and that the transactions are collateralised by appropriate securities and cash. In this section, we will consider the players from the perspective of the buy side and the sell side. Buy-side motivation is basic; sell-side motivation is more complex.

12.3.2 The Buy Side

Q&A

Question

What do the following buy-side institutions usually have in common?

- Central banks
- Commercial banks
- Mutual funds
- Exchange-traded funds
- Pension funds
- Insurance companies
- Sovereign wealth funds
- Corporate treasuries
- Fund/asset/investment managers

> **Answer**
>
> These institutions usually have one or more of the following characteristics in common:
>
> 1. They are cash-rich;
> 2. They beneficially own deep pools of securities;
> 3. They manage cash and securities assets on behalf of clients;
> 4. They tend to be risk averse;
> 5. They tend to hold their assets for medium/long-term periods of time.

These characteristics can be attractive to potential borrowers requiring access to cash and/or securities.

There is only one reason why any of the above buy-side institutions would want to lend its securities and cash: to earn a return. This return can be explicit in terms of earning fees or interest on cash balances or implied in terms of reduced custody fees incurred by the institution. It is also true that securities lending and securities-specific repo and sell/buy-back transactions increase securities liquidity in the market.

12.3.3 The Sell Side

There are several reasons why any institution might require access to securities and cash. These include:

- To cover a short position (securities);
- To finance an inventory position (cash);
- To benefit from a temporary transfer of ownership (securities).

> **Q&A**
>
> **Question**
>
> What types of institutions might wish to benefit from one or more of these three reasons?
>
> **Answer**
>
> The following institutional types might wish to utilise securities borrowing:
>
> - Market-makers
> - Hedge funds
> - Broker/dealers
> - Central banks (they facilitate central bank operations using the repo market)

Reasons include:

- Covering short positions in securities;
- Funding long positions in securities;
- Preventing settlement fails;
- Reducing funding costs;
- Reducing risk through the use of collateral;
- Ensuring liquidity in the secondary markets;
- Hedging derivatives activities;
- Preventing/containing market "squeezes" that can lead to settlement problems and disorderly markets;
- Permitting shorter settlement cycles to occur;
- Allowing more efficient use of capital.

Let us take a look at some examples of the reasons for borrowing securities and cash.

12.3.4 Borrowing to Cover Short Positions

Settlement Fails Management   You purchase USD 5,000,000 of a bond from one counterparty and sell USD 4,000,000 of the same bond to another counterparty, both for the same settlement date. On the settlement date the purchase fails; this leaves you short of bonds for the sale, which results in a second settlement fail. By borrowing USD 4,000,000 of the bond you will be able to settle the sale. This situation gives you two benefits:

1. As you have not had to pay for the purchase, you have "use of funds";[2] and
2. You have the sale proceeds which you can make use of.

On settlement of the purchase, you will be able to repay the loan of USD 4 million of the bond. The funding benefit of your positive cash flow should outweigh the cost of borrowing the bonds.

We covered the subject of fails management in more detail in Chapter 8.

Short Selling   You are a dealer and you take the view that shares in a company are about to go down in price. You do not have a position in the shares. In order to benefit, you sell the shares now and plan to buy them back at some unspecified future time when, hopefully, the price has gone down. As you have executed a sale, you have an obligation to deliver shares that you do not have. In order to settle your sale, you will need to borrow the shares until such time as you buy them back.

---

[2]The term "use of funds" means that, in theory, you can reinvest this cash until it is required to cover the purchase settlement. In practice, however, you would leave the cash idle in the settlement account.

Market Making   As a market maker, you have the obligation to make a two-way price under any market conditions. If the market comes to you with more "buy orders" than "sell orders", you might be going short of securities to deliver. In this case, you will need to borrow some from securities and return them when your inventory goes long.

Arbitrage Trading   An arbitrage strategy involves going long in one security and short in another, often related, security. The short position will need to be covered by borrowing the securities.

An example would be a convertible bond arbitrage where the arbitrageur buys a convertible bond and sells the equivalent number of underlying shares. For this strategy to work, the arbitrageur will need to borrow the shares until such time as the arbitrage is closed (i.e. buy the shares, sell the convertible bond and repay the loan of shares).

Derivatives Activities   A derivatives trader writes call options on a single stock in the expectation that he will not be called upon to exercise and deliver the underlying shares.

Q&A

Question

Under what circumstances would the trader have to deliver the underlying shares and what are the main risks and benefits?

Answer

- A writer of a call option hopes that the underlying share price does not increase beyond the break-even price. He is therefore vulnerable if the share price increases and can expect to be exercised against.
- To cover the possibility of an exercise, the dealer should either have the underlying shares or, if not, then he/she should borrow them to cover a "naked" position.
- If the option is European style, then there is just the one date on which exercise can take place; for an American-style option, exercise can take place at any time and this could require the trader to borrow the underlying shares from the moment he wrote them.
- The benefit for the writer is the premium received when the contract is executed.

12.3.5 Borrowing Cash to Finance Inventory

When a dealer buys one or more securities, it can finance the purchase costs using repo or sell/buy-back transactions. The dealer can either repo the purchased securities straight back to the original selling counterparty or repo other securities using the cash to finance the original transactions.

12.3.6 Temporary Transfer of Ownership

Arbitrage opportunities can arise when ownership of equities is temporarily transferred. However, securities lending in these situations may not be regarded as acceptable practice. There are three examples to consider:

- Dividend arbitrage;
- Scrip dividend arbitrage;
- Exercising voting rights.

Dividend Arbitrage   This is a tax-avoidance scheme used by investors based in a country that does not have a double taxation agreement with the country in which the investment is located and taxed (foreign investor). If the tax rate is 25%, then the foreign investor will receive 75% of the dividend.

With a dividend arbitrage, the shares are lent through an intermediary to a local company (borrower) over the dividend period. The borrower receives the dividend with a tax credit of 30%, enabling it to reclaim part of the tax paid by the corporation. Therefore, for every 1.00 of dividend, it is worth 1.43 to the borrower [1.43 * (100% − 30%) = 1.00].

The shares are then returned to the original lender (the foreign investor) and the increase in dividend shared between the three parties involved, with the lender receiving either an extra lending fee or a manufactured dividend.

Q&A

Question

How much extra dividend is received and what is the consequence for the local tax authority?

Answer

The extra dividend amounts to 0.68 (i.e. original tax deduction of 0.25 plus the tax credit of 0.43). The local tax authority "loses" 0.68.

Scrip Dividend Arbitrage   Arbitrage opportunities can arise when a company announces a dividend and gives the shareholder the option of receiving either cash or more shares. An arbitrageur will borrow the shares over the dividend period with an agreement that he will pay cash to the lender. The borrower will know how many shares are available based on an average of several days' closing prices following the ex-dividend date.

However, the decision as to whether to take cash or shares does not have to be made for several weeks. Depending on what the share price subsequently does, the borrower will either take cash or shares which can then be sold for a profit as the example in Tables 12.2 and 12.3 illustrates.

TABLE 12.2 Scrip dividend arbitrage

Holding	10,000	Shares		
Dividend	0.50	per share =	5,000.00	Cash
Average Closing Price	25.00	per share		
New Shares *in lieu* of cash dividend	200	Shares	i.e. [5,000/25]	

TABLE 12.3 Decision – cash or shares?

Share Price Movement	Price	Action Taken by Borrower	Result	Cash
Increases to	30.00	Take shares in lieu, sell them and pay dividend to lender	Sell 200 shares @ 30.00	6,000.00
			Pay dividend to lender	−5,000.00
			Profit:	**1,000.00**
Decreases to	20.00	Take cash dividend and pay dividend to lender	Receive dividend	5,000.00
			Pay dividend to lender	−5,000.00
			Profit:	**0.00**

On the decision date, the borrower must decide whether to take cash or shares (Table 12.3).

Q&A

Question

Why would the borrower not accept shares if the market price had declined to 20.00?

Answer

The borrower would make a loss of 1,000.00.

The sale proceeds of 4,000.00 (200 shares @ 20.00) would not cover the dividend of 5,000.00 payable to the lender.

This arbitrage has been made to look as if the borrower was effectively holding a call option – either take the shares (exercise) or not (take the dividend).

Exercising Voting Rights   An organisation could influence the corporate governance of a company without being a beneficial owner by borrowing shares and voting on them at an AGM or EGM. The UK's Bank of England addressed this point in its 2009 Code of Guidance.

Firstly, it noted that: "… securities should not be borrowed solely for the purpose of exercising the voting rights…" and secondly, that lenders should: "… consider their corporate governance responsibilities before lending stock over a (AGM/EGM) period…".[3]

12.3.7 Summary

We have seen that there are various reasons why companies should want to borrow securities and that some might be questionable in terms of tax avoidance or corporate governance issues. It is for these reasons that the regulators allow securities lending and borrowing to take place for so-called permitted purposes. These permitted purposes can be summarised as follows:

- Facilitating the settlement of a trade;
- Facilitating delivery of a short sale;
- Financing the security;
- Lending to another borrower who is motivated by one of these permitted purposes.

12.4 INTERMEDIARIES

12.4.1 The Relationship between Lender and Borrower

It is highly unlikely that a beneficial owner of securities will lend directly to the ultimate borrower of securities. There could be a "chain" or "conduit" of borrowings starting with the lender, who lends to the first borrower, who, in turn, lends to the second borrower. In this scenario, the lender could not know who the second borrower was.

There are two types of intermediary: agent intermediaries and principal intermediaries.

12.4.2 Agent Intermediaries

Agent intermediaries will, in all probability, be offering other services to their clients wishing to lend their securities. Take the example of a pension fund. A pension fund will appoint a fund manager to manage its assets. The pension fund (or its fund manager) will appoint a custodian to look after its assets including clearing and settlement, safekeeping and asset servicing.

The pension fund is the beneficial owner and might wish to take advantage of securities lending activities. It would be unlikely that the pension fund would have the resources and expertise to directly manage its own securities lending programme, and so it might appoint either its fund manager or its custodian to manage a programme on a discretionary basis.

In addition to fund managers and custodian banks, there are third-party agents that specialise in the management of securities lending programmes. These three types of intermediary act as agents on behalf of their clients; they will deal with the borrowers, manage the programme and share in the fees earned. Whilst they have a duty of care towards their clients, agent intermediaries do not take principal risk.

---

[3]*Source:* Bank of England (July 2009) "Securities Borrowing and Lending – Code of Guidance" Section 7.4 p.18. Available from http://webarchive.nationalarchives.gov.uk/20100114080129/http://www.bankofengland.co.uk/markets/gilts/stockborrowing.pdf [Accessed Monday, 30 December 2013]

12.4.3 Principal Intermediaries

Principal intermediaries can act either on their own behalf as borrowers or on behalf of their clients. The main differences between a principal and an agent intermediary are that a principal intermediary can perform the following roles:

- Providing a credit-based intermediary service; for example, the lender might be happy to lend to the principal from a credit point of view but might not be willing to lend directly to the borrower.
- Assuming liquidity risk by borrowing from a lender on an "open" basis and lending on a "term" basis to a borrower.
- Establishing a "one-to-many" type of relationship between lender and borrower; for example, the principal intermediary might be able to satisfy a single borrower's request from many lenders (and also vice versa).

Examples of principal intermediaries include:

- Broker/dealers in order to support proprietary trading, market making and on behalf of clients such as prime brokers.
- Specialist intermediaries, who might only provide a service between the lenders and, for example, market makers.
- Prime brokers servicing the needs of hedge funds and managers of alternative investment funds.

12.4.4 Choices for the Lenders and Borrowers

We have, on the one hand, institutions that are willing to lend their securities and, on the other hand, institutions that wish to borrow the securities. The question arises as to what would be the best way for a borrower to obtain the securities it requires.

Before we can answer this, we need to know what makes a good lender – a "good lender" from the point of view of the borrower. Which of the portfolio types in Table 12.4 do you think would be of more interest to a potential borrower?

TABLE 12.4 Lenders' portfolio characteristics

Portfolio Characteristics	Portfolio "A"	Portfolio "B"	Portfolio "C"
Size	USD 10 million	USD 1 billion	USD 20 billion
Average size of each holding	USD 250,000	USD 5,000,000	USD 10,000,000
Average number of holdings	40	200	2,000
Investment strategy	Passively managed	Actively managed	Passively managed
Diversification	Domestic equities and bonds	Global equities	Global equities and bonds
Attitude to risk	Risk averse – high quality collateral required	Medium risk – wider range of acceptable collateral	Risk flexible – wide range of acceptable collateral across most asset classes

A potential borrower might be attracted to all three portfolios as they could contain many of the securities it requires. However, the borrower should consider the following possible hurdles:

- **Portfolio "A":** This portfolio is somewhat limited in terms of geographical reach (domestic securities), has relatively few holdings, each with an average size of USD 250,000 and is somewhat cautious in terms of risk (will only accept high quality collateral). On the positive side, this is a passively managed portfolio, suggesting that the holdings do not change frequently.
- **Portfolio "B":** This is a larger portfolio than "A" with a greater number of holdings and a somewhat more flexible approach to collateral requirements. The portfolio is reasonably diversified albeit in one asset class only. A possible disadvantage is that the portfolio is actively managed, suggesting that any securities that the borrower takes could be recalled at any moment.
- **Portfolio "C":** This portfolio would appear to be the more attractive proposition. It has a large number of holdings, each of a good size, it is passively managed and well diversified. In addition to this, the portfolio has a flexible approach to collateral.

Taking these factors into account and with all things being equal, you might expect most borrowers would want to approach Portfolio "C" in the first instance. It might well be the case that the other two portfolios might only ever be approached occasionally, if at all.

If Portfolios "A" and "B" wish to lend securities, their only choice might be to use an agent intermediary such as their custodian and participate in its managed lending programme on a pooled basis. On the other hand, Portfolio "C" might be attractive enough that principal intermediaries would wish to deal directly with that portfolio.

12.5 AGREEMENTS AND CODE OF GUIDANCE

12.5.1 Introduction

You will recall that the definitions of securities financing imply from a legal standpoint that the lender is, in fact, disposing of its securities and the borrower is acquiring them. One of the purposes of a legal agreement is to turn the disposal/re-acquisition concept into an economically temporary and short-term collateralised lending transaction. For this to occur, securities financing is supported using legally accepted agreements. These agreements were traditionally negotiated bilaterally between lender and borrower/agent. Over time, these agreements have become globally standardised.

Copies of these agreements can be found on the appropriate website and are free to download. Please note that there might be two or more versions of an agreement as these are updated periodically.

12.5.2 Securities Lending Agreements

The master agreements for the securities lending business can be found on the International Securities Lending Association's website at www.isla.co.uk/index.php/master-agreements where you will find the documents shown in Table 12.5.

TABLE 12.5 ISLA documentation

Documentation	Version	Date
Global Master Securities Lending Agreement (GMSLA)	GMSLA 2010	July 2012 with minor changes to the 2010 version
	GMSLA (US Tax Addendum 2013)	November 2013
	GMSLA (UK Tax Addendum 2014)	December 2013
	Freshfields' Guidance Notes	April 2010
	...together with previous versions and an archive.	
Netting opinions	Available on subscription only	
Securities Lending Set-Off Protocol	▪ Adherence Letter Submission Process ▪ ISLA 2009 Securities Lending Set-Off Protocol text ▪ Form of Adherence Letter ▪ Form of Revocation Notice	
Industry documentation	Key aspects of working practice, including the Bank of England's "Securities Lending and Repo Committee – Stock Borrowing and Lending Code of Guidance – July 2009".	

You can also find a list of current best practice papers on the website (www.isla.co.uk/index.php/bestpractices) which includes the titles in Table 12.6.

TABLE 12.6 Best practice papers

Title	Date
ISLA Agency Lending Disclosure Approval of Principals – Best Practice Paper	October 2013
Statement of Market Guidance: Securities Lending (Fixed Income) Contract Compare	April 2013
Fixed Income Loan Redemptions and Coupon Collection	February 2010
Billing Statement Report Format for Equity Loans	July 2009
Mark to Market for Equity Loans	June 2009
Contract Compare	April 2009
Mark to Market Report Formats for Equity Loans	March 2009
Billing Compare	December 2008
Returns and Recalls	December 2008
Manufactured Income Collection	January 2008

If you have not already done so, please download the GMSLA 2010 and familiarise yourself with the main topics noted therein. We will refer to this agreement when we go through the lifecycle in Section 12.6 below.

12.5.3 Repurchase Agreements

The International Capital Market Association (ICMA), together with what is now the Securities Industry and Financial Markets Association (SIFMA), introduced the first version of the Global

Master Repurchase Agreement (GMRA) in 1992. The agreement has been updated three times, with the current version being the GMRA 2011.

Three versions (1995, 2000 and 2011) are available on the ICMA website (www.icmagr oup.org/Regulatory-Policy-and-Market-Practice/short-term-markets/Repo-Markets/global-m aster-repurchase-agreement-gmra/#list). For the 2011 version, you can also find the following documents:

- Revised version of the GMRA Protocol;
- GMRA 2011 black-lined to show changes from GMRA 2000;
- Guidance Notes to the GMRA 2011;
- Buy/Sell-Back Annex to the GMRA 2011;
- Bills Annex to the GMRA 2011;
- Agency Annex to the GMRA 2011;
- Equities Annex to the GMRA 2011;
- Russian Annex to the GMRA 2011;
- Russian Translation of the GMRA 2011.

In order to cover the validity of the GMRA and the enforceability of the netting provisions contained within the agreement, ICMA has obtained legal opinions covering 62 countries (plus a supplement for Switzerland). These are referred to as the 2013 GMRA Legal Opinions and they consist of a Core Opinion of the GMRA and various SLAs plus specific appendices covering each of the agreements.

12.5.4 Code of Guidance

The Bank of England's Securities Lending and Repo Committee published the *Securities Borrowing and Lending Code of Guidance* in 2009 and the *Gilt Repo Code of Guidance* in 2008. These are currently under review[4] and are available on request.[5] The 2009 Code of Guidance can also be found on the ISLA website (www.isla.co.uk/index.php/master-agree ments/industrydoc).

12.6 SECURITIES LENDING LIFECYCLE

In this section we will look at the lifecycle of a securities loan. There are three phases that we will look at in more detail:

Phase 1: Loan initiation;

Phase 2: Loan maintenance;

Phase 3: Loan closure.

Securities lending is another example of a collateralised activity; you will recall that we previously looked at collateral for non-centrally cleared derivatives in Chapter 9.

---

[4]Refer to Bank of England (online) "Codes of Guidance". Available from www.bankofengland.co.uk/ markets/Pages/gilts/slrc.aspx. [Accessed Friday, 9 May 2014]

[5]Available on request: The Secretary to the Securities Lending and Repo Committee, Bank of England (HO-1), Threadneedle Street, London EC2R 8AH.

Remember that there are several ways in which the beneficial owner is able to lend securities through the appointment of:

- A local/global custodian as agent;
- A third-party specialist as agent;
- A principal as an intermediary;
- A proprietary principal;
- A combination of the above.

Whilst these approaches will differ in detail, the concepts will remain fairly similar.

12.6.1   Phase 1: Loan Initiation

Borrower Approaches Lender   Loans can be initiated in several ways that range from an *ad hoc* approach, to automatic lending and borrowing, and to the use of electronic trading platforms specifically set up for this purpose.

It is more usual for the borrower to make the initial approach; however, the more proactive lenders (or their agents) may offer securities that are "in demand" to potential borrowers.

In addition, a borrower acting as principal might be free to deal with a lender depending on the relationship and the size and constitution of the lender's lendable portfolios. Conversely, an agent might very well have to allocate loans to its lenders' accounts in proportion to the available balances.

Example 1

A borrower acting in a principal capacity is more likely to approach a lender with whom it has a good working relationship in terms of securities availability, a diverse range of securities and contractual arrangements. It is less likely to deal with a smaller lender that lacks the size of the previous lender, has fewer attractive securities and is more restrictive in terms of loan initiation and loan recalls (see Table 12.7).

TABLE 12.7   Lending example 1

Size of Loan: 100,000 Shares			
Client	**Available Position**	**Loan Debited**	**Remaining Position**
Lender A	250,000	100,000	150,000
Lender B	20,000	0	20,000
Lender C	15,000	0	15,000
Lender D	40,000	0	40,000
Total:	325,000	100,000	225,000

Although all four lenders have positions in the shares, the borrower has chosen to take one delivery from Lender A. If this situation was to be repeated, then Lenders B, C and D may not benefit very much.

Example 2

A borrower approaches an agent such as a global custodian and is able to borrow the full amount of securities it has requested. The global custodian has a number of lendable clients from which it will apportion the loan, as noted in Table 12.8.

TABLE 12.8 Lending example 2

Size of Loan: 100,000 Shares			
Client	Available Position	Loan Debited	Remaining Position
Client A	50,000	40,000	10,000
Client B	20,000	16,000	4,000
Client C	15,000	12,000	3,000
Client D	40,000	32,000	8,000
Total:	125,000	100,000	25,000

In this scenario no one client is able to satisfy the borrowing requirement. In any event, the global custodian will satisfy the borrowing by making one delivery but will debit the clients' positions in proportion to their available positions. The global custodian can be seen to be treating its clients in a fair and equitable manner.

Whether acting in a principal or intermediary role, a borrower might experience difficulties in obtaining the quantity of securities it requires. The particular security might be *on demand* (also referred to as being *special*) and perhaps rather illiquid.

Example 3

A borrower approaches each of the four potential lenders in turn, finding that none of them is able to satisfy the borrowing in one amount. In fact, the requirement can only be satisfied by taking shares from all four lenders (see Table 12.9).

TABLE 12.9 Lending example 3

Size of Loan: 100,000 Shares			
Client	Available Position	Loan Debited	Remaining Position
Lender A	25,000	25,000	0
Lender B	20,000	20,000	0
Lender C	15,000	15,000	0
Lender D	40,000	40,000	0
Total:	100,000	100,000	0

There is a means by which a borrower who has unsuccessfully approached a lender is able to temporarily place a "hold" on some of the securities that he needs. We refer to this "hold" as *icing* and in the example above, the borrower would request Lender A to ice 25,000 shares.

The icing might only last for a short period of time, but it enables the borrower to go elsewhere in the certain knowledge that it has at least some of the shares it needs. The borrower repeats this process with Lenders B and C (60,000 shares iced) before finally finding the remaining 40,000 shares with Lender D. The icing should only be used for this purpose and not to prevent other borrowers from being able to get hold of the shares. Icing is a short-term facility which usually expires after a few hours or by close of business on that same day.

This process can be speeded up through the use of electronic platforms that enable lender (or agent) and borrower to communicate available positions and borrowing requests in a timely manner.

Terms are Negotiated Once the borrower has found the securities it needs, it then needs to agree to the terms of the borrowing.

These terms include those listed in Table 12.10.

TABLE 12.10 Borrowing terms

Terms		Comments
Duration of loan	Term	The securities are required for a specific period, e.g. one week, 30 days, etc.
Acceptable collateral	Open	The securities can be recalled by the lender or returned by the borrower at any time.
	Cash	Currency acceptable to both parties.
Fees	Non-cash	Eligible assets, e.g. government securities, letters of credit, etc.
	Rebate rate	Cash collateral.
Delivery instructions	Premium or fee rate	Non-cash collateral.
	Loaned securities and collateral	Bank account and settlement details.

Transaction is Confirmed The loan transaction should be confirmed as soon as possible, in a similar way to any other type of transaction, and details should include the contract date, the settlement date and the terms noted in Table 12.10.

In Table 12.11 we have an example of a securities lending transaction.

TABLE 12.11   Loan transaction

Transaction Date	Mon, July 7, 2014	Date loan is negotiated	
Settlement Date	Mon, July 7, 2014		Date loan commences
Term	Open		Open = At call
Security	Marks & Spencer	Ordinary shares	
Ticker	MKS:LSE	Stock exchange ticker symbol	
Security Price (GBX)	441.40	Pence per share	
Quantity	5,000,000	Shares	
Loan Value	GBP 22,070,000.00	Quantity × Price	
Delivery	DVP	From lender's account <number> to borrower's account <number>	
Lending Fee	25	Basis points	per annum
Collateral	DBVs	Type of collateral	
Margin	5.00%	Typical margin rate for non-US securities	
Collateral Required	GBP 23,173,500.00	Based on the margined value of the loaned securities	
Lending Income	GBP 151.16	Per day	Value of loan at the lending fee per day

Securities are Delivered and Collateral Received   Ideally, collateral should be received at the same time as the securities are delivered. This is achievable where cash is provided as collateral (on a delivery versus payment basis). There are difficulties, however, when non-cash is delivered as collateral, as simultaneous delivery versus delivery may not be possible. Assuming the securities and non-cash collateral are exchanged on the same day, at the very least there will be daylight exposure, as both securities and collateral will be delivered at different times of the day.

Depending on the relationship between the lender and borrower, it might be possible for the collateral to be delivered before the securities (i.e. pre-collateralisation), in which case the exposure risk is transferred to the borrower. There is an alternative to pre-collateralisation known as *delivery by value* (DBV) and we will cover this in Section 12.8.5.

Ideally, the securities lent and non-cash collateral given should both be settled as soon as possible, certainly within the normal market convention for the assets concerned. For example, the market convention for regular settlement is T+3, with delivery of loans and returns/recalls on T+0. Having shorter delivery periods enables the lending and borrowing process to be more efficient, especially in terms of accuracy and timeliness.

The loan commencement, i.e. the delivery of securities to the borrower, is shown in Figure 12.2.

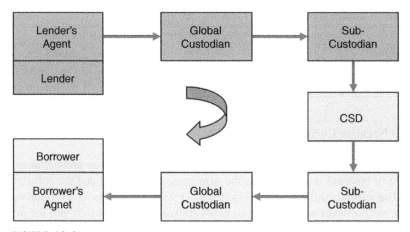

FIGURE 12.2   Loan commencement

This is the end of the first phase in which the loan has been initiated. Until such time as the securities are returned by the borrower or recalled by the lender, the loan has to be maintained and the collateral managed.

12.6.2   Phase 2: Loan Maintenance

Margin   Throughout the life of a loan, it is necessary to ensure that the value of collateral always exceeds the value of the loan. This is to ensure that there will always be sufficient collateral to liquidate and with the cash proceeds replace the securities lent.

Q&A

Question

Do you think that the value of the loan will increase or decrease as the value of the collateral increases or decreases?

Answer

The answer depends on the correlation between the loaned assets and the collateral assets. If these two assets are perfectly positively *correlated,* then, as the value of the loan increases, so the value of the collateral increases. By contrast, if the two assets are perfectly *negatively* correlated, then, as the value of the loan increases, so the value of the collateral decreases (and vice versa).

The example shown in Table 12.12 will illustrate the situation outlined in the Q&A section above.

TABLE 12.12 Correlation between loaned securities and collateral

	Value of Loan	Value of Collateral	Difference	Result
Start of business	100,000	105,000	5.00%	Acceptable
Close of business §1	95,000	106,000	11.58%	Over-collateralised
Close of business §2	105,000	107,000	1.90%	Under-collateralised

Example of Negative Correlation

At the start of business, the difference between the values of the loan and collateral is 5%. By the close of business in scenario §1, the loan value has dropped and the collateral value increased. The resulting difference has widened to 11.58% and the loan is over-collateralised. In this case, the borrower would expect to recall sufficient collateral to return the difference to 5%.

Example of Positive Correlation

By the close of business in scenario §2, the values of both the loan and the collateral have increased (albeit not by the same percentage). The difference has narrowed so that the loan is under-collateralised. If the borrower were to default at this stage, then there would be only just sufficient collateral to cover the replacement of the loan, placing the lender at risk.

So, one element of our loan maintenance is to ensure that there is sufficient collateral at all times and furthermore that the difference between the valuations is at a pre-agreed level. We refer to this difference as the loan *margin* and in the example above, the margin is 5%. Whilst there are no specific rules in this regard, market convention tends to follow the values shown in Table 12.13.

TABLE 12.13 Margin percentages

Market(s)	Margin
USA securities	2%
Rest of the world securities	5%

Please note that these margin levels are negotiable, and in markets where the operations are more problematic (e.g. settlements and custody), the margin could be higher.

Q&A

Question

How frequently should we be performing these revaluations?

> **Answer**
>
> Revaluation of the loans and non-cash collateral should be performed at least once per day. Assets such as equities tend to be more volatile than the non-cash collateral, such as bonds, being given.

A daily revaluation (also known as a *mark-to-market*) is usually sufficient under normal market conditions. Lenders, or their agents, do have the right under the SLA to call for extra margin during a day (an *intra-day margin call*).

Margin calls can be settled as soon as they are requested or, if there is an agreed threshold in place, as soon as the threshold has been exceeded (see Table 12.14).

TABLE 12.14   Margin calls and thresholds

	Loan Value	Collateral Value	Threshold	Action Required	New Collateral Balance
A	110,000	105,000	None	Borrower pays extra 10,500 margin	115,500
			25,000	Extra margin accounted for but not paid	
B	95,000	105,000	None	Lender repays 5,250 margin to borrower	99,750
			25,000	Reduced margin accounted for but not paid	

In example A in Table 12.14, the loan value has exceeded the collateral value and the lender calls for extra margin/collateral from the borrower. If there is no threshold then a delivery is made; if the threshold is, say, 25,000, then no actual deliveries are made but the extra amount is accounted for in the books and records.

In example B in the table, we have the opposite situation, where the loan value has dropped and the borrower requests a repayment of margin/collateral from the lender. Again, if there is no threshold, then a delivery is made; with a threshold, no deliveries are made and entries are passed in the books and records.

Application of Margin   Every day, using the previous day's closing prices, you should revalue the securities that are "on loan" and the collateral that has been taken, ensuring that the correct margin level is maintained. Subject to any threshold, the lender will call for more margin if the margin level has decreased below the required level, or the borrower will request a return of some collateral if the margin level has increased. An example, using a small portfolio of European equities, is shown in Table 12.15.

TABLE 12.15　Portfolio of European securities

Equities Lent	Quantity	Price (EUR)	Value (EUR)
Aegon, shares	170,000	6.91	1,174,700.00
BASF, shares	15,000	76.59	1,148,850.00
Lafarge, shares	25,000	54.08	1,352,000.00
Repsol, shares	75,000	18.13	1,359,750.00
Value of loan portfolio:			5,035,300.00
Margin level @		5%	251,765.00
Collateral required:			5,287,065.00

We can see that the amount of collateral required to cover a loan portfolio worth approximately EUR 5 million can be calculated to be just under EUR 5.3 million.

Haircut　Whenever non-cash collateral is given, there is the risk that the value of the underlying assets will decline. We therefore have a combination of issuer risk and market risk. The riskier the underlying security, the greater is the chance that the issuer might default or the market value decline.

In addition to margining the securities loan, the collateral taker will reduce the market value of the collateral by a certain percentage (the *haircut*). For the collateral giver, this means that extra collateral must be given, i.e. an *excess*.

Q&A

Question

Collateral can be ranked in terms of riskiness. How would you rank the following asset types (where 1 is low risk and 5 is high risk)?

- Cash
- Equities on a main index
- Equities (other) listed on an exchange
- Gold
- Non-sovereign debt
- Sovereign debt

Answer

These assets can be ranked as follows:

Cash	1
Sovereign debt	2
Non-sovereign debt	3
Equities on a main index	4=
Gold	4=
Equities (other) listed on an exchange	5

Asset types with a low risk will attract a low haircut; the riskier the asset type, the greater the haircut. We can also factor credit ratings and maturities into our risk ranking, as the following exercise will illustrate.

Table 12.16 shows some standard supervisory haircuts. We can draw some conclusions as to the degree of haircut required for the different asset classes.

TABLE 12.16 Standard supervisory haircuts

Issue Rating for Debt Securities	Residual Maturity	Sovereigns	Other Issuers
AAA to AA−	< 1 year	0.50%	1.00%
	1 to 5 years	2.00%	4.00%
	> 5 years	4.00%	8.00%
A+ to BBB−	< 1 year	1.00%	2.00%
	1 to 5 years	3.00%	6.00%
	> 5 years	6.00%	12.00%
BB+ to BB−	All	15.00%	
	Main index equities (including convertible bonds) and gold	15.00%	
	Other equities listed on an exchange (including convertible bonds)	25.00%	
	Cash in the same currency	0.00%	

We can come to the following conclusions:

- Sovereign borrowers that have good credit ratings and have issued securities with less than 12 months to maturity require a lower haircut compared with borrowers with poorer credit ratings and securities with more than five years to maturity.
- With debt securities, the longer the time to maturity, the greater the risk of default. Longer-term debt securities therefore require greater haircuts.

- Equities in general require greater haircuts than sovereign and non-sovereign issuers, although listed equities that are not on a main index (e.g. DAX, CAC, etc.) attract a greater haircut than equities that are on the main index.
- Cash in the same currency does not attract any haircut; cash foreign currency is exposed to FX risk and might therefore need to be assessed for a haircut.

Income and Corporate Actions   You will recall that legal title to securities that are lent and collateral that is given changes from giver to taker. Under the terms of the Securities Lending Agreement, the securities borrower and the collateral taker are obliged to "manufacture" any benefits and pass them back to the securities lender and the collateral giver. In effect, the income payer is simply a cash payer, with the cash representing the amount of income; hence, we use the term *manufactured income*. (This makes sense as an issuer is only able to pay a particular dividend or coupon once and manufacturing income overcomes the problem of a multiple income payment.)

Income   The amount of income (dividends and coupons) payable should be the amount that the beneficiary would have received if it had not lent the securities or given the collateral.

Any difference in the amount will be for the account of the payer. For example, ABC announces a dividend of 2.00 per share. A securities lender has lent 100,000 shares to a borrower. ABC pays the dividend to the borrower with a 20% withholding tax deduction. The lender is entitled to receive dividends with a 10% deduction (see Table 12.17).

TABLE 12.17   Cost to borrower through WHT differences

	Party	Gross Amount	WHT Rate	Net Amount
Dividend paid	Borrower	200,000.00	20%	160,000.00
Dividend owed to	Lender	200,000.00	10%	180,000.00
Cost to borrower				−20,000.00

In this example, had the lending institution not lent 100,000 ABC shares, then the amount of dividend receivable would have been 180,000.00.

This situation would not arise for gross-paying securities, e.g. Eurobonds.

Voting Rights   It is not possible to manufacture voting rights and therefore the securities lender loses the right to vote. The only way the lender (as the beneficial owner of the securities) can vote is to recall the securities in time to exercise the vote and hope that they can re-lend after the vote has taken place.

Corporate Actions   Securities lenders are entitled to benefit from the many different types of corporate action (e.g. bonus issues, rights issues, takeovers, etc.). In Chapter 11, you saw some examples of these corporate action events, and there will be different ways of approaching them from a securities lending point of view. In general, however, the securities lender is made good by the borrower (and the collateral giver by the collateral taker).

12.6.3   Phase 3: Loan Closure

At some stage the loan will be repaid. When repayment takes place depends on whether the original duration was on a term basis or an open basis.

Term Loan   The loaned securities must be delivered by the borrower to the lender and an appropriate amount of collateral returned by the lender to the borrower, in accordance with the original transaction terms.

Open Loan   The lender can recall a loan at any time and the borrower can return a loan at any time (with an appropriate amount of collateral). A typical reason for a lender recall is that the lender has sold some or all of the securities being lent.

Recalls and returns are covered under Section 8: Delivery of Equivalent Securities of the GMSLA. The lender must give notice of no less than the standard settlement time for the securities. By contrast, the borrower simply has to deliver the securities to the lender.

One risk for the lender is that it might not initiate a recall sufficiently early for the sale transaction to be settled on time. Another risk is that the borrower fails to return the securities to the lender.

Failure to deliver securities or collateral is covered in Section 9 of the GMSLA:

Para. 9.1: Borrower's failure to deliver equivalent securities
    The lender may either continue the loan or terminate the loan.

Para. 9.2: Lender's failure to deliver equivalent collateral
    The borrower may either continue the loan or terminate the loan.

Para. 9.3: Failure by either party to deliver
    The failing transferor pays all reasonable costs and expenses to the transferee. These can include, for example, interest charges and buy-in costs.

The return of securities to the lender is shown in Figure 12.3.

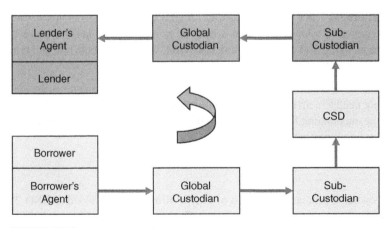

FIGURE 12.3   Loan completion

12.6.4 Lending Fees

The lending fees accrue on a daily basis and are usually paid monthly. How they are calculated depends on the type of collateral provided by the borrower. You will recall that collateral can either be in cash or non-cash.

Cash Collateral   When the borrower gives cash, it will demand a return on that cash. This return is known as the *rebate rate*. The lender will reinvest the cash and expect to earn a return, known as the *reinvestment rate*, on that cash. The reinvestment return should be greater than the rebate return and the difference, the *spread*, represents the benefit to the lender.

Example

A beneficial owner is lending US equities worth USD 10 million. The borrower is providing cash, margined at 2%, as collateral. The borrower has requested a rebate rate of 25 basis points. The benefit to the lender, assuming a reinvestment rate of 95 basis points, can be calculated as shown in Table 12.18.

TABLE 12.18   Loan spread

Loan Value	USD 10,000,000.00	
Margin	2%	US equities
Cash Collateral	USD 10,200,000.00	
Rebate Rate	25	Basis points
Rebate Amount	USD 70.83	per day (360 basis)
Reinvestment Rate	95	Basis points
Reinvestment Amount	USD 269.17	per day (360 basis)
Spread	USD 198.33	per day (360 basis)

In this example, the spread amounts to 70 basis points and the benefit amounts to USD 198.33 per day. The daily spread will change as the value of the loan changes.

Non-Cash Collateral   For loans of securities secured with non-cash collateral, the benefit to the lender is quoted as a lending fee (known as the *non-cash premium*) based on the market value of the loan. (This is in contrast to cash collateral, where the rebate rate and reinvestment rate are calculated on the collateral.)

Fee calculation for non-cash collateral is more straightforward to manage, as the lender (or its agent) does not need to actively manage cash. Instead, both the lender and the borrower know the value of the outstanding loans, know the agreed lending fee and can therefore calculate the daily accrual without any problems.

Example

A beneficial owner is lending a portfolio of Pacific-Rim equities, valued at USD 25 million, at a non-cash premium rate of 100 basis points. The benefit to the lender can be calculated as shown in Table 12.19.

TABLE 12.19   Loan fees

Loan Value	USD 25,000,000.00	
Non-Cash Premium	100	Basis points
Fee	USD 694.44	per day (360-day basis)

The daily fee accrual will change as the value of the loan changes. Please note that the amount of non-cash collateral is not taken into account for fee calculation purposes.

Q&A

Question

You are a buy-side lender of securities with a market value USD 100 million and have accepted non-cash collateral margined at 5%. The types of assets used as collateral together with their market values are shown in Table 12.20. Applying the collateral haircuts in Table 12.16 above, what would the collateral excess/shortfall be? What action would you need to take?

TABLE 12.20   Collateral valuation

Assets used as Collateral	Residual Maturity	Market Value	Credit Rating	Haircut Required	Collateral Value
UK gilts	4 years	USD 30,000,000	AA+		
US Treasury bonds	8 years	USD 40,000,000	AAA		
Country "A" Treasury bonds	15 years	USD 15,000,000	A–		
Country "B" Treasury bonds	10 years	USD 5,000,000	BB		
Main index equities	–	USD 8,000,000			
Other equities	–	USD 5,000,000			
Gold	–	USD 2,000,000			
Totals:		USD 105,000,000			
	All values stated in USD terms				

Answer

As a result of the haircut exercise, there is a USD 6.6 million shortfall in collateral (see calculations in Table 12.21). You will need to call for more collateral, ensuring that it meets the acceptance criteria stated in the agreements.

TABLE 12.21 Impact of collateral haircut

Assets used as Collateral	Residual Maturity	Market Value	Credit Rating	Haircut Required	Collateral Value
UK gilts	4 years	USD 30,000,000	AA+	2%	USD 29,400,000
US Treasury bonds	8 years	USD 40,000,000	AAA	4%	USD 38,400,000
Country "A" Treasury bonds	15 years	USD 15,000,000	A–	6%	USD 14,100,000
Country "B" Treasury bonds	10 years	USD 5,000,000	BB	15%	USD 4,250,000
Main index equities	–	USD 8,000,000	–	15%	USD 6,800,000
Other equities	–	USD 5,000,000	–	25%	USD 3,750,000
Gold	–	USD 2,000,000	–	15%	USD 1,700,000
Totals:		USD 105,000,000			USD 98,400,000
				Shortfall:	USD (6,600,000)
	All values stated in USD terms				

12.7   REPURCHASE AGREEMENT LIFECYCLE

12.7.1   Motivations

A repurchase agreement (otherwise known as a classic repo, or simply a repo) is a mature, money market instrument widely used in the USA, Europe and Asia. It enables:

- Companies to borrow and lend cash that is secured against collateral such as bonds;
- Market makers to go short in securities (by reversing securities in against cash) and to finance a long securities position (by buying the securities and immediately repoing them out against cash).

Unlike securities lending and borrowing, where the securities are the motivator, with repo, both cash and securities are the motivators. Those institutions that are cash-motivated are less concerned about what collateral is taken than they are about making sure that it meets certain quality criteria. This type of collateral is known as *general collateral* (or GC). Securities-motivated repo is known as *special*. The greater the demand for specials, the lower the price (the repo rate) will be.

For a cash borrower, the repo rate is usually lower than bank financing rates. For a cash lender, a repo can provide an attractive yield on what is a short-term, secured transaction in a very liquid market.

Title to the collateral passes from the collateral giver to the collateral taker, although the economic benefits of the collateral remain with the giver.

The motivations for repo buyers and sellers are shown in Table 12.22.

TABLE 12.22 Repo motivations

Repo	Securities Motivation	Cash Motivation
Buyer	Securities borrower	Collateral taker
	Collateral giver	Cash lender
Seller	Securities lender	Collateral giver
	Collateral taker	Cash borrower

Please note that the direction of a repo transaction is from the securities' perspective. If an investor sells a repo, it is selling the securities (i.e. lending the securities).

12.7.2 Repurchase Agreement Types

There are two types of maturity: term and open.

Term Repo   A term repo is transacted with a specified repurchase date that can range from overnight (O/N) to typically 12 months.

Open Repo   These are contracts that have no fixed repurchase date when negotiated but are terminable on demand by either counterparty.

Repurchase agreements can be transacted in several ways:

- Directly negotiated;
- Voice brokerage;
- Alternative trading system (ATS);
- An ATS linked to a CCP;
- Voice-assisted systems.

There are several types of repo that are conceptually the same but differ in detail.

Classic Repo   A classic repo transaction is negotiated between two counterparties where the collateral can either be a basket of securities (general collateral or GC) or a specific security (e.g. ABC 5% bonds due in 2030). Two examples are given in Tables 12.23 and 12.25: in Example A, the motivation is cash-driven and in Example B, it is securities-driven.

TABLE 12.23 Example A: Cash-driven repo

Background	Investor "A" wants to borrow USD 25,000,000 cash against a specific security for one month	
Counterparty	Dealer "B"	
Repo rate	0.22%	1 month
Trade date	Tuesday, 8 July 2014	
Settlement date	Friday, 11 July 2014	
Termination date	Monday, 11 August 2014	
Collateral	EDF 4.60% bonds due on 27 January 2020	Eurobond (30E/360)
Clean price	112.7771	YTM 2.13%
Accrued interest	2.0956	per USD 100 nominal
Dirty price (start)	114.8727	Clean price + accrued interest
Cash amount	USD 25,000,000.00	Cash-driven

In Example A, we know the cash amount but not the nominal amount of the EDF bonds. By taking the usual formula for calculating the cash amount of a bond transaction and rearranging it, we can calculate the face value, as shown in Figure 12.4.

$$\text{Cash Amount} = \text{Nominal} \times \text{Dirty Price} \quad \text{rearranged as:}$$

$$\text{Nominal} = \frac{\text{Cash Amount}}{\text{Dirty Price}}$$

$$\text{Nominal} = \text{USD} \frac{25,000,000.00}{114.8727\,\%}$$

$$\text{Nominal} = \text{USD } 21,763,000 \text{ (to nearest USD } 1,000)$$

FIGURE 12.4 Nominal amount of bonds required

The exact nominal amount would have been USD 21,763,221.37. However, as the board lot size of the bond is USD 1,000, it would not be possible to deliver this amount. We have therefore rounded the nominal amount down to USD 21,763,000, giving us a cash amount of USD 24,999,745.70 (a small shortfall of USD 254.30). Securities such as government bonds can have a minimum transferable amount of 0.01, enabling a much closer match between the nominal amount and the required cash amount.

On the settlement date, Investor A delivers the bonds to Dealer B against payment of the cash amount. As this is a term repo, the transaction will terminate one month later on Monday, 11 August 2014 when the bonds will be returned and the cash repaid plus interest of USD 4,736.06 (see Table 12.24 for the calculation).

TABLE 12.24 Example A interest calculation

Cash amount	USD 24,999,745.70
Repo rate	0.22%
Term (days)	31
Repo interest	USD 4,736.06

It should be noted that:

- The dirty price at the start of the transaction remains the same on termination of the transaction.
- This transaction was cash-driven. We calculated the amount of collateral using the dirty price. It is more usual to apply a margin to the securities and we will cover this later in this chapter.

Example A demonstrated a transaction where cash was the motivating asset, with Investor A wishing to borrow cash. In Example B, we will examine a classic repo transaction where a counterparty (Dealer C) wishes to borrow a particular (specific) security from Investor D (see Table 12.25).

TABLE 12.25 Example B: Securities-driven repo

Background	Dealer "C" wants to borrow USD 25,000,000 BHP Billiton 2.125% bonds due on 29 November 2018 against cash for three months	
Counterparty	Investor "D"	
Repo rate	0.21%	3 months
Trade date	Tuesday, 8 July 2014	
Settlement date	Friday, 11 July 2014	
Termination date	Friday, 10 October 2014	
Borrowed security	BHP Billiton 2.125% bonds due on 29 November 2018	Eurobond (30E/360)
Clean price	106.5765	YTM 0.60%
Accrued interest	1.3104	per USD 100 nominal
Dirty price (start)	107.8869	Clean price + accrued interest
Nominal amount	USD 25,000,000	Securities-driven
Cash collateral	USD 26,971,725.00	

On the settlement date, Investor D delivers the bonds to Dealer C against payment of the cash amount. As this is a term repo, the transaction will terminate after three months (91 days) on Friday, 10 October 2014 when the bonds will be returned and the cash repaid plus interest of USD 14,317.49, calculated as shown in Table 12.26.

TABLE 12.26 Example B interest calculation

Cash amount	USD 26,971,725.00
Repo rate	0.21%
Term (days)	91
Repo interest	USD 14,317.49

Cross-Currency Repo In both examples above, the currencies of both the cash and securities were the same, in our case US dollars. *Cross-currency repo*, by contrast, involves two different currencies; an example is shown in Table 12.27.

TABLE 12.27   Cross-currency repo

Cash	vs.	Securities
USD	vs.	Euro-denominated securities such as German Bunds, French OATs, Italian BTPs, Belgian OLOs, etc.
JPY	vs.	US treasury bonds
GBP	vs.	Japanese government bonds (JGBs)

There will be the extra complication of foreign exchange exposure when ensuring that the transaction remains fully collateralised.

Equity Repo   These are contracts where the collateral given/taken is made up of shares rather than bonds.

This type of repo works best in markets where the delivery of shares is as efficient as the delivery of government securities and corporate bonds. If, for example, it takes several days to re-register shares out of the deliverer's name into the receiver's, then the vast majority of transactions will be delayed for this reason. The ideal situation here would be instantaneous re-registration on settlement of the share deliveries.

Floating-Rate Repo   These are contracts with a floating repo rate that is reset at specified intervals. This repo type is often used when the collateral also has a floating coupon rate (e.g. an FRN). The repo reset date coincides with the FRN coupon dates.

12.7.3   Sell/Buy-Backs

As mentioned above, sell/buy-backs (or buy/sell-backs) are simply two outright transactions, dealt simultaneously, both with the same trade date but with separate settlement dates. The first transaction is therefore a sale at a spot price and a repurchase at a forward price. In Example C (see Table 12.28), we will use the same information as in Example B. You will notice that whilst the cash flows are the same, the prices are different.

TABLE 12.28   Example C: Sell/buy-back

Background	Dealer "C" wants to borrow USD 25,000,000 of a bond against cash for three months (buy/sell-back)	
Counterparty	Investor "D"	Lends the bond against cash (sell/buy-back)
Pricing rate	0.21%	3 months
Trade date	Tuesday, 8 July 2014	
Settlement date	Friday, 11 July 2014	
Termination date	Friday, 10 October 2014	
Borrowed security	BHP Billiton 2.125% bonds due on 29 November 2018	Eurobond (30E/360)
Purchase price (clean)	106.5765	YTM 0.60%
Accrued interest	1.3104	per USD 100 nominal to 11 July 2014
Purchase price (dirty)	107.8869	Clean price + accrued interest

TABLE 12.28 (*Continued*)

Nominal amount	USD 25,000,000	Delivered by Investor "D" to Dealer "C"
Cash amount	USD 26,971,725.00	Paid by Dealer "C" to Investor "D"
Interest	USD 14,317.49	Cash amount @ 0.21% for 91 days
Sell-back amount	USD 26,986,042.49	Cash amount + interest
Sell-back price (dirty)	107.9442	Total cash repayment/nominal bond amount
Accrued interest	1.8358	per USD 100 nominal to 10 October 2014
Sell-back price (clean)	106.1084	Dirty price minus accrued interest

Please note that the cash flows at the start and at the end are the same as for a classic repo. The difference for a buy/sell-back (or a sell/buy-back) is that the forward price is calculated as a clean price. This is the repayment amount (dirty price) less the accrued interest up to the forward settlement date.

Sell/buy-backs are now mostly documented within the GMRA. Those transactions that are not documented are more risky than those that are. Undocumented transactions contain no provision for variation margin calls, are not subjected to a legal agreement and the seller has no legal right to any coupons.

It is useful to gain some insight into the comparative use of repurchase agreements and sell/buy-back transactions. The ICMA publishes a semi-annual survey on the European repo markets and the surveys can be found on the ICMA website[6] (see Tables 12.29, 12.30, 12.31 and 12.32).

TABLE 12.29 Contract types – ATS and tri-party

Contract Type	December 2013	ATS	Tri-Party
Repurchase agreements	86.0%	67.3%	100.0%
Documented sell/buy-back	12.4%	32.7%	0.0%
Undocumented sell/buy-back	1.6%	0.0%	0.0%
Total:	100.0%	100.0%	100.0%

Source: ICMA European Repo Survey §26 (December 2013) published in January 2014.

TABLE 12.30 Rate comparison – ATS and tri-party

Repo Rate Comparison	December 2013	ATS	Tri-Party
Fixed rate	78.8%	88.3%	48.2%
Floating rate	8.6%	11.7%	0.0%
Open repo	12.6%	0.0%	51.8%
Totals:	100.0%	100.0%	100.0%

Source: ICMA European Repo Survey §26 (December 2013) published in January 2014.

---

[6]*Source:* ICMA (online) Surveys available from www.icmagroup.org/Regulatory-Policy-and-Market-Practice/short-term-markets/Repo-Markets/repo/latest/. [Accessed Sunday, 9 November 2014]

TABLE 12.31 Trading analysis

Trading Analysis	December 2013
Directly negotiated	53.2%
Voice brokered	15.1%
Alternative trading systems (ATSs)	31.7%
Total:	100.0%

Source: ICMA European Repo Survey §26 (December 2013) published in January 2014.

TABLE 12.32 Cash currency analysis

Cash Currency Analysis	December 2013
EUR	66.3%
GBP	10.2%
USD	14.8%
DKK, SEK	2.5%
JPY	4.9%
CHF	0.1%
Other currencies	1.3%
less Rounding:	−0.1%
Total:	**100.0%**

Source: ICMA European Repo Survey §26 (December 2013) published in January 2014.

12.7.4 Settlement

The settlement of repo transactions can occur in three forms:

1. Specified delivery.
2. Tri-party repo.
3. Hold-in-custody repo.

Specified Delivery Most securities transactions are normally settled on a delivery versus payment (DVP) basis. This mode should be adopted wherever possible in repo and sell/buy-backs where specific securities have been identified as collateral.

Securities can also be delivered on a free of payment (FoP) basis but extra care is required to ensure that both halves of any transaction are delivered/received on the same intended settlement date.

Figures 12.5 and 12.6 summarise the asset flows in a repo and sell/buy-back respectively.

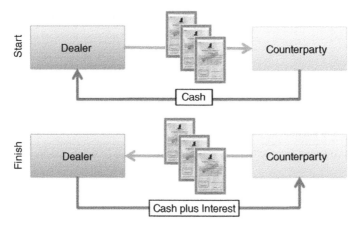

FIGURE 12.5   Repurchase agreement

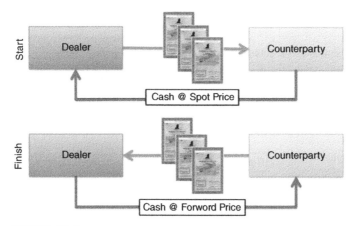

FIGURE 12.6   Sell/buy-back

Tri-Party Repo   Dealers might wish to outsource the post-trading processing to a third-party custodian. The custodian will enter into a tri-party agreement with its two counterparties – the buyer and seller.

The third-party agents in Europe are typically the two international central securities depositories (Euroclear Bank and Clearstream Banking Luxembourg), SIX Securities Services, JP Morgan Chase and Bank of New York Mellon. In the USA, the repo market is dominated by JP Morgan Chase and Bank of New York Mellon.

The tri-party agent does not assume any of the risk involved with each transaction; that remains between the buyer and seller. Furthermore, the tri-party agent does not provide the trading venue; the counterparties continue to negotiate either directly with each other or utilise one of the ATMs.

A tri-party agent will process and maintain repo transactions, as shown in Table 12.33 and Figure 12.7.

TABLE 12.33 Tri-party agent's processing

Process	Comments
1. Agent receives instructions from both counterparties and attempts to match them.	
2. Agent selects collateral from seller.	Collateral has to satisfy the credit and liquidity criteria, concentration limits and initial margins pre-set by the buyer.
3. Collateral delivered DVP to the agent's account.	Seller credited with cash and debited with collateral.
4. Cash debited from the buyer's account.	Agent holds collateral as per the section on Hold-in-Custody Repo below.
5. Agent manages the process: ■ regular marking-to-market the securities/collateral; ■ margining; ■ income collection on the collateral; ■ substitution of collateral at seller's request.	Collateral substitution can occur if: ■ The seller requests it (e.g. sale of securities previously selected as collateral); ■ The collateral no longer meets the buyer's specified quality criteria.

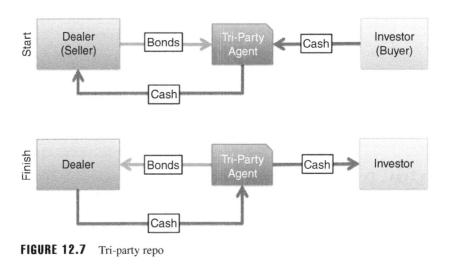

FIGURE 12.7 Tri-party repo

Hold-in-Custody Repo We have seen that the more secure types of repo involve either the actual delivery of collateral by the giver to the taker or the use of a third party as in tri-party repo. There is a third type of repo known as *hold-in-custody repo* (HIC repo), and this is especially attractive in the USA for repo transactions against general collateral (see Figure 12.8).

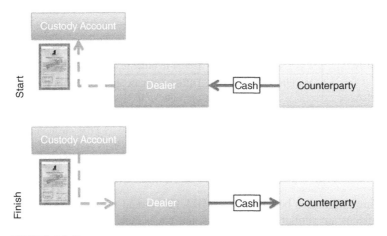

FIGURE 12.8 HIC repo

The similarity with tri-party repo is that the seller does not deliver collateral to the buyer. Instead, the seller holds the collateral, enabling it to reduce settlement costs and provide flexible collateral substitution whenever appropriate. The buyers do not need to directly manage the collateral. The disadvantage for the buyers is that they run the risk that the sellers do not hold collateral of sufficient quantity or quality and/or have perhaps pledged the same collateral to other HIC transactions.

12.8 COLLATERAL AND MARGIN

12.8.1 Terminology

The use of the words "collateral" and "margin" is informal and, in concept, both words mean the same thing. Repo originated from the bond markets and securities lending out of equities markets. Today, there is equity repo and securities lending includes bonds.

As we have seen, the market associations are different, with the ICMA for repo and the ISLA for securities lending.

The Associations' Master Agreements for repo (GMRA) and securities lending (GMSLA) use the terminology in the ways shown in Table 12.34.

TABLE 12.34 Master Agreement terminology

Activity/Agreement	Terminology	Description
Repo/GMRA	Margin (securities)	Refers to the underlying purchased securities
Repo/GMRA	Collateral	Term often used when referring to margin
Repo/GMRA	General collateral (GC)	The buyer is not concerned with the exact purchased securities (only that they meet pre-specified quality criteria)
Repo/GMRA	Special (collateral)	Used when specific collateral is being purchased/delivered

(continued)

TABLE 12.34 (*Continued*)

Activity/Agreement	Terminology	Description
Securities lending/GMSLA	Collateral	Refers to assets that the borrower provides to the lender in order to collateralise the loan
Securities lending/GMSLA	Margin	Difference between the value of the collateral and the value of the loan (e.g. by 5%)
Repo and securities lending	Haircut	This is a discount to the market value of the securities and acts as a risk cushion. For example, if a 3% haircut is applied to a security worth USD 100, the collateral value is USD 97.

Whilst there are differences between the GMRA (2011) and the GMSLA (2010), many of the core provisions are similar from a contractual perspective (e.g. with default events and close-out netting provisions).

12.8.2 Types of Collateral

The ideal type of collateral should have no credit exposure and should be highly liquid. Price discovery for this collateral should be certain, it should be easy to sell and quick to obtain the cash proceeds.

Q&A

Question

With these characteristics, what type of asset would match this ideal?

Answer

The ideal type of collateral would be a highly liquid, AAA-rated[7] government security, traded on an exchange and settled on a T+0 basis. Cash also makes an attractive alternative.

12.8.3 Repurchase Agreements (and Sell/Buy-Backs)

The most commonly used types of collateral are securities issued by creditworthy central governments, government-guaranteed agency debt and bonds issued by the supranational institutions (e.g. the World Bank). In securities-driven repo, cash is the collateral.

---

[7]Refer to Appendix 12.1 for the ratings issued by the credit rating agencies together with their meanings.

Other types of collateral can include the following:

- Delivery by value (DBV) (see below for more details);
- Corporate bonds (typically senior unsecured debt);
- Covered bonds (e.g. German *pfandbrief*);
- Equities (especially shares that are major index constituents, e.g. S&P 500);
- Convertible bonds;
- Money market securities (e.g. treasury bills, certificates of deposit and commercial paper);
- Bank loans (these should be transferable);
- Asset-backed securities (ABS);
- Structured securities such as collateralised debt obligations (CDOs), collateralised loan obligations (CLOs), credit-linked notes (CLNs), etc.;
- Residential and commercial mortgage-backed securities (RMBS and CMBS);
- Gold.

Remember that collateral in the context of repo is divided into general collateral and specials.

12.8.4 Securities Lending

Eligible collateral that is acceptable includes many of the types listed above:

- Cash;
- Government securities;
- Corporate bonds;
- Convertible bonds;
- Equities (especially constituents of major indices);
- Letters of credit;
- Money market instruments (e.g. certificates of deposit);
- Warrants;
- Delivery by value (DBV).

Remember that collateral in the context of securities lending is divided into cash collateral and non-cash collateral.

12.8.5 Delivery by Value (DBV)

We noted above that one particular type of eligible collateral for all three versions of securities financing was *delivery by value*. DBV was designed as an alternative form of collateral to cash; in other words, in the form of non-cash collateral.

Without DBV, the collateral giver would have to select securities from its securities portfolio and have them delivered to the collateral taker. This involves submitting delivery instructions to the appropriate clearing house. With DBV, however, the collateral giver instructs its clearing house to assemble a package of securities up to a specified value and quality. The DBV package is then delivered by the clearing house to the collateral taker.

In terms of the quality of the securities contained within the DBV package, there are 29 securities categories with a wide range of credit quality and geographical breadth. Some examples are shown in Table 12.35.

TABLE 12.35   DBV class list – selection

DBV Class List	Description
F10	Equities in the FTSE100 index
GIL	All UK gilts
E30	Equities in the Eurotop 300 index
INT	All international securities
USS	US securities

The full list can be found in Appendix 12.2 at the end of this chapter.[8]

Collateral givers can request the clearing house to pass a diversified portfolio of collateral by applying a concentration limit; this limit ensures that the value of any single security does not exceed 10% of the total value of the package of securities being transferred. Margin can be added to the amount of securities delivered.

There are two versions of DBV:

- **Overnight DBV:** Collateral is issued at the end of the day and returned the next morning. This version is suitable for overnight repo, for example.
- **Term DBV:** These have maturities ranging from one day to two years. This version is suitable for term financing and removes the daily requirement to reissue overnight DBVs throughout the duration of the term financing.

12.8.6   Repo Exposure, Haircuts and Margin

Repo exposure refers to the counterparty risk between the buyer and the seller and is measured by calculating the difference between each counterparty's exposure to its counterparty. By way of an illustration, a buyer and a seller enter into a single repo transaction without any haircut.

1. The buyer purchases USD 1,000 securities (e.g. a bond) with a market value of USD 1,000 (see Figure 12.9).

FIGURE 12.9   Initial purchase

---

[8]*Source:* ISLA DBV Class List. Available from http://isla.hostinguk.com/docs/Appendix%205-%20 DBV%20Class%20List.pdf. [Accessed Friday, 10 January 2014]

2. On the purchase date there is no exposure as the value of the securities equals the value of cash (see Figure 12.10).

Securities
Market Value: USD 1,000
Exposure = 0

Cash: USD 1,000

Exposure = 0

FIGURE 12.10 Exposure on purchase date

3. A period of time has elapsed and the securities are now worth USD 1,300. In the meantime, repo interest of USD 50 has accrued. We now have a situation where one party is exposed to the other, as shown in Figure 12.11.

Securities
Market Value: USD 1,300
Exposure = 0

Cash: USD 1,000
Repo Interest: USD 50
Exposure = USD 250

FIGURE 12.11 Exposure on a forward date

4. The buyer's exposure to the seller is the difference between what the seller owes the buyer and what the buyer owes the seller. In this case, the buyer has no exposure.
5. The seller's exposure to the buyer is the difference between what the buyer owes the seller and what the seller owes the buyer. In this case, the seller has an exposure that is covered through a margin call on the buyer. If the buyer defaults, the seller has insufficient cash with which to replace the securities.
6. The seller therefore calls margin from the buyer and reduces its exposure to zero (as shown in Figure 12.12).

Margin Call: USD 250

Securities
Market Value: USD 1,300

Exposure = 0

Cash: USD 1,000
Repo Interest: USD   50
Margin Call: USD   250
Exposure = USD   0

FIGURE 12.12 Exposure after margin call

In the example above, we considered just the one transaction.

Q&A

Question

If you had entered into a number of transactions (both purchases and sales) with another counterparty, would you make these exposure calculations for each and every transaction?

Answer

In theory, there is no reason why not; indeed, you could make separate margin payments/receipts for each transaction as well. This would certainly result in a large number of payments! A more efficient way would be to look at your net exposure to each of your various counterparties.

In order to calculate your net exposure you would need to take into account the following:

- All cash paid to or by the counterparty plus any accrued interest on that cash, *plus*
- The value of all securities transferred to or by the counterparty, *and*
- Any coupons that have been paid by the issuer but have not yet been repaid by or to the counterparty (i.e. manufactured coupons due).

12.9 DEFAULT AND CLOSE-OUT PROVISIONS

12.9.1 Introduction

We have seen in this chapter that securities financing consists of collateralised lending transactions of one form or another. Collateralisation is one of the tools used to mitigate counterparty risk (i.e. the risk that one or other of the counterparties defaults). The use of master agreements, haircuts and margin also helps in this process.

The master agreements for repo and securities lending contain provisions for unwinding transactions should a default occur. First, though, we need to know what event(s) could cause a default.

12.9.2 Event of Default

Both agreements contain similar descriptions of what constitutes an event of default. You will find a summary of the events in each agreement's Section 10.

2010 GMSLA (as Amended in July 2012)

Please refer to Section 10: Events of Default (pp. 18–19) and Section 11: Consequences of an Event of Default (pp. 19–23).

The following situations constitute an event of default:

- Failure to pay or repay cash collateral or deliver non-cash collateral;
- Failure to comply with manufactured dividend obligations;
- Failure to deliver equivalent securities or equivalent collateral;
- Act of insolvency of lender or borrower;
- Incorrect or untrue warranties;
- Admission of inability/unwillingness to perform obligations under the agreement;
- Regulatory involvement where a material part of the assets is transferred pursuant to legislation;
- Declaration of default or expulsion from a securities exchange, failure to meet financial resource requirements;
- Failure to remedy within 30 days any failure to perform other obligations under the agreement.

2011 GMRA

Please refer to Section 10 (a): Events of Default (pp. 17–18).

The following situations constitute an event of default:

- Failure to pay the purchase price or the repurchase price on the applicable date;
- Failure to deliver purchased securities on the purchase date or equivalent securities on the repurchase date within the normal settlement period;
- Failure to pay any sum when due;
- Failure to make a margin transfer on time;
- Failure to pay income payments when due;
- Act of insolvency of buyer or seller;
- Incorrect or untrue representations made by buyer or seller;
- Admission of inability/unwillingness to perform obligations under the agreement;
- Declaration of default or expulsion from a securities exchange, failure to meet financial resource requirements;
- Failure to remedy within 30 days any failure to perform other obligations under the agreement.

12.9.3   Consequences of an Event of Default

There are similarities in the way in which the obligations between buyer/seller (GMRA) and lender/borrower (GMSLA) are treated. Of the two parties involved, one will be the defaulting party and the other the non-defaulting party. The first step will be the delivery of a default notice by the non-defaulting party to the defaulting party.

Should an event of default occur, both parties' payment and delivery obligations to each other are replaced by a single obligation of one party to pay a cash sum to the other. It is the non-defaulting party that determines the amount of cash payable by determining the market value (referred to as the *default market value*) of deliverable and receivable securities together with cash collateral and any other cash.

This reduction of all the obligations into one single obligation is a key element of the agreement, as this netting should ensure that that the non-defaulting party receives or pays the correct amount. Netting also helps to prevent the defaulting party from utilising some of the collateral to offset other obligations.

You can refer to the actual agreements for more details:

> 2010 GMSLA (as amended July 2012) – Paragraph 11: Consequences of an Event of Default (pp. 19–23).
>
> 2011 GMRA – Paragraph 10 (b) to (g) and (j) to (n) (pp. 18–24).

12.10 CENTRAL COUNTERPARTY (CCP) SERVICES

12.10.1 Introduction

We looked at clearing houses and CCPs in Chapter 5 and noted their key role in the post-trade environment. Not all of these provide specialist services for securities financing, although this situation is changing.

Except for transactions that are executed using the alternative trading systems (ATS), securities financing has been an OTC product with bilateral negotiation. The post-transaction processing was predominantly managed in-house using internal systems and/or external, third-party solutions.[9]

The clearing houses and CCPs would be involved at the delivery and payment stages; in fact, the clearing houses may not necessarily have been aware of the purpose of delivery and payment. This situation has changed and continues to evolve, with regulatory demands for OTC transactions to be cleared centrally. This results in the clearing houses and CCPs becoming involved much sooner after a transaction.

In this final section we will take a look at three CCPs and the two international CSDs that operate in this business:

- The Options Clearing Corporation (CCP) – www.theocc.com
- Eurex Clearing (CCP) – www.eurexclearing.com
- LCH.Clearnet (CCP) – www.lchclearnet.com
- Clearstream Banking Luxembourg (ICSD) – www.clearstream.com
- Euroclear Bank (ICSD) – www.euroclear.com

12.10.2 The Options Clearing Corporation (OCC)

The OCC manages two programmes in which it acts as a CCP on behalf of its clearing members:

1. **Stock Loan/Hedge Programme:** This programme allows lenders and borrowers to negotiate bilaterally and send their instructions to the OCC, where they are processed through DTC's systems. Settlement takes place at the DTC with the OCC managing the mark-to-market processing, margin requirements and reporting. DTC handles any corporate actions.

---

[9]Refer to Appendix 12.3 for a list of vendors and their website URLs.

2. **Market Loan Programme:** Similar to the StockLoan/Hedge Programme above, this programme differs insofar as the OCC is acting as a clearer for transactions executed on AQS, an automated marketplace for securities lending and borrowing. Loans executed on AQS are processed through the OCC acting as a CCP.

12.10.3 Eurex Clearing

Eurex Clearing offers CCP services for both securities lending and repo transactions.

- **Lending CCP service:** Participants can execute transactions either bilaterally on electronic trading platforms such as SL-X (www.sl-x.com) and Pirum (www.pirum.com). Clearing services for loans in equities, fixed-income securities and ETFs in the European markets are covered. Cash collateral (USD and EUR) and non-cash collateral are accepted. Non-cash collateral includes the following securities types:
  - Bonds issued by the major central governments (e.g. USA, Japan and Luxembourg, etc.);
  - Bonds issued by the supranationals (e.g. EBRD, IBRD, EIB, etc.);
  - Bonds issued by the European Central Bank and Swiss National Bank;
  - Repo-eligible corporate bonds (AAA to BBB);
  - Equities listed in the major indices from Europe, Asia-Pacific and North America (e.g. CAC40 – France, S&P ASX20 – Australia and S&P TSX60 – Canada);
  - Selected ETFs.
  - (NB: Structured bonds are excluded.)
- **Euro repo market:** Participants can trade anonymously in both general collateral and specials segments with Eurex Clearing acting as a CCP. There are some 5,000 EUR-denominated fixed-income securities (divided into 21 different baskets) available for repo trading in both segments. The available securities consist of:
  - European government bonds;
  - Jumbo-Pfandbriefe and Pfandbriefe;
  - KfW/Laender bonds;
  - European covered bonds;
  - Agency bonds;
  - European corporate bonds.
- **GC pooling market:** This market operates an open order book that provides participants wishing to obtain secured USD and EUR funding with anonymous trading. Eurex Clearing will process the transactions and enable participants to re-use collateral for further money market transactions. Participants can select collateral from standardised baskets of fixed income and equities that are tradable in USD and EUR.

12.10.4 LCH.Clearnet

LCH.Clearnet clears repo trades through its RepoClear service. It accepts classic fixed-rate repos with first leg settlement on $T+0$ or with a forward start with a term of up to 12 months. RepoClear clears transactions in the following government bond markets:

- Austria
- Belgium

- Finland
- Germany
- Ireland
- Portugal
- Slovakia
- Slovenia
- Spain
- United Kingdom
- German Jumbo-Pfandbriefe
- Supranationals, agency and sovereign bonds.

RepoClear can accept transactions executed directly, by voice broker and screen trading systems (ATSs) with LCH.Clearnet assuming the counterparty risk through novation.

For transactions that are delivery settled, RepoClear nets all deliveries due for next-day settlement, resulting in one delivery of securities against a single payment. Settlement netting might result in multiple deliveries depending on cross-border settlement requirements or limits on the maximum delivery size.

Where no actual bond delivery takes place, the cash amounts from both ATS-and bilaterally-traded transactions are netted out per currency and paid through the protected payments system (PPS).

12.10.5 Clearstream Banking Luxembourg (CBL)

CBL manages two automated securities lending services for participants and manages all the administrative activities:

- **Automated Securities Lending and Borrowing (ASL):** CBL automatically identifies ASL lenders' available positions and attempts to cover ASL borrowers' failed trades. CBL acts as a lending agent, collateral agent and guarantor so that the lenders and borrowers are unknown to each other. As soon as the borrowers' failed trades have settled, CBL returns the bonds to the lender. If the lenders subsequently sell their loaned bonds, CBL recalls them.
  CBL also provides a case-by-case variation of ASL allowing participants to manage their own strategies (e.g. a participant might choose to delay borrowing to cover a failed transaction).
  Collateral is pledged to CBL as guarantor and its quality and quantity monitored by CBL on a daily basis.
- **Securities Lending Services (ASLplus):** If ASL is a short-term fails prevention tool for the participants' Operations departments, ASLplus is geared to borrowers wishing to consider longer-term opportunities and lenders wishing to maximise the returns on their portfolios. CBL acts as principal borrower, typically lending to proprietary desks, repo desks and other intermediaries (i.e. the Front Office).

12.10.6 Euroclear Bank

Euroclear enables its participants to manage their settlement fails by automatically borrowing sufficient bonds from lenders in order to settle the transactions. Acting as agent, Euroclear identifies the borrowing requirements, administers the asset servicing and manages recalls as they are needed.

Participants can tailor their participation in the lending programme by excluding certain asset classes or individual securities (e.g. lending only USD-denominated Eurobonds, excluding bonds issued by a particular issuer). The provision and revaluation of collateral is also managed by Euroclear.

12.11 SUMMARY

Securities financing is a powerful tool that allows us to perform a variety of activities:

- Manage our settlement fails;
- Optimise our long securities positions;
- Borrow and lend cash on a secured basis;
- Implement trading strategies that require us to borrow securities.

Securities lending, repurchase agreements and sell/buy-backs are the three types of securities financing. Securities lending is primarily driven by the need to borrow securities using either cash or non-cash collateral as security.

Repo and sell/buy-back are driven by the need to either borrow cash (using margined securities as collateral) or lend specific securities (specials) using cash as collateral.

By contrast, reverse repo and buy/sell-back are driven by the need to either lend cash or borrow specific securities.

There can be some confusion in terminology, for example, on "margin", "haircuts", etc. Margin generally refers to the difference between the value of the loan and the collateral that secures it. So, if the loan is worth USD 100.00, the collateral should be worth, say, USD 105.00 and this "gap" should always be 5% in this example.

A haircut considers the collateral value of an asset rather than its market value. So, a bond with a market value of USD 1,000.00 might have a 2% haircut; its collateral value will be lower, i.e. USD 980.00.

Traditionally, securities financing was an OTC product with transactions dealt off-exchange, deliveries made by each counterparty and each responsible for monitoring the transactions (income, mark-to-market, corporate actions, etc.) and calling or returning collateral as needed. Today, we see CCPs playing an active role as quasi-exchange and clearer/administrator and the ICSDs offering automated, automatic lending and borrowing services, with the ICSDs acting in the middle as agent between the lenders and borrowers.

APPENDIX 12.1: CREDIT RATINGS – LONG TERM

Rating Description	Moody's	S&P	Fitch
	Long-term	Long-term	Long-term
Investment grade:			
Prime	Aaa	AAA	AAA
High grade	Aa1	AA+	AA+
	Aa2	AA	AA
	Aa3	AA−	AA−
Upper medium Ggade	A1	A+	A+
	A2	A	A
	A3	A−	A−
Lower medium grade	Baa1	BBB+	BBB+
	Baa2	BBB	BBB
	Baa3	BBB−	BBB−
Non-investment grade:			
Speculative	Ba1	BB+	BB+
	Ba2	BB	BB
	Ba3	BB−	BB−
Highly speculative	B1	B+	B+
	B2	B	B
	B3	B−	B−
Substantial risks	Caa1	CCC+	CCC
	Caa2	CCC	
	Caa3	CCC−	
Extremely speculative	Ca	CC	
		C	
In default	C	D	RD

Source: Moody's Investor Services (www.moodys.com/researchandratings); Standard & Poor's (www.standardandpoors.com); Fitch Ratings (www. fitchratings.com).

APPENDIX 12.2: DELIVERY BY VALUE (DBV) CLASS LIST

DBV Class List		
DBV Class List	**Description**	**Security Categories**
F10	FTSE 100	FTSE 100
F25	FTSE250	FTSE 250
OTH	Other Equities	Other UK and Irish
F35	FTSE350	FTSE 350
UKE	All UK Equity	ALL UK and Irish Equities
UBG	Unstripped BGS	Unstripped British Government Debt
BGS	All BGS	All British Government Securities
UBN	Unstructured BGS & NBG	Unstripped British Government and Non-British Government Securities
GIL	All Gilts	All gilts
E30	Eurotop 300	Eurotop 300
EGS	EGS	Eurotop Tier 1 Collateral (includes securities of unrated issuers
OIS	Other International	Other International securities
INT	All International	All international securities
USS	U.S. Security	U.S. Securities
TSY	Treasury Bill	Treasury bills
ELG	OMO Eligible Sec's	OMO eligible bills
BB1	Eligible Bank Bills	Eligible bank bills
OMM	Other Bills	Other (including LA bills and ineligible bank bills)
CD1	CDs Band1	CDs rated Aaa-Aa3
CD2	CDs Band2	CDs rated A1-A3
CD3	CDs Band3	CDs rated Baa1-Baa3
CD4	CDs Band4	CDs rated below Baa3
CP1	CP Band1	CP rated Aaa-Aa3
CP2	CP Band2	CP rated A1-A3
CP3	CP Band3	CP rated Baa1-Baa3
CP4	CP Band4	CP rated below Baa3
ACD	All CDs	All CDs (specified in conjunction with Issuer ID)
ACP	All CP	All CP (specified in conjunction on with Issuer ID)
ISS	All CDs and all CP	All CDs and all CP (specified in conjunction with Issuer ID)

APPENDIX 12.3: TECHNOLOGY VENDORS

Company	URL
4Sight	www.4sight.com
Anetics	www.anetics.com
BondLend	www.bondlend.com
Broadridge Financial Solutions	www.broadridge.com
EquiLend	www.equilend.com
eSecLending	www.eseclending.com
Helix Financial Systems	www.helixfs.com
ION Trading	www.iontrading.com
Lombard Risk	www.lombardrisk.com
OnlineStockLoan	www.OnlineStockLoan.com
Pirum Systems	www.pirum.com
PrimeOne Solutions	www.primeonesolutions.com
Quadriserv & Automated Equity Finance Markets, Inc. (AQS)	www.tradeaqs.com
Stonewain Systems	www.stonewain.com
Sungard	www.sungard.com/securitiesfinance

CHAPTER 13

Accounting for Securities

13.1 INTRODUCTION

Part IV of the book will take you through two elements of monitoring and control: accounting and reconciliation.

13.1.1 Accounting and Why We Need It

Let me ask you a very simple question: how much are you worth? Make a list of the sort of things that you own and estimate what these are worth. This will be your net worth.

Of course there will be no definitive answer to this question, as every person is unique and every person's net worth will differ. But why do you need to know how much you are worth? Perhaps the most obvious answer would be that you are interested in knowing. However, you are not the only person who either needs to know or has to know your worth.

For example, your government has an interest as your salary will be taxed; whilst this income tax is typically deducted at source, the government, through its revenue agency, will be keen to ensure that you have paid sufficient tax.

Another example would include an application to borrow money from your bank; it needs to be assured that you have the ability to service that loan. To do this, it might require documentary evidence of your salary and other assets that you might own. The list goes on!

To summarise the above, there are certain entities that need to know certain information about our wealth.

Q&A

Question

Consider a corporate entity, such as the organisation which employs you. How much is the organisation worth, who needs to know and why?

Answer

Some examples of the various parties that would be interested in a typical corporate entity are shown in Table 13.1.

TABLE 13.1   An organisation's worth – who needs to know

Who Needs to Know?	Why Do They Need to Know?
Business managers	Business managers require information in order to make good decisions.
Owners	Owners/investors look for profits and resultant distributions from those profits (e.g. dividends).
Creditors	Creditors are concerned about the company's ability to repay its obligations.
Government agencies	Government agencies are concerned about tax payments and that any regulatory requirements are being adhered to.
Financial analysts	Financial analysts need to form opinions on companies for investment purposes.
Employees	Employees want to work for successful companies and might have bonuses or option schemes that are dependent on the company performing well.

The source of much of the information required by these interested parties will be financial information of one form or another. Those working in the business (e.g. the business managers) will need management accounting for their internal reporting purposes. By contrast, financial accounting is concerned with reporting to external parties outside the company.

It is not the purpose of this chapter to go into any great depth on the topic of accountancy and accounting, but to concentrate on the financial information that is generated by the day-to-day securities transactions and the corporate action events that flow from this. By the end of this chapter, you should be able to:

- Define assets and liabilities and understand the concept of the accounting equation;
- Understand how the Profit & Loss Statement and the Balance Sheet are affected by securities transactions;
- Distinguish between the main Front Office "books" such as the Trading Book, the Available-For-Sale and the Hold-To Maturity Book;
- Understand the accounting lifecycle for transactions and its impact on the Profit & Loss Statement and the Balance Sheet.

13.2 THE ACCOUNTING EQUATION

Any corporate entity is a collection of assets and the corresponding claims against those assets. We refer to these claims as liabilities and these are made up of creditors' claims and the owners' claims:

| Assets equal liabilities plus owners' equity |

Assets: These are the economic resources owned by the company and utilised for future economic benefits for the owner. These assets include tangible assets (e.g. cash, accounts receivable, inventories, buildings and equipment) and intangible assets (e.g. patents and legal rights).

Liabilities: These are the resources used to finance the assets. These are amounts that the company owes to other entities and represent an obligation to pay these entities. Liabilities include borrowed funds (e.g. amounts due to banks), issued debt securities (bonds) and other financial liabilities.

Owners' equity: This is the "interest" that an owner or investor has in the company. This interest is represented in terms of shares originally issued by the company (in exchange for cash through an IPO). The shares are negotiable and transferable and can be issued on a stock exchange, providing a platform from which investors can buy and sell the shares.

13.2.1 Key Financial Statements

Two of the principal financial statements that companies prepare are the Profit & Loss Statement and the Balance Sheet. You will find examples of these two statements below, as prepared by a fictitious company ABC.

Profit & Loss Statement   This statement, shown in Figure 13.1, captures the income and expenses borne by ABC for a particular period; in this case, for the 12 months that ended 31 December 2013. In ABC's Annual Report, there would be explanatory notes accompanying this statement to highlight the constituent elements to each line of the statement. For our purposes, only explanations for securities- and derivatives-related items will be included.

for the year ended 31 December 2013	Notes		2013
amounts in millions of euros			
Income			
Interest income banking operation		EUR 60,000	
Interest expense banking operations		EUR (48,000)	
Interest from banking operations	8		EUR 12,000
Investment income	9		EUR 7,500
Gross commission income		EUR 3,000	
Commission expense		EUR (1,000)	
Commission income	10		EUR 2,000
Valuation results on non-trading derivatives	11		EUR (3,000)

FIGURE 13.1   ABC – Profit & Loss Statement

Net trading income	12		EUR 2,000
Total income			EUR 20,500
Expenses			
Addition to loan loss provisions			EUR 2,000
Intangible amortisation and other impairments			EUR 300
Staff expenses			EUR 7,300
Other operating expenses			EUR 6,000
Total expenses			EUR 15,600
Profit before tax			EUR 4,900
Taxation			EUR 700
Net Profit after Tax			EUR 4,200

FIGURE 13.1 (*Continued*)

Notes: Interest from banking operations (8): Interest income from loans and securities less interest paid on loans, deposits and securities.

Investment income (9): Includes dividends, coupons, and realised profits/losses from selling investments (e.g. equities and bonds).

Commission income (10): Includes brokerage fees, advisory fees, fund management fees, transfer fees, custody fees, etc.

Valuation results on non-trading derivatives (11): Included here are the fair value movements on derivatives used to economically hedge exposures, but for which no hedge accounting is applied. The fair value movements on the derivatives are influenced by changes in the market conditions, such as stock prices, interest rates and currency exchange rates.

Net trading income (12): Includes the results of making markets in securities (e.g. government bonds, equities and money-market instruments) and interest rate derivatives (e.g. swaps, options, futures and forward contracts). Foreign exchange transaction results include gains and losses from spot and forward contracts, options, futures and translated foreign currency assets and liabilities.

Balance Sheet   In contrast to the Profit & Loss Statement which covers a particular period in time, the Balance Sheet is a snapshot on one particular date. The Balance Sheet shows the resources owned by the company and the claims against those resources. What the Balance Sheet does not do is indicate the situation one day before or one day after the particular date. Figure 13.2 shows the Balance Sheet for ABC.

As at 31 December 2013	Notes	2013
amounts in millions of euros		
ASSETS		
Cash and balances with central banks		EUR 50,000
Amounts due from banks		EUR 40,000
Financial assets at fair value through profit and loss	1	
– trading assets		EUR 110,000
– non-trading derivatives		EUR 14,000
– designated as at fair value through profit and loss		EUR 5,000

FIGURE 13.2   ABC – Balance Sheet

Investments	2	
– available-for-sale		EUR 200,000
– held-to-maturity		EUR 8,000
Loans and advances to customers		EUR 500,000
Assets Held for Sale	3	EUR 3,000
Total assets		EUR 930,000
EQUITY		
Shareholders' equity	4	EUR 60,000
Retained earnings		EUR 30,000
Total equity		EUR 90,000
LIABILITIES		
Subordinated loans	5	EUR 10,000
Debt securities in issue	6	EUR 160,000
Other borrowed funds		EUR 30,000
Amounts due to banks		EUR 40,000
Customer deposits and other funds on deposit		EUR 460,000
Financial liabilities at fair value through profit & loss	7	
– trading liabilities		EUR 85,000
– non-trading derivatives		EUR 20,000
– designated as at fair value through profit and loss		EUR 15,000
Liabilities held for sale	3	EUR 20,000
Total liabilities		EUR 840,000
Total equity and liabilities		EUR 930,000

FIGURE 13.2 (*Continued*)

Notes: Financial assets at fair value through profit and loss (1): These include assets used for trading purposes and non-trading derivatives.

Investments (2): These are investments that are either "available-for-sale (AFS)" or "held-to-maturity (HTM)". AFS investments can be either equities or debt securities; HTM investments can only be debt securities.

Assets and liabilities held for sale (3): Disposal through a stand-alone sale transaction rather than a sale from normal day-to-day (continuing) operations. This could include

    (a) a sale that is highly probable but not yet agreed or

    (b) an agreed sale that has not yet closed.

Shareholders' equity (4): This includes share capital (authorised share capital minus unissued share capital) made up of ordinary shares and, where appropriate, preference shares (common and preferred stock in US parlance) and the various reserves that are either distributable or non-distributable.

Subordinated loans (5): Loans that have a lower priority than other bonds of an issuer in case of bankruptcy.

Debt securities in issue (6): This includes fixed-interest and floating-rate debt securities, usually analysed by maturity of the debt.

Financial liabilities at fair value through profit & loss (7): See (1) above.

Some of the terms mentioned in the notes to Figure 13.2 are defined in Table 13.2.

TABLE 13.2 Terminology

Term	Definition
Trading assets	A financial asset acquired principally for the purpose of selling in the short term or if designated by management as such.
Non-trading derivatives	Derivative instruments that are used by the company as part of its risk management strategies, but which do not qualify for hedge accounting are presented as non-trading derivatives. Non-trading derivatives are measured at fair value, with changes in the fair value taken to the Profit & Loss account.
Held to maturity	Non-derivative financial assets with fixed or determinable payments and fixed maturity for which the company has the positive intent and ability to hold to maturity and which are designated by management as HTM assets are initially recognised at fair value plus transaction costs. Subsequently, they are carried at amortised cost using the effective interest method less any impairment losses. Interest income from HTM debt securities is recognised in interest income in the Profit & Loss account using the effective interest method. HTM investments include only debt securities.
Available for sale	These are non-strategic investments; neither held for trading nor HTM. An AFS investment must have a readily available market price.
Fair value (aka mark-to-market)	The fair values of financial instruments are based on quoted market prices at the Balance Sheet date where available. The quoted market price used for financial assets held by the Group is the current bid price; the quoted market price used for financial liabilities is the current ask price. The fair value of financial instruments that are not traded in an active market is determined using valuation techniques. A variety of methods is used and assumptions made that are based on market conditions existing at each Balance Sheet date.

13.3 THE ACCOUNTING LIFECYCLE FOR SECURITIES

13.3.1 Introduction

At the moment a buyer and seller agree to a transaction, both parties have a contingent liability to do something:

- The buyer is committed to pay cash (in exchange for the purchased securities);
- The seller is committed to deliver securities (in exchange for the sale proceeds).

The accounting entries should reflect these commitments at the earliest possible opportunity (ideally on the trade date). Transactions are not usually settled on the trade date; most are settled at a later date in accordance with market convention for the product being settled. Due to these timing differences, these entries will have to be split into two stages:

1. Trade date – to reflect the commitment.
2. Settlement date – to discharge the commitment.

The entries are passed using the appropriate general ledger accounts using a system of double-entry bookkeeping.

13.3.2 Trade Date

As we saw above, on the trade date the company takes the liability onto its books. Let us look at an example where the company purchases securities costing USD 10,000. Using the "T-account" format, the accounting entries for this purchase would be posted as shown in Table 13.3.

TABLE 13.3   Accounting entries (a)

Details	Dr		Details	Cr
Securities at cost	USD 10,000		Cash	USD 10,000

There are two problems with this posting:

1. It assumes that the cash has, in fact, been paid. Even for same-day settlement, there will be a timing difference between the actual trade execution and the actual payment of cash.
2. The posting does not reflect the counterparty's part in this transaction. Until such time as the transaction settles, the counterparty is the company's creditor.

A better way would be to post the trade date entries as shown in Table 13.4.

TABLE 13.4   Accounting entries (b)

Details	Dr	Details	Cr
Securities at cost	USD 10,000.00	Creditors (counterparty)	USD 10,000.00

If the securities were equities and the transaction included brokerage fees of, say, USD 100.00, then the entries would be posted as shown in Table 13.5.

TABLE 13.5   Accounting entries (c)

Details	Dr	Details	Cr
Securities at cost	USD 10,000.00	Creditors (counterparty)	USD 10,100.00
Brokerage	USD 100.00		
Total:	USD 10,100.00	Total:	USD 10,100.00

Let us change the transaction to a bond purchase with a nominal amount of USD 100,000 and a price of 101.2500. Interest has accrued at 4% p.a. for 65 days (30E/360). Convention has it that the securities at cost should be calculated at the clean price and any accrued interest added separately, as shown in Table 13.6.

TABLE 13.6   Accounting entries (d)

Details	Dr	Details	Cr
Securities at cost	USD 101,250.00	Creditors (counterparty)	USD 101,972.22
Accrued interest	USD 722.22		
Total:	USD 101,972.22	Total:	USD 101,972.22

Finally, if this same bond is sold some days later at a clean price of 101.50 plus 75 days' accrued interest, the entries would be posted as shown in Table 13.7.

TABLE 13.7   Accounting entries (e)

Details	Dr	Details	Cr
Debtors (counterparty)	USD 102,333.33	Securities at cost	USD 101,500.00
		Accrued interest	USD 833.33
Total:	USD 102,333.33	Total:	USD 102,333.33

Entries across the securities at cost ledger would be sub-divided into one of the several asset/liability accounts and reflected on the Balance Sheet.

13.3.3   Settlement Date

On settlement of a transaction, the cash is paid or received and entries posted to contra the creditor/debtor account and credit/debit the cash (bank) account. The net result would be (a) above, i.e. the purchase of securities has been debited to Securities at cost and credited to Cash. The Creditor account has been cleared by the two compensating entries.

Q&A

Question

Please refer back to the transactions (b) to (e) above. What are the settlement entries?

Answer

The answers to the four scenarios are shown in Figure 13.3.

(b) Settlement of securities purchase			
Details	**Dr**	**Details**	**Cr**
Creditors (Counterparty)	USD 10,000.00	Cash	USD 10,000.00

(c) Settlement of equities purchase			
Details	**Dr**	**Details**	**Cr**
Creditors (Counterparty)	USD 10,100.00	Cash	USD 10,100.00

(d) Settlement of bond purchase			
Details	**Dr**	**Details**	**Cr**
Creditors (Counterparty)	USD 101,972.22	Cash	USD 101,972.22

(e) Settlement of bond sale			
Details	**Dr**	**Details**	**Cr**
Cash	USD 101,500.00	Debtors (Counterparty)	USD 101,500.00

FIGURE 13.3   Settlement entries

13.3.4   Revaluation

We revalue a particular security or a portfolio of securities to establish how much they are worth. The true valuation of any security can only occur when you dispose of a long position (or cover a short position). Otherwise you can only have an estimate of that value, even though the price that you obtain can be regarded as being accurate.

For example, you may have purchased 100 shares at a price of JPY 1,000 per share and wish to revalue them. The price on the Tokyo Stock Exchange is JPY 1,200 per share and shows a potential profit of JPY 200 per share. You decide that now is the time to take your profit and sell the shares. You go into the market and find that its best bid price is JPY 180 per share. If you then decide to execute the transaction you will certainly have made a profit, but not as much as you had first thought.

So, taking any price for a revaluation is, at best, only ever going to be an indicative figure. The situation can become more complicated in the OTC markets, where a price may not be readily available. In this situation, you might need to get opinions from several market participants, who may have, at some stage, been buyers or sellers, or make use of an appropriate mathematical model that would calculate a price.

The topic of revaluation becomes more important in the mutual fund industry where the price of a fund is calculated from the net asset value (NAV) of the fund. To do this, the fund manager must calculate the value of each of the underlying securities in the fund, less any liabilities.[1]

---

[1]The NAV of a collective investment scheme such as a mutual fund is calculated by reference to the total value of the fund's portfolio less its accrued liabilities (money owed to lending banks, fees owed to service providers [such as investment managers, brokers, custodians, etc.] and other liabilities).

Any errors in pricing will cause the NAV to be inaccurate and the subsequent price of shares in the fund will be either understated or overstated. The consequences of incorrect pricing will almost certainly lead to a loss for the fund manager, mainly as a result of refunding cash to sellers or giving extra shares to purchasers.

This type of revaluation is commonly known as *mark-to-market* (MTM), and is performed on a daily basis with the results being fed through to the Profit & Loss account.

Securities are always quoted with a bid price and an offer price. As an investor, which of these two prices would you use to revalue your portfolio of, say, equities? If you are not sure of the answer, think about your portfolio from the point of view of its disposal. What price would you get if you were to sell the shares? You would get the market's bid price (the market is bidding to buy from you as a seller). By contrast, if your portfolio contains short positions, what price would you get if you had to cover the short? You would get the market's offer price (the market is offering to sell to you as a buyer).

Q&A

Question

You own a portfolio of Singapore-quoted equities (as shown in Table 13.8a) and you wish to revalue them. Using the prices in Appendix 13.1, at the end of this chapter, what is the MTM value of your portfolio and by how much has the overall value of the portfolio changed?

TABLE 13.8a Portfolio revaluation

Issue	Quantity	Opening Price	Opening Value	Closing Price	Closing Value
Charisma Energy Services	1,000,000	0.060	SGD 60,000		
DBS Group Holdings Ltd	5,000	17.09	SGD 85,450		
Global Logistic Properties	25,000	3.13	SGD 78,250		
Jardine Cycle & Carriage	2,500	34.21	SGD 85,525		
Singapore Airlines	7,500	10.33	SGD 77,475		
		Total:	SGD 386,700	Total:	
				Gain/(Loss)	

Answer

The portfolio is now worth SGD 390,300, with an overall gain of SGD 3,600, as shown in Table 13.8b.

TABLE 13.8b   Portfolio revaluation

Issue	Quantity	Opening Price	Opening Value	Closing Price	Closing Value
Charisma Energy Services	1,000,000	0.060	SGD 60,000	0.059	SGD 59,000
DBS Group Holdings Ltd	5,000	17.09	SGD 85,450	17.30	SGD 86,500
Global Logistic Properties	25,000	3.13	SGD 78,250	3.26	SGD 81,500
Jardine Cycle & Carriage	2,500	34.21	SGD 85,525	34.42	SGD 86,050
Singapore Airlines	7,500	10.33	SGD 77,475	10.30	SGD 77,250
		Total:	SGD 386,700	Total:	SGD 390,300
				Gain/(Loss)	SGD 3,600

13.4   GAINS AND LOSSES

13.4.1   Introduction

Our portfolio of Singaporean equities showed an overall gain of SGD 3,600, with the share prices of DBS, Global Logistic and Jardine Cycle all increasing. These are theoretical gains only, as we would not benefit from them unless we sold the shares. We therefore refer to these gains as *unrealised gains*. Notice that the share prices for Charisma and Singapore Airlines decreased – we would show these losses as *unrealised losses*.

Our basic accounting approach depends on the type of investment that we have made (see Table 13.9).

TABLE 13.9   Type of investment

Type of Investment	Basic Accounting Approach	Assessment Guidelines
Trading	Fair value (mark-to-market) with gains/losses posted to Operating Income	We intend to buy and sell for short-term profits
Held-to-maturity	Amortised cost	We intend to buy and hold until a fixed maturity date
Available-for-sale	Fair value with gains/losses posted to Other Comprehensive Income	Default category; similar to Trading except in the manner in which gains and losses are treated

13.4.2   Fair Value (Mark-to-Market)

If we mark-to-market our assets on a daily basis, we account for any gains and losses at the same time; in other words, we drip-feed gains and losses throughout the period in which we are holding the assets. By contrast, if we value at historic cost, then the assets are valued at the original purchase/sale price and only show the total gain or total loss on the eventual sale of the long position (or purchase to cover a short position).

Let us take one of these securities and follow the daily MTM revaluation process, as shown in Table 13.10.

TABLE 13.10   Revaluation process

Jardine Cycle & Carriage Ltd, Shares (C07)		Trading Book
Date	Details	Price
7 April 2014	You purchase 6,000 shares	SGD 36.77
7 April 2014	Closing price	SGD 35.65
8 April 2014	Closing price	SGD 36.16
9 April 2014	Closing price	SGD 35.00
10 April 2014	Closing price	SGD 34.06
11 April 2014	Closing price	SGD 34.21
14 April 2014	You sell 3,500 shares	SGD 34.78
14 April 2014	Closing price	SGD 34.42

We can observe that 6,000 shares were purchased at SGD 36.77. The loss on the sale of 3,500 shares was SGD 1.99 per share (SGD 34.78 − SGD 36.77) totalling SGD 6,965 (3,500 shares at a loss of SGD 1.99 per share).

By concentrating on the 3,500 shares sold, marking the position to market every day and accounting for any gains and losses on a daily basis, we can see in Figure 13.4 the way in which the loss was spread over the seven days.

Date	Details	Number Shares	Price	Amount	Gain/ Loss	Balance
7 Apr 2014	Purchase	3,500	SGD 36.77	SGD (128,695)	Cost	SGD (128,695)
7 Apr 2014	Closing price	3,500	SGD 35.65	SGD 3,920	Loss	SGD (124,775)
8 Apr 2014	Closing price	3,500	SGD 36.16	SGD (1,785)	Gain	SGD (126,560)
9 Apr 2014	Closing price	3,500	SGD 35.00	SGD 4,060	Loss	SGD (122,500)
10 Apr 2014	Closing price	3,500	SGD 34.06	SGD 3,290	Loss	SGD (119,210)
11 Apr 2014	Closing price	3,500	SGD 34.21	SGD (525)	Gain	SGD (119,735)
14 Apr 2014	Sale	3,500	SGD 34.78	SGD 121,730	Proceeds	SGD 1,995
				Unrealised Gain/ Loss - B/Dwn		SGD (8,960)
				Realised Gain/ Loss on Sale		SGD (6,965)

FIGURE 13.4   Sale of 3,500 Jardine Cycle & Carriage shares

Notes:

(1) Although the original purchase was for 6,000 Jardine Cycle & Carriage Ltd shares, we are focusing on the quantity that was sold on 14 April.

(2) The result of the daily MTM calculations resulted in an unrealised loss of SGD 8,960 (refer to the tinted fields in the Amount and Balance columns of the figure).

(3) The sale on 14 April showed a gain of SGD 1,995; that was because the sale price of SGD 34.78 was compared with the closing price on the previous business day (11 April) of SGD 34.21.

(4) Overall, therefore, the realised loss was the sum of the unrealised loss plus the gain on the sale date.

(5) If we re-combine the original purchase, the sale and the balance of these shares, we have a final position of 2,500 shares valued at SGD 86,050, as shown in Figure 13.5.

Date	Details	Number Shares	Price	Amount	Gain/ Loss	Balance
7 Apr 2014	Purchase	6,000	SGD 36.77	SGD (220,620)	Cost	SGD (220,620)
7 Apr 2014	Closing price	6,000	SGD 35.65	SGD 6,720	Loss	SGD (213,900)
8 Apr 2014	Closing price	6,000	SGD 36.16	SGD (3,060)	Gain	SGD (216,960)
9 Apr 2014	Closing price	6,000	SGD 35.00	SGD 6,960	Loss	SGD (210,000)
10 Apr 2014	Closing price	6,000	SGD 34.06	SGD 5,640	Loss	SGD (204,360)
11 Apr 2014	Closing price	6,000	SGD 34.21	SGD (900)	Gain	SGD (205,260)
14 Apr 2014	Sale	3,500	SGD 34.78	SGD 121,730	Proceeds	SGD (83,530)
14 Apr 2014	Reversal Unrealised Gain/Loss			SGD (8,960)		SGD (92,490)
14 Apr 2014	Reversal Realised Gain/Loss			SGD 6,965		SGD (85,525)
14 Apr 2014	Closing price	2,500	SGD 34.42	SGD (525)	Gain	SGD (86,050)

FIGURE 13.5   Final position of Jardine Cycle & Carriage shares

13.4.3 Amortised Cost

The clean price of a bond depends on several factors such as:

- The creditworthiness of the issuer;
- The remaining time to maturity of the bond;
- The overall market conditions including the yield.

We wish to purchase a bond, issued by ABC, with a coupon rate of 3% p.a. (paid annually) and with exactly ten years to maturity. We can calculate the clean price, all things being equal, using an appropriate yield. In Table 13.11 we can see, for a selection of yields, the clean prices of this bond would be:

TABLE 13.11   Bond prices using yields

ABC 3% Bonds due for Maturity in 10 Years			
Face Value	**Yield**	**Price**	**Price is at:**
100,000	2.0000%	108.9826	A premium to par
100,000	3.0000%	100.0000	Par
100,000	4.0000%	91.8891	A discount to par

Note: Prices calculated using the bond function of a Texas Instruments BAII Plus calculator.

As we are holding this bond to maturity and the bond matures at par, we can identify two features:

1. The issuer will only pay the cash proceeds from the bond on maturity of the bond (i.e. in ten years' time in our example).
2. Buying the bond at a premium will result in a loss (and at a discount, a gain).

Q&A

Question

Assuming we purchase the bond at each of the above prices, what would the overall gain or loss be?

Answer

Table 13.12 shows the gains and losses.

TABLE 13.12　Gains and losses on redemption

100,000	ABC 3% Bonds due for Maturity in 10 Years		
Price	Cost	Redemption Value	Gain/(Loss)
108.9826	108,982.60	100,000.00	(8,982.60)
100.0000	100,000.00	100,000.00	0.00
91.8891	91,889.10	100,000.00	8,110.90

Having checked your answers, please note that:

1. If you purchased the bond at a price above par, you would only receive par on maturity, i.e. you would lose 8,982.60.
2. Conversely, if you purchased the bond at a price below par, you would still receive par on maturity, i.e. you would gain 8,110.90.
3. There would be neither a gain nor a loss if you had purchased the bond at par.

For scenarios 1 and 2 above, the gain/loss would be amortised over the remaining life of the bond (i.e. ten years in our example) rather than as one amount on the maturity of the bond. The term *amortise* can therefore be described as: "an amount drip-fed (or 'recognised') in the financial accounts over the life of the bond".

The following spreadsheets illustrate the cash treatment for the amortisation.

Bonds Purchased at Par　As there is neither a gain nor a loss, we only need to account for the purchase cost, regular coupon payments (3,000.00 p.a.) and redemption proceeds (100,000.00) – see Figure 13.6.

Date	Cash Received		Coupon Income		Investment in ABC Bonds
Today	−100,000.00	CR			100,000.00
Year 1	3,000.00	DR	3,000.00	CR	
Year 2	3,000.00	DR	3,000.00	CR	
Year 3	3,000.00	DR	3,000.00	CR	

FIGURE 13.6　Bonds purchased at par

Date	Cash Received		Coupon Income		Investment in ABC Bonds
Year 4	3,000.00	DR	3,000.00	CR	
Year 5	3,000.00	DR	3,000.00	CR	
Year 6	3,000.00	DR	3,000.00	CR	
Year 7	3,000.00	DR	3,000.00	CR	
Year 8	3,000.00	DR	3,000.00	CR	
Year 9	3,000.00	DR	3,000.00	CR	
Year 10	3,000.00	DR	3,000.00	CR	
Year 10	100,000.00	DR			−100,000.00
	30,000.00	=	30,000.00		0.00

FIGURE 13.6 (*Continued*)

Bonds Purchased at a Premium The loss of 8,982.60 will be amortised over the ten-year period and will be recognised as a reduction of the coupon income. In this example, the loss will be 898.26 p.a. and will be deducted from the annual coupon of 3,000.00. This premium/loss will be recognised over the life of the bond as a decrease in interest income – see Figure 13.7.

Date	Cash Received		Coupon Income		Premium Amortisation		Investment in ABC Bonds
Today	−108,982.60	CR					108,982.60
Year 1	3,000.00	DR	2,101.74	CR	898.26	CR	108,084.34
Year 2	3,000.00	DR	2,101.74	CR	898.26	CR	107,186.08
Year 3	3,000.00	DR	2,101.74	CR	898.26	CR	106,287.82
Year 4	3,000.00	DR	2,101.74	CR	898.26	CR	105,389.56
Year 5	3,000.00	DR	2,101.74	CR	898.26	CR	104,491.30
Year 6	3,000.00	DR	2,101.74	CR	898.26	CR	103,593.04
Year 7	3,000.00	DR	2,101.74	CR	898.26	CR	102,694.78
Year 8	3,000.00	DR	2,101.74	CR	898.26	CR	101,796.52
Year 9	3,000.00	DR	2,101.74	CR	898.26	CR	100,898.26
Year 10	3,000.00	DR	2,101.74	CR	898.26	CR	100,000.00
Year 10	100,000.00	DR	0.00		0.00		0.00
	21,017.40	=	21,017.40		8,982.60		

FIGURE 13.7 Bonds purchased at a premium

Bonds Purchased at a Discount This will be similar to the premium treatment, only in reverse. The gain will be amortised at 811.09 plus the annual coupon of 3,000.00. This discount/gain will be recognised over the life of the bond as an increase in interest income – see Figure 13.8.

Date	Cash Received		Coupon Income		Discount Amortisation		Investment in ABC Bonds
Today	−91,889.10	CR					91,889.10
Year 1	3,000.00	DR	3,811.09	CR	811.09	DR	92,700.19
Year 2	3,000.00	DR	3,811.09	CR	811.09	DR	93,511.28
Year 3	3,000.00	DR	3,811.09	CR	811.09	DR	94,322.37
Year 4	3,000.00	DR	3,811.09	CR	811.09	DR	95,133.46
Year 5	3,000.00	DR	3,811.09	CR	811.09	DR	95,944.55
Year 6	3,000.00	DR	3,811.09	CR	811.09	DR	96,755.64
Year 7	3,000.00	DR	3,811.09	CR	811.09	DR	97,566.73
Year 8	3,000.00	DR	3,811.09	CR	811.09	DR	98,377.82
Year 9	3,000.00	DR	3,811.09	CR	811.09	DR	99,188.91
Year 10	3,000.00	DR	3,811.09	CR	811.09	DR	100,000.00
Year 10	100,000.00	DR	0.00		0.00		−0.00
	38,110.90	=	38,110.90		8,110.90		

FIGURE 13.8   Bonds purchased at a discount

13.4.4   Calculation Conventions

In the previous section, the gain or loss calculation for Jardine Cycle & Carriage was straight-forward as there was only one purchase and one sale. It becomes slightly more complicated when you have a security which is actively traded, with several purchases and sales. In the following example you will see there are several purchases followed by one sale; the question here will be how much gain or loss has the sale made?

There are three approaches to this, and each gives a different answer:

1. **First In, First Out (FIFO):** The sale price is compared with the price of the first purchase.
2. **Last In, First Out (LIFO):** The sale price is compared with the price of the last purchase.
3. **Weighted Average Cost (WAC):** The sale price is compared with the average weighted cost of all the previous purchases.

You will see in Figure 13.9 that there are several purchases and one sale in the shares of French supermarket company, Carrefour SA (CA:PAR).

Operation	Quantity	Price	Consideration	WAC
Purchases				
Purchase	100	EUR 27.56	EUR 2,756.00	EUR 27.56
Purchase	200	EUR 27.66	EUR 5,532.00	EUR 27.63
Purchase	400	EUR 27.20	EUR 10,880.00	EUR 27.38
Purchase	1,000	EUR 27.25	EUR 27,250.00	EUR 27.30
Purchase	250	EUR 27.38	EUR 6,845.00	EUR 27.31

FIGURE 13.9   Transactions in Carrefour shares

Operation	Quantity	Price	Consideration	WAC
Purchase	500	EUR 27.38	EUR 13,690.00	EUR 27.33
Total shares	2,450		EUR 66,953.00	EUR 27.33
Sales				
Sale	1,000	EUR 27.41	EUR 27,410.00	
Profit or Loss				
FIFO			EUR (150.00)	Loss
LIFO			EUR 30.00	Profit
WAC			EUR 82.24	Profit

FIGURE 13.9 (*Continued*)

The sale of 1,000 shares at a price of EUR 27.41 per share generates sale proceeds of EUR 27,410.00. Depending on the calculation convention adopted, the amount of profit or loss differs:

- **FIFO:** There is a loss of EUR 150.00, as the first purchase was at a higher price of EUR 27.56 per share;
- **LIFO:** There is a profit of EUR 30.00, as the most recent purchase was at EUR 27.38 per share;
- **WAC:** There is also a profit of EUR 82.24 per share.

We therefore have a situation where, depending on which calculation convention we adopt, there are three different profit/loss outcomes. The question is: which of these three is correct? The answer is that all three are correct. You might therefore be tempted to choose the one convention that suits your situation at any particular time; for example, you might choose the WAC if you wanted to maximise your profit or FIFO if you wanted to reduce your tax liability. However, one of the accounting profession's concepts and conventions is concerned with consistency. You would be expected to be consistent in the accounting treatment of items such as Profit & Loss calculations; if you start by using WAC, then you should continue in the same way.

Realised gains feed through to the Profit & Loss account as a credit and realised losses as a debit.

13.5 THE ACCOUNTING LIFECYCLE FOR DERIVATIVES

13.5.1 Introduction

In much the same way that securities held in a trading book are initially measured at fair value (and any changes are recorded in income as they happen), derivative instruments are also measured at fair value.

The key difference between cash market securities and derivative instruments is that in the latter we expect to either pay or receive any gains/losses as they occur. Why should this be the case? To answer this, you need to appreciate what is perhaps the main distinction between securities and derivatives. In the case of securities, you are expected to settle the transaction both in full and within a short period after the original trade date; settling the transaction eliminates the original counterparty risk between buyer and seller.

With derivatives, however, you may (or may not) be expected to pay the full economic cash value of the underlying derivative asset until some future date. The amount of time could be several weeks or months or years after the trade date and this exposes one counterparty to the risk of default of the other counterparty. By paying or receiving the change in the daily mark-to-market valuation, both counterparties reduce their economic exposures to each other on an overnight basis rather than intra-period.

We will take a look at how exchange-traded derivatives (ETDs) and OTC derivatives are treated in the next two sections. Please be aware that the situation on the OTC side is fundamentally changing due to pressure from industry regulators. We will look at this later in the section.

13.5.2 Exchange-Traded Derivatives

You will recall from a previous chapter that once an ETD transaction has been executed, both trading counterparties register their trades with a clearing house. Once the clearing house has matched the buyer's and seller's information, it becomes the counterparty to the buyer and separately the counterparty to the seller (novation). This means that should either the buyer or the seller default, it becomes the clearing house's responsibility to manage the subsequent un-winding of the position. Clearly, this puts the clearing house in a potentially risky situation, especially in a crisis situation where several counterparties are defaulting. For this reason, the clearing house has to have a robust risk-management system, and part of the risk mitigation is to request margin from counterparties that clear through the clearing house. Margin can be paid either in cash or in eligible non-cash assets such as high-grade treasury bonds, corporate bonds and money-market instruments.

The term *margin* therefore refers to the changes in fair value, payable or receivable by a counterparty to/from the clearing house. For any ETD product it is the clearing house that specifies how much margin is payable and what the deadlines are for its payment.

There are two variants of margin: initial margin and variation margin.

Initial Margin   This represents a returnable deposit by the clearing member to the clearing house and is an amount based on the risk profile of the contract. The purpose of initial margin is to allow the clearing house to hold sufficient funds on behalf of each clearing member to offset any losses incurred between the last payment of margin and the close out of the clearing member's positions should the clearing member default. Initial margin is usually calculated by taking the worst probable loss that the position could sustain over a fixed amount of time, and can be paid in either cash or non-cash collateral. Initial margin is a Balance Sheet item.

Traditionally, each and every open contract would have been margined as a separate exercise. Today, most clearing houses have adopted the process of collating similar derivative contracts into a "portfolio", stress testing the portfolio and calculating one amount of margin. The original framework, known as Standard Portfolio Analysis of Risk (SPAN), was developed by the Chicago Mercantile Exchange and subsequently licensed to a number of other international clearing houses. This one-stop-shop approach provides for a more accurate netting of risk and a more efficient use of collateral.

Variation Margin   This represents the profits or losses on open positions which are calculated daily in the mark-to-market process and then paid or collected. Variation margin is usually calculated at the end of each business day by the clearing house, and then settled the next business day. Unlike initial margin, which is kept by the clearing house until a position is closed out or reaches expiry, variation margin is collected from the loss-making side of the contract by the clearing house, and then paid to the profit-making side of the contract. Variation margin is a Profit & Loss account item.

As an example of how initial and variation margin work, let us take a look at the traditional methodology using an index futures contract, the FTSE 100 Index Future (see Figure 13.10).

Contract Specification		
FTSE 100 Index Futures		
Trading code – Z	Market – NYSE LIFFE London	Product type – Index future
Unit of trading	Contract valued at GBP 10 per index point (e.g. value GBP 66,000 at 6600.0)	
Quotation	Index points (e.g. 6600.0)	
Tick size/Value	0.5/GBP 5.00	
Delivery months	March, June, September, December (nearest four available for trading)	
Contract standard	Cash settlement based on the exchange delivery settlement price (EDSP)	

FIGURE 13.10   Index futures contract

Source: NYSE LIFFE (online) Available from https://globalderivatives.nyx.com/en/products/index-futures/Z-DLON/contract-specification. [Accessed Monday, 18 November 2013]

Our transaction details are shown in Table 13.13.

TABLE 13.13   Transaction details

Details		Price
Delivery month:	December 2013 contract	
Transaction:	Investor buys (to open) 10 contracts @	6,712.00
Trade date:	Day 1	
Contract size:	GBP 10.00	per contract
Initial margin:	GBP 1,000.00	per contract
FTSE 100 Index on Day 1	6703.50	
FTSE 100 Index on Day 2	6666.50	
FTSE 100 Index on Day 3	6683.00	
Day 4	Investor sells (to close) 10 contracts @	6,715.50

We can see here that the transaction was profitable overall (we opened at 6,712.00 and closed at 6,715.50). Notice, though, that the transaction was losing money by the end of Day 1, as the contract closed lower at 6,703.50. The next two tables will show the daily mark-to-market prices plus the impact on initial margin and variation margin (see Table 13.14) and the accounting treatment of the cash items (see Table 13.15).

TABLE 13.14 Margin calculations

Date	Direction	Contracts	Price	EOD Price	Initial Margin	Variation Margin	Pay/ Receive
Day 1	Buy	10	6,712.00		GBP (10,000.00)		Pay
	CFWD	10		6,703.50		GBP (850.00)	Pay
Day 2	BDWN	10	6,703.50				
	CFWD	10		6,666.50		GBP (3,700.00)	Pay
Day 3	BDWN	10	6,666.50				
	CFWD	10		6,683.00		GBP 1,650.00	Receive
Day 4	BDWN	10	6,683.00				
	Sell	10		6,715.50	GBP 10,000.00	GBP 3,250.00	Receive
					GBP 0.00	GBP 350.00	
Overall P/L	GBP 350.00	Profit					

TABLE 13.15 Accounting entries

Date	Details	DR	CR	Comments
Day 1	Initial margin on futures	GBP 10,000.00		Balance Sheet asset
	Variation margin on futures	GBP 850.00		P & L account
	Bank		GBP 10,850.00	Balance Sheet asset
Day 2	Variation margin on futures	GBP 3,700.00		P & L account
	Bank		GBP 3,700.00	Balance Sheet asset
Day 3	Variation margin on futures		GBP 1,650.00	P & L account
	Bank	GBP 1,650.00		Balance Sheet asset
Day 4	Initial margin on futures		GBP 10,000.00	Balance Sheet asset
	Variation margin on futures		GBP 3,250.00	P & L account
	Bank	GBP 13,250.00		Balance Sheet asset
	Reconciliation	**DR**	**CR**	**Balance**
Totals:	Initial margin on futures	GBP 10,000.00	GBP 10,000.00	GBP 0.00
	Variation margin on futures	GBP 4,550.00	GBP 4,900.00	GBP 350.00
	Bank	GBP 14,900.00	GBP 14,550.00	GBP (350.00)

13.5.3 OTC Derivatives

In the centrally cleared world of ETD transactions, margin is one element in the clearing house's risk mitigation. With the notable exception of SwapClear (launched in 1999 by LCH.Clearnet), OTC derivative contracts are not generally cleared centrally. It is the responsibility of the buyer and the seller to make suitable arrangements to mitigate the counterparty risk exposures.

It is usual to revalue an OTC contract on a daily basis (in much the same way as in the centrally cleared environment), and an amount of collateral representing the value of the contract will be delivered by the counterparty with the exposure to the counterparty with the risk. This is very much a bilateral activity, but formalised under agreements produced by the International Swaps and Derivatives Association (ISDA). The main agreement types[2] include the following:

- ISDA Master Agreement;
- ISDA Credit Support Documentation;
- ISDA Definitions;
- Regulatory documentation.

According to the ISDA's 2014 Margin Survey (published in April 2014), 91% of all cleared and non-cleared OTC derivatives trades were subject to collateral agreements, of which 87% were ISDA agreements.[3]

In order to be able to calculate the correct amount of collateral, it is necessary to value the contracts. This would be straightforward if prices were available centrally, for example, through an exchange or a clearing house. However, due to the bilateral nature of OTC derivatives trading, there is no central pricing facility. Instead, market participants have to use a range of pricing systems and models in order to establish a fair price. It is quite possible for the counterparties to the same trade to have different revaluation prices.

It is intended that by 2014 all non-cleared OTC derivative contracts will be cleared through a clearing house. For their part, clearing houses will, theoretically, become comfortable clearing OTC derivative contracts on condition that they (a) understand the contracts and (b) are able to revalue them. Hence, SwapClear clears a range of vanilla interest rate swaps.[4] SwapClear revalues clearing member positions daily using zero-coupon yield curves which are published and made available to the members. This is one of the key features of the service and ensures the independence of the valuation process.

---

[2] Available from www.isda.org/publications/pubguide.aspx. Documents are either for ISDA members only or non-members to purchase/download for free.

[3] Source ISDA (online) ISDA 2014 Margin Survey. Available from www2.isda.org/search?headerSearch=1&keyword=surveys. [Accessed Monday, 14 April 2014]

[4] SwapClear initially cleared plain vanilla interest rate swaps in four major currencies. Today it clears swaps in 17 currencies: USD, EUR and GBP out to 50 years, JPY to 40 years, AUD, CAD, CHF and SEK to 30 years, NZD out to 15 years and the remaining eight currencies out to 10 years. It also clears overnight index swaps out to 30 years in EUR, GBP and USD and out to 2 years in CHF and CAD. Source: LCH.Clearnet (online) Available from www.lchclearnet.com/swaps/swapclear_for_clearing_members. [Accessed Tuesday, 19 November 2013]

13.6 SUMMARY

In this chapter we have seen the importance of making our financial activities "open and transparent" to our various stakeholders. This requires us to maintain appropriate records of our activities, which, in our business world, include details and cash movements associated with:

1. Our securities and derivatives transactions.
2. Our income (coupons and dividends).
3. Corporate actions activities.
4. Maintenance of our open positions through margin payments.

We also noted that processes do change from time to time, including the requirement to centralise OTC derivatives clearing activities. It remains to be seen whether the trading of OTC derivatives will migrate to exchange in the foreseeable future.

APPENDIX 13.1: CLOSING PRICES FOR SINGAPORE EQUITIES (SGX)

Issue	Closing Price
Charisma Energy Services	SGD 0.0590
DBS Group Holdings Ltd	SGD 17.3000
Global Logistic Properties	SGD 3.2600
Jardine Cycle & Carriage	SGD 34.4200
Singapore Airlines	SGD 10.3000

Source: Singapore Stock Exchange – Market Information (www.sgx.com).

CHAPTER 14

Reconciliation

14.1 INTRODUCTION

Irrespective of what part of the company you are involved with, you will always need to know what your positions are, whether they are securities-related or cash-related. A problem arises when the position that you think you have either does not exist or indicates a different amount to what you actually have. In other words, you need to be sure that the position you think you have does actually exist. In this chapter you will see why you need to know this and how we can achieve it.

After reading this chapter you will:

- Understand the importance of maintaining an efficient reconciliation system;
- Be able to compare the different types of reconciliation and evaluate their strengths and weaknesses;
- Be able to perform a reconciliation and assess the effectiveness of the operational unit responsible;
- Be able to describe the regulatory requirements;
- Be able to take a manual reconciliation process and design an automated system.

As an example of a potential problem, your records show that you have USD 1,000.00 in your bank account. You receive a bank statement showing a credit balance of USD 1,000.00. You then make a payment of USD 900.00 on the assumption that you have sufficient funds in your account.

Thinking that you have a credit balance of USD 1,000.00, you are surprised when you receive a subsequent statement stating that you are several hundred US dollars overdrawn. In addition to being overdrawn, you will be liable for overdraft interest. Why are you overdrawn? What has gone wrong on your bank account?

This is where a reconciliation would have been helpful. A thorough investigation would have shown, for example, that you had recently issued a cheque for USD 350.00 but failed to book it into your records. Had you done so, your records would have shown a balance of USD 650.00 (not USD 1,000.00), and it would have been clear that making the payment of USD 900.00 would have taken your account into debit (i.e. overdrawn).

The fact that the cheque had not cleared only made the situation worse, as you looked at the bank balance before deciding to pay the USD 900.00.

14.2 IMPORTANCE OF RECONCILIATION

Accurate and timely reconciliation will ensure that both the Front Office and Operations will know, with a high degree of confidence, *what* their asset balances are and, just as importantly, *where* these assets are being held.

We can consider the concept of reconciliation from two points of view:

1. Comparing our *internal* records (our ledger) with those of an *external* entity (e.g. a bank statement, depot statement, broker statement, audit request, etc.);
2. Comparing *ownership* of an asset (proprietary, client) with its *location* (bank, counterparty, custodian, etc.).

14.2.1 Internal vs. External Records

Table 14.1 shows an example of *internal* versus *external* cash records.

TABLE 14.1 Internal vs. external cash records

Ledger (Our Nostro Account)		Bank Statement (ABC Bank)	
Opening balance	USD 80,000.00	Opening balance	USD 80,000.00
		less Cleared item(s)	USD (5,000.00)
Closing balance	USD 80,000.00	Closing balance	USD 75,000.00

Both opening balances agree (USD 80,000.00 credit).
Your ledger closing balance does not agree with the bank statement. There is a reconciliation break that needs investigation.

Q&A

Question

Which one of the following statements would be the most likely outcome from your investigation?

(a) Cash you were expecting has not been received, or
(b) An unexpected cash payment has been made.

Answer

The correct answer is (b); it would appear that a payment had been cleared by your bank and that you have not passed the appropriate entry in your records. There could be reasons for this, including:

(a) You forgot to pass the entries;
(b) You passed the entries with a value date after the statement date;
(c) You made the payment earlier than the (correct) value date;
(d) This is an unauthorised payment.

Having identified the reason, you should take corrective action, depending on the cause (as shown in Table 14.2).

TABLE 14.2   Reconciled account – items (a) to (c)

Ledger (Our Nostro Account)		Bank Statement (ABC Bank)	
Opening balance	USD 80,000.00	Opening balance	USD 80,000.00
less Payment(s)	USD (5,000.00)	*less* Cleared items	USD (5,000.00)
Closing balance	USD 75,000.00	Closing balance	USD 75,000.00

(a) Pass the correct entries;
(b) Reverse the incorrect value date and backdate to the date of the payment;
(c) Either request the payee to refund you and make the payment on the correct value date or, more likely, alter the value date;
(d) Make an investigation into the unauthorised payment, referring the case to a higher level of authority in your organisation.

Corrective actions (a) to (c) will result in a reconciled ledger/bank balance. However, with action (d), the first step might be to pass an entry over Sundry Payments (or other temporary account) so that the ledger reconciles with the bank during your investigations (see Table 14.3).

TABLE 14.3   Reconciled account with unauthorised payment – item (d)

Ledger (Our Nostro Account)		Bank Statement (ABC Bank)	
Opening balance	USD 80,000.00	Opening balance	USD 80,000.00
less Unauthorised payment	USD (5,000.00)	*less* Cleared items	USD (5,000.00)
Closing balance	USD 75,000.00	Closing balance	USD 75,000.00

14.2.2   Ownership vs. Location

Table 14.4 shows an example of ownership versus location for securities.

TABLE 14.4   Reconciled bond position

BNP 2.50% Bonds due 30 June 2025			
Ownership	Quantity	Quantity	Location
Trading desk	EUR 5,000,000.00	EUR (5,000,000.00)	SGSS
Clients' accounts	EUR 150,000.00	EUR (150,000.00)	BNYM
Totals:	EUR 5,150,000.00	EUR (5,150,000.00)	

In this example, the total ownership is split between our own assets (the trading desk's proprietary position) and those of our clients. The assets are located at two custodian banks (Société Générale Securities Services and Bank of New York Mellon).

Q&A

Question

Does the information in the "Location" column suggest that the underlying transactions have settled?

Answer

Yes, the transactions have settled and the purchases have been delivered by the selling counterparty to our designated custodians.

Q&A

Question

What would you expect to see if EUR 3,000,000 bonds purchased from counterparty "Broker" had not settled?

Answer

You would expect to see the EUR 2,000,000 bond held by SGSS and the USD 3,000,000 held by "Broker", as noted in Table 14.5, which shows the reconciled bond position together with a failed settlement. You might wish to contact the broker and request confirmation that the transaction is outstanding.

TABLE 14.5 Reconciled bond position with failed settlement position

BNP 2.50% Bonds due 30 June 2025				
Ownership	Quantity		Quantity	Location
Trading desk	EUR 5,000,000.00		EUR (2,000,000.00)	SGSS
			EUR (3,000,000.00)	Broker
Clients' accounts	EUR 150,000.00		EUR (150,000.00)	BNYM
Totals:	EUR 5,150,000.00	vs.	EUR (5,150,000.00)	Therefore settlement system reconciles

What you have seen in the above examples are straightforward reconciliations of cash and non-cash assets. It is important to appreciate that the reconciliation process tends to compare the trade-dated position in the company's ledger with the actual (i.e. settled) position as recorded by the external entity (e.g. the custodian or bank).

In order to be more thorough, we must collect data that relate to the following:

Non-cash assets
- Individual trades per asset;
- Traded position per asset (i.e. total of individual trades per asset);
- Trades that are open (i.e. traded but have not yet reached the intended settlement date);
- Trades that have failed to settle (i.e. trades that have reached the intended settlement date);
- Positions subjected to other movements (e.g. corporate actions and securities lending and borrowing activities);
- Trades that have settled;
- Settled position per asset (i.e. total of settled trades per asset).

Cash
- Items recorded as receipts by the company in its ledger but not credited by the bank, e.g. cheques received from clients but which the company has yet to pay in at the bank or, alternatively, credits still in the bank's clearing system.
- Items recorded as payments by the company in its ledger but not debited by the bank, e.g. cheques issued to a supplier which have not been presented for payment or have been presented but not yet cleared.
- Items deducted by the bank but not recorded in the company's ledger, e.g. bank charges which the company has yet to enter into the ledger.
- Items credited by the bank but not recorded in the ledger by the company.

We will take a look at some examples later in this chapter. In the meantime, we need to consider the different types of reconciliation, remembering that we are always comparing "our" position with "their" position.

14.3 TYPES OF RECONCILIATION

There are five basic types of reconciliation, as shown in Table 14.6.

TABLE 14.6 Reconciliation types

Type	Involves	Comments
1. Trade-by-trade	Individual trades	Front Office positions vs. Operations' positions
2. Traded position	Totals of trades recorded within a trading book/for a client	Front Office positions vs. Operations' positions
3. Open trades	Individual trades	Operations' positions vs. custodian/broker/counterparty
4. Depot position	Totals of securities positions held within a trading book/for a client	Operations' positions vs. custodian
5. Cash position	Cash balances and movements within a nostro account	Operations' positions vs. custodian/bank

Types 1 and 2 in Table 14.6 are *internal* reconciliations that ensure the dealers' blotters agree with the settlement systems in the Operations Department.

Types 3, 4 and 5 are *external* reconciliations:

- Type 3 handles both the asset and the cash counter-value;
- Type 4 handles non-cash assets only;
- Type 5 handles cash only.

14.3.1   Reconciliation Methods

The reconciliation of a securities portfolio can be performed by reconciling all the securities as at the same date, e.g. 30 June. This is known as the *total count method*. This is the more usual, standard method used in most organisations.

There is an alternative method, known as the *rolling stock method*, where a particular security is reconciled on one date and other particular securities reconciled on other dates. However, all the securities have to be fully reconciled during a reasonable period, typically six months.

Q&A

Question

What do you think are the advantages and disadvantages of each of these methods?

Answer

The advantages and disadvantages are shown in Table 14.7.

TABLE 14.7   Total count vs. rolling stock method

Total Count Method		Rolling Stock Method	
Advantage	Disadvantage	Advantage	Disadvantage
The reconciliation focuses on one date	This can result in a heavy workload over a long period	The workload can be spread more evenly over the six-month period	There is the risk that one or more securities positions might be missed and not reconciled

The Reconciliation Department must have systems and controls in place to mitigate the risk of missing one or more positions in the rolling stock method from occurring.

14.3.2   Reconciliations – Worked Examples

We will perform two reconciliations: the first a nostro (bank) reconciliation and the second a depot reconciliation.

Nostro Reconciliation   Cononley Supplies Ltd has, today, received its bank statement, which shows the balance at the close of business on 31/MMM/YYYY as GBP 4,290.00. The accountant cannot understand this, as its own records indicate the balance should only be GBP 2,700.00.

We will prepare a bank reconciliation using our ledger (see Table 14.8) and the corresponding bank statement (see Table 14.9) to explain the difference(s).

TABLE 14.8   Ledger statement

Ledger as at 31 MMM YYYY					
Date	**Credits**	**Amount**	**Date**	**Debits**	**Amount**
01 MMM	Balance b/d	GBP 2,000.00	02 MMM	Purchases	GBP 400.00
08 MMM	V. Carlton	GBP 1,000.00	06 MMM	Purchases	GBP 200.00
11 MMM	T. Horton	GBP 750.00	10 MMM	Wages	GBP 500.00
28 MMM	B. Radley (a)	GBP 600.00	30 MMM	Utility bill	GBP 200.00
			30 MMM	Purchases (b)	GBP 350.00
			31 MMM	Balance c/f	GBP 2,700.00
	Total:	GBP 4,350.00		Total:	GBP 4,350.00

TABLE 14.9   Bank statement

Bank Statement as at 31 MMM YYYY					
Date	**Details**	**Note**	**DR**	**CR**	**Balance**
01 MMM	Opening balance			GBP 2,000.00	GBP 2,000.00
08 MMM	Cheque 01234		GBP (200.00)		GBP 1,800.00
10 MMM	Cash	(c)	GBP (500.00)		GBP 1,300.00
12 MMM	Insurance premium	(c)	GBP (300.00)		GBP 1,000.00
13 MMM	Credit			GBP 1,750.00	GBP 2,750.00
15 MMM	Cheque 01233		GBP (400.00)		GBP 2,350.00
25 MMM	Credit	(d)		GBP 2,150.00	GBP 4,500.00
30 MMM	Electricity company		GBP (200.00)		GBP 4,300.00
31 MMM	Bank charges	(c)	GBP (10.00)		GBP 4,290.00
31 MMM	Closing balance				GBP 4,290.00

This is the procedure:

■ Check that the opening balances of the ledger and the bank statement agree. In this example, they do and we can, therefore, proceed.

■ Tick off the entries which are common to both records. Note: a credit on the bank statement may be made up of a number of cheques received from various customers, e.g. on 13 MMM, the credit of GBP 1,750.00 was made up of cheques received from:

V. Carlton	GBP 1,000.00
T. Horton	GBP 750.00
	GBP 1,750.00

Also note that cheques are not necessarily presented for payment in the order in which they were issued, so you may have to search for common entries.

At most, you will be left with four sets of unmatched items. The letters (a) to (d) can be referenced back to the notes in the ledger and bank statement:

(a) Items recorded as receipts by the company in its ledger but not credited in the bank statement, e.g. cheques received from suppliers but which the company has yet to pay in at the bank or, alternatively, bank giro credits still in the bank's clearing system.
(b) Items recorded as payments by the company in its ledger but not deducted in the bank statement, e.g. cheques issued to a supplier which have not been presented for payment.
(c) Items deducted in the bank statement but not recorded in the ledger by the company, e.g. standing orders and bank charges which the company may easily forget.
(d) Items credited in the bank statement but not recorded in the ledger by the company.

Items (c) and (d) may, therefore, need entering in the ledger to bring it up to date. It is also possible, however, that (c) and (d) represent items credited or debited in error by the bank, which would need to be brought to the bank's attention.

The next step is to draw up a bank reconciliation statement, i.e. start with the bank statement balance and work towards the cashbook balance (see Table 14.10) by entering the unmatched items.

TABLE 14.10   Bank statement reconciled to ledger

Bank Reconciliation Report as at 31 MMM YYY		
	GBP	**GBP**
Balance per bank statement		GBP 4,290.00
(a) *add* items not credited		GBP 600.00
	sub-total:	GBP 4,890.00
(b) *less* cheques not presented		GBP (350.00)
	sub-total:	GBP 4,540.00
(c) *add back* outgoings not entered into ledger:		
Insurance premium	GBP 300.00	
Bank charges	GBP 10.00	GBP 310.00
	sub-total:	GBP 4,850.00
(d) *less* receipts not entered in the ledger as per bank statement	GBP (2,150.00)	
	Total:	GBP 2,700.00

The total of GBP 2,700.00 reconciles with the ledger balance carried-forward figure.

Conversely, we can draw up a bank reconciliation statement starting with the cashbook balance and working towards the bank statement balance (see Table 14.11).

TABLE 14.11   Ledger to bank statement

Bank Reconciliation Report as at 31 MMM YYYY		
	GBP	**GBP**
Balance per ledger		GBP 2,700.00
(a) *less* items not credited		GBP (600.00)
	sub-total:	GBP 2,100.00
(b) *add* cheques not presented		GBP 350.00
	sub-total:	GBP 2,450.00
(c) *less* outgoings not entered into ledger:		
Insurance premium	GBP (300.00)	
Bank charges	GBP (10.00)	GBP (310.00)
	sub-total:	GBP 2,140.00
(d) *add* receipts not entered in the ledger as per bank statement		GBP 2,150.00
	Total:	GBP 4,290.00

The total of GBP 4,290.00 reconciles with the bank balance closing figure.

Depot Reconciliation   You manage assets for your client Threshfield Investors and you want to reconcile the depot positions against your client's custodian, Big Bank plc. (see Table 14.12).

TABLE 14.12   Depot reconciliation

Asset	Depot Position	Custodian Position	Difference	Position Reconciles Y/N
BARC:LSE	1,200	1,200	0	Yes
BP:LSE	400	600	200	No
GSK:LSE	200	200	0	Yes
HSBA:LSE	400	0	−400	No
RDSB:LSE	100	100	0	Yes
VOD:LSE	2,400	1,200	−1,200	No

It would appear that three positions do not reconcile (i.e. there is a reconciliation break). We need to investigate the reason why these breaks have occurred. For this we need more information. Investigations show that the transactions listed in Table 14.13 have problems.

Please note that, even though the BARC:LSE position does reconcile (i.e. there is zero difference in Table 14.12), there are two outstanding trades that compensate each other (see Table 14.13).

TABLE 14.13   Transaction problems

Asset	Details	Quantity	Problem
BARC:LSE	Our purchase	500	CSEC
BARC:LSE	Our sale	500	USEC
BP:LSE	Our sale	200	Open trade
HSBA:LSE	Our purchase	400	CSEC
VOD:LSE	1:1 bonus issue	1,200	Bonus shares not yet received

CSEC: Counterparty does not have availability.
USEC: You do not have availability.

The complete reconciliation report is shown in Figure 14.1.

| Opening Securities Balances & Reconciliation Date: | | | | DD MMM YYYY | | | | | |
Short Code	Depot Balance	Custodian Balance	Difference	Trade Fails	Pending C/Actions	Stock Lending	Other Pending	Difference	Reason(s) for Difference
BARC:LSE	1,200	1,200	0	+500 −500	0	0	0	0	Purchase 500 shares S/D yesterday: reason CSEC. Sale 500 shares S/D yesterday; reason USEC
BP::LSE	400	600	200	(200)	0	0	0	0	Open trade for S/D tomorrow
GSK:LSE	200	200	0	0	0	0	0	0	
HSBA:LSE	400	0	(400)	400	0	0	0	0	Trade failed: reason CSEC
RDSB:LSE	100	100	0	0	0	0	0	0	
VOD:LSE	2,400	1,200	(1,200)	0	1,200	0	0	0	Bonus shares not received

FIGURE 14.1 Securities Reconciliation Report

This portfolio does reconcile, although there are breaks that need to be chased in order to ensure prompt settlement. The expected receipt date for the bonus shares would already have been notified to the Corporate Actions Department.

14.4 AUTOMATION OF RECONCILIATIONS

Traditionally, reconciliations were performed with the internal ledger balances on the one hand and the external statement on the other. The reconciler then ticked off one position in the ledger against its corresponding entry on the statement. Once this had been completed, the reconciler prepared a schedule of reconciliation breaks; these were circulated to the appropriate departments for action to be taken. It was the job of the reconciliation clerk to ensure that investigations were completed without undue delay. Reconciliation was, therefore, a paper-based process that was both manually intensive and time-consuming.

Q&A

Question

What are the disadvantages of this approach and why might this be the case?

Answer

There are several disadvantages, as shown in Table 14.14.

TABLE 14.14   Disadvantages of manual reconciliation

Disadvantage	Comments
Reconciliation of a particular asset type	Reconciliations were performed on one particular asset type regardless of whether it was associated with another asset type, e.g. securities versus cash transactions. Any problem would result in two exceptions, one for the cash and another for the securities.
Timing issues	Manual reconciliation is a reactive process, undertaken some time after the event being reconciled has occurred. By the time any investigations have been made, it might be too late to avoid a problem with its associated delays and costs.
Operational risk issues	Reconciliations with high volumes of breaks and pending investigations result in Front Office and Operations Departments not being 100% certain of their positions. For example, if you do not know how many shares you own (and where they are held), any corporate action becomes a problem that could lead to financial loss.
Cost issues	There are the resource costs of performing the reconciliation, investigating the breaks and resolving the problem. These are in addition to any costs that might arise to correct the problem.
Volume issues	The reconciliation process can be made more problematic if there are large volumes of transactions across multiple asset classes (e.g. cash, equities, bonds, derivatives, etc.)

Today, we rely on automation to make the initial comparison of ledger vs. statement and to prepare the reconciliation break report. It is at this stage that human intervention takes place.

Reconciliation software is designed to track any transaction throughout its lifecycle, from confirmation through settlement to custody and asset servicing and beyond. This means that at any point in the lifecycle, a reconciliation "match" can be automatically made in real time and with automated exception processing, investigation and follow-ups. This helps to reduce operational costs and operational risk. Ideally, the reconciliation software should form part of an overall system that automates, tracks and controls financial transactions and internal processes within the firm and beyond (e.g. between a fund manager and its global custodian).

14.5 SUMMARY

Reconciliation of all asset classes is important so that "what you think you have" is actually "what you know you have" and the "assets are located in the right place". Not only does a completed reconciliation give you this confidence, but it also ensures that you are complying with regulatory rules.

In a reconciliation, we compare two sets of records. These can be our *internal* records (the ledger positions) and *external* records (bank statements, custody balances, counterparty statements, etc.). We could also compare internal records, e.g. our dealing records (blotter) with our settlement records; in other words, Front Office vs. Back Office.

Operations reconciliation staff perform reconciliations from a settlement date perspective, as they are concerned with what has (or should have) happened. This contrasts with the Front Office, which considers its activities from a trade date perspective. This results in Operations staff having to be aware of assets which have been traded but not yet settled (open trades) or those which have failed to settle.

About the Author

Keith Dickinson is Director of The Settlement & Management Research Consultancy Limited and Principal of Financial Markets Training Limited. After 20 years working in Operations in the City of London, Keith runs training courses for investment firms around the world and, more recently, teaches within academia.

For seven years, Keith was a Visiting Fellow at the University of Reading/ICMA Centre and a Programme Director at the ICMA Executive Education/ICMA Centre. Currently, he is a Senior Teaching Fellow at the International Business School Suzhou/Xi'an Jiaotong-Liverpool University, Suzhou.

Keith has written three workbooks published by the Securities Institute, London (now known as the Chartered Institute for Securities & Investment) as part of its Investment Administration Qualification (IAQ) and International Capital Markets Qualification (ICMQ):

- IAQ *Global Custody* (1994/2001);
- IAQ *Bond Settlements* (1995);
- ICMQ Module 4 *Settlement & Custody of Securities* (1995).

Index